SOCIAL INFLUENCE

The Sydney Symposium of Social Psychology series

This book is Volume 3 in the Sydney Symposium of Social Psychology series. The aim of the *Sydney Symposia of Social Psychology* is to provide new, integrative insights into key areas of contemporary research. Held every year at the University of New South Wales, Sydney, each Symposium deals with an important integrative theme in social psychology, and the invited participants are leading researchers in the field from around the world. Each contribution is extensively discussed during the Symposium, and is subsequently thoroughly revised into book chapters that are published in the volumes in this series. The themes of forthcoming Sydney Symposia are announced, and contributions from interested participants are invited around June every year. For further details see website at www.sydneysymposium.unsw.edu.au

Previous Sydney Symposium of Social Psychology volumes:

SSSP 1. FEELING AND THINKING: THE ROLE OF AFFECT IN SOCIAL COGNITION* (Edited by J.P. Forgas). Contributors: Robert Zajonc *(Stanford)*, Jim Blascovich & Wendy Mendes *(UCSanta Barbara)*, Craig Smith & Leslie Kirby *(Vanderbilt)*, Eric Eich & Dawn Macauley *(British Columbia)*, Len Berkowitz et al. *(Wisconsin)*, Leonard Martin *(Georgia)*, Daniel Gilbert *(Harvard)*, Herbert Bless *(Mannheim)*, Klaus Fiedler, *(Heidelberg)*, Joseph Forgas *(UNSW)*, Carolin Showers *(Wisconsin)*, Tony Greenwald, Marzu Banaji et al. *(U.Washington/Yale)*, Mark Leary *(Wake Forest)*, Paula Niedenthal & Jamin Halberstadt *(Indiana)*.

Comments on 'Feeling and Thinking'

"At last a project that brings together the central findings and theories concerning the interface of social cognition and affect. This important new volume is sure to become the sourcebook . . . must reading for anyone interested in the vital role of affect in social life." Prof. Tory Higgins, Columbia University.

"I am filled with admiration for the contribution I believe this book makes to our understanding of affect and cognition and its facilitation of future research on the subject. I've benefited a great deal from the scholarship in this work." Prof. Ellen Berscheid, University of Minnesota

"I can't imagine a more interesting collection of affect researchers under one roof! Joseph Forgas has brought together the best minds in psychology, young and old, to reflect on the interface between emotion and thought . . . this volume will make you wish you had traveled to Sydney to attend the original symposium. Excellent investigators showcase their best work." Prof. Peter Salovey, Yale University.

SSSP 2. THE SOCIAL MIND: COGNITIVE AND MOTIVATIONAL ASPECTS OF INTERPERSONAL BEHAVIOR* (Edited by J.P. Forgas, K. R. Williams & Ladd Wheeler). Contributors: William & Claire McGuire *(Yale)*, Susan Andersen *(NYU)*, Roy Baumeister *(Case Western)*, Joel Cooper *(Princeton)*, Bill Crano *(Claremont)*, Garth Fletcher *(Canterbury)*, Joseph Forgas *(UNSW)*, Pascal Huguet *(Clermont)*, Mike Hogg *(Queensland)*, Martin Kaplan *(N. Illinois)*, Norb Kerr *(Michigan State)*, John Nezlek *(William & Mary)*, Fred Rhodewalt *(Utah)*, Astrid Schuetz *(Chemnitz)*, Constantine Sedikides *(Southampton)*, Jeffrey Simpson *(Texas A&M)*, Richard Sorrentino *(Western Ontario)*, Dianne Tice *(Case Western)*, Kip Williams & Ladd Wheeler *(UNSW)*.

Comments on 'The Social Mind':

"At last . . . a compelling answer to the question of what is 'social' about social cognition. The editors have assembled a stellar cast of researchers . . . and the result is eye-opening and mind-expanding . . . the contributors to this project make a convincing case that, for human beings, mental life IS social life." Marilynn B. Brewer, Ohio State University

"The Sydney Symposium has once again collected some of social psychology's best researchers, and allowed them to . . . explore how the world within the mind represents, creates, interacts with, and is influenced by the world without. The bridge between social relations and social cognition has never been sturdier, and scientists on both sides of the divide won't want to miss this. . . ." Daniel Gilbert, Harvard University

* Volumes from the first two Symposia were published by Cambridge University Press.

SOCIAL INFLUENCE
Direct and Indirect Processes

Edited by

Joseph P. Forgas
University of New South Wales

and Kipling D. Williams
Macquarie University

USA	Publishing Office:	PSYCHOLOGY PRESS *A member of the Taylor & Francis Group* 325 Chestnut Street Philadelphia, PA 19106 Tel: (215) 625-8900 Fax: (215) 625-2940
	Distribution Center:	PSYCHOLOGY PRESS *A member of the Taylor & Francis Group* 7625 Empire Drive Florence, KY 41042 Tel: 1 (800) 634-7064 Fax: 1 (800) 248-4724
UK		PSYCHOLOGY PRESS *A member of the Taylor & Francis Group* 27 Church Road Hove E. Sussex, BN3 2FA Tel.: +44 (0) 1273 207411 Fax: +44 (0) 1273 205612

SOCIAL INFLUENCE: Direct and Indirect Processes

1 2 3 4 5 6 7 8 9 0

Printed by Edwards Brothers, Lillington, NC, 2001.
Cover design by Marja Walker.

A CIP catalog record for this book is available from the British Library.
∞ The paper in this publication meets the requirements of the ANSI Standard Z39.48-1984 (Permanence of Paper).

Library of Congress Cataloging-in-Publication Data
Social influence: direct and indirect processes / edited by Joseph P. Forgas and Kipling D. Williams.
    p. cm.
  Includes bibliographical references and index.
    ISBN 1-84169-038-4 (hc. : alk.paper) — ISBN 1-84169-039-2 (pbk. : alk. Paper)
    1. Social influence. 2. Interpersonal relations. 3. Influence (Psychology) I. Forgas, Joseph P. II. Williams, Kipling D.

HM1176 .S635 2001
303.3'4—dc21

2001016242
CIP

*To Teesh, Paul, and Peter, and to
Kory, Kitty, Cooper, and Dylan*

Contents

II. THE ROLE OF COGNITIVE PROCESSES
AND STRATEGIES IN SOCIAL INFLUENCE

III. SOCIAL INFLUENCE AND GROUP BEHAVIOR

About the Editors

Joseph P. Forgas received his DPhil and subsequently a DSc from the University of Oxford. He is currently Scientia Professor of Psychology at the University of New South Wales, Sydney, Australia. He has also spent various periods of time working at the Universities of Giessen, Heidelberg, Stanford, Mannheim, and Oxford. His enduring interest is in studying the role of cognitive and affective processes in interpersonal behavior. His current project investigates how mood states can influence everyday social judgments and social interaction strategies. He has published some 14 books and over 130 articles and chapters in this area. He has been elected Fellow of the Academy of Social Science in Australia, the American Psychological Society, and of the Society of Personality and Social Psychology, and he is recipient of the Alexander von Humboldt Research Prize (Germany) and a Special Investigator Award from the Australian Research Council.

Kipling D. Williams received his BS at the University of Washington, where he began his research career testing whether rats preferred to work or free-ride for their food. He then received his MA and PhD in Social Psychology at The Ohio State University. There, he began his collaboration with Bibb Latané and Stephen Harkins, working on the causes and consequences of social loafing. Before coming to Macquarie University, Professor Williams taught at Drake University, University of Washington, Purdue University, University of Toledo, and the University of New South Wales. His recent research focus is on ostracism—being excluded and ignored, on which his book, "Ostracism—The Power of Silence" will be published in 2001. He also has interests in psychology and law, including research on the tactic of stealing thunder, eyewitness accuracy, and the impact of crime heinousness on jury verdicts.

Contributors

Herbert Bless, Faculty of Social Sciences, University of Mannheim, Germany.

Martin J. Bourgeois, Department of Psychology, University of Wyoming, USA.

Shannon Butler, Department of Psychology, University of Arkansas, USA.

Robert B. Cialdini, Department of Psychology, Arizona State University, USA.

Barbara David, Division of Psychology, Australian National University, Australia.

Ap Dijksterhuis, Department of Social Psychology, University of Nijmegen, The Netherlands

Lara Dolnik, School of Psychology, University of New South Wales, Australia.

Joseph P. Forgas, School of Psychology, University of New South Wales, Australia.

Stephen G. Harkins, Psychology Department, Northeastern University, USA.

Michael A. Hogg, School of Psychology, University of Queensland, Australia.

Miles Hewstone, Department of Psychology, Cardiff University, UK.

John T. Jost, Graduate School of Business, Stanford University, USA.

Eric S. Knowles, Department of Psychology, University of Arkansas, USA.

Bibb Latané, Department of Psychology, Florida Atlantic University, USA.

Martin Lea, Department of Psychology, University of Manchester, UK.

Jay A. Linn, Department of Psychology, University of Arkansas, USA.

Robin Martin, School of Psychology, University of Queensland, Australia.

Thomas Mussweiler, Department of Psychology, University of Würzburg, Germany.

Sik Hung Ng, Department of Psychology, City University of Hong Kong, Hong Kong.

Richard E. Petty, Department of Psychology, Ohio State University, USA.

Tom Postmes, Department of Social Psychology, University of Amsterdam, The Netherlands.

Mark Schaller, Department of Psychology, University of British Columbia, Canada.

Gretchen B. Sechrist, Department of Psychology, University of Maryland, USA.

Russell Spears, Department of Social Psychology, University of Amsterdam, The Netherlands.

Charles Stangor, Department of Psychology, University of Maryland, USA.

Fritz Strack, Department of Psychology, University of Würzburg, Germany.

James T. Tedeschi, Department of Psychology, State University of New York at Albany, USA.

Deborah J. Terry, School of Psychology, University of Queensland, Australia.

John C. Turner, Division of Psychology, Australian National University, Australia.

Eva Walther, Department of Psychology, University of Heidelberg, Germany.

Susan E. Watt, Department of Social Psychology, University of Amsterdam, The Netherlands.

Kipling D. Williams, Department of Psychology, Macquarie Univeristy, Australia.

Preface

*I*nfluencing, and being influenced by others is the very essence of interpersonal behavior, and is the key mechanism that makes coordinated social life possible. Indeed, the ability to act in a smoothly cooperative, interdependent, and orderly manner is one of the main achievements of our species, and probably one of the secrets of our remarkable evolutionary success. Being human is to be social, and to be social is to influence and be influenced by others. Our thoughts, judgments, and actions all seem to be profoundly dependent on what other people think and do. It is rather surprising to find then that social psychologists have traditionally conceptualized social influence phenomena in a rather more limited and restrictive way, largely focusing on unidirectional and face-to-face influence processes such as conformity, obedience, compliance, and persuasion. Of course, these are exceedingly important effects, and many of the most dramatic results in our discipline come from these fields. When we want to impress our grandmothers with the importance of what we do, it is probably classic studies on conformity and obedience that first spring to mind as among the more important achievements of our discipline.

The main objective of this book is to provide an informative, scholarly, yet readable overview of recent advances in social influence research; at the same time we also want to advocate a greatly expanded and more integrated conceptualization of the social influence domain. Contributions to this volume will argue that social influence includes both direct and indirect influence processes, that can operate at the interpersonal, group, or socio-cultural level. Social influence involves effects that may be subconscious or conscious, and can impact on our thoughts, judgments, or observable behaviors. Further, a proper study of social influence requires a dynamic, interactive framework that simultaneously focuses both on the source and the target of influence. That is, we need to pay equal attention to the strategies of the influence agent, and the way recipients interpret, resist, or accede to influence attempts.

Indeed, one of the key themes of this book is that cognitive processes involving the thoughts, imagination and memories of influence agents and recipients play a key role in how influence strategies are delivered and responded to. In other words, we propose a new, expanded conceptualization of social influence that also incorporates the latest developments of research on social cognition and social motivation. Given the recent rise of social cognition research, we believe that this is a particularly fortuitous time to suggest such an integrated approach, as by linking these two approaches, the cognitive and the behavioral, we can enrich and expand both social influence research, and the social cognitive paradigm.

The chapters offer important new insights into the way everyday influence processes operate, and address a variety of intriguing questions such as: What kinds of influence strategies are preferentially used by 'compliance professionals', and why? How can we reduce resistance to social influence by disrupting recipients' cognitive strategies? Can we simulate dynamic influence processes using computer algorithms? Can social influence be exercised subliminally? What roles do influence processes play in the establishment and maintenance of cultural norms? How does group membership influence the use of stereotypes, and the way persuasive messages from minority and majority subgroups are processed? What is the role of mood states in the way people exercise, and respond to influence strategies? Are there times when being thoughtful makes us more susceptible to social influence?

Of course, no single book could possibly include everything that is interesting and exciting in contemporary social influence research. In selecting and inviting our contributors, we aimed to achieve a comprehensive and representative coverage, but of course we cannot claim to have fully sampled all of the relevant areas. The chapters are arranged into three sections: dealing with I, fundamental issues in influence research; II, the role of cognitive processes in social influence; and III, social influence and group behavior. The introductory chapter presents a historical overview of influence research, and outlines the case for a more comprehensive and integrative conceptualization of the field (Forgas & Williams).

The chapters in Part I discuss some of the cognitive influence strategies used by 'compliance professionals' (Cialdini), as well as strategies that can reduce resistance to influence attempts (Knowles et al.). It turns out that dynamic influence processes can be effectively modeled using computer simulations (Latané & Bourgeois), and we find that spontaneous influence between people can play a key role in how cultural norms are maintained or changed (Schaller). Social influence can also operate subconsciously, when merely activating a stereotype can produce stereotype-consistent behaviors (Dijksterhuis). In the last chapter of this section, Tedeschi outlines a social interactionist theory of aggression as one of the more dramatic influence strategies people use.

The chapters in Part II examine the role of cognitive processes in social influence. Paradoxically, being thoughtful may sometimes increase people's susceptibility to subtle influence strategies (Petty), and affective states can also impact on how social influence strategies are used and responded to (Forgas). Social influence also plays a role in purely cognitive phenomena, such as memory performance (Bless, Strack & Walther). Ng identifies three conceptually distinct levels of social influence (face-to-face, indirect, and subliminal influence) and uses this framework to analyze the way language is used in creating emergent power relationships within groups. The role of various cognitive strategies in counteracting social influence is discussed by Strack and Mussweiler, and Williams and Dolnik describe one such influence strategy, stealing thunder— exposing an audience to potentially negative information first.

Part III focuses on social influence in group settings. Stangor, Sechrist, and Jost discuss how group consensus influences individuals' confidence in their stereotypic beliefs, and in-group norms can also influence whether people be- have in accordance with their attitudes (Terry & Hogg). Harkins shows that evaluations by others often appear to exert greater influence on people than do their self-evaluations. David and Turner use self-categorization theory to ex- plain majority and minority influence phenomena in a variety of experimental and field settings. Martin and Hewstone analyze how persuasive messages from minority or majority groups are processed. Finally, Spears, Postmes, Lea and Watt develop their SIDE model (the Social Identity model of Deindividuation Effects) to explore how contextual factors impact on social influence processes within groups.

THE SYDNEY SYMPOSIUM OF SOCIAL PSYCHOLOGY SERIES

This book is the third in the Sydney Symposium of Social Psychology series, held every year at the University of New South Wales, Sydney. We want to emphasize that this is not simply an edited book in the usual sense. Perhaps a few words are in order about the origins of this volume, and the Sydney Sympo- sium of Social Psychology series in general. The objective of the Sydney Sym- posia is to provide new, integrative understanding in important areas of social psychology by inviting leading researchers in a particular field to a three-day residential Symposium in Sydney. This Symposium has received generous fi- nancial support from the University of New South Wales, allowing the careful selection and funding of a small group of leading researchers as contributors. Draft papers by all contributors were prepared well in advance of the sympo- sium and were made available to all participants before the meeting. Thus, par- ticipants had an opportunity to review and revise their papers in the light of everyone else's draft contribution even before they arrived in Sydney.

The critical part of the preparation of this book has been the intensive three-day face-to-face meeting between all invited contributors. Sydney Sym- posia are characterized by open, free-ranging, intensive and critical discussion between all participants, with the objective to explore points of integration and contrast between the proposed papers. A further revision of each chapter was prepared soon after the Symposium, incorporating many of the shared points that emerged in our discussions. Thanks to these collaborative procedures, the book does not simply consist of a set of chapters prepared in isolation. Rather, this Sydney Symposium volume represents a collaborative effort by a leading group of international researchers intent on producing a comprehensive and up-to-date review of social influence research. We hope that the published papers will succeed in conveying some of the sense of fun and excitement we all shared during the Symposium.

Two previous volumes of the Sydney Symposium series have been published. The first, *Feeling and Thinking: The Role of Affect in Social Cognition*, was edited by Joseph Forgas, and was published by Cambridge University Press, New York, 2000 (ISBN 0521 64223X). This book explored the role that affective states play in social cognition and social behavior, with contributions by Robert Zajonc, Jim Blascovich, Craig Smith, Eric Eich, Len Berkowitz, Leonard Martin, Daniel Gilbert, Herbert Bless, Klaus Fiedler, Joseph Forgas, Carolin Showers, Tony Greenwald, Mahzarin Banaji, Mark Leary, Paula Niedenthal, and Jamin Halberstadt among others. The second volume, *The Social Mind: Cognitive and Motivational Aspects of Interpersonal Behavior*, was also published by Cambridge University Press, 2001; ISBN 0521 770920, and featured chapters by William and Claire McGuire, Susan Andersen, Roy Baumeister, Joel Cooper, Bill Crano, Garth Fletcher, Joseph Forgas, Pascal Huguet, Mike Hogg, Martin Kaplan, Norb Kerr, John Nezlek, Fred Rhodewalt, Astrid Schuetz, Constantine Sedikides, Jeffrey Simpson, Richard Sorrentino, Dianne Tice, Kip Williams, Ladd Wheeler, and others.

Given its comprehensive coverage, this book should be useful both as a basic reference book, and as an informative textbook to be used in advanced courses dealing with social influence phenomena. The main target audience for this book comprises researchers, students, and professionals in all areas of the social and behavioral sciences, such as social, cognitive, clinical, counselling, personality, organizational, and applied psychology, as well as sociology, communication studies, and cognitive science. The book is written in a readable yet scholarly style, and students both at the undergraduate and at the graduate level should find it an engaging overview of the field and thus useful as a textbook in courses dealing with social influence. The book should also be of direct interest to people working in applied areas where using and understanding social influence is important, such as marketing and advertising, organizational psychology, counselling, clinical psychology, and health psychology.

We want to express our thanks to people and organizations who helped to make the Sydney Symposium of Social Psychology, and this third volume, in particular, a reality. Producing a complex multi-authored book such as this is a lengthy and sometimes challenging task. We have been very fortunate to work with such an excellent and cooperative group of contributors. Our first thanks must go to them. Because of their help and professionalism, we were able to finish this project without any delays and in fact, somewhat ahead of time. Past friendships have not frayed, and we are all still on speaking terms; indeed, we hope that working together on this book has been as positive an experience for them as it has been for us.

The idea of organizing the Sydney Symposia owes much to discussions with, and encouragement by Kevin McConkey, and subsequent support by Chris Fell, Merilyn Sleigh, and numerous others at the University of New South Wales. We want to express our gratitude to Alison Mudditt, Editorial Director at Psychology Press who has been amazingly helpful, efficient, and supportive through all the stages of producing this book. We are also grateful to Elizabeth Ebersole, Production Editor at Psychology Press for her professional and efficient handling of the production process. Our colleagues at the School of Psychology at UNSW, Stephanie Moylan, Cherie Robbins, Vera Thomson, Lisa Zadro, Christopher Koletti, Simon Latham, Lara Dolnik, Cassie Govan, and others have helped with advice, support, and sheer hard work to share the burden of preparing and organizing the symposium and the ensuing book. Financial support from the Australian Research Council and the University of New South Wales were of course essential to get this project off the ground. Most of all, we are grateful for the love and support of our families who have put up with us during the many months of work that went into producing this book.

We are obliged to finish this Preface on a rather sad note. Jim Tedeschi, a key contributor to this project, tragically and suddenly passed away just a few weeks after he completed work on the copyedited manuscript of his chapter. Jim has been a particularly thoughtful and stimulating member of our group, and his contributions to our discipline are too numerous to list here. We want to express our sympathy and condolences to his family; his loss will be keenly felt in our discipline, and by all of us who knew him.

Joseph P. Forgas and Kipling D. Williams
Sydney, January 2001

PART *I*

SOCIAL INFLUENCE: FUNDAMENTAL PROCESSES AND THEORIES

1

Social Influence
Introduction and Overview

JOSEPH P. FORGAS
KIPLING D. WILLIAMS

*T*he study of social influence processes is one of the core issues in psychology. All interpersonal behavior involves mutual influence processes, and coordinated interaction by larger social units, such as groups, and even whole societies, is only possible because our behavior is guided by pervasive and shared forms of social influence. The remarkable capacity of human beings to cooperate and collaborate with each other, and to establish ever-more com-

This work was supported by a Special Investigator award from the Australian Research Council, and the Research Prize by the Alexander von Humboldt Foundation to Joseph P. Forgas, and an Australian Research Council grant to Kipling D. Williams. The contribution of Stephanie Moylan and Lisa Zadro to this project is gratefully acknowledged. Please address all correspondence in connection with this chapter to Joseph P. Forgas, at the School of Psychology, University of New South Wales, Sydney 2052, Australia. E-mail: jp.forgas@unsw.edu.au, or Kipling D. Williams, Department of Psychology, Macquarie University, Sydney, NSW, 2109, Australia. E-mail: kip@psy.mq.edu.au

3

plex forms of social organization provides ultimate evidence for our highly developed ability to influence, and to be influenced by others (see Schaller, this volume). Social influence is thus arguably the main currency of social life. Indeed, Allport's (1924) classic definition of social psychology as the study of how individuals are influenced by the real or imagined presence of others clearly illustrates how crucial influence processes are to all aspects of social life (see also Ng, this volume).

Surprisingly, social psychologists typically think about social influence processes in a much more restrictive way. Although all our textbooks contain key sections on 'social influence' processes, what is discussed there is usually limited to dramatic illustrations of various forms of direct interpersonal influence, such as social facilitation effects, conformity, obedience, and persuasion. It seems that our fascination with these impressive demonstrations of direct influence in classic experiments by Sherif, Asch, and Milgram perhaps limited our interest in the much more general and pervasive aspects of influence processes.

We want to argue in this book that social influence should be conceptualized in a much more broad and inclusive manner. All forms of human interaction involve mutual influence processes, and these function at a variety of levels—cognitive, interpersonal, and cultural. Further, influence is frequently indirect rather than direct. Others often influence us in ways we are not even aware of (see Dijksterhuis, this volume), and social influence shapes not only our behaviors, but also our thoughts, memories, and cognitive representations (see Bless, Strack, and Walther, also Petty, and Strack and Mussweiler this volume). This book, then, seeks to provide an informative, scholarly yet readable overview of recent advances in this field. But this is not all; we also hope to advocate a new, radically expanded vision of what social influence entails.

Rather than merely focusing on traditional research areas mainly concerned with direct, face-to-face influence processes, contributions to this volume advocate an expanded theoretical approach that also incorporates many of the insights gained from contemporary research on social cognition and motivation. Few attempts have been made so far to integrate the contributions to social influence research made by these distinct theoretical frameworks, or to directly link research on social influence processes with recent work on social cognitive and motivational processes. Yet with the rapid accumulation of empirical evidence, there is now a pressing need for such a more inclusive and integrative theoretical treatment of this field. This is one of the main objectives of this volume.

The book is organized into three main sections. After this general introductory chapter by the editors the first section considers some fundamental processes and theories applicable to social influence research (chapters by Cialdini, Knowles, Latané & Bourgeois, Schaller, Dijksterhuis, and Tedeschi). The second section of the book also contains six chapters, and looks at the role of cognitive processes and strategies in social influence phenomena (chapters by Petty, Forgas, Bless, Ng, Strack, and Williams & Dolnik). The third section of the book turns to perhaps the most complex domain of social influence research: the operation of social influence mechanisms in group settings (chapters by Stangor & Sechrist, Terry & Hogg, Harkins, David & Turner, Martin & Hewstone, Spears, Postmes, Lea, & Watt). This introductory chapter surveys the major themes covered in the book, highlights the links between the various chapters, and proposes future avenues for research in this area.

SOCIAL INFLUENCE IN SOCIAL PSYCHOLOGY

Of course, the study of social influence processes has a long and proud tradition in social psychology. Indeed, our textbooks continue to feature social influence research prominently, and some of our most intriguing research findings come from this area. When we want to impress our students, friends, and mothers-in-law with the importance and relevance of our discipline, the work of Sherif, Asch, and Milgram on conformity and obedience are often the first examples that come to mind. Despite this proud tradition, it is fair to say that contemporary interest in direct social influence processes has been somewhat in decline. Very few people continue to do this kind of research. At a recent meeting of experimental social psychologists, Eliot Aronson commented on the sad demise of what he called "impactful" research on "real" interpersonal behavior. What has happened?

Social psychology has undergone something like a paradigmatic revolution since the "crisis" of the 1970s. With the emergence of the social cognitive paradigm, we now spend much more time studying the internal cognitive representations, thoughts, and motivations of isolated social actors rather than their reactions to real social situations. During the past few decades social psychology has increasingly adopted an individualistic social cognitive paradigm that has mainly focused on the study of individual thoughts and motivations (Forgas, 1981); as a consequence, the study of direct interpersonal behaviors has declined in relative importance (Wegner & Gilbert, 2000). Although we have made major advances in understanding how people process information about the social world, relatively few attempts have been made to explore how processes of social cognition and motivation may find expression in interpersonal influence behaviors.

Within the social influence field, this shift towards social cognition has been reflected in a growing interest in persuasive communication phenomena, and in particular, research on the influence of different information processing strategies on how individuals respond to persuasive messages (Petty & Cacioppo, 1986). Clearly both approaches are necessary if we are to understand social influence processes. However, perhaps the time has come when we should look toward a greater integration between impactful, behavioral research, and cognitive and motivational approaches. As several contributors to this volume argue, social influence research has been handicapped by a rather restrictive conceptualization of what influence entails. We now know that social influence often works not because people are exposed to explicit pressures, but because they are encouraged to imagine events (Cialdini, this volume), experience particular moods (Forgas, this volume), are subconsciously influenced by incidental observations (see chapters by Dijksterhuis and by Petty, this volume), or engage in spontaneous group interactions (Latané & Bourgeois, Stangor & Jost, Sechrist & Jost, Terry & Hogg, David & Turner, this volume). In other words, in addition to highly familiar direct and face-to-face influence phenomena, influence also operates at cognitive, group, social, and cultural levels.

Mass societies function well because they have developed efficient ways of influencing and coordinating the behavior of 'strangers' in ways of which we are barely aware. We are constantly bombarded with influence messages designed by a new class of 'social influence professionals' (see chapter by Cialdini, this volume), and we certainly need to understand better how these often invisible influence processes operate (see chapters by Schaller, Dijksterhuis, Petty, Ng, Terry & Hogg, David & Turner).

We also want to argue in this volume that the traditional juxtaposition of the 'behavioral' and the 'cognitive' aspects of social influence is neither helpful nor necessary. A meaningful explanation of social influence phenomena must be based on an integrated analysis of the thoughts and motivations of individual social influence agents and recipients (see, for example, chapters by Cialdini, Knowles, Butler, & Linn, Forgas, Ng, this volume). On the other hand, social influence always occurs in real social settings, and we must pay careful attention to the personal relationships, group memberships, and cultural expectations that provide the pragmatic context for all influence processes (see Terry & Hogg, David & Turner, Spears, Postmes, Lea, & Watt, this volume). In a way, the dichotomy between cognitive and behavioral, and indirect and direct influence processes reflects one of the oldest debates in the history of psychology. Should psychology be primarily the study of 'mind,' or the study of 'behavior' (Hilgard, 1980)?

We believe that understanding social influence processes, by definition, requires paying as much attention to the thoughts, motivations, and feelings of social actors—the 'mental world'—(Bless & Forgas, 2000) as to actual interpersonal behaviors. Thus, the proper focus of influence research should be the analysis of the interaction between the mental (cognitive) and the behavioral aspects of social influence processes. We referred to 'direct' and 'indirect' processes in the title of this book intentionally, to signify the close interdependence between the mental (cognitive) and the behavioral, interpersonal aspects of social influence.

Surprisingly, the important insights gained from the cognitivist paradigm that has dominated social psychology for the past few decades have only rarely been applied to enrich our understanding of social influence processes. One important objective of this book is to rectify this imbalance by focusing on both the study of explicit, direct influence strategies, and implicit, indirect influence mechanisms as they interact in many kinds of real-life influence episodes.

The terms direct and indirect social influence also indicate another, related distinction. Social influence doesn't always operate in a direct, observable way as one person's behavior is manifestly influenced by an influence agent. Often we are influenced in more indirect ways. For example, the norms, values, and beliefs of the social groups we belong to all exert a profound influence on our thoughts and behaviors in subtle and not so subtle ways—yet people are not always aware of such influences. Social influence can thus be exercised not only by direct person-to-person mechanisms such as social facilitation, conformity, obedience, or persuasion, but also by more indirect, diffuse means such as attempts to change the attitudes and norms of larger social groups. Further, many kinds of influence mechanisms operate in ways that influence recipients are not even aware of. Cognitive and behavioral priming effects as discussed by Dijksterhuis and Petty in this text represent examples of such indirect influence processes.

Some contributors to this volume, such as Ng, argue that we should distinguish between three fundamentally different kinds of influence phenomena. According to Ng, Level 1 influence involves direct, person-to-person influence. Level 2 influence relies on the indirect manipulation of group norms and customs and social and cultural attitudes. Level 3 influence is the most elusive and indirect, when influence recipients are not even aware that their thoughts and behaviors have been influenced by others (see chapters by Dijksterhuis, Petty, Bless, Strack, & Walther, and Strack & Musswieler this volume). The contributors to this book were selected so as to cover a broad spectrum of these different influence processes. The aim is to demonstrate that social influence includes a far richer and more multifaceted range of phenomena than traditionally assumed by social psychologists. The chapters in this volume all report theories and research that illustrate the benefits of adopting such an integrative approach to the analysis of social influence processes.

SOCIAL INFLUENCE AND SOCIAL INTEGRATION

The sophisticated ability of human beings to influence, and be influenced, by each other is probably one of the cornerstones of the evolutionary success of our species, and the foundation of the increasingly complex forms of social organization we have been able to develop. Homo sapiens is a highly sociable species. The astounding development of our mental and cognitive abilities, and our impressive record of achievements owes a great deal to the highly elaborate strategies we have developed for getting along with each other and coordinating our interpersonal behaviors. In fact, we argue that social influence processes constitute the essential 'glue' that holds families, groups, and even whole societies together.

Understanding the various ways that people influence each other, and the role of cognitive, motivational, and affective mechanisms in these processes has probably never been of greater importance than today. As modern industrialized societies become ever more complex and impersonal, and as our interactions increasingly involve people we only know superficially, our social influence strategies had to become more sophisticated, indirect, and subtle. Complex mass societies present us with a social environment that is far more problematic and demanding than was the case in earlier epochs. The last few hundred years produced a form of social living that is profoundly different from the way human beings lived throughout previous millenia. Our past evolutionary history scarcely could have prepared us for life in the kind of anonymous mass societies we now find ourselves in.

Since the dawn of evolution, human beings lived mostly in small, close, face-to-face groups. From our earliest hunter-gatherer societies to life in small-scale villages that was dominant everywhere as recently as in the eighteenth century, human social interaction typically involved intimately known others, mostly members of our small, immediate group. The eighteenth century brought with it a fundamental revolution in social relationships. Several historical factors contributed to the rapid disappearance of traditional, face-to-face society, and the fundamental change in social influence processes and social integration that occurred (Durkheim, 1956). The philosophy of the enlightenment laid the conceptual groundwork for the image of the liberated, self-sufficient, and mobile individual, freed from the restrictive influence of unalterable social norms and conventions. This ideology found its political expression in the French, and American Revolutions. Industrialization produced large-scale dislocation and the reassembly of massive working populations as required by technologies of mass production. These developments had crucial consequences for the way people related to each other.

In stable, small-scale societies social relationships are highly regulated. One's place in society is largely determined by ascribed status and rigid norms. Mobility is restricted, and social influence strategies mainly function at the direct, interpersonal level. Compare this with life in modern mass societies. Most people we encounter are strangers. Our position in society is flexible, personal anonymity is widespread and mobility is high—yet social influence strategies continue to play a key role in achieving our objectives in such a fluid social environment. The fact that most people we deal with are not intimately known to us makes the appropriate use of influence strategies ever more problematic. It is perhaps no coincidence that the emergence of psychology and social psychology as a science of interpersonal behavior so clearly coincided with the advent of mass societies. For the first time, social interaction—once a natural, automatic process almost entirely enacted within the confines of involved relationships with intimately known others—has become uncertain and problematic, and thus, an object of concern, reflection, and study (Goffman, 1972). To be able to influence others, we need to rely on ever-more sophisticated and elaborate cognitive and motivational strategies.

Emile Durkheim, the father of modern sociology described this profound shift in social relationships in terms of a change from organic solidarity to mechanical solidarity (Durkheim, 1956). Organic solidarity refers to the complex web of face-to-face interdependencies and social influence processes that provide cohesion and unity to small-scale, primary social groups. Organic solidarity is based on direct, personal influence relationships. Mechanical solidarity, in turn, refers to the indirect, impersonal, and disembodied web of relationships and interdependencies that characterize mass societies based on the anonymous division of labor. We have come depend on, and be influenced by strangers we never meet, and our relationships are increasingly regulated by rules and contractual expectations that are no longer based on personal contact. Many of the chapters here discuss the operation of anonymous social influence processes in indirect, diffuse social contexts (see chapters in this volume by Schaller, Dijksterhuis, Petty, Ng).

SOCIAL INFLUENCE: SOME HISTORICAL ANTECEDENTS

The kind of close integration between the mental and the behavioral aspects of influence phenomena we want to advocate here is far from new. Indeed, a number of classical social science theories have argued for such an approach, emphasizing the close interdependence between symbolic mental processes and direct interpersonal behavior. Symbolic interactionism, a comprehensive theory of interpersonal behavior developed by George Herbert Mead (Mead, 1934), offers one important example of such an integrative framework for the study of social influence processes. For Mead, social cognition and social behavior were not distinct, separate domains of inquiry, but intrinsically related. Mead explicitly sought to reconcile the behaviorist and the phenomenologist, mentalistic approaches to human behavior. He argued that social influence functions because of the symbolic representations and expectations formed by social actors as they experience interpersonal episodes.

Our mental representations of how to behave in any given situation are partly 'given,' determined by our prior experiences and symbolic representations of past social encounters. However, behavior is not fully determined; to some extent, social actors are free to construct their encounters in unique and individualistic ways. According to Mead (1934), our uniquely human ability for symbolic representations allows us to abstract and internalize social experiences, and it is such mental models that are the key to understanding interpersonal behavior in general, and social influence processes in particular. A number of the chapters (e.g., by Petty, Bless et al., Terry & Hogg, David & Turner, Spears et al., and others) in this volume describe research that is strongly reminiscent of Mead's emphasis on symbolic representations in explaining behavior.

It is perhaps unfortunate that symbolic interactionism has never become an important theory within social psychology, probably because the absence of suitable methodologies for studying individual symbolic representations at the time. The currently dominant social cognitive paradigm has changed much of this, as it essentially deals with the same kinds of questions that also were of interest to Mead: How do the mental and symbolic representations that people form of their interpersonal encounters come to influence their interpersonal behavior? Recent social cognitive research has produced a range of ingenious techniques and empirical procedures that for the first time allow a rigorous empirical analysis of the links between mental representations and strategic behaviors (e.g., Bless & Forgas, 2000; Forgas, 1995; Wegner & Gilbert, 2000). Several chapters (e.g., Forgas, Williams & Dolnik, etc.) included here provide excellent illustrations of how the merging of cognitive and behavioral approaches can give us important new insights into the nature of social influence phenomena.

Another important, yet frequently neglected, approach that could inform contemporary theorizing about social influence processes is associated with the name of Max Weber. Weber always assumed a close and direct link between how an individual thinks about and cognitively represents social situations, and the individual's actual interpersonal behaviors. For Weber, it was precisely these mental representations and ideas about the social world that provided the crucial link between understanding individual behaviors, and the operation of large-scale social and cultural systems. The chapter here by Schaller offers an almost Weberian analysis of social influence processes properly located within their larger social and cultural context. Perhaps the best example of Weber's cultural analysis is his theory linking the emergence of capitalism with the spread of the values and beliefs—and behaviors—associated with the protestant ethic. This work is profoundly social psychological in orientation, in that its key emphasis is on individual social behaviors as they are influenced by diffusely shared beliefs and norms, and as they in turn create large-scale and enduring social systems (Weber, 1947). The same kind of approach is also directly applicable to understanding how social influence mechanisms operate.

The tangible social and economic system that surrounds us and exerts such a profound influence on our everyday behaviors is, in the last analysis, simply a product of the shared symbolic representations and spontaneous socially influenced behaviors of countless individuals and the choices and decisions made by members of our society. Weber assumes that individual beliefs and motivations—for example, the spreading acceptance of the protestant ethic—are the fundamental influences that ultimately shape large-scale social structures and cultures such as capitalism (Weber, 1947).

The richness of Weber's approach to the study of social influence processes is particularly well illustrated by his seminal work on bureaucracies (Weber, 1947). This analysis probes the intricate relationship between the rigid external rules and norms that are an intrinsic feature of mechanistic bureaucratic systems, and the subjective internal representations and beliefs of the inhabitants of such systems, the bureaucrats. On the one hand, the explicit rule systems that define bureaucracies play a critical role in shaping and maintaining the mental world and behavior of the bureaucrat. On the other hand, the mental worlds of bureaucrats cannot but impact on the functioning of the bureaucratic organization. Max Weber also was among the first to show that a clear understanding of the effects of social influence processes on behavior must involve both the study of externally observable behavior, as well as the subjectively perceived meanings that are attached to an action by the actor. In fact, Max Weber is probably one of the intellectual originators of the kind of integrative social psychological research that is becoming increasingly popular today and is represented by several contributions to this book. This approach seeks to unify the insights derived from the social cognitive approach, with a genuine concern with real-life social behavior and its role in larger social systems.

Of course, Weber was not a social psychologist; because of his primary interest in larger social systems, experimentation was not one of his methods. However, he was a creative empiricist and he pioneered a variety of ingenious techniques to obtain reliable empirical data about social influence processes. A number of chapters included in this volume also feature innovative ways to study influence mechanisms. These techniques, relying on participant methods and field studies, will certainly enrich the methodological armory of social influence researchers (see chapters in this volume by Cialdini, Dijksterhuis, Terry & Hogg, David & Turner, etc.).

Even though the work of Max Weber and George Herbert Mead is rarely acknowledged by social psychologists, it nevertheless exerts an important, albeit indirect, influence on our discipline. The microsociological tradition represented by the work of Erving Goffmann (1972) and others owes much to Weber's theories, and in turn, it has had a definite impact on social psychologists. Goffmann produced some illuminating analyses of the delicate interaction between the influence of externally imposed norms and roles on social behavior on the one hand, and an individual's thoughts, plans, and self-presentational strategies in public encounters on the other. Goffman used the metaphor of the theater to study interpersonal behavior, and his dramaturgical account of social influence strategies continues a unique tradition in our field. The work of Cialdini (this volume) represents a nice illustration of how participant observation of the strategies used by everyday influence agents, in the best Goffmanesque tradition, can provide intriguing new insights into influence strategies. Other chapters offer similarly useful illustrations of the important role that microsociological approaches continue to play in the study of social influence processes (e.g., chapters by Schaller, Terry & Hogg, David & Turner).

Yet another important conceptual orientation that is highly relevant here is the rich phenomenological tradition in our discipline. In fact, the work of classic theoreticians in our discipline such as Fritz Heider and Kurt Lewin owe much to the phenomenological perspective. For example, Fritz Heider's pioneering work (Heider, 1958) explored the kind of information gathering strategies and implicit inferences that social actors must rely on as they plan and execute their social influence strategies. Heider's phenomenological theorizing produced some of our most popular empirical paradigms, including work on such key questions as attribution processes and person perception phenomena, balance and dissonance theories, and research on attitude organization and attitude change.

The other great figure of classical social psychology, Kurt Lewin, also was profoundly committed to the study of interpersonal behavior as it is influenced by the mental representations and motivations of individuals. Lewin's field theory in particular represents a framework that allows us to conceptualize social influence processes not as external events, but as subtle changes that occur within the subjectively defined life-space of individuals (see Knowles, Butler, & Linn, this volume). The Lewinian approach affirms the principle that the way people mentally represent and experience social influence situations should be the focus of our research. Lewin's emphasis on the subjective life-spaces of social actors gave us some of our most productive research paradigms, including much research on group behavior (see chapters by Terry & Hogg, David & Turner, Martin & Hewstone, Spears et al.).

Mead, Weber, Heider, and Lewin represent just a few of the classic social science theorists for whom the internal and external world of social actors was integrally related. In referring to their work, we simply want to demonstrate that our discipline has an impressive tradition of theorizing that is directly relevant to the objectives of this book. The very same questions that occupied the minds of these authors continue to be reflected in the contributions to this volume. To what extent is social influence exercised through subtle, often subconscious cognitive mechanisms? How can we conceptualize influence processes as dynamic interpersonal events where reactions by the recipient are as much part of the influence process as are the strategies of influence agents? How do groups and societies construct shared belief systems? How does imagining an event influence subsequent behaviors? How do perceptions of groups dynamically develop into shared interaction experiences? How can resistance to change be lowered? How do individual states, such as moods impact on how people use, and respond to influence strategies? These are just some of the questions contributors to this volume will explore.

OUTLINE OF THE BOOK

The 19 chapters in this book were selected so as to represent a broad a cross-section of contemporary social influence research. Contributions are arranged into three sections: chapters that deal with fundamental theoretical and methodological issues relevant to social influence research (Part 1), chapters that explore the role of mental representations and cognitive processes in social influence phenomena (Part 2), and chapters that discuss the operation of social influence mechanisms in a group context (Part 3).

PART I. SOCIAL INFLUENCE: FUNDAMENTAL PROCESSES AND THEORIES

The first part of the book presents chapters that illustrate some of the basic approaches to social influence research.

Cialdini starts off by observing that many social influence tactics have withstood the test of time through an evolutionary process of survival of the fittest.

Essentially, through trial-and-error use by compliance professionals, particularly those in marketing and sales, some methods prove quite successful and robust. But this is where the contribution of compliance professionals ends, because they typically do not know *why* these methods work. Thus, we can look to compliance professionals in the real world to inform us about successful social influence tactics, but we must rely on careful experimental work to figure out why they work, and what their boundary conditions are.

One such example is inducing potential customers to imagine a situation in which the product being sold would be necessary. Does this tactic work because it provides consumers with ideas they had not previously considered, especially by eliciting fear? Cialdini thought that a more basic process was at work, one that might underlie most social influence phenomena: the availability heuristic. When people can more easily imagine circumstances where having what is being sold would be rewarding, they will be more likely to comply to sales pitches for that product. Using both field and laboratory investigations, Cialdini provides strong support for his simple, yet elegant principle. The implications are far-reaching, and provide a useful foundation for many of the other forms of social influence discussed in this volume by illustrating how mental representations and imagination play a key role in many influence situations.

In the next chapter, Knowles, Butler, and Linn astutely observe that most theories of social influence focus primarily on the approach side of the social influence conflict dynamic. That is, social influence tactics used for persuasion and compliance emphasize bolstering the approach tendencies. Most persuasion and compliance techniques work by adding incentives to promote persuasion or compliance. Knowles, Butler, and Linn take a step back, and conceptualize social influence in a Lewinian framework, in which the individual who is approached by a social influence agent is caught between a combination of approach and avoidance forces. Every opportunity to be influenced has potential costs and benefits. They argue that most social psychological research has focused on how, by increasing the perceived benefits, compliance increases.

Their interest is in showing how to increase compliance by reducing resistance. Resistance, they argue, is an important component of most social influence situations. Any attempt of social influence that fails, does so because there is resistance. Even with successful influence, resistance may persist to produce reservation and doubt. Yet, resistance has played a very minor role in the study of social influence. Knowles, Butler, and Linn consider a large number of tactics from this perspective, but also forge new ground by exploring techniques that undermine mental resistance. Among other techniques, Knowles and his colleagues use very subtle and clever word disfluencies in field and laboratory experiments, and show how disrupting thought when costs would normally be considered will increase compliance. Like Cialdini's insight, this is quite simple and elegant, yet has important implications in such diverse areas as clinical therapy, sales, and marketing.

Latané and Bourgeois begin with the principle of a very successful static theory of social influence: Latané's social impact theory. This theory provided an excellent conceptual and mathematically precise fit to all sorts of social influence phenomenon based upon two tenets: that social influence was a function of the number, strength, and immediacy of others, and that this impact could either be multiplied (if the others are sources of impact) or diffused (if the others share the impact with the target individual). This metatheory, as they call it, can be applied to describing a large body of social influence research, including conformity, compliance, stage fright, helping, help-seeking, productivity, and obedience.

The authors then argue for the importance of recognizing the dynamic aspect of social influence. In typical interchanges between individuals, within groups, or between groups, it is rarely the case that only one person talks to another, while the other passively listens without giving any feedback or reaction. Rather than simply giving lip service to the frequent admission that social influence phenomena are more complicated than that usually depicted in stimulus-response paradigms, Latané and Bourgeois make theoretically derived predictions of dynamic influence and test them in computer simulations and in real life influence networks. They also developed clever games, like the conformity game and the deviance game, to investigate the dynamic influence of minorities, persuasion, and conformity, in complex situations in which individuals differ from each other in terms of their physical distance, the positions they take on attitude issues, and their persuasiveness. Through simulations and experiments, Latané and Bourgeois examine several important principles in dynamic social influence: consolidation, clustering, correlation, and continuing diversity.

The next chapter by Schaller expands social influence research in yet another direction. Schaller takes a broader view of social influence, invoking a social-evolutionary framework to explain the processes in the construction and change of cultural norms—the socially shared information that describes a human population. Schaller argues that change in cultural norms occurs often without the explicit intention of individuals or society. The aim of his chapter is to discuss what psychological process contributes to the unintended changes in the contents of cultural norms?

To illustrate how these processes operate, Schaller discusses two seemingly unrelated phenomena: The disappearance over several decades of the trait "superstitious" from stereotypes of African Americans, and the apparent anti-innovation bias in the editing process of scientific journals. Schaller argues that it is through subtle communication processes, the way people talk about their experiences, that cultural norms are created and maintained. It is not what one believes so much as it is how one talks about these norms that determine their persistence. Thus, social influence is not only produced by shared norms (as Terry & Hogg discuss), but it affects the contents of the norms as well. Schaller's analysis shows some affinity both with Mead's classical theories, and Weber's cultural sociology.

In yet another approach, Dijksterhuis examines automatic social influence processes that operate at a level below awareness. He invokes the century-old concept of ideomotor action: That merely thinking about an action leads automatically to tendencies to engage in that action. To the extent that these thoughts can be triggered by others, we have instances of automatic social influence. Dijksterhuis reviews recent literature that demonstrates how neurophysiological changes that accompany the mere *thought* of simple and complex behaviors mirror neurophysiological changes during the *action* of what those thoughts represent.

He interprets two social influence phenomena as evidence for this automatic social influence: behavior matching and priming. In some cases activation of behavior representations resulted from a perception process, while in others the manipulations used came closer to manipulations of mental simulation (similar to Cialdini's discussion of the potent effects of imagining). Dijksterhuis argues that perception of behaviors leads to activation of behavior representations. In both cases behavior representations are activated, ultimately leading to the increased likelihood of performance of this behavior. Thus, for Dijksterhuis social influence represents the interplay between perception, cognition, and action. Whereas behavior matching is more direct, social influence caused by priming is likely to be mediated by trait activation. For instance, Dijksterhuis and his colleagues showed that activation of the stereotype of the elderly led to forgetfulness, but only among participants who associated elderly with forgetfulness. Thus, stereotypes can automatically affect behavior because they activate, through the priming of traits and of behavior representations, motor programs that are consistent with these stereotypes.

The next chapter by Tedeschi deals with aggression. At first glance this may seem out of place in a volume on social influence, but this is precisely the view that Tedeschi wants to challenge. To him, the isolation of aggression within the field of social psychology as a distinct social phenomenon is arbitrary and capricious. He regards aggression as harm-doing or threats of harm-doing that is related to, and is on a continuum with other social influence phenomena that are motivated by interpersonal goals. As such, he takes a strong position that aggression is, by definition, instrumental. People use harmful actions as a means of social influence—to compel or deter others. Tedeschi develops a power-oriented social interactionist theory to explain aggressive behavior. He sets forth three primary motives for aggressive behavior as an influence strategy: to control others, to maintain justice, and to establish or defend social identities. Causes of aggression are due to social cognitive processes of the actors and the social context in which the action takes place. The net result of this theoretical framework is to bring the study of aggression into the fold of social influence. In so doing, there are surprising similarities between his analysis of aggression, and analyses of other social behaviors more commonly thought to be those affected by social influence, such as persuasion, conformity, and compliance.

Another key contribution of Tedeschi's chapter is drawing attention to the source of social influence rather than, as is the typical focus, the target of it. Similar to Ng's and Forgas's (see their chapters) interests, Tedeschi argues that the field of social psychology artificially separates social influence by its focus on targets or sources. He states, "when the source of influence is the focus of interest, it is usually referred to as leadership, self-presentation, prosocial behavior, and aggression, and not theoretically interpreted in terms of power and influence." This sort of distinction serves to separate rather than integrate common processes within the field. He argues, as do others in this volume, that a more complete theory of social influence would incorporate an analysis of sources together with an analysis of targets as is also done, for example, in Williams and Dolnik's chapter.

PART II. THE ROLE OF COGNITIVE PROCESSES AND STRATEGIES IN SOCIAL INFLUENCE

Petty's chapter explores the general principles of subtle and automatic social influence and asks, What are the conditions under which these subtle effects will have the most influence, and who is most susceptible? Is it the case that all people are similarly affected by such subtle influences because cognitive effort by the targets of influence is generally absent? Or is it the case that subtle effects are weaker for those who are most thoughtful? Petty argues for a third, counterintuitive perspective: that subtle influences will be most powerful on those who are most thoughtful. He reasons that in thoughtful situations, or with thoughtful people, subtle influences permeate and guide behavior because "the more cognitions one has, the more bias that can occur." Similar counterintuitive principles were previously advocated by Forgas (1995), who in a series of experiments also found that affective states have a greater impact on judgments and behavior when individuals have to engage in thoughtful, extensive processing in order to solve a problem (see also Forgas, this volume).

Three social influence contaminants are described: effects of overt head movements on attitudes, effects of cognitive primes on behavior, and effects of mood state on judgments, attitudes, and behavior. For each of these contaminants, Petty demonstrates that thoughtful people can be more susceptible to a variety of subtle assimilative influences on their thoughts, judgments, and behavior than less thoughtful people, and even more surprising, that the power of the influence attempt also is stronger on thoughtful people as it becomes more blatant—but its influence now drives behavior in the opposite direction. His research leads to the ironic conclusion that it is the most thoughtful people who will sometimes show the most bias in their judgments and behaviors because of irrelevant contextual variables. This work stands against the common belief that it is the least thoughtful individuals who should be most susceptible to assimilative biases, whereas highly thoughtful individuals should be most susceptible to contrastive biases.

The chapter by Forgas takes a fundamentally cognitive orientation, and argues that both the social influence strategies of influence agents, and the reactions of recipients are significantly influenced by such factors as their temporary moods, and the information processing strategies they happen to adopt.

This chapter represents a good example of how the application of methods and theories taken from social cognitive research can enrich our understanding of social influence phenomena. As Forgas notes, despite many decades of social influence research, the mental states of influence agents and recipients, such as their mood states have rarely been taken into account. Yet intuition—and more recently, experimental research—suggests that how people feel can have a profound influence on their strategic interpersonal behaviors. Forgas describes a series of experiments that show that even mild temporary changes in mood, induced by such simple manipulations as watching a brief film, produce significant changes in influence behaviors.

For example, a series of experiments showed that people who experience temporary negative moods tend to produce persuasive arguments that are rated as of higher quality and more persuasive than arguments produced by happy people. These mood effects are consistent with other research suggesting that positive mood promotes a less attentive and more schematic thinking style, while negative moods facilitate more focused and more attentive thinking strategies. Other studies showed that mood also influences the level of confidence people display in their choice of compliance-gaining strategies, such as requests. Happy people prefer and use more confident, impolite, and direct requests, while sad people rely on more cautious, polite, and hedging request forms. These differences confirm theoretical predictions that moods can selectively prime access to mood-congruent memories and ideas, and these in turn can influence judgments, decisions, and behaviors. Happy persons may selectively recall positive memories giving them greater confidence in their compliance gaining strategies, and end up using more direct (and impolite) requests. Forgas also argues, however, that these effects are not universal. They only occur when social actors adopt constructive, substantive information processing strategies that facilitate affect priming processes.

Bless, Strack, and Walther summarize their ingenious research program on how social influence effects memory. Their findings suggest that social influence is not restricted to individuals' attitudes and behaviors. Rather individuals' memory performances can also be susceptible to social influence. Their research picks up where Loftus's (1979) research left off, which found that individuals cannot correctly discriminate whether their memory traces result from their exposure to a particular event or suggestions made by other sources of information. Bless, Strack, and Walther's approach emphasizes the social and constructive aspect underlying social influence on memory.

These authors' premise is that individuals may feel uncertain about what it means if they do not have a recollective experience about an event to which they were exposed. In line with Festinger's (1954) social comparison theory, Bless, Strack, and Walther argue that in such instances, people reduce their uncertainty by relying on information that is directly or indirectly provided by others. From this perspective, they examine whether uncertainty is affected by the metacognitive processes about the memorability of an item, and by how the information is provided by others.

Based upon four experiments, Bless et al. found that social influence on memory was highly dependent on whether or not participants judged the event to be memorable: If it was judged to be memorable, social influence was diminished. When participants were uncertain as to the memorability of the event, then Bless, Strack, and Walther found ample evidence for social influence. This research provides a nice complement to the other contributions in this volume by extending social influence research into the domain of memory, and highlighting the subtle links that exist between subjective metacognitive judgments, the behavior of others, and actual memory performance.

In the next paper, Ng provides an insightful theoretical review in which he discusses the different forms of social influence studied by social psychologists. He argues that there has been a disproportionate emphasis on the recipient of social influence, to the relative neglect of the psychology of the influence agent, and the processes by which influence is communicated. Ng identifies three conceptually distinct levels of influence: the kind of immediate and face-to-face influence most commonly studied by psychologists, indirect influence achieved through the manipulation of social values and practices, and influence that is achieved by planting thoughts and attitudes in the recipient's mind that determine future actions, without the influencee becoming aware of any external influence. This distinction is particularly useful in the context of the present book, as it clearly maps out areas of light and darkness in terms of our present knowledge about influence processes.

Research on social facilitation, conformity, obedience, and persuasion are all examples of Level 1 influence processes. Ng proposes an extension of our interests to Level 2 and Level 3 influence processes, and suggests that language plays a critical role in how social influence is exercised at these levels. Language is used not only to communicate power, according to Ng, but also to create and manipulate power. Ng applies this analysis to the study of emergent power relationships within groups, and the role of language in these processes in particular. Following Bales' (1950) pioneering work, Ng and his colleagues studied the role of speech in establishing intragroup and intergroup influence systems.

Like a few others in this volume, Strack and Mussweiler focus their attention on resisting influence, and how different correction goals affect judgment. They report three studies in which people are asked to form an impression of a target person while they are asked to avoid stereotypic influences. Their findings suggest that people may strategically counteract the influence of information on their judgment, not by directing their attention to the source of the influence, but rather by appealing to social goals to decontaminate their judgments. These goals, they find, do not necessarily eliminate bias, because sometimes participants overcompensate their correction, suggesting that they are still mindful and reactant to the stereotypes. The implication of this, they argue, is that trying to correct for biases necessarily means that those biases must be accessed. Thus, whereas the immediate judgment may be free from bias, subsequent judgments when awareness for bias is low may become more distorted because stereotypes are now more highly accessible.

Strack and Mussweiler's research implies that many influence attempts operate on an automatic level and lie outside awareness. But, they also find that self-knowledge can be applied to the regulation of stereotyped judgments. An individual may not only know the content of a stereotype but also may know the circumstances under which the stereotype is most likely to affect him or her. In situations that afford self-reflection, the objective to decontaminate a judgment can be achieved if the individual can recompute or adjust it based upon knowledge of the contaminating influence, the direction of its impact, and its strength. As the authors suggest, this may not always be as easy as it seems.

In a similar vein, Williams and Dolnik examine a specific tactic that, when employed, causes resistance to social influence. The tactic is called *stealing thunder*. This occurs when in anticipation of a social influence attempt whose aim is to discredit an individual, the individual (or his or her agent) can admit to the potentially damaging information first. In their review of over 13 studies, they show how, in most cases, simply revealing the worst first is sufficient to reduce, and sometimes eliminate, the negative impact of that potentially harmful information.

Much of Williams and Dolnik's chapter is devoted to understanding the boundary conditions for this tactic, which also allow them to uncover the mechanisms by which it works. As yet, stealing thunder works just as well with highly negative as mildly negative information, and it works better if it is not accompanied by a positive spin. These results suggest that although source credibility may contribute to its effectiveness, it is not a sufficient explanation. Instead, Williams and Dolnik argue that message recipients, in an attempt to make sense of such a startling revelation, change the meaning of not only the negative information, but also of the other contextual information. Their findings are extended to a variety of applications, including legal, political, and interpersonal domains where neutralizing negative information is an important and recurring influence goal.

PART III. SOCIAL INFLUENCE AND GROUP BEHAVIOR

Stangor, Sechrist, and Jost ask how we are affected by stereotypes. In terms of underlying mechanisms, their research provides evidence for stereotypes fulfilling an informational function of indicating perceived consensus. Individuals express more confidence in their beliefs if others validate them, and individuals who are less confident show more belief change toward the opinions of others. However, these authors suggest that it may not be necessary for participants to identify with the groups that provide the source of the information. Indeed, in none of their studies has the manipulation or measurement of identification been found to influence the extent of stereotype change, and change was even found in students as the result of exposure to the opinions of faculty members at a different university (with whom they were unlikely to identify). Thus, Stangor, Sechrist, and Jost conclude that it is not a prerequisite that individuals identify with the group providing the consensus information in order to be influenced by that information, although it is possible that identification does play some role. They also note that it is more likely for people to be in contact with ingroup, rather than outgroup members, so as a matter of practice, shared ingroup information is likely to be more important.

Stangor, Sechrist, and Jost's position is that stereotype development and change must take into consideration the importance of perceptions of shared beliefs. They argue that children and adults alike, are likely to talk about their stereotypes and share them with each other, which will create and reinforce their beliefs. This emphasis on shared 'talk' as creating a social reality is reminiscent of Mead's (1934) and Weber's (1947) theoretical ideas, as well as the work presented in this volume by Schaller and by Ng. The results of several experiments by Stangor et al. demonstrated that changing participants' perceptions of the beliefs of others significantly changed the participants' racial stereotypes. Thus, people hold their stereotypes in large part because they perceive (accurately or inaccurately) that others do, too, and assume that shared beliefs must represent consensual reality. In other words, many of the perceptual and individual mental consequences of stereotyping can also by understood as a special case of implicit, indirect social influence processes.

Terry and Hogg take on the recent controversies surrounding the importance of norms for attitude-behavior consistency. Whereas Schaller asked why and how cultural norms change, Terry and Hogg explore when these cultural norms affect our attitudes and behaviors; they are particularly interested in the consistency between the two. Norms are the social influence component within the attitude-consistency question, but some relegate norms to playing a minor role. Terry and Hogg use social identity to provide a theoretical framework, and specific predictions as to when norms can account for attitude-behavior consistency. Their central prediction is that the attitudinal congruence of an ingroup norm will influence attitude-behavior consistency. In a series of laboratory and field studies, they found that participants were more likely to behave in accordance with their attitude when exposed to attitudinally congruent ingroup norms.

These authors argue that exposure to attitudinally congruent ingroup norms should strengthen attitude-behavior consistency because they confirm that attitudinally congruent behavior is appropriate for group members. A second pattern of results that supports their perspective is that the strength of this effect is related to the extent that group membership is salient. Terry and Hogg's research thus demonstrates that the consequence of discrepant behaviors and attitudes depend not only on intrapsychic variables such as attitude accessibility and mode of behavioral decision-making, but also on the implicit social influence represented by strongly held ingroup beliefs. Overall, their results serve to reaffirm the important and central role that social influence processes play in attitude-behavior relations.

Harkins examines how social influence of others, notably authority figures like experimenters, combines with the influence of the individual's own goals and evaluations of his or her own performances. Noting that goal setting theories and research typically argue for the importance of self-evaluation in motivating performance, Harkins asks which source of evaluation is more important. Surprisingly for goal setting researchers, but in line with Harkins's predictions, when both sources of evaluation (other and self) are available, other-evaluation generally supersedes self-evaluation. The importance of this discovery for performance and other related behaviors is discussed. The relevance of this idea extends to a variety of applied domains, suggesting that task performance is more likely to be influenced by evaluations by others, rather than self evaluations.

Harkins' research uncovers specific conditions that must be met before the potential for self-evaluation motivates performance to the same extent or even more than does the potential for external evaluation. However, his findings show that the potential for social evaluation, an important component of social influence, motivates performance more than the potential for self-evaluation under a wider variety of conditions. Even when self-evaluation is motivating, Harkins believes that this motivational force will dissipate faster than social evaluation. Clearly, Harkins' results challenge many self-evaluation and goal setting theorists who maintain the dominance of self-evaluation over social evaluation. The implications for motivation and productivity are particularly critical.

David and Turner use self-categorization theory to explain and test another important social influence phenomenon: the operation of majority and minority influence processes within groups. They summarize the basic theoretical principles underlying social influence as specified by self-categorization theory, and then show that the various outcomes of majority and minority influence can be explained by means of the same set of general theoretical principles. David and Turner also present a series of studies which suggest that the influence process really begins because a conflict is created when individuals disagree with people who are similar to them or agree with people who are different from them. When this conflict occurs, people search for ways of maintaining current beliefs, by focusing on the source and examining if their perception of their similarity or dissimilarity is, in fact, accurate. Alternatively, individuals may also question the accuracy of their perception of the others' views. This inquiry can cause individuals to change the meaning of what others said to help clarify the apparent inconsistency.

Whether individuals employ both strategies equally, or use one more than the other, is a function of interactions between their relevant, salient, self-categorization, whether they are part of the majority or minority within their ingroup, their representation of the source in relation to themselves, and the perceived normativeness of the message. If cognitive elaboration does not explain away the conflict, individuals are likely to change their attitudes. The interesting implication of this theory is that when such inconsistencies are encountered, people may be driven to shift from being merely the targets of influence to becoming sources of active social influence themselves.

Martin and Hewstone are concerned with how people process persuasive information from others. They argue that it depends not only upon the ability and motivation of the individual to process the message, but also upon whether the communicator of the message is a member of a numerical majority or minority.

An analysis of prior research generally indicated more systematic processing for majority sources. However, these studies often employed messages that advocated a position undesirable to the source and the participants' bias. Martin and Hewstone argue that it is important to examine whether majority sources lead to greater message processing when employing a message that does not invoke such a bias. Their results show that in such conditions systematic processing occurs for the minority, but not the majority, source.

Their next group of studies show that processing of a majority or minority message is largely dependent upon an individual's ability and motivation to engage in message elaboration. Tasks that led to a low level of message processing resulted in only heuristic processing. When moderate levels of processing were elicited, there was systematic processing of only the minority source. For tasks that require high levels of message elaboration, systematic processing of both a majority and minority source occurred. These findings indicate an important new direction in the questions researchers should be asking about social influence. Rather than simply asking whether the majority or minority is more effective in producing change, the question should be under what conditions are majority and minority messages likely to instigate systematic versus heuristic processing.

Finally, Spears, Postmes, Lea, and Watt summarize a program of research in which they investigate social influence phenomena from the perspective of the Social Identity model of Deindividuation Effects (SIDE). This model extends and develops self-categorization explanations of social influence effects, which understands social influence in terms of levels of a target's social identifications (person, group) and how these relate to the influencing source. SIDE adds an analysis of contextual influences that can impinge on the salient level of self. The authors focus in this chapter on the contextual factors of anonymity, identifiability, and isolation within groups.

Spears et al. present evidence that the SIDE analysis has been more successful in explaining social influence in crowds than traditional deindividuation theories. Spears, Postmes, and Lea also present pioneering research into social influence that occurs within computer-mediated environments. Again, the results are often counterintuitive, showing that in certain circumstances, the anonymity assumed to cause deindividuation in computer-mediated communication actually increases adherence to established sources of social identity. This is an exciting new theory that integrates traditional theories of social influence with contemporary theories of social identity and self-categorization.

CONCLUSION

Understanding the way people plan, use and respond to social influence processes has long been one of the key tasks of social psychology, and remains one of the most important questions for social science to deal with. For some decades, social influence was understood in our discipline as primarily the study of observable behavioral changes in response to exposure to manipulated influence processes. Research on social facilitation, conformity, and obedience are examples of such classic research domains. With the adoption of a much more cognitive orientation during the last few decades, interest in direct influence phenomena declined. The insights of social cognitive research have not, so far, been applied to social influence phenomena in any systematic way, except perhaps in the domain of persuasive communication research.

In their various ways, all contributors to this book argue that there is much to be gained from an integration of recent advances in research on social cognition and social motivation with established research paradigms on social influence processes. Several key themes recur throughout the book. One key message is that social influence cannot be considered as purely a behavioral phenomenon, but something that first occurs in the minds of social actors. As Cialdini (this volume) shows, imagining what it would be like facing life without an 'essential' service or good can be as effective a persuader to make a purchase as are more tangible inducements. Behavioral changes are often precipitated by such subtle and often subconscious ideas and influences we are exposed to throughout our daily lives, as the work of Dijksterhuis, Knowles et al., Strack and Mussweiler, and Petty also suggest. Even slight fluctuations in mood states, elicited by such ephemeral variables as the weather, can have a systematic influence on how people use and respond to social influence strategies, as the experiments by Forgas show. However, cognitive activity can be both the antecedent, as well as the consequence of social influence. As Bless et al. show, even intrinsically private experiences—such as our memory for what we saw—are open to subtle social influence pressures.

Nor is social influence something that occurs only at the individual level, as Ng persuasively argues. We are continuously exposed to social influence pressures at the group and the cultural levels as well (Schaller, this volume). Groups represent powerful sources of influence, and whether we are members of minorities or majorities, and how such memberships impact on our sense of self and identity can play a critical role in how we respond to influence attempts, as David and Turner, Spears et al., and Martin and Hewstone show in their chapters. Even such apparently purely cognitive constructs as stereotypes exert their powerful effects on us largely because they come to be seen as symbolic representations of consensual social reality as defined by a reference group, according to Stangor et al. In a similar vein, the apparently personal goals that seem to drive much of our behavior may also turn out to be surprisingly dependent on how others see and evaluate us, according to Harkins.

A further recurring theme throughout the book is that social influence is not a static, but a dynamic, interactive phenomenon. Latané and Bourgeois present a formal model to analyze such dynamic social influence processes. Schaller suggests that dynamic influence processes operate continuously and shape our thoughts and behaviors not only at the individual, but also at the social and cultural levels. A related point is made both by Ng and Tedeschi, who argue that aggression should also be analyzed within such a dynamic framework of influence phenomena. Within such a dynamic conceptualization of social influence, we also need to pay closer attention to how resistance to influence operates, as Knowles et al. suggest, and to how anticipated influence attempts can be deflected, as the work of Williams and Dolnik illustrates.

In conclusion, we hope that contributions to this, the third volume in the Sydney Symposium of Social Psychology series will achieve their objective of stimulating new ways of thinking about social influence phenomena. Often, an intense period of discussion and exchange between highly productive researchers can bring new insights and integration. We certainly had a feeling of new insights being achieved during our meeting at the University of New South Wales, Sydney. Our aim with this book was to preserve and communicate to a wider audience that sense of discovery and excitement that would otherwise have been a more ephemeral experience. We hope that readers will find these papers as interesting as we did.

REFERENCES

Allport, F. H. (1924). *Social psychology*. Boston, MA: Houghton-Mifflin.

Bales, R. F. (1950). *Interaction process analysis*. Reading, MA: Addison-Wesley.

Bless, H., & Forgas, J. P. (Eds.). *The message within: The role of subjective experience in social cognition behavior*. Philadelphia: Psychology Press.

Durkheim, E. (1956). *The division of labor in society*. New York: The Free Press.

Festinger, L. (1954). A theory of social comparison processes. *Human Relations, 7*, 117–140.

Forgas, J. P. (1981). *Social cognition: Perspectives on everyday understanding*. New York: Academic Press.

Forgas, J. P. (1995). Mood and judgment: The Affect Infusion Model (AIM). *Psychological Bulletin, 116*, 39–66.

Goffman, E. (1972). *Strategic interaction*. New York: Ballantine Books.

Heider, F. (1958). *The psychology of interpersonal relations*. New York: Wiley.

Hilgard, E. R. (1980). The trilogy of mind: Cognition, affection and conation. *Journal of the History of the Behavioral Sciences, 16*, 107–117.

Loftus, E. F. (1979). *Eyewitness testimony*. Cambridge, MA: Harvard University Press.

Mead, G. H. (1934). *Minds, self and society*. Chicago: University of Chicago Press.

Petty, R. E., & Cacioppo, J. T. (1986). The elaboration likelihood model of persuasion. In L. Berkowitz (Ed.), *Advances in experimental social psychology* (Vol. 19, pp. 123–205). New York: Academic Press.

Weber, M. (1947). *The theory of social and economic organisation*. (T. Parsons, Ed.). Glencoe, IL: The Free Press.

Wegner, D. M., & Gilbert, D. T. (2000). Social psychology: The science of human experience. In H. Bless & J. P. Forgas (Eds.), *The message within: Subjective experience in social cognition and social behavior* (pp. 1–9). Philadelphia: Psychology Press.

2

Systematic Opportunism
An Approach to the Study
of Tactical Social Influence

ROBERT B. CIALDINI

I am not the sort who remembers jokes. So, I thought it odd several years ago when I heard one that stuck stoutly in my mind. The joke goes as follows:

A man is leaving a restaurant one night and spots a friend looking around at the ground under a street lamp. He says that he'd dropped his car key and would appreciate some help in locating it. After some time spent searching, the pair come up with a few things (a coin, an interesting button, an earring) but no key. Exasperated, the first man asks, "Are you sure this is where you lost the key?" His friend replies, "No, actually. I think I lost it when I was getting out of my car across the street." Incredulous, the first man asks, "Then why aren't you looking for it there?" "Because the light's better over here," answers his friend.

As I considered why, of all jokes, this not-especially-funny one should be so memorable, it occurred to me that perhaps I saw myself in the story's main

Address for correspondence: Robert Cialdini, Department of Psychology, Arizona State University, Tempe, AZ 85287-1104, USA. E-mail: robert.cialdini@asu.edu

character. That is, my approach to research at one time could have been seen as all-too-frequently akin to his approach to finding the key. For the most part, I was doing my work in highly-controlled laboratory settings. And I was deciding what effects to study in those settings on the basis of theoretical considerations and the prior experimental literature.

It struck me that, as a social psychologist, this controlled experimental approach—in which methodological precision is valued and all extraneous influences to the one under study are removed or controlled away—was fine provided I was confident that the phenomena I was investigating were important in the course of naturally-occurring human behavior. But neither theory nor the prior literature addresses the issues of the strength, prevalence, or prominence of predicted effects in everyday interaction. Rigorous experimental procedure certainly doesn't answer the question either. If anything, the precision of technique and measurement may mislead us by allowing for the discovery of replicable and statistically significant influences that are so trivial in their size and impact outside of the experimental setting as to never manifest themselves when other factors are allowed to vary. I realized that I was bringing the factors of theory, prior literature, and experimental precision to bear too early in the sequence of my investigation. These were things that would tell me, once I had something important to examine, what exactly it was that I had.

Like the laughable character in our joke, I was deciding what to study based on where I was afforded the best light (by prior theory, prior literature, and experimental precision). But, as in the joke, what was under the light wasn't necessarily what I should have been looking for. Finding out what was important enough to study in the first place had to occur by some other process than theory-based experimentation. One such process that seemed potentially fruitful to me was systematic personal observation (i.e., the careful examination of naturally occurring behavior for its powerful and regular effects). I have used this process frequently to guide my own decisions of what in the realm of compliance action is worthy of focused examination—is worth bringing under the light. The sequence usually proceeds from (1) the recognition of a powerful and interesting influence upon the compliance process to (2) an initial scientific test of the validity of the observation, which if successful leads to (3) further scientific investigation, this time of the conceptual and theoretical underpinnings of the effect.

SYSTEMATIC PERSONAL OBSERVATION

I have employed two main varieties of systematic personal observation. First is a spontaneous kind in which I have found myself exposed to a highly effective influence process and then decided to study the generality and mediation of the process. For example, this is how I began to investigate such phenomena as basking in reflected glory (Cialdini, Borden, Thorne, Walker, Freeman, & Sloan, 1976; Cialdini, Finch, & DeNicholas, 1989), the even-a-penny-will-help technique (Cialdini & Schroeder, 1976), and the door-in-the-face tactic (Cialdini, 1990; Cialdini, Vincent, Lewis, Catalan, Wheeler, & Darby, 1975).

The second type of systematic personal observation is a more purposive kind and is akin to participant observation. It is fine to stand ready and waiting to be struck in the course of one's daily affairs by a phenomenon worthy of scientific pursuit; but there is no reason to be only reactive in these matters. This is especially the case in an area like social influence, where there are all sorts of organizations dedicated to influencing us to comply with their requests. It is possible to actively interact with these agencies in order to observe from the inside the nature of the techniques they regularly and effectively employ. See the chapter by David and Turner, and by Terry and Hogg (this volume) for an instructive variant of this approach.

This is a valuable sort of observation because the effects that appear consistently across a range of different compliance settings are likely to be the most influential ones. That is, these organizations serve as natural proving grounds for procedures that work. They have to work—a rule not unlike natural selection assures it. Therefore, when we examine them in controlled experimental settings to learn why they work, we can do so with the knowledge that these are genuinely powerful phenomena that we are studying. It is worthy of note, however, that this analysis applies primarily to direct *commercial* compliance professionals whose economic welfare is highly related to the success of the compliance practices they employ. That is, we should not expect a body of adaptive procedures to develop and proliferate to the same degree among noncommercial compliance organizations, in which the invisible hand of the market does not sweep away inefficient practices over time.

Schaller (this volume) makes a compelling case for why direct commercial influence settings are particularly likely to be characterized by effective compliance practices, whereas other kinds of influence settings may not spawn the most potent tactics. For example, patient compliance with various medical regimens (medication, diet, exercise) is notoriously poor (Colon, Popkin, Matas, & Callies, 1991; Eracker, Kirscht, & Becker, 1984). One reason may be that, unlike the direct commercial compliance situation wherein a noncompliant target person departs from and impoverishes the system, in a medical care system, a noncompliant person stays and enriches it. Thus, in seeking evidence as to the most regular and potent influences on the compliance process, we are well advised to pay principal attention to the compliance repertoires of longstanding commercial compliance professions.

This is what I resolved to do, then, to observe from the inside the compliance practices of all of the influence organizations I could get access to whose principle goal it is to get us to say yes. In a nearly three year study, I became a spy of sorts, infiltrating the training programs of as many influence professions as I could get access to and learning from the inside how people can be led to say yes to requests in sales, fundraising, marketing, negotiation, and recruitment settings. Occasionally, I ventured outside of traditional business circles to find out how other influence professionals generated "yes." For example, I interviewed political lobbyists and cult recruiters to learn what they did to produce their own brand of powerful influence.

Through it all, I watched for commonalties, for parallels. I thought that, if I could identify which psychological principles were being used successfully by individuals selling insurance and industrial machinery and computer equipment and portrait photography and if these were the same principles being used successfully by advertisers and negotiators and fundraisers and recruiters and lobbyists, then I would know something very important. I would know that these must be the most powerful and flexible principles of influence available, because *these* are the principles that work across the widest range of influence professions, influence practitioners, and influence opportunities. See Cialdini (2001) for a fuller description of the method and outcomes of this study.[1]

It is important to recognize, however, that even though compliance professionals know the procedures that work—that, after all, is their job—they don't necessarily know why they work. That's *my* job, as an influence researcher. To illustrate, let me tell you about one such procedure that I came across while investigating the tactics of insurance salespersons.

IMAGINING MAKES IT SO

In order to understand the practices of successful insurance salespersons, I enrolled in a training program for new insurance sales agents. During the program, we were advised as follows by a veteran insurance sales instructor:

> If you're selling auto insurance, start by getting 'em alone in a quiet place and making 'em imagine that they just totaled the car. If you're selling health insurance, first make 'em suppose that they're laid up in the hospital too sick to work. If your selling theft, get 'em to think how it would be to come home from vacation and find everything gone. And take 'em through every picture, every step along the way.

If somehow we had missed the point, we also were given copies of an article from, 'The American Salesman,' an influential trade magazine advising life insurance salesmen to urge the client to construct a mental picture of the exact event the salesperson wanted the client to insure himself against. The article entitled "Add a picture—Make a sale" went further to suggest that the salesper-

---

1. There are longstanding criticisms of participant observation as a research tool, mostly involving the subjectivity of the observer at the critical point of data collection. This is a legitimate concern, especially when those data are the only ones taken—that is, when they serve as the end point of the data gathering activity. But this problem drops away when, as advocated here, participant observation is used to start the investigatory process, thereby allowing the impressions of personal observation to be submitted to more objective methods of data collection.

son should arrange to have the client imagine the event precisely in the way that would most benefit the salesperson.

> In order to keep in full command of the situation—in order to get the prospect to create the kind of picture the *salesperson* wants—see what an important difference it makes when a forceful picture is planted. . . . 'Suppose something were to happen to *you*. Would your children be *brought up by strangers?* . . . by some unknown matron in an orphanage or some unknown social worker in an institution?' Phrased in that manner, the only picture the prospect can get is the picture the salesperson wants him to get. The picture of his loved ones being 'brought up by strangers' is a shocker he may never have thought of. The pictures of an 'unknown matron' and 'orphanage' and an 'institution' are pictures that will keep haunting him until his family is provided with adequate coverage."

So insurance companies, at least, believe that having a prospect imagine an event the way the salesperson wishes will make the prospect more willing to buy insurance against the event's occurrence. Their information suggests that the imagination procedure works for one or both of two reasons:

1. New information that the target hadn't considered: images prospects "may never have thought of."
2. Fear: images that "shock" and "haunt" prospects into compliance.

I was willing to grant they are right that this technique works, because that's the sort of thing that compliance professionals are good at—knowing what works. But that's all I was willing to grant them, because my experience told me that they weren't especially good at the explanations. Returning to this chapter's opening street lamp metaphor, now it was time to bring this effect under the light. Now that there was suggestive evidence of a potent and pervasive influence on the influence process in everyday life, it was time to undertake a full scientific analysis of it. That meant, first, validating the insurance professionals' view that actively imagining an event spurs individuals to believe that the event will occur and take appropriate behavior steps. But, more importantly, it meant testing the possible conceptual and theoretical explanations for the effect should it appear as predicted.

It seemed to me that other factors besides the insurance professionals' favorites (new information and fear) could account for the effect. One struck me as especially worthy of consideration: Tversky and Kahneman's (1973) availability heuristic—a mental shortcut through which one estimates the likelihood of an event by the ease with which instances of that event come to mind. We store things in memory so that those we see as most true or likely to occur spring to mind easily (i.e., are cognitively available). That's adaptive because we would want to have easiest access to the ideas that are likely to hold true. It's not unlike the way we stock a cupboard, putting those things that are most useful to us in the front where we can have the most ready access to them. Therefore, as a kind of rule of thumb, the more cognitively accessible an image is, the more we believe it (Bacon, 1979).

Because this rule is only a rule of thumb, it often leads to errors. That is, other factors besides the perceived validity of an idea can make it spring easily to mind. For example, repeated presentations (Boehm, 1994), vivid presentations (Kisielius & Sternthal, 1986), as well as analogy and metaphor (Read, Cesa, Jones, & Collins, 1990; Reinsch, 1971) have this effect and are often used by influence professionals. Actively imagining the event also seemed to me likely to increase the event's cognitive accessibility for a pair of reasons. First, generating an image should make that image easier to generate from that point on. After an image is once imagined, it no longer needs to be cognitively constructed, only reconstructed. Second, once the image is produced, a mental set will be created that is likely to hinder the ability to see the idea or event in other ways.

To test the impact and mediation of an imagination procedure on subsequent responding, Larry Gregory, Kathleen Carpenter, and I (Gregory, Cialdini, & Carpenter, 1982) decided to undertake research designed to achieve three major goals. First, we sought to determine whether imagining would work as powerfully as the insurance professionals suggested on consequential forms of behavior. Second, we sought to determine whether it would work when the explanatory possibilities of new information and fear arousal were removed. Finally, we wanted to see if an imagination procedure would work according to availability predictions—that imagining an event would increase the perceived likelihood of the event's occurrence, which would then influence behavior appropriately.

STUDY 1: WHEN IMAGINING MAKES IT SO

The study proceeded as follows. Homeowners scheduled for marketing by the area cable TV company within one month's time were contacted by a female experimenter who said she was doing a survey on attitudes toward cable TV for a class at Arizona State University. All who agreed to the interview were told that in order to acquaint them with the features of cable TV, a brief description of the features of cable TV, taken from company promotional materials, would be read to them. Half (those in the Information condition) were asked to consider the features of cable TV as they heard the features presented in straight informational terms, "Cable TV will provide a broader entertainment service to its subscribers." The other half (those in the Imagination condition) were asked to imagine themselves experiencing those features, "Take a moment and imagine how cable TV will provide you with a broader entertainment service." Immediately afterward, all participants were administered a questionnaire concerning cable TV and were given a card they could mail to the company if they wanted more information.

Sometime within the month, the participants were canvassed via the standard marketing operation of the cable TV company. In a first visit by a company representative who was blind to the experimental condition participants were offered a free week of service. During a second marketing visit, participants were asked to subscribe. Two months after our contact, we checked the company's records to see what happened on the behavioral measures. The time delay between the interview measures and the last two behavioral measures was important for two reasons. First, if the imagination procedure proved to be more effective after the passage of substantial amounts of time, the results would be a testament to the potency and durability of imagination effects. Second, these results would not be susceptible to an alternative explanation based on the more favorable mood that the imagination procedure may have created in our participants. See the chapter by Forgas (this volume) indicating that mood can have powerful effects on responding while the mood is present. However, such a more favorable mood would have long dissipated by the time these behavioral measures were assessed.

Results

Questionnaire Responses. Participants' reactions to the questionnaire items, which were administered immediately after exposure to one of our experimental conditions, are summarized in Table 2.1. The first two questionnaire items asked participants, respectively, how much prior information regarding cable TV they felt they had been exposed to and how favorable they felt toward cable TV as a consequence. Fortunately, there were no significant differences between participants in the Information and the Imagination conditions on these measures of prior information about or prior attitudes toward cable TV. For the remaining three questions, significant differences between the two groups were found. Imagination condition participants reported that they were significantly more likely to want cable TV, had significantly more positive attitudes toward cable TV, and were significantly more likely to subscribe to cable TV than the Information condition participants. It seems clear from these questionnaire data that causing participants to imagine (rather than

TABLE 2.1. Mean Scores for the Major Nonbehavioral Measures

	Information Condition	Imagination Condition
Prior information	3.473	3.636
Impression of prior information	5.055	5.236
Likely cable TV will be as popular as regular TV	5.709	5.927
Likely will want cable TV°	4.109	5.109
Attitude toward cable TV°	4.618	5.418
Likely will subscribe to cable TV°°	3.655	4.418

°° $p < .1$ ° $p < .05$
N = 41 in the Information condition and 38 in the Imagination condition; all responses were made on 7-point scales, with larger scores indicating greater amount or favorability.

merely to consider) the benefits of cable TV led to more favorable beliefs, attitudes, and expectancies toward this entertainment service.

Behavioral Measures. For us, however, the real test of the imagination procedure's effectiveness came from an examination of its influence on our behavioral measures. We took three behavioral measures: (1) whether participants requested more information about the cable TV service via the postcard given to them at the interview's end; (2) whether they agreed to take a sample free week of the service; and (3) whether they subscribed to the service. The latter two measures were collected by cable TV company salespeople (who were blind to the experimental manipulations) during the course of the standard marketing of the participants' neighborhood 2–6 weeks after our interviews. Participants' scores on these measures were obtained from company records approximately 2–3 months following the interview contact; they are presented in Table 2.2.

As can be seen in Table 2.2, the two experimental groups differed slightly in their postcard return rates. However, the data were slightly opposite to prediction in that 9.7% of Information condition participants mailed the postcard while only 5.2% of Imagination condition participants did so. We can see one possible way of reconciling this lack of effect with the strong positive reactions toward cable TV that we found on our questionnaire measures. Perhaps the favorability of the Imagination condition participants was sufficiently strong by the end of our interview that they felt no need to mail the postcard to obtain additional information regarding the service's value. Whatever the explanation, we did not find a significant effect on our first behavioral measure.

However, chi-square analyses of the remaining behavioral data revealed striking differences between the groups in the direction of prediction. Imagination condition participants were significantly more likely to accept the free week of service offer than were Information condition participants (65.8% versus 41.4%). Most importantly, they also were significantly more likely to subscribe to the service when asked to do so 2–6 weeks after our manipulations (47.4% vs. 19.5%).

At this point, we felt that we had accomplished two of the three goals we set for the study. That is, we had demonstrated, first, that imagining could work powerfully on consequential forms of behavior and, second, that it could work when the explanatory possibilities of new information and fear arousal were

TABLE 2.2. Percent Compliance on Behavioral Measures

	Information Condition (N = 41)		Imagination Condition (N = 38)	
Returned postcard	$n = 4$	9.7%	$n = 2$	5.2%
Obtained free week°	$n = 17$	41.4%	$n = 25$	65.8%
Subscribed°°	$n = 8$	19.5%	$n = 18$	47.4%

° $p < .05$. °° $p < .01$

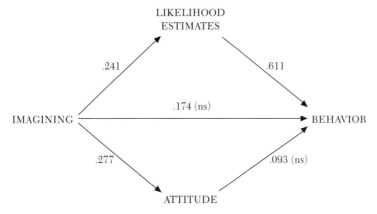

FIGURE 2.1.   Path Analysis of the Impact of Imagining on Behavior

removed. What remained was the achievement of our final goal—a demonstration that the imagination procedure we employed worked according to availability predictions, such that imagining an event would increase the perceived likelihood of the event's occurrence, which would then influence behavior appropriately. We had not demonstrated such a sequence, as it was possible that the imagination procedure had influenced behavior not because it led to greater perceived likelihood estimates regarding cable TV, but because it led to more positive attitudes toward cable TV. To test these alternative accounts, we conducted a path analysis that investigated the relationship among (1) our imagination procedure, (2) the decision to subscribe to the cable TV service, and (3) the two potential mediating variables of likelihood estimates and attitudes regarding cable TV. The results of that path analysis are depicted in Figure 2.1. They show that, although our imagination procedure led to both greater likelihood estimates and favorable attitudes toward cable TV, only the likelihood estimates were causally related to the decision to subscribe to the service—just as would be predicted by an availability heuristic perspective.

FULL-CYCLE SOCIAL PSYCHOLOGY: ONE MORE TURN

In the past (Cialdini, 1980, 1995), I have written about a favored research orientation called Full-Cycle Social Psychology, in which I have suggested, with no special claims to originality, that the proper approach to social psychology involves a continual interplay between (1) field observation of interesting phenomena, (2) theorizing about the causes of the phenomena, and (3) experimental tests of the theorizing. If there was anything original about the suggestion, it was the depiction of this relationship as a cycle rather than a progression. (See Fig. 2.2, for a graphical depiction of the distinction between a progression model and a cyclical model.) The cycle begins with a field observation of some interesting and seemingly important behavioral phenomenon, which leads to theoretical hypotheses regarding the underlying causes of the phenomenon, which leads, in turn, to experimental tests of the hypotheses. Although it is a vitally important link, social psychologists frequently spend *all* of their time on the path between theory and experimentation.

As I have argued so far, we need to spend more time on the link between field observation and theory to determine which phenomena are worth theorizing about and experimenting on in the first place. But what I haven't yet discussed is the arc in the cycle that has traditionally received the least attention: that between experimentation and field observation. This is the connection that often provides us with a unique source of information about the validity and generality of our experimental findings, and can then inform theory, and can form the basis for predictions in the field to be checked by field observation. So the connections in the cycle always allow for a bidirectional flow.

As an example, let's consider the data I just described to you: these data seemed, at first glance, all I could ask for: (1) The imagination procedure had produced effects on both verbal and behavioral measures; (2) the behavioral effects were breathtaking; and (3) we had evidence in support of one conceptual mediator of our behavioral effects—cognitive accessibility—and against several others—information, fear, and attitude change. In short, we had everything a good social psychologist is taught to look for.

I realized upon further reflection that there was something wrong with our findings: They were too good to be true. The size of the most important behavioral effect was remarkable—more than a doubling of effectiveness from the use of this small imagination procedure. If what I was suggesting earlier was

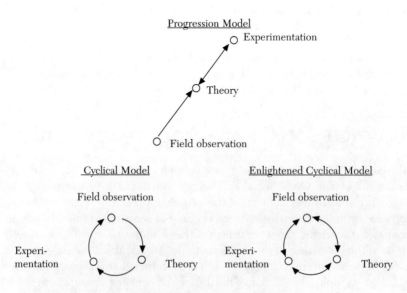

FIGURE 2.2. Research Models

true about the evolutionary character of effective influence techniques, then this practice should have evolved to widespread use in a variety of influence professions. But, it hasn't. We should see compliance pros of all stripes asking us to imagine our brains out. But, we don't.

No, there was clearly something wrong with our data. First, I looked to see if the problem came from inside the study. Could it be that our imagination procedure didn't enhance compliance but that our information procedure suppressed it? After all, because we had done a saturation sample of the neighborhoods, we hadn't included a no-contact control group to use as a baseline against which to compare our effects. Maybe there was something about the information interview—perhaps it was boring—that decreased participants' interest in cable TV. Then our result would show, not that the imagination device was stunningly effective but that the information interview was the opposite. So, I called the general sales manager of the cable TV company—someone who had not been associated with our study—and asked him to tell me what the standard response on our two behavior measures was in the city where we did our study. His answers were reassuring. The average response to the free week offer was 40%, while the average subscription rate after solicitation in the home was 21%, virtually identical to our Information condition figures but greatly below our Imagination condition. So, the possibility that our imagination device was ineffective seemed remote.

I next checked and double-checked the cable TV company's records to assure that there was no recording error there. There was not; the requests for free weeks and the subscription rates were correct. Finally, I interviewed the salespeople to find out if they had somehow learned of the conditions of our experiment to which homeowners had been assigned and had treated them differently when contacting them. To my relief, they hadn't even been aware that a study had been conducted and, consequently, were oblivious to the issue of experimental condition.

At this point, I stopped asking questions of internal validity and turned to matters of external validity. I already knew there was one compliance profession, insurance sales, that used and believed in the effectiveness of the imagination procedure, but that there were many other professions that didn't. I also knew my results supported the presumptions of the insurance salespeople. So I looked for features that our research setting had in common with the sales setting of the insurance salesperson.

The first place I looked was to the lessons of the insurance sales trainers. Recall what they were saying, "If you're selling auto insurance, start by getting 'em alone in a quiet place . . . and take 'em through every picture, every step along the way." In other words, make it easy for people to picture what you want them to imagine; get them someplace where there are no competing stimuli, no likely disruptions or distractions, and where you can spoon-feed them the relevant images so they don't have to work hard to construct them.

The next place I looked was to our procedure, where I found that we had done exactly what the insurance trainer had recommended. We got people to stop and participate in our study in a quiet place with the TV off and the kids banished to another part of the house or outside, at which time we gave them already-structured images to experience.

Finally, I looked at what Tversky and Kahneman (1973) said about the availability heuristic and what other researchers have confirmed (Schwarz, Bless, Strack, Klumpp, Rittenauer-Schatka, & Simons, 1991; Wanke, Bless, & Biller, 1996): It is the ease or difficulty of generating an image that serves as the cue to its likelihood. Thus, the probability of an event will not necessarily increase because one has recently imagined it. Rather, this will be the case only when the imagination of the event can be achieved easily and with little effort. In fact, according to the availability heuristic, hypothetical events for which images are difficult to construct should appear as relatively improbable.

STUDY 2: WHEN IMAGINING MAKES IT WORSE

To test this proposition, I, along with my colleagues Jim Sherman, Donna Schwartzman, and Kim Reynolds (Sherman, Cialdini, Schwartzman, & Reynolds, 1985), conducted a study in which participants were asked to imagine events that varied in their ease or difficulty of imaginability. We predicted that, compared to a group of control participants who did not imagine the event, those who imagined an easy-to-construct outcome would increase their subjective likelihood estimates for that event, whereas those who imagined a difficult-to-construct outcome would decrease such estimates.

We chose to test this prediction in a laboratory setting because we already knew that the phenomenon under consideration was a powerful one in the course of naturally occurring behavior. Now was the time to bring this phenomenon under the bright light that laboratory procedures provide. In brief, participants were told about an illness (Hyposcenia-B) that was becoming increasingly prevalent on their campus. In the *easy-to-imagine* condition, the symptoms of the disease were concrete and had probably been experience by most participants (low energy level, muscle aches, and frequent severe headaches). In the *difficult-to-imagine* condition, the symptoms were far less concrete (a vague sense of disorientation, a malfunctioning nervous system, and an inflamed liver). Half of the participants in each of these conditions were asked to simply read about the symptoms (*Read-only* condition), whereas the other half were asked to also imagine experiencing them (*Imagine* condition). Next, all participants were asked to rate their perceived likelihood of contracting the disease.

As can be seen from Table 2.3, the pattern of obtained findings confirmed our prediction. That is, the resultant (statistically significant) interaction pattern was composed of two separate effects working in combination: a tendency for participants imagining easy-to-imaging symptoms to rate their probability of contracting Hyposcenia-B as greater than control participants *and* a tendency for participants imagining difficult-to-imagine symptoms to rate their probability of getting the disease as smaller than controls.

TABLE 2.3. Judgments of Disease Likelihood for Self

	Accessibility of Symptoms	
	Easy-to-Imagine	Difficult-to-Imagine
Imagine (N = 20)	5.25	7.70
Read only (N = 20)		
Control (N = 20)	6.20	6.55

Note: *N* = 20. 1 = very likely; 10 = very unlikely.

CONCLUSION

Thus, our results explain why not all advertisers or marketers would use the device of active imagery: It will only be adaptive when ease of imagery is possible, such as in the controlled settings that insurance agents are typically able to structure for their prospects. Moreover, it will be maladaptive when such imagery is difficult, which would be the case with many other types of commercial influence attempts. It is important to note that we were led to these insights not by the surface successes of our cable TV study or by the extent to which the findings of that study aligned well with the prior data and theory concerning the availability heuristic. To the contrary, the outcomes of Study 1 gave us nothing but encouragement that we had identified a compliance procedure that would be useful to all users.

Thus, it wasn't the surface successes of Study 1 that were instructive; it was an obscured failure—the failure of the findings to align with the widespread practices of commercial compliance professionals. The impetus for Study 2 came only when we looked for confirmation of our conclusions, not to the traditional sources of experimentation and theory, but to the rarely employed source of field observation. Without a glance back to the evidence of the field, aided by the earlier participant observation work I had done, I would have never thought to ask the telling experimental questions of the follow-up research. There would have been no reason; all the important questions had seemed answered. Accordingly, as the "enlightened cyclical model" depicted in Figure 2.2 illustrates, field observations can profitably serve to both initiate and validate experimental efforts.

Indeed, I am pleased to report that a more recent field observation has helped validate the findings of Study 2, which demonstrated that imagining procedures are only likely to be effective when the relevant images are easy to generate. Recall that insurance companies frequently train their agents to use such procedures because they have traditionally been able to structure the influence setting to remove the competing stimuli, disruptions, and distractions that would make active imagining difficult. But times are changing for the insurance companies.

Because of an increase in single-parent households in the United States, some American insurance companies are no longer able to guarantee that the home can offer their agents an interruption-free, quiet place in which they can ask parents to imagine the likelihood of various kinds of misfortune. According to Tom Kaetner, an agent for Mutual Service Insurance, "The kids are all over the place. They want to play with my computer; they're up on parents' laps. It becomes very distracting" (The Art of Selling, 1994). So, Kaetner and his company have hit on a strategy to restore a quiet environment where a parent can imagine things easily. Now, agents come to the home equipped with coloring books for the children, who can then be counted on to allow the adults at least several peaceful moments. Kaetner claims that the coloring books have been a successful selling tool because, "If we're going into people's homes, we need to have this" (The Art of Selling, 1994). Here, then, is an example of how looking back to the natural environment to confirm laboratory results can be not just confidence shaking—as it was after our cable TV study—but confidence enhancing, as well.

More generally, the issues discussed in this chapter illustrate how social influence processes operate at a number of direct and indirect levels, many of them well known to influence professionals, but often ignored by social psychologists. Observing what influence professionals do can thus provide us with novel insights into the many ways human beings influence each other. As other contributions to this volume also clearly illustrate, the time is certainly ripe for a broader and more inclusive reconceptualization of social influence mechanisms by psychologists than has been the case in the past.

REFERENCES

Bacon, F. T. (1979). Credibility of repeated statements. *Journal of Experimental Psychology: Human Learning and Memory, 5,* 241–252.

Boehm, L. E. (1994). The validity effect: A search for mediating variables. *Personality and Social Psychology Bulletin, 20,* 285–293.

Cialdini, R. B. (1980). Full-cycle social psychology. In L. Bickman (Ed.), *Applied Social Psychology Annual* (Vol. 1, pp. 21–47). Beverly Hills, CA: Sage.

Cialdini, R. B. (1990). Perspectives on research classics: A door opens. *Contemporary Social Psychology, 14,* 50–52.

Cialdini, R. B. (1995). A full-cycle approach to social psychology. In G. G. Brannigan & M. R. Merrens (Eds.), *The social psychologists: Research adventures* (pp. 52–71). Boston: McGraw-Hill.

Cialdini, R. B. (2001). *Influence: Science and Practice* (4th ed.). Boston: Allyn & Bacon.

Cialdini, R. B., Borden, R. J., Thorne, A., Walker, M., Freeman, S., & Sloan, L. (1976). Basking in reflected glory: Three (football) field studies. *Journal of Personality and Social Psychology, 34,* 366–375.

Cialdini, R. B., Finch, J. F., & DeNicholas, M. (1989). Strategic self-presentation: The indirect route. In M. Cody & M. McLaughlin (Eds.), *The psychology of tactical communication* (pp. 194–206). London: Multilingual Matters.

Cialdini, R. B., & Schroeder, D. A. (1976). Increasing compliance by legitimizing paltry contributions: When even a penny helps. *Journal of Personality and Social Psychology, 34,* 599–604.

Cialdini, R. B., Vincent, J. E., Lewis, S. K., Catalan, J., Wheeler, D., & Darby, B. L. (1975). A reciprocal concessions procedure for inducing compliance: The door-in-the-face technique. *Journal of Personality and Social Psychology, 31,* 206–215.

Colon, E. A., Popkin, M. K., Matas, A. J., & Callies, A. L. (1991). Overview of noncompliance in renal transplantation. *Transplantation Reviews, 5,* 175–180.

Eracker, S. A., Kirscht, J. P., & Becker, M. H. (1984). Understanding and improving patient compliance. *Annals of Internal Medicine, 100,* 258–268.

Gregory, W. L., Cialdini, R. B., & Carpenter,

K. M. (1982). Self-relevant scenarios as mediators of likelihood estimates and compliance: Does imagining make it so? *Journal of Personality and Social Psychology, 43,* 89–99.

Kisielius, J., & Sternthal, B. (1986). Examining the vividness controversy: An availability-valence interpretation. *Journal of Consumer Research, 12,* 418–431.

Read, S. J., Cesa, I. L., Jones, D. K., & Collins, N. L. (1990). When is the federal budget like a baby? Metaphor in political rhetoric. *Metaphor and Symbolic Activity, 5,* 125–149.

Reinsch, N. L. (1971). An investigation of the effects of metaphor and simile in persuasive discourse. *Speech Monographs, 38,* 142–145.

Schwarz, N., Bless, H., Strack, F., Klumpp, G., Rittenauer-Schatka, H., & Simons, A. (1991). Ease of retrieval as information: Another look at the availability heuristic. *Journal of Personality and Social Psychology, 61,* 195–202.

Sherman, S. J., Cialdini, R. B., Schwartzman, D. F., & Reynolds, K. (1985). Imagining can heighten or lower the perceived likelihood of contracting a disease. *Personality and Social Psychology Bulletin, 11,* 118–127.

The art of selling (1994, September, 30). Interview, KOY radio, Phoenix, AZ.

Tversky, A., & Kahneman, D. (1973). Availability: A heuristic for judging frequency and probability. *Cognitive Psychology, 5,* 207–232.

Wanke, M., Bless, H., & Biller, B. (1996). Subjective experience versus content of information in the construction of attitude judgments. *Personality and Social Psychology Bulletin, 22,* 1105–1113.

3

Increasing Compliance by Reducing Resistance

ERIC S. KNOWLES
SHANNON BUTLER
JAY A. LINN

> *. . . all who seek to bring about change experience resistance to their efforts.*
>
> (Anderson & Stewart, 1983, p. 1.)

> *Resistance is very important. Once you learn to use it, you really have come to a point where you can be effective.*
>
> (Paul Watzlawick, cited in Ard, 1982, p. 3)

Address for Correspondence: Eric Knowles, Department of Psychology, University of Arkansas, Fayetteville, AR 72701, USA. E-mail: eknowles@uark.edu

APPROACH-AVOIDANCE CONFLICT MODEL OF PERSUASION

*S*ocial influence often creates an approach-avoidance conflict for the recipient (Dollard & Miller, 1950; Miller, 1944, 1959; Wheeler, 1966). A request, an offer, a command, or a suggestion engages two opposing reactions. On the one hand, the target of the request wants to help, wants to own, wants to enjoy, wants to participate, but at the same time the target is resistant to the expense, to the effort, or to the commitment that comes from complying.

Lewin (1951) conceived of behavior as a "quasi-stationary equilibrium" that averaged the field of forces existing at that moment. The equilibrium point was that behavior that balanced the approach forces and the avoidance forces (Knowles, 1980). For instance, a request that you let me use your car for a while can establish a variety of approach forces (preserve our friendship, viewing self as a helper, strategically creating the opportunity for reciprocity, etc.), and also can create a variety of avoidance forces (concern about the safety of the car, desire to minimize inconveniences, wanting to avoid self-view as submissive, etc.). Whether I get to use your car depends on whether these forces come into equilibrium on the 'Yes' side or on the 'No' side of your decision criterion. If the approach forces are sufficiently strong, then you will agree, though with some reservations. If the approach forces are sufficiently weak, then you will decline, though with some regret.

TWO TARGETS FOR SOCIAL INFLUENCE

The approach-avoidance conflict model provides two diametrically different strategies for moving the quasi-stationary equilibrium in a particular direction. One may increase the promotive forces for movement in the desired direction, that is, add to the strength, number, or availability of the approach forces. Alternatively, one may decrease the resistive forces that prevent movement in that direction, that is, diminish the strength, number, or availability of the avoidance forces.

Theories of social influence focus primarily on the approach side of the social influence conflict dynamic (Eagly & Chaiken, 1993). Persuasion, marketing, attitude change, and other studies of influence aim primarily, often exclusively, at bolstering the approach tendencies. Persuasion is often defined as the attempt to provide additional incentives for compliance. Cialdini (1993), for instance, identified six major principles of social influence: reciprocity, commitment and consistency, social proof, authority, scarcity, and liking. Each one of these principles creates its influence by adding something to the approach forces promoting compliance. Reciprocity, for instance, is the addition of an interpersonal obligation to the reasons for complying; liking is the addition of interpersonal incentives to the reasons for complying.

Few theories, few approaches, few techniques of social influence have focused on diminishing resistance as an avenue for increasing compliance. Among those occasional voices are Ladd Wheeler (1966) who proposed that contagion occurs when the avoidance gradient in an approach-avoidance conflict is diminished and Schachter and Hall (1952) who attempted to influence volunteering by reducing restraints against volunteering. This chapter revisits and extends the approach-avoidance model of persuasion by proposing four strategies to social influence, each one concerned with reducing the impact of resistance. The first strategy is to redefine the social influence so as to avoid activating resistance in the first place. Relationship selling or redefining a selling interaction as a consultation are examples of this strategy. The second strategy is to directly attack resistance and focus at least part of the persuasive attempt on reducing resistance. A money-back-guarantee adds no value to a product, but does undermine reasons for resisting a purchase. A third strategy is to disrupt or distract resistance so that it is not allowed to contest the social influence. This third strategy has produced more psychological research and thinking than the other two strategies have. It has both a blatant side, as in Festinger and Maccoby (1964) presenting a comedy film to distract young fraternity men from an anti-fraternity persuasive message, and a subtle side, as in our research on the Disrupt-Then-Reframe technique (Davis & Knowles, 1999), where we add a disrupting twist of a phrase just before an offer. The fourth strategy is to turn the resistance into a partner rather than an adversary. Double binds, such as predicting the resistance, are examples of this strategy. This chapter explores and demonstrates each of these strategies.

RELATIONSHIP TO OTHER CHAPTERS

The focus of this chapter is motivational, dynamic, strategic, and molecular. It focuses on the motivations for compliance and examines ways to influence by changing the impetuses for action. Williams and Dolnik's (this volume) chapter on stealing thunder looks strategically at when it is better to diffuse resistance The motivational emphasis joins this chapter with others that explore the functional nature of social influence (e.g., Schaller, this volume; Tedeschi, this volume; Harkins, this volume; David & Turner, this volume) and distinguishes this chapter from a number of others that concentrate on the automatic implementation of activated schema (e.g., Dijksterhuis, this volume; Bless, Strack, & Walther, this volume; Stangor, Sechrist, & Jost, this volume; Spears, Postmes, Lea, & Watt, this volume). Williams and Dolnik's chapter (this volume) by addressing when and how "stealing thunder" might diffuse an adversary's main criticism, shares, at least in part, a specific focus on overcoming resistance to persuasion.

This chapter is founded on a dynamic theory of behavior, that is, a theory that sees behavior as the product of a complex set of often opposing forces. One changes behavior by changing the mix of forces operating on those forces. In some situations, dynamic systems may operate linearly (i.e., $Y = a + bX$), but in other cases the system may be nonlinear. The two hallmarks of nonlinear systems are paradoxical stasis (as when the addition of strong forces produces no change in behavior) and paradoxical change (as when the addition of weak forces creates great change). In this chapter we review a program of research on the disruption of resistance that shows paradoxical change: Relatively minor changes in the wording of an offer create great differences in the compliance rate. The treatment of influence as a dynamic process is an assumption shared most clearly by Latané and Bourgeois (this volume) who apply dynamic theory at the level of the group and society.

This current chapter takes a strategic approach to social influence. It proposes four different strategies that can be used to reduce the impact of the resistance forces on behavior. This strategic focus is shared by a number of other chapters in this volume, particularly Cialdini, Strack and Mussweiler, and Williams and Dolnik.

Finally, the present chapter takes a subtle and molecular approach to social influence. The focus of much of this chapter is on influence that operates through the nuances of communication. The success of the persuasion we present depends not simply on what is said, but how it is said. Ng (this volume) presents the larger language-based context for influence. The chapters by Bless, Strack, and Walther (this volume), Cialdini (this volume), Dijksterhuis (this volume), Petty (this volume), Stangor, Sechrist, and Jost (this volume), and Strack and Mussweiler (this volume) along with this chapter show how small changes in what is presented or how it is presented can produce large consequences.

NATURE OF RESISTANCE

Resistance to persuasion is well known to anyone who has offered advice, delivered a sales pitch, counseled another, or tried to enlist others in a plan of action, and probably also to anyone who has received these persuasive attempts. Brehm (1966) defined resistance as an aversive motivational state, initiated when one perceives that ones' freedom is threatened, and directing thought and action toward regaining the threatened freedom. Two sets of ingredients determine the amount of resistance (Brehm, 1966; Brehm & Brehm, 1981). One set concerns the freedoms that are threatened. The more numerous and ego-centric the freedoms, the greater the resistance to losing them. A second set of factors concerns the nature of the threat. Arbitrary, blatant, direct, and demanding requests will create more resistance than legitimate, subtle, indirect, or delicate requests.

Like an attitude, resistance has three components: an affective component ("I don't like it!), a cognitive component ("I don't believe it!"), and a behavioral component ("I won't do it!"). Most of the work in social psychology on resistance to persuasion has focused on the cognitive component, where resistance is identified by the counterarguments to a persuasive message. Brock (1967) introduced this definition of resistance, as well as the cognitive response method of measuring resistance. In a deceptively simple insight, Brock had respondents list their thoughts about a persuasive message. The number (or proportion) of counterarguing thoughts, thoughts that were critical of the message or the position it advocated, was used as the measure of resistance to the message. Brock (1967) and others showed that attitude change towards the position advocated by the message decreases, and even reverses, as the proportion of counterarguing thoughts increases.

The affective and behavioral components of resistance are central issues for other theories of change. Milton Erickson (1964; Erickson, Rossi, & Rossi, 1976; Haley, 1973; Sherman, 1988; Zeig, 1982) founded a psychotherapy that explicitly addressed resistance. For Erickson, resistance is a motivating force, originating outside of awareness, that influences feeling, thought, and action. Erickson realized that people came to him desiring to be treated, often through hypnosis, but also were resistant to the treatment. The therapist's task, he understood, was to neutralize the resistance and engage the underlying desire. Erickson (Erickson et al., 1976; Haley, 1973) discussed a number of strategic ways to sidestep resistance, and even to use it in service of the resisted change.

A strategy for neutralizing resistance was to occupy it with a diversion. Erickson's (1964) confusion techniques for hypnotic induction provided clear examples. He would engage a script with which the patient felt comfortable, move with the script for a while, then violate the script in a confusing way, creating disorientation and uncertainty, and finally provide a prescription to heal or go into a hypnotic trance. He enacted this general form through stories and actions, sometimes of very short duration. Erickson believed that the confusion did two things. First, the confusion occupied the resistance motivation, leaving little energy left to counteract the persuasive message. Second, the confusion set up a motivation for certainty that could be satisfied by a clear and unambiguous statement, such as a blatant persuasive message. Erickson (1964) told of employing the confusion technique through a handshake. A patient who wanted to be hypnotized came to Erickson's office. The patient extended his hand in greeting. Erickson took the patient's hand, began a standard handshake, then slowly lifted the patient's hand up to the level of his head, and said, "You are here to be hypnotized. You can go into a trance now." Erickson reported, that the patient immediately went into a trance. The unconventional conclusion to the prosaic handshake had (1) occupied the patient's resistance, leaving none left over to counteract the hypnotic suggestion, and (2) created a desire for clarity that motivated acceptance of the clear prescriptions that followed.

RESISTANCE AND SOCIAL INFLUENCE

The approach-avoidance conflict model proposes that resistance to persuasion is as much a part of the social influence equation as are extra inducements for compliance. Our understanding of social influence can be greatly expanded by focusing on resistance, particularly on methods used to avoid it, minimize it, disarm it, or use it in service of persuasion. The next sections of this chapter review four strategies for increasing compliance by reducing the influence of resistance to persuasion.

STRATEGY 1: SIDESTEPPING RESISTANCE

Perhaps the most effective way to deal with resistance is to not raise it in the first place. Brehm's (1966) theory of reactance suggests two general ways to minimize resistance: (1) minimize the importance of the action to be influenced, and (2) minimize the strength of the threat.

Minimizing Importance

Trivializing the action that is requested is a way of minimizing resistance. Perhaps this realization is why many interpersonal requests tend to be for a "small favor." Strategic therapists often give patients homework assignments that seem trivial, but are designed to evoke major consequences. Watzlawick, Weakland, and Fisch (1988) describe treating a case of writer's block by concocting with the patient a game of devising the most creative and ridiculous faux pax and social gaffs, and then experiencing them. For instance, the patient walked into a Chinese restaurant and ordered a taco, and hailed a cab to take him to an address that was exactly where the cab picked him up. The patient had great fun creating these situations, and reported back on the astonished looks and amusing comments that his hoaxes had created. Watzlawick et al. report that soon the patient resumed writing again and finished his project on time. Watzlawick et al.'s analysis was that it would have been fruitless to try to persuade the patient to not be afraid of failure and embarrassment. Instead, the therapist made an apparently unrelated request that was easy, even fun, to fulfill. But, this homework assignment delivered the message that failure was under one's control and that embarrassment could be lived with.

Minimizing Strength of Threat

Erickson's psychotherapy often employed storytelling, where he would tell a story about some apparently trivial or external experience (Rosen, 1991). Since the story was not explicitly about the patient, its message raised little resistance. However, Erickson chose the story carefully to describe metaphorically the patient's situation or therapeutic actions. The message was direct, but not directed at the patient.

Several forms of social influence may inadvertently use the strategy of minimizing the strength of the threat. One aspect of the foot-in-the-door technique (Freedman & Fraser, 1966) is that it involves a small initial request that raises relatively little resistance, thus is easily accepted. The next, larger request seem less of a step when it comes after the small request, than when it comes by itself.

Similarly, the door-in-the-face technique (Cialdini, Vincent, Lewis, Catalan, Wheeler, & Darby, 1975) also has elements of minimizing resistance. The influence agent begins with a very large request that is almost certain to be rejected, and follows it with the request that was intended all along. The door-in-the-face minimizes the strength of the intended request by contrasting it with the much larger previous request.

Marketing has many suggestions for minimizing the strength of the threat. Jolson (1997) advised salespeople to sidestep resistance by redefining the sales situation as a long-term consultative relationship. Thus, your photocopier salesperson calls to help you assess your photocopy needs, rather than to sell you a photocopier. In a version of this strategy called "Straight Shooter Selling," D. K. Straight (1996) counseled salespeople to avoid the immediate sales pitch and instead begin by exploring the interests and needs of the buyer to see if a mutually acceptable basis for doing business may be established. Redefining the purpose of the interaction can diminish the resistance to it. A sales pitch engenders wariness and opposition; a consultation promotes cooperation. These forms of relationship selling often have multiple features, such as adding liking, reciprocity, and consistency to the mix of inducements for compliance, but they also reduce resistance to the offer by reducing the strength of the threat.

STRATEGY 2: DIRECTLY REDUCING RESISTANCE

A second set of strategies implied by the conflict model is to direct some of the persuasive attention to the resistance itself. For instance, an offer of a warranty or a guarantee precisely addresses a major source of resistance to a purchase, the concern that the product may not perform satisfactorily. A guarantee has monetary and persuasive value because it minimizes the buyer's risk. Wal-Mart stores, for instance, give customers the option to return any product for any reason. Presumably, the slightly greater returns Wal-Mart receives are sufficiently outweighed by the greater sales that come from buyers' perception that any unwanted purchases can be returned. Guarantees are effective inducements for sales, not because they upgrade or improve the product, but because they take away a major class of resistance to the sales.

Whether persuasive messages should address or avoid possible counterarguments has a long history in the study of communications (Hovland, Lumsdaine, & Sheffield, 1949). A one-sided message is one that gives only supportive arguments for the thesis. A two-sided message gives supportive arguments, but also mentions and attempts to discount possible counterarguments to the thesis. Research has shown a number of complex findings concerning the effectiveness of one- and two-sided communications. For instance, Lumsdaine and Janis (1953) found that both kinds of messages produced equal attitude change for their respondents, but that the two-sided communication left respondents less susceptible to a later counterattack on their attitude.

One- and two-sided communications have been found to be effective in different ways in different situations (Chu, 1967; Hovland et al., 1949). It appears that people who are uninformed or uninterested in a topic are generally more persuaded by a one-sided communication. People who are knowledgeable and interested in a topic are generally more persuaded by a two-sided communication. Sorrentino, Bobocel, Gitta, Olson, and Hewitt (1988) explain this effect in terms of cognitive responsiveness. If people are motivated to use heuristic processing, then one-sided works better, but if they are motivated to use systematic processing, then two-sided communications work better. So, the general principle seems to be that if resistance is high enough to spontaneously produce counterarguments, then a message is more effective if it can address, frame, and nullify those counterarguments. Otherwise, a simple one-sided message works best, presumably because it does not introduce doubt to the message.

STRATEGY 3: DISRUPTING RESISTANCE

A third strategy for minimizing the effects of resistance is to interfere with its operation or application. Distractions, disruptions, misdirections, or other interferences can be done in several ways, some blatant, some subtle.

Blatant Distraction of Resistance

Festinger and Maccoby (1964) asked fraternity men to listen to a speech criticizing the role of fraternities on college life. Some of the men watched a film of the speaker, other men watched a lively, colorful, and amusing film while listening to the speech. Festinger and Maccoby found that the distracting film enhanced acceptance of the anti-fraternity position advocated in the speech. At about the same time, Janis, Kaye, and Kirschner (1965) reported more persuasion for participants who eat while reading persuasive essays than for participants who did not eat. Distraction, however, sometimes had the opposite effect of making people less responsive to a persuasive message (Haaland & Venkatesan, 1968).

In thinking about these studies, Osterhouse and Brock (1970) believed that the effect of distraction was to reduce counterarguing. Because the Festinger and Maccoby (1964) study employed a message that clearly would be counter attitudinal for fraternity members, the unfettered response would be for the fraternity members to be resistant to the message and to counterargue its points. Because counterarguing a message takes more effort than understanding the message, distraction interfered more with the resistance to the message than with the understanding of the message (Gilbert, 1991).

To demonstrate the effects of distraction on counterarguing, Osterhouse and Brock (1970) asked undergraduates to list their thoughts after listening to a six-minute message advocating a tuition increase at the students' university. The position advocated by the message was clear, but unpopular with the students.

While listening to the message, the students had to monitor four lights, labeled 1 through 4, mounted on the corners of a wooden panel, and voice the number of the light when it flashed. In a no distraction condition, the lights did not flash. In a low distraction condition, the lights flashed 12 times a minute. In a high distraction condition, the lights flashed 24 times a minute. Distraction did not interfere with students ability to recall the message, but did reduce the number of counterarguments that students were able to report, and did increase acceptance of the message.

Petty, Wells, and Brock (1976) reasoned that if distraction interfered with people's ability to develop counterarguing thoughts about a message, it should also interfere with people's ability to develop favorable thoughts about a message. They conducted two studies that varied the degree of distraction (0, 4, 12, or 20 presentations per minute of a stimulus to be tracked), and the quality of the message that students heard while attending to the distraction. Both messages advocated a tuition increase at the students' university, but the high quality message supported this position with very strong arguments that were difficult to counterargue (e.g., average salary of graduates would increase), while the low quality message contained weak arguments that were easy to counterargue (e.g., improved lighting was needed in classrooms to cut down on student headaches). Increasing distraction reduced the effectiveness of the high quality message but increased the persuasiveness of the low quality message. Inspection of the thoughts that students listed about the message showed that distraction decreased the number of favorable thoughts about the high quality message, and decreased the number of counterarguments to the low quality message. These results clearly implied that distraction affected attitude change because it interfered with people's ability to think about the message. When those distracted thoughts would have been negative, then distraction produced more acceptance of the message, but when those distracted thoughts would have been favorable, then distraction decreased acceptance of the message.

Two theories in particular help explain the effects of blatant disruptions on persuasion and compliance: Petty and Cacioppo's (1986) elaboration likelihood model of attitude change and Gilbert's (1991) two stage model of judgment.

Elaboration likelihood model (ELM) of persuasion.   Petty and Cacioppo's (1986) Elaboration Likelihood Model (ELM) of persuasion suggests that distraction reduces someone's ability to process a message thoughtfully by carefully considering and evaluating the content of the message. Petty and Cacioppo call this thoughtful processing the central route to persuasion. Disrupting access to this central route leaves people with only heuristic cues to evaluate their attitude, what Petty and Cacioppo call the peripheral route to persuasion. This model, already discussed in terms of blatant distraction (Petty & Brock, 1981; Petty et al., 1976), predicts that distraction will increase acceptance of a message that would normally be counterargued, but decrease acceptance of a message that would produce spontaneous, favorable elaborations.

Gilbert's two stage model of judgment.   Gilbert (1991) suggested that judgments resulted from two sequential stages of information processing. When a message or situation is noticed by a person, that person first needs to comprehend the situation, then later evaluate it. The comprehension stage requires an automatic and uncritical acceptance of the proposition in order to understand its meaning. To comprehend the utterance that a university tuition should increase requires that a recipient assume, embrace, visualize, or otherwise accept the statement being uttered. As soon as a statement is comprehended, it becomes available for evaluation. At this evaluation stage, the statement can be checked against other information, compared to other beliefs and positions, evaluated for internal and logical consistency, and so forth. It is at this second stage that resistance, particularly counterarguing, would be influential.

Gilbert (1991) showed, in many ways, that the evaluation stage required more cognitive effort than the comprehension stage. Consequently, if an influence target is under any cognitive load, such as a distraction, the evaluative stage would be disrupted sooner and more easily than the acceptance stage. This means that a distraction would promote an automatic acceptance of the proposition, no matter what position was advocated by the message, no matter what the prior position of the target was, and no matter whether strong or weak arguments were used in the message.

Subtle Momentary Disruption of Resistance

Most of the studies commonly considered as assessing the effects of distraction on attitude change have used potent and continuous distracting tasks. These are sledgehammer-like distractions that smash cognitive responses while demanding attention. We have become interested in a class of distractions that are much more unobtrusive and momentary, subtle distractions that also increase acceptance of a favorable message.

We have studied a social influence technique that we call the Disrupt-Then-Reframe (DTR) technique (Davis & Knowles, 1999). The technique employs a mild disruption to the ongoing script of a persuasive request, followed by a persuasive message. We call this persuasive message a "reframe" because it asks the listener to reframe the request, that is, understand the issue in a new way. For instance, in one study, a male solicitor went door-to-door introducing himself as a college student seeking donations to a local center for developmentally disabled children. In the normal solicitation condition, he described the center, then said, "Would you be interested in donating some money to the Richardson Center?" Then he added a simple persuasive message, the reframe. He said, "You could make a difference!" He was successful in gaining contributions from 30% of the households. In the DTR condition, he said, "Would you be interested in donating money some to the Richardson Center? You could make a difference!" The only change in the script was that the DTR contained an unexpected reversal of two words, "money" and "some." In this condition, the donations increased dramatically to 65% ($p < .03$). This subtle technique introduced a minor disruption to the script, followed by a "reframing" persuasive message. It was developed from two lines of thinking: Milton Erickson's (1964) confusion approaches to hypnosis, and Vallacher and Wegner's (1985, 1987) Action Identification Theory.

Ericksonian confusion techniques. I've previously described some of Milton Erickson's (1964; Gilligan, 1987) approaches to overcoming resistance. His contribution to the DTR was to show the subtlety of the disruption process. Among his many techniques for inducing hypnosis (Erickson et al., 1976; Haley, 1973; Rosen, 1991) were ones he called the confusion techniques (Erickson, 1964; Lankton, 1987). Gilligan (1987) described a number of Ericksonian confusion techniques, including nonsequiturs, syntactical violations, inhibition of motoric expression, interruption of cues correlated with counterarguing (such as glancing up and to the left), as well as interrupting a handshake. Erickson believed that the disruption occupied a patient's resistance and established a desire for certainty. For both reasons, confusion was likely to increase compliance with whatever suggestion immediately followed.

Action Identification theory. Action Identification Theory is a theory of change (Vallacher & Wegner, 1985, 1987; Nowak & Vallacher, 1998) that comes out of a social cognitive framework. It also focuses on the role of disruption in establishing a new framing of the situation, but specifies a different mechanism. An action identification is a person's label for and understanding of a particular action. For any particular act, many identifications are possible. These identifications may be ordered hierarchically, from low-level characterizations that attend to details and parts of the action, to high-level labels that capture the purpose, goals, or implications of the action (Vallacher & Wegner, 1987).

To move from being a novice to an expert at an activity, be it golf, writing, or stealing, one usually moves in a natural progression from the novice's focus on the minute details of the action to the expert's focus on the entire action sequence. Whereas golf, for the novice, is in fact the action of setting an overlapping grip, keeping the knees bent, keeping the feet at shoulder width, raising the club, keeping the eye on the ball, pulling not pushing the club, and a hundred other details, for the expert this action is identified as driving the ball toward the hole.

Comprehension and mastery over an activity allows for higher and higher levels of identification. But these higher level characterizations also make the particulars of the activity more remote. The performance demands of the task are best met by attending to the details of the activity. But, a focus on the details obscures the integration of the action. Thus, an action identification is the equilibrium point in a double approach-avoidance conflict between the goals of integrating the meaning and purpose of the action and effectively controlling the details of action (Vallacher & Wegner, 1985, 1987). The expert is able to achieve this equilibrium at a much higher level of identification than the novice.

It is unlikely that one high-level action label will be replaced by an alternative high-level label, unless the quasi-stationary equilibrium of the first label is disrupted. The disruption causes the person to move to lower level representations in order to recapture efficient control of the action. The attention to the details of action allows mastery to be regained. The reclaimed control over the action then allows the person to adopt a higher level identification of the action. It is at this stage that a new, high-level representation of the action may be substituted for the previous one. The new representation, then, is a reframed understanding of the action. Vallacher and Wegner (1985) established these reframings through biased questionnaires, where the questions were all loaded in the direction of the reframing, or through declarative assertions (e.g. "Coffee drinkers seek/avoid stimulation").

The instigators of action identification change that Vallacher and Wegner describe are subtle, swift, and outside of focal attention. For instance, in one study, students were instructed to eat Cheetos with their hands or with a pair of chopsticks (Vallacher & Wegner, 1985). In another, students drank coffee from a normal cup or from a cup made very awkward by a pound of shot in its base (Wegner, Vallacher, Macomber, Wood, & Arps, 1984). The students who performed the actions as they normally would were unresponsive to imbedded influence techniques and, if anything, showed more resistance to the influence attempt. However, students whose normal behavior had been disrupted by the awkward apparatus proved quite susceptible to the social influence. The disruption made them susceptible to the reframing suggested in the influence attempt, and they adopted the reframed action identification.

Requirements for Disrupt-Then-Reframe

Ericksonian (1964) confusion techniques and Vallacher and Wegner's (1985, 1987) Action Identification Theory provide different explanations for similar phenomena. Taken together, though, they suggest the requirements for the DTR. For both theories, the disruptions that the authors used were unexpected elements in the normal script for the interaction, anomalous but not the focus of the interaction. They were seemingly part of the script, albeit a odd part. The research participants in Vallacher and Wegner's disruption conditions were still trying to eat Cheetos or drink coffee. Erickson's hypnotic subjects were still trying to make sense out of the induction even when Erickson seemingly got his phrases backwards. We assume that if the participants had been forced to change the focus of action away from eating Cheetos or drinking coffee to a focus on manipulating chopsticks or hefting that cup, then they would not have been as susceptible to the influence attempt. So, the disruption has been subtle, disrupting to the script of the interaction, but not disrupting targets away from the script.

In contrast, the reframings used by Erickson and by Vallacher and Wegner were as brazen as the disruptions were subtle. Erickson followed a confusing phrase with the assertion, "You are falling deeper into trance." Vallacher and Wegner followed their disrupting activity with reframing assertions such as "college education impairs one's sex life" or "coffee drinkers seek stimulation." It appears that when the subtle disruption works, the reframing can be startlingly direct.

The Disrupt-Then-Reframe Technique

Over the past several years, we have studied DTR change procedures consistent with Erickson (1964) and Vallacher and Wegner (1985) that would work in more everyday situations. The first version of the technique offered a subtle disruption to a sales script (stating the price in pennies rather than in dollars) and followed it with an explicit new characterization ("It's a bargain"; Davis & Knowles, 1999).[1] Salespeople went door-to-door in different neighborhoods selling packets of note cards, the profits from which supported a local center for developmentally delayed people. The packets contained envelopes and eight cards with different pictures drawn by clients of the center.

The homes sampled were single family detached and duplex dwellings in a metropolitan area with a population of 125,000 people. A household participated in this experiment when a resident answered the doorbell and listened long enough to hear the entire sales script. The salesperson introduced him- or herself, presented the cards, and said, "I would like to show you some cards made by clients of the Richardson Center. Are you familiar with the Richardson Center? Then you know that it is a nonprofit organization that has great programs for developmentally disabled children and adults. These cards are made by clients at the center and come eight to a package. Would you like to know the price?"

Then, depending on a random schedule, residents were assigned to one of the differently worded offers. The various studies included the following conditions.

> DTR. In this condition, the salesperson said, "This package of cards sells for 300 pennies." After a 2-second pause, she said, "That's three dollars. It's a bargain." We believed that the "300 pennies" occurring first provided the disruption to the ongoing script. We followed this after several seconds with the price stated in dollars so that all conditions would have the price stated in the same way at least somewhere in the offer.
>
> Price only. In this control condition, the salesperson stated, "This package of cards sells for three dollars."
>
> Reframe only. A second control condition was added in which the salesperson stated, "This package of cards sells for three dollars," then, after a 2-second pause, added, "It's a bargain."
>
> Disruption Only. In the disruption only condition, the salesperson provided a subtle disruption to the usual offer–response action sequence.

---

1. These studies were carried out by Barbara Davis. She was assisted in this work by Kimberley Phipps, Jennifer Atkinson, Jason Boaz, Jennifer Bullington, Samantha Hill, Scott McDaniel, Nirika Morris, Rupal Patel, and Kelvin Tay.

She said, "This package of cards sells for 300 pennies." Then, after a two-second pause, the salesperson added, "That's three dollars."

Reframe-then-disrupt. This condition reversed the order of the two components. The salesperson said, "The package of eight note cards is a bargain." After a two-second pause, she said, "It's 300 pennies, that's three dollars."

After the offer, the salesperson waited for a response from the resident. A purchase of any number of packages was recorded as complying with the request. The percentage of households that purchased cards is presented in Table 3.1 for each condition in each study. The results are quite clear. First, the DTR script sold substantially more cards than any other condition, typically showing nearly a doubling of the sales. This is a large effect. Second, the phenomenon identified here was replicated in several subsequent studies. This is a reproducible effect. Third, the various comparison conditions showed that both the disruption and the reframe were required, and that they must be presented in that order. This is a specific effect. When either element was presented alone, or the reframe preceded the disruption, then the compliance rate dropped to the level of the price-only condition. Fourth, Study 4, which used a between-salesperson design, where salespeople learned and delivered only one script, demonstrated that the effect was not dependent upon salespeople knowing the comparison conditions.

In Study 4, we videotaped the salespeople delivering the same control script, and used ratings of their presentations to match pairs of salespeople which we then randomly assigned to conditions. Subsequent videotapes and ratings showed that the experimental scripts did not alter ratings of the salespeople's friendliness, nervousness, persuasiveness, comfortableness, eagerness, likability, or overall presentation. In short, there was no evidence that the scripts altered viewer's impression of the salesperson even though they altered compliance.

TABLE 3.1. Percentage of Respondents who Complied in Each Condition
($N = 20$)

Condition	Study 1	Study 2	Study 3	Study 4
DTR (Disrupt then reframe)				
They're 300 pennies, that's $3.00, it's a bargain	65%	70%	65%	90%
Price only:				
They're $3.00	35%	25%	30%	—
Reframe only:				
They're $3.00, it's a bargain	35%	30%	—	50%
Disruption only:				
They're 300 pennies, that's $3.00	—	35%	—	—
Reframe-then-disrupt				
It's a bargain, they're 300 pennies, that's $3.00	—	—	25%	—

Note: For studies 1, 2, and 3, one or two salespeople enacted all conditions, with 20 respondents per condition. Study 4 matched salespeople for quality of presentation and assigned them to one condition or the other, with 20 respondents per condition.

Two conceptual replications, using different disruptions and different reframes, also show a subtle but strong effect on compliance rates. Both of these replications also attempted to test the idea that a subtle disruption would work better than a blatant disruption.

The Cupcake study.[2]   The first replication sold cupcakes on campus for the Psychology Club. Young women sat at a Psychology Club table with a box of large frosted cupcakes. When people asked the price, they were answered in one of three ways. In the control condition, they were told, "These cupcakes are 50 cents; they're really delicious!" In a mild disruption condition, they said, "These halfcakes are 50 cents; they're really delicious!" In the severe disruption condition, they said, "These petit gateau are 50 cents; they're really delicious!" The sales showed a significant effect of condition, with the mild disruption condition showing more compliance (74%) than the control condition (46%), and the severe disruption condition showing a somewhat increased effectiveness (67%) that was not significantly different from either of the other conditions.

The Donation study.[3] The second replication asked for donations for the Richardson Center, and was described earlier. The college student received donations from 30% of the households when he asked people to donate "some money," but received donations from 65% of the households when he asked people to donate "money some." When he invoked a more severe disruption by reversing the order of "money" and "some" and reversing the order of "Richardson" and "Center," he received donations from only 25% of the households. Both of the lower percentages were significantly less than the 65% in the mild disruption.

These replications add several important pieces of information about the DTR. First, they eliminate several alternative explanations for the "300 pennies" studies. It is clear that the DTR is not dependent on a numerical contrast between 3 and 300, or between pennies and dollars. These replications bolster the claim that it was the unexpectedness of 300 pennies that produced the original effect. Second, it appears that only a mild disruption works to make the reframing persuasive; what seems like a more severe disruption was less effective. Apparently, the disruption needs to perturb the processing of the script, but not to be so potent that it become a focus of attention itself.

The subtle disruptions may work through different mechanisms than do the blatant distractions described earlier. Erickson (1964) believed that the subtle disruptions increased acceptance of any subsequent suggestion. Petty et al. (1976) showed that a blatant distraction increased the acceptance of an easily counterargued message, but decreased the acceptance of a strong argument that normally inspired supporting thoughts. The specific mechanisms involved in the DTR still need to be studied.

----

2. This study was conducted by Shannon Butler, Amanda Talley, and Helen Woodyard.
3. This study was conducted by Scott McDaniel.

Subtle disruptions may not be so rare as an influence technique. Our work with the That's-Not-All (TNA) technique suggests that it too may work through a disruption, but with an implicit reframing (Pollock, Smith, Knowles, & Bruce, 1998). To demonstrate the TNA technique, Burger (1986) sold cupcakes on campus. The standard sales pitch said "These cupcakes are 75 cents," whereas the TNA sales pitch said, "These cupcakes were one dollar but are now 75 cents." The hallmark of the TNA technique is that an offer is begun, then amended to make the offer look better. The typical finding is that the offer after an amendment is accepted much more often than the same offer without the amendment. The TNA seems to be in the family of DTR techniques, one that creates the disruption by changing the offer, and provides a reframing implicitly by the comparison of the new with the old offer. Interestingly, our DTR studies suggest that if Burger (1986) had changed his TNA sales pitch to say, "These cupcakes are 75 cents, but they used to be one dollar," he would not have found his effect. Presenting the information in this order does not disrupt the understanding of the offer. We suspect that there are a number of other influence techniques that fall within this family. It is not difficult to find a number of television advertisements that seem to insert subtle disruptions in the message.

STRATEGY 4: TURNING RESISTANCE FROM AN ADVERSARY INTO AN ALLY

When resistance is so prevalent or so strong that it becomes automatically applied, then it becomes susceptible to the ironic vulnerability of a "double bind." In a double bind, the target of influence is presented with a choice, where both alternatives subtly lead to the same end. Prescribing the resistance is a prime example. For instance, when a therapist tells a particularly resistant patient, "You will find it hard to complete this assignment," the patient is placed in conundrum. The highly resistant patient can only resist the therapist's suggestion by finding it easy to finish the assignment. If the patient finds it hard to complete the assignment, then the therapist has gained compliance of a different sort, making further compliance easier. Either way, the patient's resistance is turned against the resistance itself.

Prescribing the symptom is one of the strategic therapies that make up the technique called paradoxical intention (Ghadban, 1995; Kim, Poling, & Ascher, 1991). The more resistant the patient, the more completely these approaches work. In sales, similar prescriptions of resistance ("You probably won't see the advantage of this policy"; "You are going to be doubtful about this offer, but I'll tell you anyway.") also create a double bind for the customer. If the customer resists the prescribed resistance, they become more accepting of the offer; if the customer goes along with the prescription and resists, then the salesperson is omniscient and trustworthy.

Brehm's (1966; Brehm & Brehm, 1981) reactance theory provides a motivational explanation for this paradoxical persuasion effect. Prescribing the resistance, "You'll find it hard to complete this assignment " encroaches on the target's freedom to choose any response to the assignment. This threatened loss of freedom creates the aversive and motivational psychological state that Brehm called "reactance." The only way to remove the reactance and to reestablish freedom of choice is to resist the encroachment, that is, to find it "easy" to complete the assignment.

Ironic processes such as these probably work in several ways (Ansfield & Wegner, 1996). Wegner's (1994) dual process model of mental control proposes that the will to resist something ("don't think about white bears") creates an intentional operating process that initiates the resistance ("think about the garden instead"), and also creates an ironic monitoring process that evaluates the effectiveness of the resistance ("are there any white bears in these thoughts?"). The operating process requires intention, effort, and energy. The monitoring process occurs automatically, without effort. When the operating process falters through fatigue, the monitoring process still keeps activating the resisted elements and making them available for intrusion. This is why slips of the tongue and other faux pax are often ironically focused on precisely what was being resisted. Although Wegner developed the dual process model as a cognitive explanation of ruminative thinking, it seems that these ironic phenomena involve many more kinds of behaviors (Shoham & Rohrbaugh, 1997) and additional motivational elements (Liberman & Förster, 2000)

CONCLUSION

Resistance is an important component of most, if not all, social influence situations. By definition, it is the most important component of any social influence attempt that fails to gain compliance. But even with successful influence, a person's resistance to the persuasion may persist to produce reservation and doubt. Surprisingly, resistance has been considered only rarely in the psychology of social influence. When it has been considered, resistance has been treated as an adversary of attitude change: Important attitudes are more resistant to change (Jacks & Devine, 1996, 2000; Krosnick, 1988). We have attempted to show here how an understanding of resistance can be used in service of attitude change and social influence.

An approach-avoidance model of social influence expands our understanding of the dynamics of social influence. Resistance is a constant component of any attitude change process. The context and features of a request, an offer, a command, or a suggestion raise both desires to comply and desires to not comply. The end result, compliance or defiance, stems from the relative strengths of these two opposing desires.

The approach-avoidance model also adds to the repertoire of techniques that can be used to increase compliance. As we have outlined here, a fuller understanding of resistance also can be used to increase compliance. We have outlined four resistance based compliance strategies: (1) don't raise resistance, (2) confront resistance, (3) distract or disrupt resistance, and (4) use resistance to further compliance.

Some chapters in this volume engage themes that we do not. These chapters add to and will eventually complete the analyses of resistance presented here. For instance, individual differences in persuasiveness and persuasability undoubtedly will become important moderators in the study of resistance persuasion. Petty (this volume) has shown how one individual difference variable, the need for cognition, has a major impact on subtle social influence. Several other chapters in this volume show individual and social identity to be a fundamental and powerful factor in social influence. The identity-related aspects of resistance invite development.

In many ways the concerns of this chapter do echo the major themes of this book and resonate with many of the topics in other chapters. We have seen in this chapter and will see in the rest of this volume, that social influence has both blatant and subtle sides. The subtlety is often so hidden that it occurs outside of awareness (Dijksterhuis, this volume; Petty, this volume; Stangor, Sechrist, & Jost, this volume), but can become so blatant that it is part and parcel of our self (David & Turner, this volume), our language (Ng, this volume), and our being (Shaller, this volume).

We also see in these themes that social influence is a dynamic processes that involves elements unfolding over time. So, in this chapter, the order and presumably timing of words makes a great deal of difference in how persuasive messages are accepted. But, in many chapters we see that unfolding, and process, and time are needed for social influence to work its way at the level both of self (Terry & Hogg, this volume) and at the level of society (Latané & Bourgeois, this volume; Shaller, this volume).

REFERENCES

Anderson, C. M., & Stewart, S. (1983). *Mastering resistance: A practical guide to family therapy*. New York: Guilford.

Ansfield, M. E., & Wegner, D. M. (1996). The feeling of doing. In P. Gollwitzer, & J. Bargh (Eds.), *The psychology of action: Linking cognition and motivation to behavior* (pp. 492–506). New York: Guilford.

Ard, B. (1982). Reality, reframing and resistance in therapy: Interview with P. Watzlawick. *AAMFT Family Therapy News, 13*, 1.

Brehm, J. W. (1966). *A theory of psychological reactance*. San Diego, CA: Academic.

Brehm, S. S., & Brehm, J. W. (1981) *Psychological reactance: A theory of freedom and control*. San Diego, CA: Academic.

Brock, T. C. (1967). Communication discrep-

ancy and intent to persuade as determinants of counterargument production. *Journal of Experimental Social Psychology, 3*, 296–309.

Burger, J. M. (1986). Increasing compliance by improving the deal: The that's-not-all technique. *Journal of Personality and Social Psychology, 51*, 277–283.

Chu, G. C. (1967). Prior familiarity, perceived bias, and one-sided versus two-sided communications. *Journal of Experimental Social Psychology, 3*, 243–254.

Cialdini, R. B. (1993). *Influence: Science and practice*. Reading, MA: Addison-Wesley.

Cialdini, R. B., Vincent, J. E., Lewis, S. K., Catalan, J., Wheeler, D., & Darby, B. (1975). Reciprocal concessions procedure for inducing compliance: The door-in-the-face technique. *Journal of Personality and Social Psychology, 31*, 206–215.

Davis, B. P., & Knowles, E. S. (1999). A disrupt-then-reframe technique of social influence. *Journal of Personality and Social Psychology, 76*, 192–199.

Dollard, J., & Miller, N. E. (1950). *Personality and psychotherapy*. New York: McGraw-Hill.

Eagly, A. H., & Chaiken, S. (1993). *The psychology of attitudes*. Fort Worth, TX: Harcourt Brace Jovanovich.

Erickson, M. H. (1964). The confusion technique in hypnosis. *The American Journal of Clinical Hypnosis, 6*, 183–207.

Erickson, M. H., Rossi, E. L., & Rossi, S. (1976). *Hypnotic realities: The induction of clinical hypnosis and forms of indirect suggestion*. New York: Irvington.

Festinger, L., & Maccoby, N. (1964). On resistance to persuasive communications. *Journal of Abnormal and Social Psychology, 68*, 359–366.

Freedman, J. L., & Fraser, S. C. (1966). Compliance without pressure: The foot-in-the-door technique. *Journal of Personality and Social Psychology, 4*, 195–202.

Ghadban, H. (1995). Paradoxical intentions. In M. Ballou (Ed.), *Psychological interventions: A guide to strategies* (pp. 1–19). Westport, CT: Preager.

Gilbert, D. T. (1991). How mental systems believe. *American Psychologist, 46*, 107–114.

Gilligan, S. G. (1987). *Therapeutic trances: The cooperation principle in Ericksonian hypnotherapy*. New York: Brunner/Mazel.

Haaland, G., & Venkatesan, M. (1968). Resistance of persuasive communications: An examination of the distraction hypotheses. *Journal of Personality and Social Psychology, 9*, 167–170.

Haley, J. (1973). *Uncommon therapy: The psychiatric techniques of Milton H. Erickson, M.D.* New York: Norton.

Hovland, C. I., Lumsdaine, A. A., & Sheffield, F. D. (1949). *Experiments in mass communication* Princeton, NJ: Princeton University Press.

Jacks, J. Z., & Devine, P. G. (1996). Attitude importance and resistance to persuasion: It's not just the thought that counts. *Journal of Personality and Social Psychology, 70*, 931–944.

Jacks, J. Z., & Devine, P. G. (2000). Attitude importance, forewarning of message content, and resistance to persuasion. *Basic and Applied Social Psychology, 22*, 19–29.

Janis, I. L., Kaye, D., & Kirschner, P. (1965). Facilitating effects of "eating while reading" on responsiveness to persuasive communications. *Journal of Personality and Social Psychology, 1*, 181–186.

Jolson, M. A. (1997). Broadening the scope of relationship selling. *Journal of Personal Selling and Sales Management, 17*, 75–88.

Kim, R. S., Poling, J., & Ascher, L. M. (1991). An introduction to research on the clinical efficacy of paradoxical intention. In G. R. Weeks (Ed.), *Promoting change through paradoxical therapy* (Rev. ed.) (pp. 216–250). New York: Brunner/Mazel.

Knowles, E. S. (1980). An affiliative conflict theory of personal and group spatial behavior. In P. B. Paulus (Ed.), *Psychology of group influence*. Hillsdale, NJ: Erlbaum.

Krosnick, J. A. (1988). Attitude importance and attitude change. *Journal of Experimental Social Psychology, 24*, 240–255.

Lankton, S. R. (1987). The scramble technique. In S. R. Lankton (Ed.), *Central themes and principles of Ericksonian therapy*. Phoenix, AZ: Milton H. Erickson Foundation.

Lewin, K. (1951). Frontiers in group dynamics. In D. Cartwright (Ed.), *Field theory in social science: Selected theoretical papers by Kurt Lewin* (pp. 188–237). New York: Harper.

Liberman, N., & Förster, J. (2000). Expression after suppression: A Motivational explanation of post-suppressional rebound. *Journal of Personality and Social Psychology, 79*, 190–203.

Lumsdaine, A. A., & Janis, I. L. (1953). Resistance to "counterpropaganda" produced by one-sided and two-sided "propaganda" presentations. *Public Opinion Quarterly, 17*, 311–318.

Miller, N. E. (1944). Experimental studies in conflict. In J. McVicker Hunt (Ed.), *Personality and the behavior disorders* (Vol. 1, pp. 431–465). New York: Ronald.

Miller, N. E. (1959). Liberalization and basic S-R concepts: Extensions of conflict behavior, motivation, and social learning. In S. Koch (Ed.), *Psychology: A study of a science* (Vol. 2, pp. 196–292). New York: McGraw-Hill.

Nowak, A., & Vallacher, R. R. (1998). *Dynamical social psychology: Dynamics of social influence*. New York: Guilford.

Osterhouse, R. A., & Brock, T. C. (1970). Distraction increases yielding to propaganda by inhibiting counterarguing. *Journal of Personality and Social Psychology, 15*, 334–358.

Petty, R. E., & Brock, T. C. (1981). Thought disruption and persuasion: Assessing the validity of attitude change experiments. In R. E. Petty, T. M. Ostrom, & T. C. Brock (Eds.), *Cognitive responses in persuasion* (pp. 55–79). Hillsdale, NJ: Erlbaum.

Petty, R. E., & Cacioppo, J. T. (1986). *Communication and persuasion: Central and peripheral routes to attitude change*. New York: Springer-Verlag.

Petty, R. E., Wells, G. L., & Brock, T. C. (1976). Distraction can enhance or reduce yielding to propaganda: Thought disruption versus effort justification. *Journal of Personality and Social Psychology, 34*, 874–884.

Pollock, C., Smith, S. D., Knowles, E. S., & Bruce, H. (1998). Mindfulness limits compliance with the That's-not-all technique. *Personality and Social Psychology Bulletin, 24*, 1153–1157.

Rosen, S. (1991). *My voice will go with you: The teaching tales of Milton H. Erickson, M.D.* New York: Norton.

Schachter, S., & Hall, R. (1952). Group-derived restraints and audience persuasion. *Human Relations, 5*, 397–406.

Sherman, S. (1988). Ericksonian psychotherapy and social psychology. In J. K. Zeig & S. R. Lankton (Eds.), *Developing Ericksonian psychotherapy* (pp. 59–90). New York: Brunner/Mazel.

Shoham, V., & Rohrbaugh, M. (1997). Interrupting ironic processes. *Psychological Inquiry, 8*, 151–153.

Sorrentino, R. M., Bobocel, D. R., Gitta, M. Z., Olson, J. M., & Hewitt, E. C. (1988). Uncertainty orientation and persuasion: Individual differences in the effects of personal relevance on social judgments. *Journal of Personality and Social Psychology, 55*, 357–371.

Straight, D. K. (1996). How to benefit by straight shooter selling. *American Salesman, 41*, 10–15.

Vallacher, R. R., & Wegner, D. M. (1985). *A theory of action identification*. Hillsdale, NJ: Erlbaum.

Vallacher, R. R., & Wegner, D. M. (1987). What do people think they're doing? Action identification and human behavior. *Psychological Review, 94*, 2–15.

Watzlawick, P., Weakland, J. H., & Fisch, R. (1988). *Change: Principles of problem formation and problem resolution*. New York: Norton.

Wegner, D. M. (1994). Ironic processes of mental control. *Psychological Review, 101*, 34–52.

Wegner, D. M., Vallacher, R. R., Macomber, G., Wood, R., & Arps, K. (1984). The emergence of action. *Journal of Personality and Social Psychology, 46*, 269–279.

Wheeler, L. (1966). Toward a theory of behavioral contagion. *Psychological Review, 73*, 179–192.

Zeig, J. K. (1982). *Ericksonian approaches to hypnosis and psychotherapy*. New York: Brunner/Mazel.

4

Successfully Simulating Dynamic Social Impact
Three Levels of Prediction

BIBB LATANÉ
MARTIN J. BOURGEOIS

*C*omputer simulation can be seen as either an alternative to experimental research for evaluating and correcting scientific theories or simply another way of stating them (Latané, 1996a). Indeed, computer programs are quickly replacing mathematical modeling as a way of working out the consequences of theoretical ideas in domains characterized by complexity and non-linear dynamics (Casti, 1994). In this chapter, we present a case history of how simulation data and empirical data can creatively inform each other in develop-

---

We thank Wim Liebrand for programming an earlier version of CAPSIM and for contributing a number of ideas that were instrumental in the development of the research presented in this chapter. We also thank Matthew Rockloff for programming the final version of CAPSIM, and Helen Harton for comments on an earlier version of this paper.

Address correspondence to: Bibb Latané, Department of Psychology, Florida Atlantic University, Boca Raton, FL 33431, USA. E-mail: latane@fau.edu

ing and testing a comprehensive social theory. By allowing empirically derived theories of human behavior to guide computer simulations, by allowing what we learn from the simulations to help us evaluate our empirical data, and by allowing what we learn from our data to help drive the next round of simulations, we can make theoretical discoveries that may not have been possible using only simulation or experimental research.

We will do so in the context of testing dynamic social impact theory (DSIT; Latané, 1996b; Latané & Nowak, 1997; Nowak, Szamrej, & Latané, 1990). DSIT is based on a static theory of individual social impact (Latané, 1981), and aims to determine the group level effects that emerge as a population of people influence each other in lawful ways.

AN EMPIRICALLY-BASED THEORY
OF INDIVIDUAL BEHAVIOR

Briefly, social impact theory (Latané, 1981), a theory of social influence at the individual level, assumes that one's behaviors, attitudes, moods (indeed, any attribute of a person that is at least in part socially determined) will vary as a function of the strength (how persuasive), immediacy (how close in physical or temporal space), and number (how many) of sources and targets of social influence that are present. These three factors—strength, immediacy, and number—combine in a multiplicative fashion to determine the degree of social impact to be expected in any given situation. Social impact theory is a metatheory that is based on a large body of experimental research on conformity, compliance, stage fright, helping, obedience, and other individual level phenomena. In this sense we can consider the theory to be data-driven, based on real world observation and experimentation.

SIMULATIONS PREDICT EMERGENT
GROUP-LEVEL PHENOMENA

What will happen if we treat a group as a complex system of people, influencing each other and being influenced, following the individual-level laws of social impact derived from the theory? This is the goal of dynamic social impact theory. Here computer simulation is very helpful in making predictions that are not intuitively obvious or easily calculated by manipulating equations. Latané (1996a) describes computer simulation as a derivation machine, a way to help us find out what an individual-level theory predicts at the group level.

Thousands of simulations using SITSIM (Nowak & Latané, 1994), a computer program that allows us to specify a population of people ranging in size from 9 to 400, have allowed theoretical discoveries of group-level emergence from the behavior of individuals. In a SITSIM run, each individual, randomly assigned a strength (persuasiveness) and a position on a target issue, is situated in a two-dimensional social space with more influence on near than far neighbors. SITSIM allows us to vary many parameters of interest such as group size, whether the group is bordered or people on the edges wrap around, minority size, and so forth. As rounds of social influence are simulated, the individual members are influenced to either change or maintain their opinions simply by the strength, immediacy, and number of the other members. Members are not influenced by any higher-order laws, nor are they even in a position to see the group-level consequences of their actions, which are unintended by the individual members, much as individual members of a colony of ants are not in a position to see the group-level consequences of their behavior.

Four predicted forms of self-organization—consolidation, clustering, correlation, and continuing diversity—typically emerge in the simulations. First, opinions at the group level become consolidated as those holding the minority opinion find themselves more exposed to counterpersuasive attempts than members of the majority. Of course, consolidation does not always happen, as research in minority influence (e.g., Latané & Bourgeois, 1996a; Moscovici, 1985) would suggest. For example, if we introduce a bias parameter into the simulations such that members are more likely to be persuaded by the minority than the majority opinion (modeling a situation in which minorities have truth on their side), minorities can gain additional members. However, varying parameters such as group size, the mean and standard deviation of persuasive strength, and so forth, does not eliminate the tendency for minorities to be reduced in size.

The second form of self-organization that typically emerges from social influence at the local level is that opinions at the group level become clustered; that is, neighbors become more likely to share similar opinions than we would expect by chance. Compared to the randomly assigned opinion distributions at the beginning of a simulation run, there is typically a clear pattern to the opinions after discussion, in which those group members who are closer to each other come to share the same opinions.

Third, this clustering on separate issues leads initially unrelated opinions to become correlated with each other to the extent that the clusters on the different issues overlap. The increased correlation is a result of the reduced degrees of freedom as individuals within a cluster, protected from counterpersuasion by being surrounded by like-minded others, come to respond as members of a subgroup instead of as individuals. This correlation is analogous to spatial autocorrelation (in which neighbors tend to share similar opinions) discussed by geographers and political scientists.

Finally, the minority opinion factions, while becoming reduced in size, do not completely disappear, but tend to persevere. This is largely the result of minority members situated close to each other giving each other social support. Although these individuals are in the global minority, they are in a local majority (Kameda & Sugimori, 1995). Therefore, because they are more influenced by these nearby others, the pressure to change does not outweigh the pressure to stay. As a result, the population achieves continuing diversity. This diversity will only result when the minority is sufficiently large (typically at least one-third of the total population size) to achieve local majorities. Smaller minorities, lacking social support, tend to be overwhelmed by majority influence.

These predicted forms of self-organization at the group level are very robust, emerging over thousands of simulations with a wide range of initial parameters and implementing assumptions (Latané & Nowak, 1997). Despite considerable variation in specific change rules, strength distributions, group size, the presence or absence of borders, the size of the minority (down to the functional limit described above), and other system characteristics, opinion distributions become clustered, correlations across issues emerge, and minorities survive, albeit reduced in size. Thus, the results of the simulation are reliable. However, are they meaningful beyond that? Social scientists, in comparison to physical scientists, seem to be biased against accepting results of computer simulations as support for theories (Latané, 1996a). Therefore, now that the simulations have told us what our individual-level theory predicts at the group level, we felt it necessary to go back to the real world to look for evidence. That is, do human systems exhibit these forms of self-organization, or are they simply amusing outcomes from computer simulation?

SELF-ORGANIZATION IN THE REAL WORLD

Cross-cultural and subcultural variation in the real world shows promising similarity to outcomes of SITSIM. English dialects provide a vivid example of real world phenomena similar to the emergent behavior shown in the SITSIM simulations: Variations in pronunciation of words change over time, are regionally clustered, are correlated, and do not often disappear (Latané, 1996b; Trudgill, 1990).

The recent abundance of research on cross-cultural differences shows a great deal of evidence for regional differences between geographically separated cultures (i.e., clustering) and correlation of attributes within and across cultures. The most prominent example of cross-cultural difference, that between western individualism and eastern collectivism (Hui, 1988), reflects differences on a whole constellation of attitudes and behaviors. Put simply, there are many differences between people who live in the Eastern and Western hemispheres. That is, people differ in their self-concepts ("me" vs. "we" orientation), their social relations (independent vs. interdependent), their child-rearing practices (emphasizing weaker vs. stronger bonds with the extended family), and their communication patterns (e.g., outward disclosure of skills and accomplishments vs. modesty) (Myers, 1995). These patterns of regional differences lead the various attributes to be correlated, with people who are more likely to disclose their skills also being more likely to be independent and to emphasize weaker bonds with their extended family.

These correlations may reflect a top-down process in which broader core values dictate more specific attitudes and behaviors. Whether such correlations result from top-down or bottom-up self-organizational processes is far from being settled, however, since other correlations characteristic of regional clustering are more clearly the result of bottom-up processes. If, for example, we find that someone who says "Y'all," who drives a pickup truck, and who listens to country music are all correlated, we are not surprised. These behavior constellations may be driven less by any unified set of underlying principles than simply by whether a person lives in Texas.

While the similarities between these regional variations in cultural elements and the results of SITSIM simulations are encouraging, there is no direct evidence that these forms of societal self-organizations emerged as a result of interpersonal influence, and it is difficult to imagine the kinds of large-scale social experiments that would be necessary to provide a rigorous test of dynamic social impact theory. However, we can use the simulation results to help design laboratory experiments to provide empirical tests of the hypothesized group-level consequences of individual social impact.

SELF-ORGANIZATION IN THE PSYCHOLOGY LABORATORY

As part of Florida Atlantic University's continuing Computer Administered Panel Study (CAPS), we regularly recruit large numbers of people to work individually at computer terminals for five one-hour sessions spaced 2–5 days apart. In a recent academic year, we configured 240 such people into ten 24-person groups, and allowed them to discuss a variety of issues by sending electronic mail messages to one another; messages sent one session were read the next. Communication took place only by electronic messages, and members of the same group were not necessarily in the same lab at the same time. Each person could send and receive messages from only four other members of their 24-person group. People were situated in a form of social space (Latané & Liu, 1996) by determining who could send and receive messages from whom. In the studies reported here, we used a hierarchical "Family" geometry in which each person communicated with the other three members of a four-person subset of the entire group as well as to one member of a neighboring subgroup.

For a clear test of the predictions of dynamic social impact theory, we wanted to maximize social influence. Therefore, we devised a conformity game that rewarded members who correctly guessed the most popular choice on six arbitrary dichotomous issues, such as who (Euler or Hilbert) will be the more frequently chosen mathematician or which color (red or blue) the majority of the group will select (Latané & Bourgeois, 1996b; Latané & L'Herrou, 1996).

At the individual level, people confronted with an opposing majority were very likely to change their choices (70% changed when 3 or 4 people they were communicating with disagreed with them). Thus, unlike the SITSIM simulations, in which individuals always change when pressure to change outweighs pressure to stay, 30% of the individual group members did not change even when confronted with an opposing majority. By contrast, fewer than 5% of the participants changed when at least half of their correspondents agreed with them.

Despite the failure of people to be quite as rational or consistent as the lifeforms inhabiting SITSIM, all four predicted forms of group self-organization emerged strongly: choices consolidated and became clustered, correlations among initially unrelated choices increased, and continuing diversity was the norm. Thus, the emergent forms of self-organization predicted by the simulations are robust, even in an outside world which is not so perfect as the virtual reality of the simulations.

Figure 4.1 summarizes the choices of a typical conformity game group of 24 people trying to predict the most frequently chosen author. The left half of the figure illustrates the 24 members in their communication networks. Each person communicates with the three others within their subgroup and to the closest outgroup member (note that the ends are assumed to wrap around so everyone talks to an outside member). The right half of the figure shows the 24 group members' predictions in a line to facilitate showing what happens over time to individual predictions. Each row represents the 24 individual choices before a given round of messages (light faces reflect a choice of Thomas Mann and dark faces reflect a vote for Jorge Luis Borges). Each column represents the history of a single group member's choices over the five sessions, with an arrow representing each change. Before discussion, the distribution of choices was essentially random. After four rounds of messages, we see that choices have become perfectly clustered, and the minority has gotten smaller. However, it still survives, and it is likely that it would continue to do so even with continued communication, as each person has reason to believe he or she is in the global majority.

OTHER FORMS OF SOCIAL INFLUENCE

Are the results responsive to the hypothesized individual-level social process of conformity, or are they some artifact of the social situation or the electronic

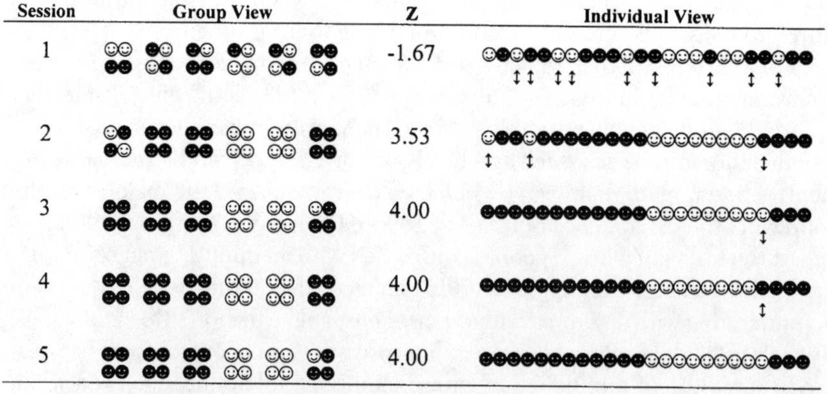

Session	Group View						Z	Individual View
1							-1.67	
2							3.53	
3							4.00	
4							4.00	
5							4.00	

FIGURE 4.1. The temporal evolution of a typical group playing the Conformity Game.

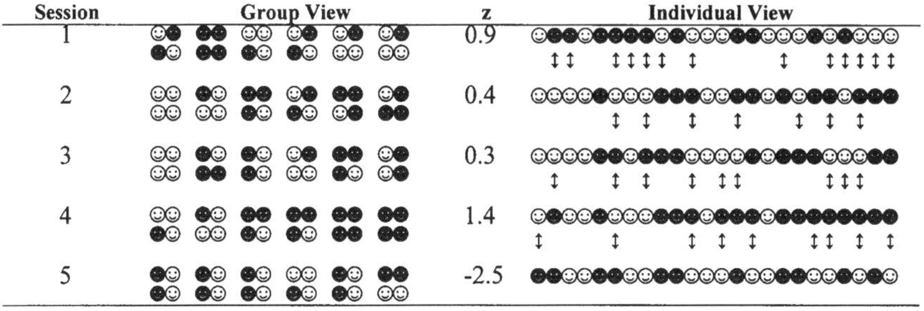

FIGURE 4.2. The temporal evolution of a typical group playing the Deviation Game.

network? To find out, in five groups we included several cases of a deviation game. This game was designed to minimize individual-level social influence and can be considered the opposite of the conformity game. Again, players were given arbitrary dichotomous choices (e.g., do you prefer Waldorf or Cobb salad?), but instead of being rewarded for being in the majority, they won if they made the less frequent choice. Therefore, any time individuals found themselves in a local majority we would expect them to be motivated to change their selection.

Figure 4.2 summarizes the data from a typical deviation game group of 24 people trying to select the least frequently chosen architect (Corbusier or Pei). Again, the left half of the figure shows people in their actual hierarchical communication networks, and the right half shows each individual's history. That is, each column represents an individual's choices through the five sessions, and arrows represent a change as a result of communication.

This example is typical—none of the forms of self-organization characteristic of the conformity game emerged in the deviation game. Minorities overall did not tend to shrink, choices did not become clustered, correlations across different issues did not emerge, and choices failed to stabilize. Instead, groups developed a continuously shifting pattern of choices. This illustrates the importance of individual-level social influence; the nature of group-level self-organization depends on whether individuals are positively or negatively influenced by their neighbors.

While this initial empirical support for the predictions generated by computer simulation was very encouraging, the conformity and deviation games model only two types of social influence, imitation and its converse. Although much social influence is due to such simple processes, one could argue that, by rewarding participants for conforming or deviating, we are essentially coercing them to act like the individual units in a simulation (although, as we noted, only 70% of the group members changed when a majority opposed them). Yet DSIT predicts social impact on any socially influenceable attribute. Therefore, we also had groups of people discuss their attitudes on 10 or 12 political and social issues within the same computer networks in which they played the Conformity Game. No rewards or other inducements for agreement were given; people were simply asked to indicate their personal opinion and to give their reasons for holding it.

People were much less influenced by the choices of their neighbors when they were discussing political issues than they were in the conformity game (in which they were paid for picking the majority selection), even though they had the opportunity to read a two-line statement of reasons for the former.

The results of this experiment are clear—the amount of emergent self-organization depended to a very large extent on the group members' response to social impact at the individual level. Consolidation, clustering, and correlation were greatest in the conformity game, less (although still significant) when people discussed political issues, and, as discussed above, not at all present in the deviation game. Before presenting these very strong results in detail, let us pause to consider a second level of prediction possible with simulation.

CAPSIM: A NEW GENERATION OF SIMULATIONS

SITSIM showed us what types of self-organization to look for, and we found them, which was very satisfying. The data also helped drive a new round of simulations, one based directly on CAPS. We found that the type of issue our CAPS participants were discussing had large effects on their susceptibility to social influence (being more open to influence on some types of issues than others), which in turn led to different amounts of self-organization. Therefore, the type of issue people are discussing is an important factor to consider.

These observations guided the development of CAPSIM, a program designed to predict the level of self-organization to be expected from different topic types. Written in Turbo Pascal (by Matthew Rockloff), CAPSIM allows us to input different change rules for different topic types (e.g., conformity game vs. deviation game), and simulate communication rounds of people in the same communication networks as our participants. CAPSIM is a simple program: Separate opinion change probabilities, depending on the number of correspondents who agree or disagree, are programmed for each topic type (conformity game, deviation game, political issues), and these change probabilities dictate whether or not any individual will change on a given communication round. Then four rounds of communication are simulated, with resulting choice distributions on each subsequent round used as input for the next communication round. Figure 4.3 shows the relative social influence operating at the individual level on the three types of issues: the conformity game, the deviation game, and political attitudes. The change probabilities programmed in for each topic type were calculated from data from our panel study shown in Figure 4.3. It is important to note that CAPSIM makes several simplifying assumptions. First, people making choices on all discussion topics within an issue type are assumed

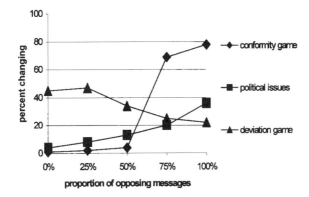

FIGURE 4.3. Individual change probabilities as a function of task and number of oppositions.

to follow the same change probability rules for each topic. Second, different agents in the simulation are assumed to follow the same change rules depending on issue type and pressure to change; that is, individual differences in strength are not part of the model.

For example, if a group member on a conformity game topic chose red over blue in the first round, and his or her four correspondents each picked blue, this member would have a 70% chance of choosing blue on the subsequent round. Thus, CAPSIM is a probabilistic simulation as opposed to a deterministic one; separate runs from the same starting distribution of opinions will lead to different (but similar) final distributions.

In order to insure realistic initial positions (and to enable the very specific predictions described below), CAPSIM was initialized with the actual first-round choices of each of the ten groups of 24 people. From the starting configuration of choices on issues for each of our ten 24-person groups, we ran 100 simulations and observed the resulting levels of three forms of self-organization predicted by dynamic social impact theory: consolidation, clustering, and continuing diversity. The predictions of the simulation can be tested against the data at three levels:

1. We can assess the fit between simulated and obtained overall levels of each form of self-organization as a function of the different types of discussion issues (conformity game, deviation game, political discussion issues).
2. We can see how well CAPSIM predicts levels of self-organization in each observed group at the level of individual topics.
3. We can determine how well the simulations predict the different levels of self-organization for different groups.

CAPSIM Predicts Different Levels of Self-Organization for Different Topic Types

Table 4.1 presents a comparison between the simulated and obtained consolidation, clustering, and continuing diversity separately for different topic types. This section summarizes the results of comparisons from each form of self-organization separately.

Consolidation, or reduction in minority size, is calculated by the formula (1– size of final minority/size of initial minority). Therefore, it is expressed as a number ranging between a variable negative number (in which the entire group ends up at the initial minority position) and +1 (in which the entire group ends up at the initial majority position). A consolidation score of 0 represents no change in the minority/majority ratio, and positive numbers reflect movement toward the initial majority position.

As Table 4.1 shows, in the actual CAPS study we found the greatest amount of consolidation on conformity game items (with majorities, on average, losing slightly more than a third of their members), significantly less consolidation on political issues (but the amount of consolidation is still significantly different from 0), and no consolidation on deviation game issues. The overall means for our simulated data showed the same overall pattern, and in fact estimated the degree of consolidation for the different issue types almost precisely. In direct comparisons between simulated and obtained consolidation, we found no difference (by paired t-tests) on any of the different types of discussion issues.

A similar comparison can be made on clustering indices between our actual and simulated groups. A numerical index of clustering (neighbors becoming more similar to each other) is calculated by counting up the total amount of agreement within the group on a given topic (i.e., how often do people who are

TABLE 4.1. Simulated and Obtained Consolidation, Clustering, and Continuing Diversity (%) by Topic Type

	Conformity game (N = 10)	Political issues (N = 10)	Deviation game (N = 5)
Consolidation			
obtained	.37°(.15)a	.15°(.08)b	.02(.14)b
simulated	.37°(.11)a	.15°(.08)b	−.09(.20)b
Clustering			
obtained	2.60°(.39)a	.93(.39)b	−.93(.94)c
simulated	2.79°(.51)A	1.26°(.14)B	−.34(.03)c
Continuing diversity			
obtained	83a	94.0b	100c
simulated	89A	99.8B	100c

Note: Numbers in the continuing diversity comparisons reflect the percent of groups that retained diversity within each topic type. Means within a row with different subscripted letters (e.g., a vs. b) are significantly different at $p < .05$. Simulated vs. obtained means whose subscripts differ in case (e.g., a vs. A) are also significantly different at $p < .05$. Standard deviations are in parentheses. Means different from 0 by one-sample t-test are marked with an asterisk.

communicating with each other agree?), and seeing how extreme this degree of agreement is relative to the 24 possible permutations of addresses in the group. From this comparison, similar in logic to a runs test, we can determine how likely it is that an observed amount of agreement resulting from discussion (in actual groups) or a simulation run within a group would be due to chance alone. These probabilities, expressed as z scores (with higher z scores reflecting higher levels of clustering), can then be analyzed for differences.

In our actual groups (see Table 4.1), we found the most clustering on the conformity game (as we expected, since people were rewarded for adopting the majority opinions of their neighbors), less (but a significant amount) on the political issues, and no clustering on the deviation game (as expected, since group members were rewarded for becoming dissimilar to their neighbors). Again, the same comparisons on our simulated data were almost identical; we found the most clustering on conformity game issues, a lesser (but significant) degree of clustering on political discussion issues, and no clustering on the deviation game. In comparing the simulated and observed clustering indices for the different topics, it seems that the simulations slightly, but consistently, overestimated the observed amount of clustering. In direct comparison between simulated and obtained clustering indices, the scores for the simulated groups were significantly higher for both the conformity game and political discussion topics.

Finally, we also tested CAPSIM predictions regarding continuing diversity (the tendency for minorities to survive after discussion, although reduced in size) on our simulated and observed data. Again, the amount of continuing diversity found in the simulations slightly overestimated that of the observed group. Compared to 91% of 180 cases where an actual group discussing a topic maintained diversity of choices or opinions, 96% of the 18,000 simulations resulted in a nonunanimous group opinion (that is, one in which not everyone in the group shared the same opinion after discussion). On the conformity game, 83% of the actual groups maintained diversity (surprisingly high considering they were paid to predict the majority opinion) compared to 89% of the 6,000 simulation runs with conformity game change rules. A similar comparison can be made with the political issues, where 94% of our 110 instances of actual groups maintained opinion diversity, compared to 99.8% of 11,000 simulation runs. In the deviation game, in which people are rewarded for becoming dissimilar to their neighbors, none of the 10 observed cases or 1,000 simulations unified. Overall, then, our simulated groups showed slightly more of a tendency towards continuing diversity then our actual groups. This may be due in part to the higher levels of clustering in the simulations. When minorities form into clusters of like-minded members, this allows continuing diversity.

Therefore, at the level of different topic types, the CAPSIM simulations provided a nearly perfect approximation of the amount of consolidation we found in our actual interacting groups, and a slight overestimation of clustering indices and continuing diversity. Interestingly, the simulation clustering scores and diversity indices still showed reliable differences across topic types that were consistent with our observed data, suggesting that the simulations are reliable if not perfectly valid reflections of the observed groups. One could think of the simulation clustering and diversity scores as thermometers that accurately detect differences in temperature, but always measure a little hot. The degree of prediction is amazing considering that the simulations do not take any individual differences into account. Although our real group members varied widely on the likelihood that they would change their opinion on a given topic as a function of whether their correspondents disagreed with them (indeed, the change rules of particular individuals varied between sessions), all the individual "people" in our simulations followed the same change rules throughout the simulation. This difference may have contributed to the tendency for the simulations to overestimate clustering and continuing diversity.

TABLE 4.2. Simulated and Obtained Postdiscussion Consolidation and Clustering by Topic for a Typical 24-Person Group

	Simulated consolidation	Obtained consolidation	Simulated clustering	Obtained clustering
Conformity game				
painter: Klee or Kandinsky	.19 (.08)	.27 (98)	3.66 (.63)	4.00 (97)
color: red or blue	.16 (.16)	.11 (39)	3.65 (.82)	3.54 (27)
note: E flat or C sharp	.65 (.29)	.28 (16)	.85 (1.20)	3.25 (98)
number: 3 or 8	.04 (.08)	.30 (99)	3.81 (.28)	2.77 (1)
magazine: Vogue or Cosmopolitan	.10 (.24)	.00 (8)	3.60 (.65)	2.51 (2)
nusician: Elgar or Handel	.89 (.22)	1.00 (38)	.02 (.21)	.00 (47)
Political attitudes				
wife won't let husband go out	.00 (.14)	.25 (75)	1.65 (1.07)	1.73 (51)
homeowner kills robber	.19 (.08)	.08 (13)	1.59 (.93)	1.66 (53)
person hospitalized against will	.15 (.19)	.09 (40)	1.35 (.93)	1.50 (54)
women required to cover faces	.00 (.15)	−.04 (25)	.64 (.98)	1.15 (71)
parents take kids out of school	.00 (.22)	−.04 (37)	.83 (1.00)	1.06 (52)
affirmative action	.30 (.24)	.40 (92)	1.79 (1.14)	.86 (23)
homosexuals can adopt kids	.01 (.15)	−.07 (4)	1.08 (1.06)	.03 (15)
US foreign military intervention	.34 (.20)	.00 (1)	.72 (1.05)	.03 (28)
smoking restrictions in public	.80 (.12)	1.00 (80)	1.31 (.98)	.00 (7)
person declared insane/locked up	.00 (.28)	−.13 (1)	.41 (.90)	−.57 (1)
legalizing marijuana	.15 (.19)	.00 (6)	1.38 (1.09)	−.65 (1)
lowering drinking age	.23 (.20)	.24 (54)	1.48 (1.03)	−.89 (1)

Correlations:

r (simulated & obtained consolidation for conformity game topics): .81
r (simulated & obtained consolidation for political issues): .87
r (simulated & obtained clustering for conformity game topics): .68
r (simulated & obtained clustering for political issues): .28

Note: The number in parentheses following simulated consolidation and clustering shows the standard deviation for the 100 simulations. The number in parentheses following obtained consolidation and clustering reflects the percentile of the 100 simulations for each topic in which the observed scores fall. We also made comparisons between the simulated and obtained clustering scores separately for each topic within the different topic types. Again, correlation coefficients were calculated separately for each group and topic type, and the rs for the ten independent groups across topics were combined meta-analytically. Here again, the strongest relationship between the simulated and observed clustering scores was in the Conformity Game, but the r for the political discussion issues was also significant.

CAPSIM Predicts Different Levels of Self-Organization for Different Individual Discussion Topics

Another way to assess the fit of the simulation data to the actual data is to calculate the correlation coefficient (Pearson's r) between the two across different discussion topics as a measure of reliability. We did this separately, for each group, within each topic type, then meta-analytically combined the r's across the ten independent groups. As we noted earlier, CAPSIM ignores differences in change probabilities across different topics.

Table 4.2 presents both simulated and obtained consolidation and clustering scores for a typical group across the 18 discussion topics. There was a significant relationship between the simulated and obtained consolidation in the conformity game and in the political discussion issues, but not in the deviation game.

These results suggest that CAPSIM does a better job at predicting the amount of consolidation or clustering at the level of individual topics for the conformity game, but still does a decent job of predicting these measures for groups of people discussing political issues. This difference is not surprising, as the individual change rules (i.e., whether or not group members change their opinions as a function of other group members' opinions) are the same in CAPSIM for each topic within a topic type. In contrast, we have found in our political discussion groups (Bourgeois & Latané, 1995) that people are much more resistant to pressure to change their opinions on some issues than others, perhaps as a function of the importance of the issue (Harton & Latané, 1997). Such a difference between topics does not appear when people are playing the conformity game, in which they are being rewarded to adopt the majority opinion. This may suggest a reason for the lesser ability of this version of CAPSIM to accurately predict consolidation and clustering at the level of individual discussion topics. Given the simplifying change rule assumption, however, CAPSIM still predicted self-organization on discussion issues quite well.

CAPSIM Predicts Different Levels of Self-Organization for Different Groups

We observed the relationship between simulated and observed amounts of self-organization across the different groups for each topic separately, then meta-analytically combined the rs across topics. This analysis tells us how well CAPSIM predicts different outcomes at the level of the individual group. That is, will CAPSIM predict how much an individual group will self-organize relative to other groups, given their different initial distributions of choices and opinions? Recall that CAPSIM ignores individual differences in strength or openness to change; therefore, if we find differences between groups on the different forms of self-organization, this would not be due to individual differences between groups, but simply a function of the different initial distributions of opinions in the different groups.

TABLE 4.3. Simulated and Obtained Consolidation and Clustering for a Typical Conformity Game Topic (Which Number: 3 vs. 8)

	Simulated consolidation		Obtained consolidation		Simulated clustering		Obtained clustering	
Group 1	.30	(.15)	.27	(24)	3.77	(.57)	4.00	(75)
Group 2	.18	(.23)	.30	(72)	3.62	(.83)	4.00	(77)
Group 3	.17	(.16)	.25	(61)	3.50	(.56)	3.00	(10)
Group 4	.06	(.20)	–.12	(1)	.69	(1.33)	2.96	(84)
Group 5	.30	(.22)	.58	(82)	3.34	(.61)	2.90	(23)
Group 6	.04	(.08)	.30	(99)	3.81	(.28)	2.77	(12)
Group 7	.34	(.24)	.45	(60)	3.32	(.50)	2.75	(10)
Group 8	.34	(.19)	.00	(6)	3.43	(.75)	2.70	(11)
Group 9	.26	(.31)	.33	(48)	3.36	(.76)	1.86	(7)
Group 10	.95	(.11)	1.00	(80)	.12	(.61)	.00	(24)

Correlations: r (simulated & obtained consolidation): .79
r (simulated & obtained clustering): .66

Note: The number in parentheses following simulated consolidation and clustering shows the standard deviation for the 100 simulations. The number in parentheses following obtained consolidation and clustering reflects the percentile of the 100 simulations for this group in which the observed scores fall. Table 4.4 summarizes results of the meta-analytic combinations of correlation coefficients across topics and across groups. As we noted, there was a significant relationship between observed and simulated consolidation and clustering both at the level of topics and at the level of groups.

Table 4.3 shows the simulated and obtained consolidation and clustering on a typical conformity game topic for each of the ten groups. In fact, the relationship between observed and simulated amounts of consolidation and clustering were significant for all the topic types in the study; the relationship again was strongest for the conformity game, but still significant for political discussion issues. This analysis suggests that groups that achieved greater clustering and consolidation scores in the discussion study also were more likely to show greater amounts of these forms of self-organization in the simulations.

Table 4.4 summarizes the results of the meta-analytic combinations of correlation coefficients across topics and across groups. As we noted, there was a significant relationship between observed and simulated consolidation and clustering both at the level of topics and at the level of groups.

TABLE 4.4. Correlation Between Simulated and Obtained Consolidation and Clustering across Topics and across Groups

	Conformity game	Politcal issues	Deviation game
Consolidation			
across topics	.85°	.38°	.65°
across groups	.83°	.51°	.85°
Clustering			
across topics	.86°	.56°	.14
across groups	.84°	.68°	.57

Note: Correlations for conformity game and political issues are based on the meta-analytic combinations of *r*s across discussion topics and groups. Significant ($p < .05$) correlations are marked with an asterisk.

CONCLUSION

Just as in our real groups, minorities in our simulations tended to be reduced in size, opinions became spatially clustered and minorities tended to survive. Not only did the simulated data show the same phenomena, but to the same degree at a surprising level of precision. CAPSIM accurately predicted differing amounts of self-organization at the general level of topic type, at the level of specific topics within a topic type (i.e., for different conformity game or political issues), and at the level of individual groups.

The CAPSIM simulations, based on a few simple change rules, provide an amazing degree of agreement to the levels of self-organization we found in our actual groups, especially when considering what the simulations leave out. As we noted earlier, there are no individual differences in CAPSIM; each person's probability to change their opinion on any issue is completely derived from the type of issue they are discussing and the number of correspondents who disagree with them. We are currently looking at ways to incorporate individual differences in strength into the simulations. Differences in openness to social influence as a function of the specific discussion topic are also ignored in the current simulations; future versions may incorporate these differences.

Given the similarity of our simulated results to those of our actual groups, we are encouraged to start the cyclical process again. That is, CAPSIM can help generate and test new predictions that are much easier to pilot test on computer than with real people. Panel studies are expensive; participants in CAPS make an average of $8 a session, with 24 people in each group. It is sometimes a herculean task to get 120 people to show up at five appointed times over a two week period without absences; real people have real problems. For example, a woman in a recent panel study who broke her leg between sessions left us with missing data for a 24 person group. In contrast, with CAPSIM, we can change one line of programming code and find out what might happen if discussion lasted 10 rounds instead of 5 (essentially saving us nearly $5,000), and look at the relative consolidation, clustering, correlation, and continuing diversity.

Another thing to look for is differing levels of self-organization in different communication geometries; we have found different amounts of clustering and consolidation in one versus two versus hierarchical networks in actual groups, but it has taken years to do so. With CAPSIM, it is a simple matter of changing who talks to whom in the simulation.

By varying the individual change probabilities we can parametrically test the relationship between individual change and the resulting levels of self-organization. How much influence at the individual level is necessary or sufficient to cause groups to self-organize? Are there upper limits to the emergent group properties, or will self-organization continue to grow given sufficient time?

The fact that we can predict levels of self-organization as a function of the particular initial opinion distributions within our groups may have immense broader implications from a social engineering perspective. The possibilities are very intriguing; one may want to encourage or discourage agreement with a majority opinion, or increase or decrease the extent to which people agree with those around them. Results of simulations that vary the location of people within a group may inform a wide range of social planners, from a host planning a dinner party to an elementary school teacher devising a seating chart to the Speaker of the House deciding where members of Congress should sit.

Of course, the process does not stop here; once we make some new discoveries from this round of simulations, we can implement them in the next round of experimental research.

REFERENCES

Bourgeois, M. J., & Latané, B. (1995). Dynamic social impact causes spatially clustered and correlated opinions. Poster presented at the annual meeting of the American Psychological Society, September, 1995, New York.

Casti, J. L. (1994). *Complexification: Explaining a paradoxical world through the science of surprise.* New York: Harper Collins.

Harton, H. C., & Latané, B. (1997).Information- and thought-induced polarization: The mediating role of involvement in making attitudes extreme. *Journal of Social Behavior and Personality, 12,* 271–299.

Hui, C. H. (1988). Measurement of individualism-collectivism. *Journal of Research in Personality, 22,* 17–36.

Kameda, T., & Sugimori, S. (1995). Procedural influence in two-step group decision making: Power of local majorities in consensus formation. *Journal of Personality and Social Psychology, 69,* 865–876.

Latané, B. (1981). The psychology of social impact. *American Psychologist, 36,* 343–356.

Latané, B. (1996a). Dynamic social impact: Robust predictions from simple theory. In R. Hegselmann, U. Mueller, & K. G. Troitzsch (Eds.), *Modeling and simulating in the social sciences from a philosophy of science point of view* (pp. 287–310). Dordrecht, The Netherlands: Kluwer Theory and Decision Library.

Latané, B. (1996b). Dynamic social impact: The creation of culture by communication. *Journal of Communication, 46,* 13–25.

Latané, B., & Bourgeois, M. J. (1996a). Commentario a "La influencia minoritaria en psicologia social: Apuntes para una reconstructon historica" (Commentary on "Minority influence in social psychology:

Points for a historical reconstruction"). *Revista de Psicologia Social, 10,* 105–109.

Latané, B., & Bourgeois, M. J. (1996b). Experimental evidence for dynamic social impact: The emergence of subcultures in electronic groups. *Journal of Communication, 46,* 35–47.

Latané, B., & L'Herrou, T. (1996). Spatial clustering in the Conformity Game: Dynamic social impact in electronic groups. *Journal of Personality and Social Psychology, 70,* 1218–1230.

Latané, B., & Liu, J. H. (1996). The intersubjective geometry of social space. *Journal of Communication, 46,* 26–34.

Latané, B., & Nowak, A. (1997). Self-organizing social systems: Necessary and sufficient conditions for clustering and polarization. In G. Barnett & F. Boster (Eds.) *Progress in communication sciences: Persuasion* (Vol. 13, pp. 43–74). Norwood, NJ: Ablex.

Moscovici, S. (1985). Social influence and conformity. In G. Lindzey & E. Aronson (Eds.) *The handbook of social psychology* (3rd ed., pp. 225–262). Hillsdale, NJ: Erlbaum.

Myers, D. G. (1995). *Exploring social psychology.* New York: McGraw-Hill.

Nowak, A., & Latané, B. (1994). Simulating the emergence of social order from individual behavior. In N. Gilbert & J. Doran (Eds.), *Simulating societies: The computer simulation of social processes* (pp. 63–84). London: University College Press.

Nowak, A., Szamrej, J. & Latané, B. (1990). From private attitude to public opinion: A dynamic theory of social impact. *Psychological Review, 97,* 362–376.

Trudgill, P. (1990). *The dialects of England.* Oxford, England: Blackwell.

5

Unintended Influence
Social-Evolutionary Processes in the Construction and Change of Culturally-Shared Beliefs

MARK SCHALLER

*T*he story told here has a simple moral: In our efforts to satisfy our personal goals, we may exert unintentional and sometimes surprising influences on the cultural norms and shared belief systems that govern our own and others' future behavior and outcomes. Before fleshing out that main story, I begin with two simpler, shorter stories. One story is about stereotypes and the other is about science.

Here's the first story. In the early 1930s, Katz and Braly (1933) conducted a descriptive study to determine the contents of the ethnic stereotypes of Ameri-

Address correspondence to: Mark Schaller, Department of Psychology, University of British Columbia, 2136 West Mall, Vancouver BC V6T 1Z4, Canada. E-mail: schaller@cortex.psych.ubc.ca

can university students. Among the stereotypes assessed were those of African Americans (or "Negroes" as they were popularly identified at the time). One hundred White Princeton students were asked to indicate the five traits that seemed most typical of "Negroes." On the basis of these data, Katz and Braly tabulated a list of the 12 traits that were most frequently identified as typical. At the very top of that list, endorsed by 84% of their subjects, was the trait "super-stitious" ("lazy" and "happy-go-lucky" followed in second and third place, re-spectively). Some 35 years later, Karlins, Coffman, and Walters (1969) dupli-cated these procedures to assess the contents of ethnic stereotypes of a later generation of Princeton students. Results revealed that a mere 13% of subjects indicated that "superstitious" was especially stereotypical, and that seven other traits (including "lazy" and "happy-go-lucky") were more frequently endorsed. More recent surveys reveal the continued fading of "superstitious" from the cultural stereotype of African Americans; results reported by Devine and Elliot (1995) revealed not a single subject who perceived the trait "superstitious" to be particularly stereotypical of African Americans.

Now here's the second story. In the 1990s, conversations between scien-tists who study social influence and stereotypes and other social psychological phenomena were commonly punctuated by remarks that the articles published in relevant professional journals just weren't interesting anymore. These com-plaints were occasionally aired in articles printed in those journals, buttressed by observations that published articles were increasingly long, redundant, and devoted to empirical support for hypotheses that seemed too obvious to be true (e.g., Schaller & Crandall, 1998; Wallach & Wallach, 1994; Wegner, 1992). On the basis of these publications trends, Higgins (1992) argued that the psycho-logical community had become increasingly concerned with methodological rigor and decreasingly attentive to the promotion of new ideas.

Each of these two stories begs a question. The stereotype story compels one to wonder why the trait "superstitious" disappeared from the stereotype of African Americans. The disappearance seems particularly striking because eth-nic stereotypes are commonly perceived to be frustratingly resistant to change. And yet, even as other elements of the stereotype persisted across generations, "superstitious" vanished. There's no evidence that "superstitious" was targeted by anyone as a trait to be eliminated from stereotypic perceptions. If particular characteristics were targeted by civil rights activists, educators, politicians, me-dia managers, and other influential parties, those traits were the more negative-charged ones (laziness, ignorance, etc.). Yet those negative traits seem to have persisted in the stereotype much more so than "superstitious." Why? Mean-while the science story compels one to wonder why the social psychological community seems to have become decreasingly concerned with discovering and promoting truly novel theories and phenomena. This trend, if true, seems par-ticularly odd because innovation is commonly perceived to be a fundamental value of scientists. And yet, even as new journals spring up to provide more outlets for social psychological research, complaints persist that published ar-ticles continue to just tell us what we already know. There is no evidence that scientific authorities deliberately target novel theories and phenomena for censure. Quite the opposite. Journal editors routinely publish pleas for innovative work, and research granting panels set up special funds earmarked for innovative, speculative projects. So, if the normative publication has become increasingly dull, it has done so despite clear intentional efforts to the contrary. Why?

Ethnic stereotypes and scientific publications are obviously different; on the surface, the disappearance of a trait from a stereotype and the rarity of innovative ideas in a scientific literature seem to have very little in common with one another. Lurking beneath these differences, however, are some conceptual similarities. Both stories pertain to cultural norms—the socially shared information that describes a human population. Each story illustrates something about persistence or change in the contents of these norms over time. And in each story, the persistence or change in these norms appears to have occurred in the absence of intention. Thus, the precise questions begged by each story are specific versions of a broader, common question: What process accounts for the unintended contents of cultural norms?

This question transcends psychology or any other single domain of inquiry. But an answer—at least one answer—to the question exists squarely in the realm of psychological inquiry. The answer lies in a simple process of social influence. The process can be considered a "social-evolutionary" process, and it operates through the act of communication.

SOCIAL-EVOLUTIONARY PROCESSES
AND THE EPIDEMIOLOGY OF CULTURAL NORMS

Within the biological sciences, the term "evolution" typically refers to a process where genes—and the phenotypic traits they generate—are transmitted from individual organisms to their offspring, and so may come to describe a population of organisms. This evolutionary process occurs inevitably as long as three things occur: (1) There is some variability in the pool of genes that might be transmitted, (2) there are selective forces operating on this gene pool so that some genes are more likely than others to be transmitted, and (3) there is some system for retaining the variants that actually are transmitted. A fundamental outcome of the process is this: Whatever genetic information is more likely to be transmitted is more likely to become common within the population.

In an analogous fashion, a "social-evolutionary" process refers to a selection process where elements of social information are transmitted from individual to individual, and so may come to describe a population of people. These elements of social information may include ideas, beliefs, behavioral strategies, fads, and fashions—all the things that have come to be referred to collectively as "memes" (Dawkins, 1989). The method of transmission occurs through the verbal and nonverbal methods by which people communicate with each other. Social-evolutionary processes occur inevitably as long as three things occur: (1) There is some variability in the pool of memes that might be communicated, (2) there are selective forces operating on the meme pool so that some memes are more likely than others to be communicated, and (3) there is some system for retaining the variants of memes that actually are communicated (cf. Campbell, 1965). All three preconditions exist in virtually every realm of social information. Consider attitudes. There is substantial diversity in attitudes within individuals and across different individuals; some attitudes are more likely than others to be expressed to other people; those attitudes that are communicated can be encoded and stored in individuals' memory structures and in a variety of cultural archives. Just as with biological evolutionary processes, there is a fundamental outcome of this social-evolutionary process: Whatever information is more likely to be communicated is more likely to become common within any population of human beings.

It is for this reason that attitudes, beliefs, and other memes can be thought of as viruses (Sperber, 1990). The analogy helps illustrate two fundamental points concerning the role of communication in the emergence and persistence of cultural norms. First, just as the spread and persistence of a virus within human populations requires a sort of social influence (individuals must transmit the virus to other individuals), so too the emergence and persistence of a culturally-shared meme depends on a sort of social influence (individuals must transmit relevant information to other individuals). Second, just as the social influence underlying the transmission of a virus typically operates outside the realm of intention or awareness, so too the social influence underlying the transmission of memes often occurs unintentionally and outside of awareness.

It is clear that cultural norms, like viral pandemics, can and do emerge and persist simply as the result of the social influence that accompanies interpersonal communication. The classic example of this sort of unintended influence is provided by Sherif's (1936) studies of mutual influence in the formation of norms under conditions of uncertainty. A more sophisticated approach to mutual influence and norm formation is provided by dynamic social influence theory and the research it has inspired (Latané, 1996; Latané & Bourgeois, this volume). Although different in many respects, these two lines of inquiry yield a shared message: Individuals influence each other unintentionally through the act of communication, and the result of this mutual influence is the emergence of shared normative beliefs and behaviors.

Just as the process of mutual influence through communication helps us understand how cultural norms emerge at all, so too it helps us understand and predict what specific norms will emerge and persist over time. Again the epidemiological analogy is useful in illustrating a simple fundamental implication of the social-evolutionary process of social influence: Just as some viruses are more highly communicable and thus more likely to become and remain widespread, so too some memes may be more likely to be communicated and thus more likely to become and remain widespread. Anything that is especially "communicable" is likely to be normative.

COMMUNICABILITY AND THE CONTENTS
OF CULTURALLY-SHARED BELIEFS

This simple point is illustrated by the somewhat-persisting but partially-changing stereotypes of African Americans over the course of the 1900s. Here we return to the question of why the trait "superstitious" disappeared from the contents of these stereotypes while other traits remained. The answer, it seems, depends in part upon the different communicability of different traits.

Katz and Braly (1933) reported a list of traits that were most stereotypic of African Americans in the early 1930s, along with numbers indicating just how stereotypic each trait was. Four studies over the course of the next several decades used similar methods and provided similar lists (Devine & Elliot, 1995; Dovidio & Gaertner, 1986; Gilbert, 1951; Karlins et al., 1969). The resulting dataset indicates the extent to which different traits were stereotypic of African Americans at different points in recent history. These data allow us to compute crude indices indicating the extent to which specific traits persisted in the stereotype over time. (e.g., one can compute a trait's persistence from the 1930s to the 1950s by subtracting its stereotypicality in the 1930s from its stereotypicality in the 1950s.) Given five separate studies reporting data at five separate points in time, one can compute persistence scores across one, two, three, and four generations for each trait considered stereotypical in the 1930s, 1950s, 1960s, and 1980s. It turns out that most of these persistence scores were negative (indicating that these traits were less stereotypic at Time 2 than at Time 1—an effect that is attributable in part to a statistical "regression toward the mean" artifact). But there was considerable variability in these persistence scores. Some traits (including "superstitious," of course) had highly negative values, indicating a lack of persistence. Other traits had persistence scores closer to zero, and some had positive scores. The key question is whether this variability was predicted by communicability: Were more communicable traits also more likely to persist in stereotypes of African Americans?

To assess the communicability of these traits, Schaller, Conway, and Tanchuk (2000) asked a sample of contemporary university students to respond to two questions about each of 76 traits: (1) "Suppose you met a person who had this trait, and now you're talking to others about this person; how likely is it that you'll tell these others that this person has this trait?" and (2) "In general, considering all the various traits of people that you talk about when you talk to others, how common is it to find yourself talking about this trait (or behaviors relevant to this trait)?" Ratings in response to those two questions were averaged to form a rough "communicability" index that was calculated separately for each of 76 traits. Included among these traits were each of the traits listed as stereotypical of African Americans by one or more of the five surveys indicated above.

Thus, for each of these target traits, we have a crude index of its communicability. ("Superstitious," it is worth noting, had a relatively low communicability score.) Consequently, we assessed the extent to which a trait's communicability predicted its persistence in the stereotype of African Americans from one point of time (Time 1) to a later point in time (Time 2), indicated by the correlation between the communicability index and the persistence score. Given the four different candidates for Time 1 (1930s, 1950s, 1960s, and 1980s), and the four different candidates for Time 2 (1950s, 1960s, 1980s, 1990s), ten different correlations were computed to test the communicability–persistence relation.

The results of each of these ten tests revealed that communicability predicted persistence. More communicable traits persisted. Less communicable traits—such as "superstitious"—fell by the wayside.

WHAT MAKES SOMETHING "COMMUNICABLE"?

If indeed the communicability of a meme is an important predictor of its tendency to become and remain normative, a more interesting question is begged: What makes a meme communicable?

It is instructive to return again to the virus metaphor. The communicability of a virus is not strictly a feature of the virus itself, but depends upon the actions of individuals already carrying the virus and on the features of uninfected individuals that make them receptive (or not) to infection. The same holds for the communicability of memes. Within a social-evolutionary framework, communicability refers simply to the likelihood that a meme will be successfully replicated from one individual to another. Successful replication requires two steps: The meme must be transmitted from a host individual to another individual (e.g., you convey some information to me), and the meme must be successfully received by the target individual (e.g., I actually incorporate that information into my existing knowledge structures). Research on persuasion processes can be viewed as addressing that second step—the extent to which designated receivers of information actually do incorporate that information into their existing repertoire of attitudes. One fundamental insight of this research is that the success of a persuasive message depends on complex interactions between the nature of the message and the features of the target. This illustrates a more general point: The "communicability" of a meme is not strictly a trait of the meme itself; it is dependent on the psychological processes of the individuals who traffic in that and other memes.

An important subset of these psychological processes pertain to the goals that individuals seek to fulfill. Therefore, the communicability of beliefs, behaviors, and other memes is a function of the extent to which they effectively satisfy the salient goals of individuals. This is an obvious statement, and some of its implications are obvious as well; but some of its implications are less obvious and imply some fairly subtle ways in which individuals' immediate goals—and their actions designed to achieve those goals—can have unintended influences on cultural norms.

The remainder of this chapter considers some of the ways in which individuals seek to fulfill specific needs, the impact of these actions on the communicability of specific memes, and the consequent unintended influence on culturally shared beliefs.

THE PERCEPTION OF POPULARITY AND ITS CONSEQUENCES

People have a fundamental need to belong, to be accepted by others (Baumeister & Leary, 1995). One way we achieve this goal is to adopt as our own whatever beliefs and behavioral tendencies are popular among those who we want to accept us. Consequently, one characteristic of a meme that influences its communicability is its perceived popularity: All else being equal, the more popular a meme is perceived to already be, the more communicable it is, and the more likely it is to become even more widespread and remain so. Research on mimicry, conformity, and other aspects of behavioral contagion reveal the obvious effects that actual popularity has on the increasing or continuing popularity of behavioral tendencies (e.g., Wheeler, 1966), including behaviors with potentially dangerous consequences, such as binge eating (Crandall, 1988).

The perception of popularity not only conveys a means to achieve social acceptance; it also conveys information. Humans have a need to understand and predict the world, and so we are intuitively inferential, drawing conclusions about reality on the basis of others' behavior. Consequently, individuals receive from others information that those others did not intend to communicate. When we mimic the behaviors of others, our actions are rarely perceived by observers as mere mimicry; instead, our actions unintentionally communicate to observers the belief that there are good reasons to engage in that same behavior. The inferred reasons may then be internalized. The impact of perceived popularity on cognitive structures is illustrated by research revealing that specific elements of group stereotypes are especially accessible and specific events especially memorable if individuals perceive that others endorse those stereotypes or remember those events (Bless, Strack, & Walther, this volume; Stangor, Sechrist, & Jost, this volume). Thus, popularly endorsed memes are especially communicable; they are more likely than other memes to be successfully transmitted between individuals and to become widespread across a population.

This tendency for popular behavior to convey information about popular opinion can have some ironic and troubling consequences. One consequence is that behavioral norms may emerge and persist unsupported by beliefs or opinions consistent with those behaviors. Prentice and Miller's (1993) work on "pluralistic ignorance" and alcohol consumption offers one striking example. Among students at Princeton University (and, one assumes, at most universities) there is a common misperception of others' attitudes toward alcohol consumption: Students believe that their peers like to drink alcohol more than they really do. In order to comply with this misperceived attitudinal norm, students drink more than they personally want to. The consequence is a population of students drinking more than they want to in order to conform to a fictional attitudinal norm, and so unintentionally conspiring to maintain that fictional norm through their own, very factual, behavior.

Another consequence is that normative behavioral strategies serving some goal imperfectly may remain normative even if better strategies are available. This phenomenon is analogous to a phenomenon common in the domain of technology, and is exemplified by the case of the QWERTY keyboard. During the development of the mechanical typewriter decades ago, the QWERTY keyboard configuration was a useful innovation because it precluded especially speedy keystroking. By slowing the fingerspeed of expert typists, it helped prevent typewriter keys from jamming at the platen. In the age of electronic word processing, key jams are no longer a problem; yet the QWERTY configuration persists despite the many alternative keyboard configurations that would facilitate faster typing. Moreover, many people mistakenly assume that the QWERTY keyboard confers maximal typing efficiency.

Similarly, suboptimal behavioral practices (and the beliefs that support them) may remain normative long after more optimal strategies become available. One example familiar to behavioral scientists pertains to the manner in which results of inferential statistical results are reported in published papers. In the early 1900s, behavioral scientists began using statistical methods to address inferential questions about results obtained in experiments—specifically, methods that allowed them to comment upon alternative explanations based on sampling error. In those precomputer times, researchers did not have the technological means of determining the exact likelihood (p) that sampling error alone could have produced an obtained experimental effect. One reasonable response to this constraint became the norm: Researchers referred to truncated tables of "critical values" for the purpose of making binary judgments about whether the actual value of p was bigger or smaller than a somewhat arbitrarily-chosen likelihood value ("alpha"). The results of these inferential statistical tests were reported in a manner that was necessarily inexact and vague (e.g., "$p > .05$" or "nonsignificant" or "ns"). Within a few decades, however, computer technology became available that eliminated these constraints on statistical inference and reporting. For at least two decades now, statistical software packages have been providing researchers with *exact* p values. And yet this more accurate inferential information typically goes unreported. Instead, it remains common for researchers to obscure those precise p values, to transform the exact value on their computer output ("$p = .085$") into the vaguer, less informative renderings of older times ("ns"). The technological constraints under which suboptimal statistical rituals emerged no longer exist; and yet, ritualized folkways of reporting statistical results persist, supported in part by beliefs attesting to the optimality of those normative rituals.

One might think that scientists—having been bred to be skeptical—would be relatively immune to this sort of "naturalistic fallacy" in inference. Ironically, it may be exactly because of the skepticism attributed to our peers that scientists may be especially vulnerable to this inferential error. Individual scientists may tacitly acknowledge the scientific community's famous fussiness about matters of accuracy and truth, and so may infer that if some behavior meets the standard of social approval, then this behavior must be the best way of doing things—better (or at least no worse) than obvious alternatives. Consequently, scientists may be especially likely to perpetuate scientific practices (like the reporting of inexact p values) that are suboptimal but are at least good enough to have attained popularity.

STRATEGIC DISCOURSE AND ITS CONSEQUENCES

The goal of social acceptance does more than merely compel people to mimic the perceived behaviors of others. The same goal also leads us to devise subtle strategies through which we can influence the impressions that others form of us. One means through which we influence these impressions is through discourse: When communicating with other people, we strategically choose what to say and what not to say in order to make a good impression. This means that whatever publicly articulated memes best serve individuals' impression management goals will be especially communicable, and most likely to emerge as widespread cultural norms.

This process is illustrated in a set of studies by Schaller and Conway (1999) that examined the effects of impression management goals on the contents of emerging group stereotypes.

In one of these studies, participants in dyads received information about two target groups—simply called the Red Group and the Blue Group. The "objective" information that participants received revealed that people in the Red Group were, on average, both more aggressive and more intelligent than those in the Blue Group. Thus, if participants formed stereotypes that focused on especially diagnostic information, emerging stereotypes would be expected to focus approximately equally on traits connoting intelligence and aggressiveness.

However, participants did not merely receive this objective information. They also were provided periodic opportunities to communicate with each other (by writing notes) about their emerging perceptions of the Red and Blue Groups. Before participants received any information of any sort, we introduced a manipulation designed to make each participant consider the manner in which he or she might be able to make a good impression on the other. Specifically, as the result of an ersatz debriefing following a "preliminary study," participants in some dyads were led be believe that they would appear especially likely to succeed in life if they communicated about the negative aspects of other people. Assuming that they want to lead others to think of them as potential success stories, we suspected that these participants would be especially likely to communicate about diagnostic traits that were evaluatively negative (e.g., aggressive). Thus, for these participants, we introduced a specific impression management goal that could be carried out through strategic discourse.

Indeed, compared to a "no goal" control condition, participants who had received the particular impression goal did communicate more about negative

characteristics. So, as a result of participants' responses to the impression management manipulation, the manipulation affected the communicability of different traits.

What impact did this have on the contents of the stereotypes that emerged
over time? Consistent with the social-evolutionary approach, the more communicable a trait was, the more central it became to the consensually shared stereotype that emerged over time. Despite the fact that the actual objective information about the groups was identical across experimental conditions, individuals
who shared the particular impression goal ended up being more likely than
controls to perceive the Red Group as aggressive and unpleasant, and were
somewhat less likely to perceive them as intelligent. This effect occurred, at
least in part, as a result of the mutual social influence that occurs through communication. This is apparent from the results that emerged in two additional
experimental conditions in which the same specific impression management
goal was introduced to individuals. In one of these conditions, subjects wrote
notes to each other, but never exchanged them. In the other condition, subjects
read notes written by prior subjects, but never wrote notes themselves. Thus, in
neither condition did the individual goal have an opportunity to exert an influence through dynamic interpersonal discourse. Results revealed that in neither
condition did stereotypes coalesce around traits connoting aggressiveness as
much as they did in the condition in which participants had the opportunity to
actually influence each other through strategic discourse. In sum, the goal of
making a good impression on others had a side effect on stereotype formation—a side effect that subjects themselves almost certainly did not intend.

One can imagine a variety of other ways in which impression management
goals may influence the communication process and thus influence cultural
norms. Accents, locutions, and attitudes that are believed to convey a desired
social status may be especially likely to be used in discourse, and so may become culturally normative. Thus, fancy phrasings and conservative economic
attitudes may be highly communicable within populations of individuals who
desire high socioeconomic status, while entirely different linguistic styles and
attitudes may be communicable among populations of individuals who desire
acceptance as urban rap musicians. The more general upshot is this: Seemingly
irrelevant impression management goals can have, through the simple act of
communication, eventual impacts on the contents of cultural belief systems.

THE DESIRE FOR EPISTEMIC COMFORT
AND ITS CONSEQUENCES

Impression management goals offer just one example of the variety of individual goals that can influence the extent to which certain beliefs, ideas, and
other memes enter the realm of public discourse. Decisions about discourse
are influenced by many other goals as well (Grice, 1975; McCann & Higgins,
1992). Some of these goals are based on our needs to understand and predict

our world—the goals we seek to satisfy in order to experience a sort of epistemic comfort. Among the things that make us uncomfortable are incoherence and inconsistency. Consequently, beliefs that are consistent with preexisting cognitive structures are more likely to be successfully communicated than inconsistent ones. Another powerful contributor to epistemic comfort is ease of understanding. Consequently, simpler beliefs are more communicable than complex ones, and are more likely to become culturally normative. (For similar reasons, behavioral strategies that are easier to imagine also may be more communicable; see Cialdini, this volume.)

The communicability of simple ideas is evident not just in casual conversation, but in more formalized forms of communication as well, such as scientific discourse. Scientists typically try to communicate parsimonious explanations for phenomena, and even when more complex explanations are transmitted, they are less readily understood and retransmitted than are simpler but less complete (and often less accurate) explanations. Thus, even within communities of individuals most accustomed to complex thinking, simple ideas are especially communicable and so especially likely to become and remain culturally normative.

Our personal epistemic goals not only govern the information that we ourselves transmit and receive, but also impact upon our judgments of what should be communicated more widely, and consequently exert unintended influences on cultural norms. The culture of science again provides an example. Here we return to the second of the stories that opened this chapter and consider why it is that conceptually novel ideas are increasingly rare in the socially shared archives of social psychological knowledge.

The pursuit of innovative ideas is necessary to the progress of science; consequently, scientists place great value on conceptually novel theories and hypotheses. But scientists value other things too, such as truth. The veracity of a theory or hypothesis is valued not merely because of its implications for the progress of science, but also because it has immediate consequences for individual scientists. As Hull (1988) has pointed out, scientists' own personal outcomes are potentially affected when erroneous inferences and false theories are admitted into the published scientific literature. Although novelty and veracity are conceptually orthogonal, they are psychologically intertwined. This is because scientists, like other people, are intuitive Bayesian statisticians: Our confidence in the veracity of a hypothesis depends not only on the implications of data bearing on that hypothesis, but also on the perceived prior probability that the hypothesis is true. Compared to truly novel ideas, more entrenched ideas have subjectively higher prior probabilities of being true. This analysis suggests that although scientists may recognize and earnestly proclaim the abstract value of original ideas, this value is trumped by the more immediate concerns about the personal consequences of a potentially erroneous idea becoming public. As a result, when judging the suitability of others' work for publication, scientists may hold truly innovative theories and groundbreaking empirical results to higher standards. Moreover, this concern may be especially pronounced

under conditions in which the innovative—and therefore potentially erroneous—ideas seem especially seductive or persuasive.

Empirical results from a study conducted by Crandall and Schaller (1998)
suggests that exactly this sort of anti-novelty bias may occur in the peer review
process. The participants in the study were social psychologists experienced in
the conduct of research and the critical evaluation of others' research. We asked
these scientists to pass judgment on a hypothetical manuscript, based on a brief
summary of that manuscript's contents. Within the summary, we manipulated
the conceptual novelty of the research reported: For some participants, the
research was described as testing a hypothesis derived from an entirely innovative, previously untested theory; for others, the research was described as testing a hypothesis derived from a well-established theory. We also manipulated
the evidential strength of the research results: For some participants the results
were strong and convincing; for others, the results were weak and less convincing. These two variables were crossed within a fully between-subjects experimental design. After reading one of these four summaries, participants offered
publication-relevant evaluations of the manuscript. They also indicated the evaluation that they thought the typical reviewer would offer.

The results revealed three interesting findings bearing on a potential anti-
novelty bias in the peer review process. First, participants who evaluated the
"novel theory" manuscript perceived that it would be less positively received by
peers, compared to those who evaluated the "established theory" manuscript.
Second, participants' own evaluations were generally more positive than their
perceptions of their peers' evaluations, and this was especially so in the also
novel theory condition. Thus, it appears that people perceive others to be anti-
novelty and themselves to be more open to original ideas. The third interesting
finding emerged by comparing participants' own evaluations across the four
experimental conditions. Under conditions in which the hypothetical results
were weak (and participants' evaluations were fairly negative) the novel theory
manuscript was evaluated somewhat more positively than the established theory
manuscript. However, when the hypothetical results were strong and compelling (and participants' evaluations were more generally positive), the novel theory
manuscript was evaluated less positively than the established theory manuscript.

One interpretation of this interaction is that when empirical results are
fairly unconvincing and rejectable, reviewers throw the authors a bone because
of the originality of the idea; but when the empirical results are sufficiently
compelling that they are at the threshold for entering the archives of public
knowledge, reviewers become risk-averse and an anti-novelty bias emerges.

If this anti-novelty bias is most likely to emerge when faced with the most
evidentially publishable manuscripts, than it is most likely to affect reviews of
manuscripts submitted to the most prestigious and visible journals in the field.
This individual tendency, when aggregated across a population of scientists,
becomes a descriptive (and perhaps a prescriptive) norm of peer-review behavior. Thus, despite individual and institutional values placed on conceptual novelty, the more immediate personal goals of scientists may lead unintentionally

to the emergence of an anti-novelty norm in individual reviewer behavior. The further cultural consequence of this individual-level bias depends on the extent to which individual-level biases of this sort actually inhibit publication of novel ideas. In sciences described by lenient editorial decision rules and low rejection rates, aggregate probabilities are such that this individual-level bias is largely offset by the editorial practice of soliciting multiple reviews on manuscripts, and so it may have minimal consequences. However, in sciences (such as psychology) marked by stringent editorial decision rules and low acceptance rates, this individual-level bias may actually be magnified by the practice of soliciting multiple reviews on manuscripts. Consequently, articles on truly innovative theories are less likely to gain entrance into the prestigious, visible journals than are articles pertaining directly to older, well-established theories. Thus, individual-level concerns with subjective veracity undermine the communicability of innovative ideas and adversely affect the subjective interest value of the published scientific literature.

There may be additional unintended consequences on norms of scientific behavior. By observing the normative behavior of reviewers (and its effects on the contents of the professional journals), scientists may draw inferences about additional things that they should and should not do in order to be successful members of the scientific culture. Inferred "shoulds" might include: Report research results within the bounds of already-accepted theoretical frameworks; use conservative techniques and decision-rules when drawing inferences about the support for hypotheses. "Should nots" may include: Do not offer conceptual frameworks that are bigger and broader than the actual results; do not speculate beyond inferences that are most immediately and obviously indicated by the actual data. Thus, abstract values favoring innovation, originality, and conceptual adventurousness do not become institutionalized at the cultural level. What do become institutionalized, unintentionally, are values favoring theoretical and inferential conservativism.

And so people lament that the journals just aren't as interesting as they used to be. These lamentations often find a receptive and agreeable audience, but that agreeable reception does not easily undo the normative trajectory of the scientific culture. This is because the emergence and persistence of these norms is typically a product of unintended influence—an unintentional byproduct of behaviors that, at the individual level, seem right.

SOME ADDITIONAL IMPLICATIONS

The examples described above all fit a common template. A psychological process operating within individuals' heads influences the nature of the information that is (and is not) transmitted between individuals. Thus different types of information—different memes—are differentially communicable within a human population. The ultimate consequence, based on multiple interactions among multiple people over time, is the emergence, persistence, and sometimes change of specific culturally-shared beliefs. Sometimes, these emergent beliefs and norms are undesired; but they emerge nonetheless, because the communication process is subtle and the mutual influence unintended.

These examples have focused primarily on the unintended consequences of individuals' needs for belongingness and epistemic comfort. There are, of course, a lot of other psychological constructs that influence the communication of information between individuals. Consider mood states. Not only do moods influence attention to and receipt of information transmitted by others, moods also influence the information individuals' transmit to others and the manner in which they do so (see Forgas, this volume). Thus, depending on the mood states of interacting individuals, different memes may be differentially communicable and so differentially likely to become normative. What exactly might the cultural consequences be? It is difficult to intuit, because social-evolutionary processes proceed in a nonlinear dynamic manner. As work by Latané and Bourgeois (this volume) reveals, the ultimate impact of mutual social influence processes magnified across time and individuals can be startlingly nonintuitive—and yet still predictable when viewed through the lens of an appropriately dynamic model. Indeed, one value of casting social influence processes within a social-evolutionary framework is that, by doing so, we may discover a lot of hypotheses about broader, population-wide consequences of the many psychological pressures that operate on local social interactions. Anything that influences interaction and influence between individuals may also have unintended consequences on cultural norms.

The social-evolutionary perspective suggests that we view with caution some of our intuitions about cultural norms and their origins. Because normative beliefs often appear peculiar, it can be tempting to think that the reasons underlying their existence must be strictly idiosyncratic—that their origins might be described historically but cannot be explained scientifically. A consideration of subtle social-evolutionary processes reveals that the origins of norms are amenable to scientific analysis. Just as easily-modeled dynamic processes predict the shape and form of culturally shared beliefs (Latané & Bourgeois, this volume), so too dynamic social-evolutionary processes help predict the specific contents of these norms as they emerge and change over time. The key to prediction, as with biological evolutionary processes, is to appreciate the manner in which individuals' actions impact upon the communicability of different types of information.

Of course, an incomplete appreciation of complex social-evolutionary processes can lead to other misleading intuitions. It is sometimes tempting to think that the norms that are shaped through social-evolutionary processes are optimally designed. This is probably rarely so. Just as biological evolutionary processes are heavily constrained by preexisting biological structures, so too social-evolutionary processes are constrained by preexisting cultural structures. The most objectively correct beliefs or most optimal behavioral strategies may have a hard time catching on, regardless of their apparent rational superiority to other available options. Social-evolutionary processes may indeed weed out entirely counterproductive memes, but they don't guarantee that the most optimal memes are sowed into the system. Moreover, memes that are counterproductive along one dimension may be very functional along another, as the example of anti-novelty bias in science reveals. As another pertinent example, consider the inferences we might logically draw from the popularity of different social influence strategies used by influence professionals (Cialdini, this volume). Existing norms may indeed offer clues about desired utility in domains where a single obvious financial goal is paramount. Individuals working on commission and selling products in direct, face-to-face interactions are almost certainly motivated primarily by financial rewards contingent upon the success of their sales strategies, and so the sales strategies that become popular are probably those that are truly influential. However, in other domains of professional influence, such as television advertising, the contingency between sales strategy and individual financial rewards is weaker, and goals other than immediate sales may impact upon the advertising strategy. Within these domains in which the communicated product serves multiple hidden goals, the normative popularity of a strategy may be a very imperfect clue as to its effectiveness in attaining its most apparent purpose. In assessing the utility of normative beliefs, we must consider not only the most obvious goals that they might serve, but also less obvious, more personal goals as well.

A social-evolutionary perspective not only helps explain past and present cultural norms, but also may offer useful insights into intervention strategies that might influence future forms of these norms. Consider strategies designed to undermine harmful group stereotypes. Some intervention strategies are designed to change individuals' attitudes and beliefs about stereotyped groups. These sorts of strategies may not be all that effective in changing cultural stereotypes that really matter, because long-held individual cognitive structures are hard to change. The social-evolutionary perspective suggests that more effective strategies for changing cultural stereotypes might focus less on individual cognitive structures and more on interpersonal communication. The idea is to create interventions that alter the communicability of stereotypic beliefs. The most effective strategies for stereotype change may be those that address norms of how one talks about groups. Although laws against hate speech and social norms proscribing linguistic bigotry (e.g., "political correctness" norms) are deservedly criticized for a variety of reasons, it may be that these norms will ultimately turn out to be a means of undoing negative stereotypes of historically disparaged ethnic groups. Of course, these effects may take time, measured not merely in years but in generations.

Communication-based interventions may also be most successful in revising scientific norms. Years of high profile criticisms of traditional statistical practices have had only the most modest impact on the actual statistical practices of behavioral scientists. Perhaps this is because these intervention strategies focused primarily on the analytic strategies scientists pursue in the privacy of their labs. More impactful interventions may be those that focus on how we talk about statistics and how we transmit statistical knowledge to novice scientists.

Similarly, in order to increase the frequency of innovative ideas in a scientific literature, interventions aimed directly at the communication process may be most effective. In this case, the communication process involves the peer-review system governing the extent to which individually-held knowledge is transmitted publicly. Interventions designed to undo tendencies of individual reviewers to hold conceptually novel work to higher standards, or designed to impede the impact of individual reviewers' anti-novelty bias on actual publication decisions (e.g., through changes in editorial decision rules) may lead to a subjectively more interesting body of scientific literature and may have positive consequences on scientific progress.

If we are more mindful of the subtle communication processes through which our own and others' communicative actions unintentionally create and sustain cultural norms, we can learn to more carefully construct and conduct these actions. In doing so, we may more successfully avoid unintended influences on culturally-shared beliefs, and we might make more headway in achieving intended influences as well.

REFERENCES

Baumeister, R. F., & Leary, M. R. (1995). The need to belong: Desire for interpersonal attachments as a fundamental human motivation. *Psychological Bulletin*, *117*, 497–529.

Campbell, D. T. (1965). Variation and selective retention in socio-cultural evolution. In H. R. Barringer, G. I. Blanksten, & R. W. Mack (Eds.), *Social change in developing areas* (pp. 19–49). Cambridge, MA: Schenkman.

Crandall, C. S. (1988). Social contagion of binge eating. *Journal of Personality and Social Psychology*, *55*, 588–598.

Crandall, C. S., & Schaller, M. (1998). How do scientists respond to truly innovative research?: An empirical inquiry. Unpublished manuscript, University of Kansas.

Dawkins, R. (1989). *The selfish gene* (New ed.). Oxford, England: Oxford University Press.

Devine, P. G., & Elliot, A. J. (1995). Are racial stereotypes *really* fading? The Princeton Trilogy revisited. *Personality and Social Psychology Bulletin*, *21*, 1139–1150.

Dovidio, J. F., & Gaertner, S. L. (1986). Prejudice, discrimination, and racism: Historical trends and contemporary approaches. In J. F. Dovidio & S. L. Gaertner (Eds.), *Prejudice, discrimination, and racism* (pp. 1–34). New York: Academic.

Gilbert, G. M. (1951). Stereotype persistence and change among college students. *Journal of Abnormal and Social Psychology*, *46*, 245–254.

Grice, H. P. (1975). Logic and conversation. In P. Cole & J. L. Morgan (Eds.), *Syntax and semantics 3: Speech acts* (pp. 95–113). New York: Academic.

Higgins, E. T. (1992). Increasingly complex but less interesting articles: Scientific progress or regulatory problem? *Personality and Social Psychology Bulletin*, *18*, 489–492.

Hull, D. L. (1988). *Science as a process*. Chicago: University of Chicago Press.

Karlins, M., Coffman, T. L., & Walters, G. (1969). On the fading of social stereotypes: Studies in three generations of college students. *Journal of Personality and Social Psychology*, *13*, 1–16.

Katz, D., & Braly, K. (1933). Racial stereotypes in one hundred college students. *Journal of Abnormal and Social Psychology*, *28*, 280–290.

Latané, B. (1996). Dynamic social impact: The creation of culture by communication. *Journal of Communication*, *46*(4), 13–25.

McCann, C. D., & Higgins, E. T. (1992). Personal and contextual factors in "the communication game." In G. R. Semin & K. Fiedler (Eds.), *Language, interaction, and social cognition* (pp. 144–172). London: Sage.

Prentice, D. A., & Miller, D. T. (1993). Pluralistic ignorance and alcohol use on campus: Some consequences of misperceiving the social norm. *Journal of Personality and Social Psychology, 64,* 243–256.

Schaller, M., & Conway, L. G., III (1999). Influence of impression-management goals on the emerging contents of group stereotypes: Support for a social-evolutionary process. *Personality and Social Psychology Bulletin, 25,* 819–833.

Schaller, M., Conway, L. G., III, & Tanchuk, T. L. (2000). Selective pressures on the once and future contents of ethnic stereotypes: Effects of the 'communicability' of traits. Unpublished manuscript. University of British Columbia.

Schaller, M., & Crandall, C. S. (1998). On the purposes served by psychological research and its critics. *Theory and Psychology, 8,* 205–212.

Sherif, M. (1936). *The psychology of social norms.* New York: Harper.

Sperber, D. (1990). The epidemiology of beliefs. In C. Fraser & G. Gaskell (Eds.), *The social psychological study of widespread beliefs* (pp. 25–44). Oxford, England: Clarendon.

Wallach, L., & Wallach, M. A. (1994). Gergen versus the mainstream: Are hypotheses in social psychology subject to empirical test? *Journal of Personality and Social Psychology, 67,* 233–242.

Wegner, D. (1992). The premature demise of the solo experiment. *Personality and Social Psychology Bulletin, 18,* 504–508.

Wheeler, L. (1966). Toward a theory of behavioral contagion. *Psychological Review, 73,* 179–192.

6

Automatic Social Influence

The Perception-Behavior Links as an Explanatory Mechanism for Behavior Matching

AP DIJKSTERHUIS

> *"Contagion is a phenomenon of which it is easy to establish the presence, but that is not easy to explain."*
>
> (Gustave LeBon, 1935/1982, p. 10)

*T*he phenomenon of behavioral contagion or behavior matching has intrigued many thinkers (Bandura, 1977; James, 1890; Koffka, 1925; Le Bon, 1935/1982; McDougall, 1908; Piaget, 1946; Scheflen, 1964; Smith, 1759/1966; Tarde, 1903). The reason that so many theorists have published about behavior matching may indeed be, as Le Bon observed, that this phenomenon is so easy to witness. It is simply hard to ignore. Many people will have observed that they take over postures or gestures of others, for instance while watching a game on television. Although our own movements aren't as smooth and impressive as the ones made by Dennis Bergkamp or Ken Griffey Jr., many of us do

Address correspondence to: Ap Dijksterhuis, Department of Social Psychology, University of Nijmegen. PO Box 9104, 6500 HE, Nijmegen, The Netherlands. E-mail: dijksterhuis@psych.kun.nl

tend to mimic the behavior of our sports heroes to at least some extent. Other examples that are easy to observe are the temporary changes in our accents (especially when speaking a second language) as a result of the different accents of the people we are interacting with. I very well remember the first day in the office after my return from a two-month stay in Scotland. I read aloud an English letter to a colleague who became more and more amused as I read. As it was hard to see how the contents of the letter could be the reason behind his increasingly good mood—it was a rejection letter—I asked him why he was laughing. "You're talking Scottish!" he replied.

These examples represent a very basic form of social influence. Our behavior is continuously and automatically adjusted to bring it more in line with our social environment. More concretely, we automatically change our behavior to match more closely the behavior of the person (or people) we perceive. This phenomenon is widespread and pertains to a very broad behavioral domain (see also Latané & Bourgeois, this volume). We match both very basic actions we perceive in others (such as gestures or accents) as well as more complex behavioral patterns (such as intellectual performance or aggressive behavior). My goal in the present chapter is to briefly review behavior matching findings and to propose the possibility that all these forms of behavioral matching—ranging from matched facial expressions to matched intellectual performance—can be explained by one and the same psychological principle, namely the principle that perception directly and automatically affects overt behavior (the "perception-behavior link"; see also Bargh & Chartrand, 1999; Bargh, Chen, & Burrows, 1996; Berkowitz, 1984; Chartrand & Bargh, 1999; Dijksterhuis & Bargh, in press; Dijksterhuis, Bargh, & Miedema, 2000; Dijksterhuis & van Knippenberg, 1998). The remainder of this chapter consists of three parts. First, I will review some of the more important findings in the literature on matching of behavior of a relatively elementary nature. In this part the literature on facial expressions, speech related variables, gestures, and postures is discussed. Second, I review some recent findings on matching behavior that is more complex and multifaceted. Finally, I argue that these findings can be accounted for by the same fundamental psychological mechanism, the perception-behavior link.

Before moving on, it is appropriate to explain the choice for the term "behavior matching" to refer to the phenomena under consideration. There are two reasons for my use of the term behavior matching. The broad term "behavior" is used exactly because it is broad in that it refers to many different kinds of psychological processes ranging from basic facial expressions to complex and multifaceted behavior such as intellectual performance. The term matching is used because it is a more accurate descriptor of the phenomenon I am referring to than some alternative terms. Mimicry and synchrony are too narrow as they are only used to refer to behavior of a rather elementary nature. Imitation is confusing as it is often used to describe more strategic forms of behavior, while the focus in this chapter is on automatic behavioral effects. Finally, the use of the term "contagion"—although essentially accurate—is disadvantageous as it is usually applied in treatments of behavior of social groups (or even societies as a whole), while the focus in this chapter is on the behavior of the individual.

MATCHING OF ELEMENTARY BEHAVIOR[1]

Although the first theoretical contributions on behavior matching appeared long ago (James, 1890; Smith, 1759/1966; Tarde, 1903), it took quite some time before the evidence for behavior matching grew strong enough to be characterized as being more than just anecdotal. Scientific demonstrations started to be published in the 1960s and 1970s (LaFrance, 1979; Mattarazzo & Wiens, 1972; Meltzoff & Moore, 1977; O'Toole & Dubin, 1968; see also Scheflen, 1964). As others have noted (Bernieri & Rosenthal, 1991; Chartrand & Bargh, 1999), three different lines of research about three different forms of behavioral matching appeared after the early publications. One line of research addresses matching of facial (often emotional) expressions, another group of studies addresses matching of variables related to speech production, while a third line of research is aimed at matching of postures, gestures, and other body movements.[2]

The evidence for matching in the domain of facial expressions is abundant. An interesting early study was conducted by O'Toole and Dubin (1968). Their experiment was focused on mother-child interactions during feeding. They observed that some mothers, while feeding their infants with a spoon, open their mouth while the spoon reaches the mouth of the child. One intuitive explanation for this effect is that mothers try to show the child what she or he has to do in order to eat. That is, mothers try to function as models hoping the child imitates the behavior and the food ends up where it is supposed to end up. O'Toole and Dubin, however, also found that in the vast majority of cases the mother opens her mouth just *after* the child does so. The mother, in other words, imitates the child (who presumably opens her or his mouth upon the perception of the spoon with the food).

In later years, evidence showing that people mimic facial expressions accumulated (Bavelas, Black, Lemery, & Mullett, 1986; Dimberg, 1982; Hatfield, Cacioppo, & Rapson, 1994; Vaughan & Lanzetta, 1980). Various contributions were made that emphasized the generalizability of the phenomenon. Facial mimicry is already present among neonates (Field, Woodson, Greenberg, &

---

1. The experiments reviewed in this section and the next section were often more complicated than is suggested here. Researchers have studies mediators, moderators, and effects of matching on other psychological variables. In this review however, I restrict myself to the matching effects themselves.
2. To avoid confusion, it should be noted that my definition of behavior matching is much broader than some of the other definitions. The research about posture and gesture sharing is often specifically referred to as behavior matching research (see e.g., Bernieri & Rosenthal, 1991), while this term is never (or seldom) used to refer to research on facial expression of speech related variables.

Cohen, 1982; Meltzoff & Moore, 1977) and even among people with various disorders regarding more controlled behavioral mechanisms such as aphasic, apraxic, and mentally retarded people (Prinz, 1990). A very interesting contribution was made by Zajonc and colleagues (Zajonc, Adelmann, Murphy, & Niedenthal, 1987). They presented their participants with photograph's of individual members of couples. Some were of partners who had been together for many years, others were of partners who recently met. As expected by the investigators, partners resembled each other more the more time they had spent together. This effect can be interpreted as a long-term behavioral matching effect. Many years of matching facial expressions causes lasting changes in facial lines (see also Chartrand & Bargh, 1999).

Evidence showing that people match each others' verbal behavior is also abundant. Mattarazzo and Wiens (1972) conducted several studies in which the length of the utterances of an interviewer was manipulated. Sometimes interviewers used relatively long sentences, sometimes they used shorter sentences. Evidence showed that interviewees (the actual participants) matched this verbal behavior. Jaffe and Feldstein (1970) showed that interviewees also matched the length of the pauses between sentences of an interviewer. When interviewers paused long between different sentences, interviewees started to use long pauses. Conversely, short pauses between sentences prompted interviewees to use short pauses.

Evidence for matching of other speech related variables has been obtained as well. Natale (1975) demonstrated in several studies that people match each others' speech intensity while interacting. Various experiments showed that we match the syntax others use (Bock, 1986; Levelt & Kelter, 1982) and the accents others have (Dell, 1986). Moreover, as with facial expression, neonates have been found to synchronize their movements and expressions to human speech (Condon & Sander, 1974).

Finally, various researchers have studied matching in gestures and postures. Although most people simply conclude that posture matching exists, until about ten years ago there was no reliable evidence as to the frequency with which it occurred. Early reports (e.g., Charney, 1966; Kendon, 1970) on posture matching suffered from methodological weaknesses, (see Capella, 1981; LaFrance, 1979) while later work was not concerned with the frequency of posture matching per se. That is, most relevant experiments were conducted to examine the relation between posture matching and liking or rapport. Indeed, several studies have obtained evidence for the relation between posture matching and liking (including impressive correlations of .74 between matching and positive affect [Bernieri, 1988] and .63 between posture matching and rapport [LaFrance, 1979]).

The first solid evidence for posture matching was obtained by Bernieri (1988), who used an ingenious paradigm (see also Bernieri, Reznick, & Rosenthal, 1988). First, two participants (A and B) were videotaped while they interacted. Later, both participants engaged in a new interaction with different participants (i.e., A interacted with C, B interacted with D). Again, both A and

B were videotaped. Subsequently, two tapes were constructed on which the behavior of both A and B were displayed. One concerned the real interaction between A and B. The other tape pictures A while he or she was interacting with C, and B while he or she interacted with D. Subsequently, judges—who are unaware of which tape displayed the real interaction between A and B—estimated the degree of posture similarity. If the degree of matching is greater on the first tape (the real interaction) than on the second, there is evidence for posture matching. Bernieri (1988) indeed obtained this evidence.

Recently, Chartrand and Bargh (1999) replicated and extended these effects. In their first experiment, a confederate was instructed to either rub her nose or shake her foot while working with a participant on a task. Their hypothesis, that participants would mimic the behavior of the confederate, was confirmed. When the confederate rubbed her nose participants engaged more in nose-rubbing than in foot-shaking, while the opposite was true for participants who were confronted with the confederate who shook her foot. They replicated and extended this finding in a second study.

In sum, people have the tendency to match facial expressions, various speech related variables, gestures, and movements. The mere perception of an act elicits the tendency to engage in this same act.

MATCHING OF MORE COMPLEX BEHAVIOR

Obviously, facial expressions, gestures, movements, and other relatively elementary actions are easily and automatically perceived in others. Importantly however, social perception does not stop there. We "see" a lot more in our fellow human beings than just facial expressions and elementary acts. Twenty years of social cognition research has demonstrated that human social perception is fairly sophisticated. Our perceptual repertoire is enriched with abstract cognitive constructs such as personality traits and stereotypes. Although one may argue that these constructs are probably better captured by the term "cognitions" than by the term "percepts," evidence shows that these constructs are very important in our daily and routine social perception processes, in that we activate these constructs *automatically* during social encounters (Bargh, 1994; Brewer, 1988; Devine, 1989; Gilbert, 1989; Winter & Uleman, 1984). That is, upon the perception of people we automatically activate social stereotypes, while upon the perception of behavior we automatically infer personality traits. Now if, as was concluded in the previous paragraph, perception indeed elicits corresponding behavior in the perceiver, the question arises whether this also is true for these more advanced "percepts"—traits and stereotypes. As is alluded to earlier, recent evidence demonstrates that this is indeed the case.

First of all, there is evidence showing that activation of social stereotypes affects motor behavior. Bargh, Chen, and Burrows (1996, Exp. 2) primed the stereotype of the elderly among half of their experimental participants by using a scrambled sentence technique (see Srull & Wyer, 1979; 1980). Among the remaining half, the stereotype of elderly was not activated. After participants had completed the scrambled sentence task, they were told that the experiment had finished. However, a second experimenter surreptitiously recorded the time it took participants to walk from the experimental room to the nearest elevator. The researchers hypothesized that participants would start to show stereotype corresponding behavior. That is, they predicted stereotype activation to lead to behavior matching. This was indeed the case. Participants primed with the stereotype of the elderly walked significantly slower than no-prime control participants. Recently, these effects of stereotype activation on motor behavior were extended to different behavior. In several experiments it was shown that activation of the stereotype of the elderly led to slower reaction latencies in a lexical decision task (Dijksterhuis, Spears, & Lepinasse, in press).

Secondly, stereotype and trait activation elicit behavior matching in the domain of interpersonal behavior. Carver, Ganellen, Froming, and Chambers (1983) subliminally primed the concept of hostility among half of their participants. The remaining half of the participants were not primed. In a second task, participants played the role of a teacher in a learning task based on the classic procedure used by Milgram (1963). That is, participants had to administer electrical shocks to a second participant (actually a confederate) whenever this second participant gave a wrong answer to a question. As expected by Carver et al. (1983), activating the concept of hostility led to more hostile behavior. Participants who were primed with hostility delivered longer shocks than no-prime control participants.

Greater hostility as a result of the activation of social stereotypes also has been demonstrated. Bargh, Chen, and Burrows (1996, Exp. 3) seated their participants behind a computer on which they had to perform a very laborious task. After they had performed this task for a while, the computer broke down which prompted the experimenter to ask the participant to start all over again. Importantly, before participants started with the boring task, half of them were subliminally primed with faces of African Americans. Both the experimenter (who was blind to conditions) as well as independent coders rated the reactions of the primed participants to the request of the experimenter to start all over again as more aggressive than the reaction made by control participants. Again, stereotype activation was shown to lead to stereotype corresponding behavior. Later, they replicated and extended this finding in another experiment (Chen & Bargh, 1997).

Other forms of interpersonal behavior were shown to be affected by traits and stereotypes as well. Bargh, Chen, and Burrows (1996, Exp. 1) primed participants with either rudeness or politeness. In a third condition, participants were not primed. Priming was again administered with a scrambled sentence task. The experimenter left the room after participants had been given the instruction necessary to complete the scrambled sentence task. Participants were requested to meet the experimenter in a different room upon finishing the scrambled sentence task. The experimenter, however, was talking to a confederate when the participant approached. Of interest was the time it took participants to interrupt the conversation. As expected, participants who were primed with rudeness interrupted more quickly than control participants, while participants primed with politeness interrupted later than control participants.

Macrae and Johnson (1998) showed that priming the concept of helpfulness led participants to be more helpful. In their experiments, participants were primed with the concept of helpfulness with the use of a scrambled sentence task. At a later stage, the experimenter "accidentally" dropped a set of objects in the presence of the participant. Of interest to the investigators were the number of objects a participant would pick up. As expected, it was shown that participants who were primed with helpfulness picked up more objects (i.e., were more helpful) than control participants. Macrae and Johnson (1998) replicated this effect in a second experiment.

Finally, Epley and Gilovich (1999) primed people with conformity or with nonconformity. Later, participants were asked to evaluate various aspects of the experiment. They did this in the presence of confederates, who expressed their (positive) evaluations before the participant did. As expected, participants primed with conformity conformed more to the confederates (i.e., evaluated the experiment more positively) than no-prime controls and than participants who were not primed. Participants primed with nonconformity however, did not conform less than no-prime controls. There are various explanations for this asymmetric finding (see Epley & Gilovich, 1999), in my view the most likely being that there was a lot of social pressure on participants to conform making the "mental hurdle" not to conform very high.

A third domain in which it has been shown that stereotypes and traits affect our own functioning concerns the domain of intellectual (or mental) performance. Dijksterhuis and van Knippenberg (1998) tested the hypothesis that intellectual performance could be improved as well as deteriorated by activating stereotypes designating good or poor intellectual ability. They primed half of their participants with the stereotype of college professors, while the remaining participants were not primed. In an ostensibly unrelated second experiment, participants were asked to answer several general knowledge questions (taken from the game Trivial Pursuit). Again, participants displayed stereotype corresponding behavior, or, in this case, intellectual performance. Primed participants answered more questions correctly than did no-prime control participants. In a subsequent experiment, it was shown that participants also could be led to perform worse on this general knowledge task by priming them with soccer-hooligans, a social group that is associated with stupidity. Finally, changes in intellectual performance also were obtained after trait priming. Priming the concept of intelligence enhanced performance, while priming the concept of stupidity reduced it.

Conceptually comparable results were obtained by Dijksterhuis and Corneille (2000) and Wheeler, Jarvis, and Petty (2000; see also, Petty, this volume). Dijksterhuis and Corneille (2000) used the stereotype of women as being bad at mathematics. They demonstrated that subliminally priming participants with the female stereotype reduced performance (of both male and female participants) on a calculus task relative to participants who were not primed. This finding was replicated in several experiments. Wheeler, Jarvis, and Petty (2000) showed that activation of the stereotype of African Americans led both Black and White participants to underperform on a standardized achievement test.

A final example of changes in mental performance after stereotype activation comes from experiments conducted by Dijksterhuis, Bargh, and Miedema (2000; see also Dijksterhuis, Aarts, Bargh, & van Knippenberg, 2000). In their research it was demonstrated that participants' memory performance could be influenced by activating the stereotype of the elderly. In their first study, participants were seated in a room in which 15 objects were displayed (a cup, a bag, a poster, etc.). Half of the participants were primed with the elderly while in this room, while others were not primed. Afterwards, participants were seated in a different room and asked to recall as many of the objects as possible. As expected, activating the elderly stereotype reduced memory performance. Primed participants recalled less objects than no-prime control participants. In later work, this finding was replicated several times.

To summarize, a great number of recent findings have demonstrated that activation of traits and stereotypes leads to corresponding behavior, or to behavior matching. The domain covered is broad. Motor behavior, desirable (e.g., helpfulness) as well as undesirable (e.g., aggression) social behavior, and intellectual performance can all be changed by automatized social perception processes, or more concretely, by activated traits and stereotypes.

IDEOMOTOR ACTION AND NEUROPSYCHOLOGICAL EVIDENCE

Are all the findings reviewed above the consequence of essentially one and the same psychological principle? That is, can we explain matched facial expressions and enhanced intellectual performance after activation of a stereotype with the same mechanism? I think we can.

About a century ago, several theorists started to publish on the topic of what they called "ideomotor action" (Carpenter, 1874; James, 1890; Jastrow, 1908). The principle of ideomotor action states that merely thinking about an action leads automatically to the tendency to engage in this action. As James (1890, p. 522) put it "Whenever movement follows unhesitatingly and immediately the notion of it in mind, we have ideo-motor action." When we translate this line of thinking in the psychological terms we use nowadays, we may say that the activation of a behavioral representation leads to the tendency to engage in this same behavior. To give an example, the activation of the mental representation of "running" should lead to the tendency to run. This is of course not surprising. It is hard to imagine that we are able to run without first activating some neural correlate of this behavior in the brain. What was important for the theorists cited earlier though, was that such behavior representations were not only activated after conscious decisions ("let's run") but instead, that a mere fleeting notion of the behavior was enough to elicit the behavior itself.

Important recent evidence from the neuropsychological domain supports the notion that merely thinking about an action is enough to evoke this action. Paus, Petrides, Evans, and Meyer (1993) have shown that thinking about a word or a gesture leads to the same pattern of activation in the anterior cingulate cortex (ACC) as actually uttering the word or making the gesture. Jeannerod and colleagues have been conducting several experiments in which they showed that imagining somewhat more complex actions (such as running or weightlifting) also leads to neurophysiological consequences comparable to engaging in an action (Decety, Jeannerod, Germain, & Pastene, 1991; Jeannerod, 1994, 1997). Crucial in these studies are so called "motor programs." They are ultimately responsible for overt behavior. And, as the researchers above have shown, imagining an action leads to activation of exactly the same motor programs as performing the action. Jeannerod (1997, p. 109) concluded on the basis of this work that "Simulating a movement is the same thing as performing it, except that the execution is blocked" (see also MacKay, 1981). This neurophysiological evidence is important as it shows how thinking about an action (or, in different terms, activation of a behavioral representation) ultimately leads to corresponding overt behavior. And, as has been shown, these behavior representations can be very specific (a single gesture) or more complex (running or weightlifting). In both cases, the activation of the behavioral representation leads to activation of the motor programs.

The fact that behavior representations activate the relevant motor programs—and therefore lead to overt behavior (except when the execution of the behavior is somehow blocked)—gives us a lead for explaining behavior matching. After all, all that is needed for overt behavioral changes are activated motor programs and all we need for activated motor programs are activated behavior representations. It is likely that in all behavior matching experiments discussed in this chapter behavior representations were indeed activated. The differences between the various experimental manipulations reviewed in this chapter constitutes the process leading to activation of these behavior representations. In some cases activation of behavior representations resulted from a perception process, while in others the manipulations used came closer to manipulations of mental simulation.

In the relevant neuropsychological experiments, activation of behavior representations was brought about by imagining the behavior; however, most of the studies on behavior matching were, of course, done with different manipulations. Behavior matching of facial expressions, speech related variables, and gestures and postures is the consequence of the perception of these behaviors in others. It is likely though, that perception of these behaviors lead to activation of behavior representations. Whether one perceives a gesture (as e.g., in Chartrand & Bargh, 1999) or whether one thinks about a gesture (as in Paus et al., 1993) makes presumably no difference. In both cases behavior representations are activated, ultimately leading to performance of this behavior.

The research on behavior matching after trait activation or stereotype activation demonstrates that wildly different priming procedures lead to the same results. Some of these priming procedures resemble more closely real perception processes. For instance, both Bargh, Chen, and Burrows (1996) as well as Dijksterhuis, Spears, and Lepinasse (in press) showed pictures of members of social groups to bring about stereotype activation. Other manipulations almost resemble imagination of behavior, such as in the cited neuropsychological studies. Examples of such priming manipulations can be found in the experiment by Dijksterhuis and van Knippenberg (1998) who asked participants to think for five minutes about their definition of the traits concepts "intelligence" or "stupidity." In sum, behavior representations can be activated by both perception and by thought (or imagination) and there is no evidence yet to suggest that these different processes differ in their consequences for behavior matching.

FROM STEREOTYPES TO MOTOR PROGRAMS

The process that ultimately led to activation of behavior representations in the behavior matching experiments reviewed in this chapter differs among different experiments. In general, one may assume that very simple behavior is elicited by direct activation of a behavioral representation, while more complex behavior is mediated by activation of several other representations. The perception of a facial expression or a gesture, for instance, directly affects the behavior representations that guide the motor programs, as the results by Jeannerod and others have shown. The same goes for various speech related variables. As discussed earlier, people match syntax and word choice of others they are interacting with (Bock, 1986; Levelt & Kelter, 1982). This can be explained with the help of the findings obtained by Paus et al. (1993) who showed that hearing a word leads to the same neurological activation as uttering the word.

Obviously, the experiments that have demonstrated effects of stereotype or trait activation on behavior matching can not be explained by the direct activation of relatively concrete behavior representations such as "running." However, it may be that the behavior representations do get activated, but that this activation is mediated by activation of various intermediate representations. An abundance of research shows that upon activation of a social category (e.g., elderly), associated stereotypic traits (e.g., slow, forgetful) are also activated (Blair & Banaji, 1996; Devine, 1989; Dijksterhuis & van Knippenberg, 1996; Dovidio, Evans, & Tyler, 1986). Indeed, it has been shown that effects of stereotype activation on behavioral matching are mediated by trait activation. Dijksterhuis, Aarts, Bargh, and van Knippenberg (2000) showed that activation of the stereotype of the elderly led to forgetfulness, but only among participants who indeed associated the elderly with forgetfulness. That is, only participants who indeed activate the trait forgetfulness after being confronted with the category elderly display actual forgetfulness. Hence, effects of stereotype activation on behavior are mediated by activation of traits (see also Dijksterhuis & Corneille, 2000).

Traits in turn, are associated with behavior representations. In concrete terms, activating the trait "slow" leads to activation of more concrete behavior representations such as "linger" or "dawdle," while the trait "intelligent" leads to activation of behavior representations such as "concentrate" and "think." In a recent study, Dijksterhuis and Marchand (2000) showed that activation of the stereotype of professors leads to activation of these concrete behavior representations. Furthermore, these effects were mediated by activation of the trait "intelligent." It follows from the work of Jeannerod and others that these behavior representations activate the appropriate motor programs. In sum, stereotypes can automatically affect behavior because they activate—mediated by activation of traits and of behavior representations—motor programs. This process can be conceived of as a three-step process. Stereotypes activate traits, traits activate behavior representations, and behavior representations activate motor programs.

CONCLUSION

Most people will have observed the often impressive synchrony of the behavior of fish in a school or birds in a flock. The fact that the behavior of a fish in a school or a bird in a flock is so well matched to that of the behavior of the others is straightforward: Perception directly affects behavior. When a fish perceives a change of direction in another fish, it simply matches this change of direction. As argued in this chapter, this direct link between perception and behavior can easily be witnessed in humans as well. We too match the behavior of others, and we too do this simply because perception directly affects action. The specific behavioral changes effects of perception can bring about differ between humans and fish, but the underlying mechanism is essentially the same. In concrete terms, when I am talking Scottish, this is simply because I share an important psychological mechanism with a haddock.

REFERENCES

Bandura, A. (1977). *Social learning theory*. Englewood Cliffs, NJ: Prentice-Hall.

Bargh, J. A. (1994). The four horsemen of automaticity: Awareness, intention, efficiency and control in social cognition. In R. S. Wyer, Jr. and T. K. Srull (Eds.), *The handbook of social cognition, Vol. 2, Basic processes* (pp. 1–40). Hillsdale, NJ: Erlbaum.

Bargh, J. A., & Chartrand, T. L. (1999). The unbearable automaticity of being. *American Psychologist*, 54, 462–476.

Bargh, J. A., Chen, M., & Burrows, L. (1996). The automaticity of social behavior: Direct effects of trait concept and stereotype activation on action. *Journal of Personality and Social Psychology*, 71, 230–244.

Bavelas, J. B., Black, A., Lemery, C. R., & Mullett, J. (1986). "I *show* how you feel": Motor mimicry as a communicative act. *Journal of Personality and Social Psychology*, 50, 322–329.

Berkowitz, L. (1984). Some effects of thoughts on anti- and prosocial influences of media events: A cognitive-neoassociation analysis. *Psychological Bulletin*, 95, 410–427.

Bernieri, F. (1988). Coordinated movement and rapport in teacher-student interactions. *Journal of Nonverbal Behavior*, 12, 120–138.

Bernieri, F., Reznick, J. S., & Rosenthal, R. (1988). Synchrony, pseudo synchrony, and dissynchrony: Measuring the entrainment process in mother-infant interactions. *Jour-*

nal of Personality and Social Psychology, 54, 243–253.

Bernieri, F., & Rosenthal, R. (1991). Interpersonal coordination: Behavioral matching and interactional synchrony. In R. S. Feldman & B. Rime (Eds.), *Fundamentals of nonverbal behavior* (pp. 401–432). Cambridge, UK: Cambridge University Press

Blair, I. V., & Banaji, M. R. (1996). Automatic and controlled processes in gender stereotyping. *Journal of Personality and Social Psychology, 70,* 1142–1163.

Bock, J. K. (1986). Syntactic persistence in sentence production. *Cognitive Psychology, 18,* 355–387.

Brewer, M. B. (1988). A dual process model of impression formation. In R. S. Wyer, Jr. & T. K. Srull (Eds.), *Advances in social cognition* (Vol. 1, pp. 1–36). Hillsdale, NJ: Erlbaum.

Capella, J. N. (1981). Mutual influence in expressive behavior: Adult-adult and infant-adult dyadic interaction. *Psychological Bulletin, 89,* 101–132

Carpenter, W. B. (1874). *Principles of mental physiology.* New York: Appleton.

Carver, C. S., Ganellen, R .J., Froming, W. J., & Chambers, W. (1983). Modeling: An analysis in terms of category accessibility. *Journal of Experimental Social Psychology, 19,* 403–421.

Charney, E. J. (1966). Psychosomatic manifestations of rapport in psychotherapy. *Psychosomatic Medicine, 28,* 305–315.

Chartrand, T. L., & Bargh, J. A. (1999). The chameleon effect: The perception-behavior link and social interaction. *Journal of Personality and Social Psychology, 76,* 893–910.

Chen, M., & Bargh, J. A. (1997). Nonconscious behavioral confirmation processes: The self-fulfilling nature of automatically-activated stereotypes. *Journal of Experimental Social Psychology, 33,* 541–560.

Condon, W. S., & Sander, L. W. (1974). Synchrony demonstrated between movements of the neonate and adult speech. *Child Development, 45,* 456–462.

Decety, J., Jeannerod, M., Germain, M., & Pastene, J. (1991). Vegetative response during imagined movement is proportional to mental effort. *Behavioural Brain Research, 42,* 1–5.

Dell, G. S. (1986). A spreading activation theory of retrieval in sentence production. *Psychological Review, 93,* 283–321.

Devine, P. G. (1989). Stereotypes and prejudice: Their automatic and controlled components. *Journal of Personality and Social Psychology, 56,* 5–18.

Dijksterhuis, A., Aarts, H., Bargh, J. A., & van Knippenberg, A. (2000). On the relation between associative strength and automatic behavior. *Journal of Experimental Social Psychology, 36,* 531–534.

Dijksterhuis, A., & Bargh, J. A. (in press). The perception-behavior expressway: Automatic effects of social perception on social behavior. *Advances in Experimental Social Psychology.*

Dijksterhuis, A., Bargh, J. A., & Miedema, J. (2000). Of men and mackerels: Attention and automatic behavior. In H. Bless & J. P. Forgas (Eds.), *Subjective experience in social cognition and behavior* (pp. 36–51). Philadelphia: Psychology Press.

Dijksterhuis, A., & Corneille, O. (2000). *On the relation between stereotype activation and intellectual performance.* Unpublished manuscript, University of Nijmegen.

Dijksterhuis, A., & Marchand, M. (2000). *The route from stereotype activation to overt behavior.* Manuscript in preparation, University of Nijmegen.

Dijksterhuis, A., Spears, R., & Lepinasse, V. (in press). Reflecting and deflecting stereotypes: Assimilation and contrast in automatic behavior. *Journal of Experimental Social Psychology.*

Dijksterhuis, A., & van Knippenberg, A. (1996). The knife that cuts both ways: Facilitated and inhibited access to traits as a result of stereotype activation. *Journal of Experimental Social Psychology, 32,* 271–288.

Dijksterhuis, A., & van Knippenberg, A. (1998). The relation between perception and behavior or how to win a game of Trivial Pursuit. *Journal of Personality and Social Psychology, 74,* 865–877.

Dimberg, U. (1982). Facial reactions to facial expressions. *Psychophysiology, 19,* 643–647.

Dovidio, J. F., Evans, N., & Tyler, R. B. (1986). Racial stereotypes: The contents of their cognitive representations. *Journal of Experimental Social Psychology, 22,* 22–37.

Epley, N., & Gilovich, T. (1999). Just going along: Nonconscious priming and conformity to social pressure. *Journal of Experimental Social Psychology, 35,* 578–589.

Field, T., Woodson, R., Greenberg, R., & Cohen, D. (1982). Discrimination and imitation of facial expression by neonates. *Science, 218*, 179–181.

Gilbert, D. T. (1989). Thinking lightly about others: Automatic components of the social inference process. In J. S. Uleman & J. A. Bargh (Eds.), *Unintended thought* (pp. 189– 211). New York: Guilford.

Hatfield, E., Cacioppo, J. T., & Rapson, R. L. (1994). *Emotional contagion*. Cambridge, England: Cambridge University Press.

Jaffe, J., & Feldstein, S. (1970). *Rhythms of dialogue*. New York: Academic.

James, W. (1890). *Principles of psychology*. New York: Holt.

Jastrow, J. (1908). *The subconscious*. Boston: Houghton, Mifflin and Company.

Jeannerod, M. (1994). The representing brain: Neural correlates of motor intention and imagery. *Behavioral and Brain Sciences, 17*, 187–245.

Jeannerod, M. (1997). *The cognitive neuroscience of action*. Oxford, England: Blackwell.

Kendon, A. (1970). Movement coordination in social interaction: Some examples described. *Acta Psychologica, 32*, 1–25.

Koffka, K. (1925). *Die grundlagen der psychischen entwicklung*. Osterwieck, Germany: Zickfeldt.

LaFrance, M. (1979). Nonverbal synchrony and rapport: Analysis by the cross-lag panel technique. *Social Psychology Quarterly, 42*, 66–70.

Le Bon, G. (1982). *The crowd: A study of the popular mind*. Atlanta, GA: Cherokee. (Original work published 1935)

Levelt, W. J. M., & Kelter, S. (1982). Surface form and memory in question answering. *Cognitive Psychology, 14*, 78–106.

MacKay, L. (1981). The problem of rehearsal or mental practice. *Journal of Motor Behavior, 13*, 274–285.

Macrae, C. N., & Johnston, L. (1998). Help, I need somebody: Automatic action and inaction. *Social Cognition, 16*, 400–417.

Matarazzo, J. D., & Wiens, A. N. (1972). *The interview: Research on its anatomy and structure*. Chicago: Aldine-Atherton.

McDougall, W. (1908). *Introduction to social psychology*. London: Methuen.

Meltzoff, A. N., & Moore, M. K. (1977). Imitation of facial and manual gestures by human neonates. *Science, 198*, 75–78.

Milgram, S. (1963). Behavioral study of obedience. *Journal of Abnormal and Social Psychology, 67*, 371–378.

Natale, M. (1975). Converge of mean vocal intensity in dyadic communication as a function of social desirability. *Journal of Personality and Social Psychology, 32*, 790–804.

O'Toole, R., & Dubin, R. (1968). Baby feeding and body sway: An experiment in George Herberts Mead's "Taking the role of the other." *Journal of Personality and Social Psychology, 10*, 59–65.

Paus, T., Petrides, M., Evans, A. C., & Meyer, E. (1993). Role of human anterior cingulate cortex in the control of oculomotor, manual and speech responses: A positron emission tomography study. *Journal of Neurophysiology, 70*, 453–469.

Piaget, J. (1946). *La information du symbole chez l'enfant*. Paris: Delauchaux & Niestle.

Prinz, W. (1990). A common coding approach to perception and action. In O. Neumann & W. Prinz (Eds.), *Relationships between perception and action* (pp. 167–201). Berlin: Springer-Verlag.

Scheflen, A. E. (1964). The significance of posture in communication systems. *Psychiatry, 27*, 316–331.

Smith, A. (1966). *The theory of moral sentiments*. New York: Augustus M. Kelley. (Original work published 1759)

Srull, T. K., & Wyer, R. S., Jr. (1979). The role of category accessibility in the interpretation of information about persons: Some determinants and implications. *Journal of Personality and Social Psychology, 37*, 1660–1672.

Srull, T. K., & Wyer, R. S., Jr. (1980). Category accessibility and social perception: Some implications for the study of person memory and interpersonal judgments. *Journal of Personality and Social Psychology, 38*, 841–856.

Tarde, G. (1903). *The laws of imitation*. New York: Holt.

Vaughan, K. B., & Lanzetta, J. T. (1980). Vicarious instigation and conditioning of facial expressive and autonomic responses to a model's expressive display of pain. *Journal of Personality and Social Psychology, 38*, 909–923.

Wheeler, S. C., Jarvis, W. B. G., & Petty, R. E. (2000). *Think unto others . . . : The self-destructive impact of negative stereotypes*. Manuscript submitted for publication.

Winter, L., & Uleman, J. S. (1984). When are social judgments made? Evidence for the spontaneousness of trait inferences. *Journal of Personality and Social Psychology, 47,* 237–252.

Zajonc, R. B., Adelmann, K. A., Murphy, S. T., & Niedenthal, P. M. (1987). Convergence in the physical appearance of spouses. *Motivation and Emotion, 11,* 335–346.

7

Social Power, Influence, and Aggression

JAMES T. TEDESCHI[1]

*P*sychologists have predominantly viewed aggression as responses "pushed out" by inner forces, such as aggressive drive, anger, hormones, or brain centers (cf. Geen, 1990; Moyer, 1987), or automatically instigated by external stimuli, such as frustration and aversive stimuli (Berkowitz, 1989). In general, traditional orientations have examined intrapsychic variables in the form of physiological and cognitive processes. This is an extremely individualistic and sometimes solipsistic view of aggressive behavior since it tends to exclude other people, except for their roles as eliciting, inhibiting or reinforcing stimuli.

Another literature in the social sciences focuses on conflicts and their resolution. Among the concepts employed in conflict theories are power, coercion, force, threats, and punishment (cf. Pruitt & Rubin, 1986). These concepts have been used to explain grievances, disputes, legal redress, escalation processes, and violence. Criminal violence is discussed in the literature on crime. This literature focuses on subcultures of violence, internal and external controls that

---

1. We learned with great shock and sadness that Jim Tedeschi passed away a few weeks after correcting the copyedited manuscript of this chapter, probably his final publication. He has made a great contribution to our discipline, in general, and our symposium, in particular. He will be sorely missed by all who knew him. The Editors.

inhibit crime, and crime as an alternative form of achievement when legitimate opportunities are blocked (cf. Tedeschi & Felson, 1994, Chapter 5).

It is curious how well segregated the literatures on aggression, power and conflict, and criminal violence are. Aggression theorists seldom discuss conflicts, threats, and punishment, conflict theorists only infrequently use the term "aggression," and criminologists usually do not refer to frustration, anger, or hormones to explain criminal violence. There are many reasons for this lack of overlap or integration of these separate literatures. For example, the various social sciences have different levels of analysis and different methodological orientations.

Tedeschi and his colleagues have developed a social interactionist theory of coercive actions that integrates these various approaches. The theory focuses on the exercise of power and influence by an actor who is motivated to achieve social goals. The goal of this chapter is to show how a power-oriented social interactionist theory explains the phenomena that have preoccupied aggression theorists. The chapter is organized into three parts. First, the basic assumptions of a social interactionist perspective are described. Second, based on a critical analysis of the concept of aggression, a common language is developed to bridge the areas of aggression and coercive power and to identify the phenomena that will circumscribe the scope of the theory of coercive actions. Third, the basic tenets of the theory are presented in terms of motives for social control, to enhance social identities, and to maintain justice.

ASSUMPTIONS OF THE SOCIAL INTERACTIONIST PERSPECTIVE

A social interactionist perspective rests on three major assumptions. First, harm-doing and threats of harm-doing are motivated to achieving interpersonal goals. Actors use harmful actions to compel and deter actions from other people. Actors who experience grievances may be motivated to enforce rules, punish blame-worthy persons, and maintain justice. Actors also may attack others as a means of achieving status and maintaining a desired social identity in front of audiences. The three social motives to control others, maintain justice, and establish or defend social identities are assumed to underlie all forms of coercive action.

Second, a social interactionist perspective is primarily a social psychological theory and hence focuses on individual actions in a social context. Social psychological processes of attribution, the assignment of blame, social motives, values and expectations, and the evaluation of decision alternatives are featured in explanations of why a person engages in harm-doing actions. Sometimes this focus requires an understanding of the phenomenology of actors, who often view their own harm-doing as legitimate and even moralistic.

Third, the social context of actions is central to an explanation of interactions between antagonists. The relationship between the parties, the dynamics of the interchange between them, and the presence or absence of third parties are all relevant for explaining harm-doing actions. While the focus is on such situational factors, it is recognized that individual differences are also important.[1]

There is a weak version and a strong version of social interactionist theory. The stronger version assumes that all harm-doing actions are instrumental. The weaker version recognizes the distinction between angry and instrumental aggression, and accepts that the theory applies only to instrumental acts. The general strategy is to proffer a strong version of social interactionist theory and to explain angry harm-doing aggression as instrumental behavior.

CONCEPTUALIZATION OF COERCIVE ACTIONS

The first task is to develop a clear set of concepts that can be used to integrate the literatures of aggression, conflict, and criminal violence. The language used by aggression theorists has failed to provide for such an integration, partly because the term "aggression" is poorly defined. A behaviorist definition of aggression as any "response that delivers noxious stimuli to another" (Buss, 1961, p. 1) focuses on the consequence to the victim. An attribution definition (Berkowitz, 1993) of aggression as "the intent to do harm" focuses on a psychological process inside the actor, which is itself undefined.

I do not believe a scientific concept of aggression is salvagable (cf. Tedeschi, Melburg, & Rosenfeld, 1981), primarily because it involves making a value judgment. Aggression is typically viewed as bad or wrong behavior. This is why aggression researchers do not study parental punishment of children, unless it is abusive, and why they do not try to explain the behavior of judges who sentence offenders to death. The problem is illustrated by the observation that when you harm me, it is aggression, but when I harm you it is necessary and legitimate.

Scholars recognize these problems with the concept of aggression, but find aggression useful as an orienting or generic concept to the phenomena of interest (e.g., Bandura, 1973). My analysis leads to the opposite conclusion. The current construct has directed research primarily to physical forms of harm-doing in the form of noxious stimulation (noise or electric shocks), and has ignored threats, conflicts, and power relationships, and focused on intrapsychic explanations that push out or pull the aggressive behavior. As an alternative, Tedeschi, Smith, and Brown (1974) proposed that the relevant phenomena be described as coercive actions, including threats, punishments, and bodily force. These actions appear to capture most of the phenomena referred to by aggression theorists, and avoid value judgments. It is legitimate for parents to threaten their children and illegitimate for robbers to threaten their victims, but both probably have the same intention—to gain compliance. Similarly, it may be le-

---

1. Space limitation does not permit discussion in this chapter of individual difference factors that may contribute as moderators of coercive actions.

gitimate for a judge to sentence an offender to death, but illegitimate for a person to hire someone to kill her spouse, although both may be motivated by a desire to punish some offense (i.e., a motive for justice). While it is important that the language of coercive actions reduces the need to make value judgments, it is equally important that it shifts attention to questions of power and influence and away from intrapsychic processes.

Power, Influence, and Coercive Actions

It is not necessary here to examine all the notions of power that have been proposed by social scientists or to choose between them. Indeed, power as a construct may be as ambiguous as the concept of aggression. Nevertheless, it is useful to recognize that social scientists have long viewed the use of threats and punishments as a central and important aspect of social interactions. Critically important for identifying power-related or aggressive events is to establish that the actor's behaviors are intentional. Unfortunately, little or no formal discussion of what is meant by intent has been provided by social scientists who study power or aggression.

Intentions. The concept of intent developed by Tedeschi and Felson (1994) has been applied to the use of threats and punishments. An act is intentional when there is an expectation that the act will have a specific outcome and when the outcome is valued by the actor. Expectancy, by itself, is inadequate to define an intention. Dentists anticipate that their patients will experience pain in a root canal procedure, but would deny that they intend to inflict pain on their patients. Dentists do not value causing pain to their patients, and if their procedures could be carried out without pain, presumably they would adopt them. In general an actor can be said to intend an act when it follows an assessment that a desired outcome will probably result from performing it.

Coercive actions involve the imposition of an outcome on a target person, where the outcome is intended. Most of the outcomes imposed are harmful since it is usually unnecessary to impose outcomes on people that they desire. However, sometimes the actor's intent is to produce compliance, and harm is an incidental outcome. This is the case in most robberies, for example. In the case of robbery, the offender expects that the victim will be harmed by the loss of material possessions but it is the loot the robber values, not harm to the victim.

Threats. A threat is a communication containing a statement of an intent to do harm. Threats can be contingent or noncontingent (Tedeschi, 1970). Contingent threats contain a demand by the source and make punishments contingent upon noncompliance. Noncontingent threats only communicate an intent to harm the target person. While both types of threats can be used for many purposes, contingent threats are more apt to be used to gain control over the behavior of the target person (compellence or deterrence). Noncontingent threats are more likely to be used to intimidate and induce fear in the target person or available audiences.

Bodily force. A person may be constrained or compelled to accept outcomes because of the application of superior bodily strength by another actor. For example a protesting child may be carried by a parent to the bedroom at bedtime. It is difficult to distinguish bodily force from punishing actions because the acts and outcomes alone might be perceived as punishing by the target person. However, the actor who uses bodily force values compliance and the actor who engages in a punishing action values harm.

Punishing acts. An act that has a significant probability of causing harm to another person and is performed with the goal of inflicting the harm is a punishing act. Any specific punishing act may or may not succeed in causing harm to another person. A fighter may throw a punch and miss the opponent, or an assassin may fire a rifle at a victim but miss the target. When a punishing act succeeds, it is a harm-doing act. Harm refers to outcomes that the target would avoid if possible. Thus, a parent who sends a naughty child to the bedroom expects that this outcome will make the child unhappy, values this harm, and therefore is engaged in a punishing action. Note that this says nothing about the motive or extended goal of the parents' action, which may be to deter future occurrences of the naughty behavior or to reform the character of the child. Note also that this definition of a punishing act would exclude acts of competition since actors do not necessarily value harm to the competitor even though they know that if they win the competition the competitor will be harmed. Lies, fraud, and trickery would also be excluded because they do not involve coercive means, although they sometimes involve an intent to harm.

Types of harm. Psychologists sometimes refer to reinforcements and punishments as if they varied only in magnitude. Tedeschi and Lindskold (1976) suggested that there are three kinds of punishments: physical, deprivations, and social. Physical punishments involve the use of external stimuli or energies to impose biological damage on or to induce unpleasant psychological states in a target person. Deprivation of resources refer to attempts to restrict opportunities, remove material possessions, or interfere with the social relationships of the target. Social punishments refer to insults and other attempts to impose negative social identities on a target.

Comparison of the Concepts of Coercion and Aggression

A vocabulary of coercive actions is preferable to the traditional vocabulary of aggression or violence for four reasons. First, it links other literatures to the aggression literature. In particular, it ties in the literature on conflict, grievances and social control, and other forms of social power and influence. It includes some behaviors that are criminal, but it does not make the definition so broad as to include noncoercive acts of crime, such as fraud. Thus while some acts of coercion are illegal, the study of coercion and crime are not the same.

Second, threats and punishing acts are less value-laden descriptions than the term "aggression." Aggression is a label often used for harm-doing that people condemn. No value judgment needs to be made in order to identify a coercive action. Thus, a mild threat by a parent directed toward a child and a robber's threat to a targeted victim are both threats, although aggression theorists appear to be interested only in the latter action. Furthermore, while parent and robber usually have different motives, they also frequently have the same intention—to gain compliance.

Third, reference to coercive actions focuses on interpersonal behavior while the definition of aggression focuses on the outcome (harm). One consequence of this difference is that the social interactionist theory includes the study of threats, which typically do not directly inflict harm. The language of coercion focuses attention on the social goals of actors who use threats, bodily force, and punishments as ways of gaining their objectives. The language of aggression focuses on biological or psychological processes within the person, such as hormones or arousal states, and tends to ignore the social functions of the relevant behavior.

Fourth, the concepts within social interactionist theory are more clearly defined than concepts of aggression. Furthermore, the notion of intent is defined in such a way that it can be tied to decision theory. If the actor is viewed as a decision maker, who generates, evaluates, and chooses between alternatives, and intent is defined as a product of expectations and values, then intent can be incorporated into an explanation of the actor's behavior. Aggression theorists have never defined what they mean by intent and no theory of aggression includes an account of the actor's intentions as part of the explanation of why she aggresses.

Motives for Coercive Actions

Motives refer to the ultimate or terminal goals of actions. Intentions, as defined here, refer to the proximal or instrumental goals. Intentions and motives are both reasons for acting. A person may issue threats with the intention of gaining compliance, but the question remains about why compliance is desired. Motives provide the reasons for desiring compliance. Similarly, the short term or proximal goal of a punitive action is to harm the target person, while motives provide the reasons for valuing the suffering of the target. Another way of stating this difference is that intentions provide the "in order to" reasons for an act, while motives provide the "because of" reasons for the act (Schutz, 1967). Thus, the actor threatens the target in order to gain compliance or punishes to inflict harm, and values compliance or harm because it is instrumental for achieving some further value.

Tedeschi and Felson (1994) proposed three general motives for explaining why actors perform coercive actions: social control, identity, and justice. All three motives evolve out of social interdependence and issues of social power. Social control motivation refers to goals that are essentially mediated by compliance by target persons. Identity motivation refers to self-presentational goals, including both assertive and protective actions that take the form of threats or punishments, or both. Justice motivation refers to coercive actions taken by an individual for the purpose of retributive justice. While each of these motives are examined independently of the other in this chapter, they may all be involved in any particular episode in which coercive actions occur.

SOCIAL CONTROL MOTIVATION

People are interdependent of their outcomes. Important resources, including money, status, love, and respect, are provided through the mediating behaviors and reactions of other people. Since it is rare that people provide these kinds of benefits to others without prodding or inducements, actors must exercise some form of influence or go without attaining many desired outcomes and relationships.

There are many ways of influencing others. The actor can use persuasion, promises, modeling, cue control, and many other tactics. Of course actors may also use threats, punishments, and bodily force to get their way with others. Social interactionist theory conceives of the actor as a decision maker who chooses between available targets and alternative means of influence to achieve interpersonal objectives. The decision maker also considers the probability and value of costs associated with both success and failure. A criterion for judging the "best" alternative is adopted, and the decision eventuates in the act or means associated with the chosen alternative. This model of human decision-making can be used to organize predictions about whether the person will choose coercive or noncoercive means.

Expectancies and Relative Efficacy of Coercion

Estimates of the probability of success, holding all else (such as the values of expected costs and gains) constant, should be directly related to exercising influence. If it is believed that positive forms of influence will not work, the person has two alternatives. One is to do nothing and give up the goal. This alternative may be associated with learned helplessness and depression. The other possibility is to use coercive means to obtaining the goal. The relative efficacy principle stipulates that when the probability assigned to the success of using coercion is higher than the probabilities assigned to other means of influence to achieve the same value, it is likely that a coercive act will be performed. To test this principle the probability and value of costs must be controlled.

There are a rather large number of factors that can make an individual pessimistic about the success of noncoercive forms of influence and therefore (by the relative efficacy principle) increase the likelihood that coercive actions will be chosen. Lack of abilities that are needed to successfully use persuasive arguments, such as intelligence, education, social skills, and articulateness increase the likelihood that a person will engage in coercive actions. People lacking these abilities assign low probabilities of success to noncoercive forms of influence. Indirect support has been found for this generalization. For example, violent criminals have lower intelligence than nonviolent criminals (Wilson & Herrnstein, 1985).

Lack of argumentative skills by either the perpetrator or the victim may lead to spouse abuse. Argumentative skills include the ability to effectively present a position and to defeat opposing positions. If one lacks this ability and is engaged in an argument, the tendency is to resort to blaming, insulting, and identity attacks. This verbal abuse may enrage the target and elicit physical forms of retaliation. Abused women tend to be deficient in communications skills (Jansen & Meyers-Abel, 1981), and male offenders frequently report being provoked by swearing and attacks on their character (Coleman, 1980).

French and Raven (1959) proposed that people who have strong power bases will be effective in influencing others. Research has shown that sources who are more expert, attractive, trustworthy, and credible and who are higher in status are more effective in using persuasive communications than are sources who are low on these power bases (cf., Tedeschi, Lindskold, & Rosenfeld, 1985). Low standing on the various power bases will engender low confidence in positive forms of influence. A person who lacks expertise, is not very attractive, has little or no legitimate authority, controls few material or informational resources, and has a reputation as an untrustworthy communicator will not be effective in influencing others by persuasion and has little or nothing to offer as inducements. People with little power and who can expect that positive forms of influence will not get them what they want from others, may resort to other means, including the use of coercion. Lower socioeconomic status people often fit this description, and it should not be surprising that much of the crime and criminal violence in society is committed by them.

The kinds of resources accessible to the individual also may affect the choice of an influence mode. A person who possesses rewarding and informational resources may offer inducements to others through promises or bribes. On the other hand, a person who has little reward power but has punitive resources may be inclined to use coercion because the estimated probability of success is enhanced by access to such resources. In a classic study Deutsch and Krauss (1960) demonstrated that the mere possession of gates in a trucking game induced subjects to employ them punitively against a peer. A number of studies have shown that subjects who possessed a unilateral power advantage frequently used threats and punishments against a peer in a mixed-motive game (cf., Tedeschi, Schlenker, & Bonoma, 1973). Furthermore, the greater the magnitude of punitive resources the individual possesses, the more frequently coercion is used (Fischer, 1969; Hornstein, 1965).

The tactics of the target in response to contingent threats also may affect the decisions of a source. Tedeschi, Bonoma, and Lindskold (1970) found that open and consistent communication of defiance by a target decreased the use of threats by a more powerful opponent. Expressions of defiance presumably lower the source's estimate of the probability of success of threats. On the other hand, yielding to coercion encourages it use. For example, the appeasing behavior of whipping boys encourages bullying behavior (Olweus, 1978). Expectations that others will yield to aggressive tactics encourages their use. Aggressive children (as compared to nonaggressive children) report being more confident that aggressive behavior will gain positive results (Perry, Perry, & Rasmussen, 1986).

The structure of relative power has been examined by Molm (1988). She proposed that imbalance in coercive power between two persons will lead to more coercive actions when it favors an actor who is disadvantaged in reward power. In other words, when someone else has what the person wants and does not have, and the person has the punitive power to coerce the target to provide it, the chances are good that coercion will be used. There may be less use of coercion between parties who have equal power. Several researchers have reported that compromise solutions are likely to occur when parties have roughly equal power (Murdoch, 1967; Thibaut, 1968; Thibaut & Faucheux, 1965).

The most important situational factor in the decision to use coercion is social conflict. Conflict is a situation in which there are scarce resources relative to the demands of two or more people. Actors can behave in one of three ways in social conflicts: let the other actor have the resource, try to share the resource, or attempt to obtain the lion's share of the resource. The latter two alternatives require that some form of influence be employed to reach the desired outcome. In the context of conflict noncoercive forms of influence, such as persuasion or inducements, are not very effective because the contender also wants the disputed resource and is apt to distrust the actor. The result is that contenders frequently use coercion to achieve outcomes in conflict situations.

Values and the Use of Coercion

People give value to ends, but they also give value to means, referred to here as procedural values. Among procedural values is the value or disvalue of using particular means in influencing other people. The actor may value controlling others, perhaps because it contributes to a lessening of anxiety, bolstering of self-esteem, or as an assertive means of projecting an identity as a powerful person. Thus, successful control of others is a secondary value or added value of influencing them. Coercive means are more controlling than other means of influence because they are imposed on other people for the purpose of compelling them to respond in a way intended by the actor. The finding that males are more aggressive than females (Maccoby & Jacklin, 1974) may be explained (at least partially) by the evidence that males value control of others more than do females (Boldizar, Perry, & Perry, 1989; Schönbach, 1990). A survey of elementary school children, who had been divided into high and low aggression groups based on peer ratings, found that aggressive children perceived control of others as more important (Boldizar et al., 1989).

While a positive procedural value for coercion will add value to associated outcomes, a negative procedure value for using physical forms of harm-doing deters the actor from using them. Mahatma Ghandi did not shrink from using coercion against the British in his fight for the independence of India, but he preferred economic sanctions as his means and shunned any use of physical violence. Similarly, some parents never use physical means of punishing their children. In American society men are more likely to use physical coercion than are women (Eagley & Steffen, 1986). Girls in Denmark are more likely than boys to use indirect means to harm others when they are angry (Bjorkqvist, Lagerspetz, & Kaukianinen, 1992). Substantial variation in the value given to violent actions across cultures has been documented (e.g., Bond & Tedeschi, in press; Chagnon, 1976).

Costs and coercion.   Principles of inhibition in aggression theories assert that the greater the expected costs for engaging in harm-doing behavior, the less apt the individual is to perform such behavior (e.g., Dollard, Doob, Miller, Mowrer, & Sears, 1939). A target may impose costs on a source of coercive action by retaliatory use of threats and punishments. In addition to tangible costs there may be social and moral costs for using coercion. Deterioration of a valued relationship with another would be a social cost. A calculus of costs— material, physical, social, and moral—has not been invented yet, but where we can measure and test, it should be expected that the higher the expected costs for using coercion, the less it will be used. It has been found that subjects used fewer threats as the cost of the punishment to back them up increased (Tedeschi, Horai, Lindskold, & Faley, 1970).

The anticipation of costs explains why coercion is often the means of last resort. In a study of conflict resolution tactics, it was found that most respondents preferred noncoercive forms of influence, but would use coercion if all other means of conflict resolution failed (Peirce, Pruitt, & Czaja, 1991). Goldstein (1981) reported that heroin users first attempt nonviolent means of getting money before resorting to violent means.

THE JUSTICE MOTIVE

A rough law of karma is taught in every human group informing individuals that good behavior will lead to positive consequences, and the harm that one does to others is ultimately repaid to the harm-doer. This rule becomes a moral rule when people believe not only that injustices *will* be redressed, but that they *ought* to be. This value for justice may motivate the individual to engage in actions to restore justice, including using punishing actions that serve as retributive justice. The imposition of penalties or harm on the perpetrator is a form of coercive power in that it is done to enforce rules, and to deter both the perpetrator and others from violating them again. Punishments can also have the goal of rehabilitating the harm-doer by changing her character or values.

The typical sequence, then, is some harm-doing action or rule violation, which through the attribution process leads to blaming a perpetrator. Generally, the process is one of assigning cause, then fixing responsibility, and when the responsibility is attributed for negative events, blame is assigned. This attribution process is affected by prior experience, relationship between the harmed person and the harm-doer, group affiliations, and many other factors (Rule & Nesdale, 1976). Blame, in turn, causes the perceiver to become angry. Anger is an emotional reaction to perceived misdeeds of others. It is important to distinguish between the experience of anger and its expression. The experience of anger has some important effects on cognition and behavior, but how and under what conditions people will express their anger is largely regulated by norms. For example, Utku Eskimos are taught to inhibit expressions of anger in public (Briggs, 1970).

The experience of anger, especially when intense, disrupts cognitive functioning (Zillmann, 1983). There is a tendency to simplify information processing and make black and white judgments (White, 1968). Strong emotions create tunnel vision so that there is a focus on the anger inducing cues produced by the perpetrator of negative events to the exclusion of other information that might help resolve the conflict. The angry person is also less articulate in expressing grievances. The angered individual is less able to develop alternative strategies for handling the precipitating incident, and is therefore more likely to engage in scripted or habitual behavior. If, for example, a person typically handles conflicts by using physical forms of coercion, it is likely that when angered he or she will impulsively engage in this type of behavior. If the individual delays reacting until anger arousal subsides somewhat, it is more likely that more constructive actions will be taken (Averill, 1983).

An angered individual's responses, will be more intense, the greater the anger that is experienced. Accusations will be expressed in a louder voice, doors will be closed more forcefully, and the foot will be heavier on the accelerator of the automobile. These more intense responses may serve to acerbate conflict because the other person may take offense by what is perceived as disrespectful, impolite, and obnoxious behavior. When the angered person uses coercion, heightened arousal will also intensify that form of behavior.

According to Tedeschi and Felson (1994), one of the most important consequences of the experience of anger is to activate a motive, which they refer to as a grievance, to restore justice. There are a number of alternative ways in which a person with a grievance might respond. One choice would be to do nothing. In a survey study carried out by Averill (1983) college students reported that they infrequently expressed their anger relative to the number of grievances they experienced. Inaction may occur because the grievant lacks confidence that any action will restore justice. The grievant may wish to avoid an embarrassing scene. Expection of unacceptable costs for a justice-restoring behavior will lead to inaction. However, the individual is motivated to restore justice and is unlikely to simply forget the incident. If a later opportunity to engage in a justice-restoring behavior occurs, the individual may take advantage of it. The grievance does not simply go away. It festers and waits for its chance.

A second alternative for an aggrieved party is to forgive the harm-doer. Often the harm-doer anticipates angry and retributive reactions by the grievant and offers an apology for the harmful action. Sometimes an apology is demanded by the grievant and tendered by the harm-doer. Forgiveness removes the resentment underlying a grievance, although it does not remove the blame. The grievant will remember that the harm-doer acted in an unjust and blameworthy way, but is no longer motivated to undertake actions to restore justice. In subsequent arguments the grievant may bring up a laundry list of such past transgressions to put the other person in a defensive position. In other words, past transgressions that were forgiven may be reactivated to add to new or current ones, increasing the amount of blame attributed by the grievant. The cumulation of blame over incidents, whether forgiven or not, may cause the grievant to appear to overreact to the precipitating incident.

A third alternative is for the grievant to reconsider the negative event and revise judgment about the other person. Often the person associated with a negative event will provide some form of explanation or account for her behavior. Such accounts may take the form of excuses or justifications. Weiner, Amirkin, Fokes, and Verette (1987) found that acceptable excuses for being late for an appointment reduced the perceived responsibility of the tardy person, reduced the anger of the person who had been waiting, and enhanced the relationship between the two strangers.

A fourth alternative that a grievant might choose is to make some claim against the perceived offender. The grievant, if unsure about the reasons for the offender's conduct, and hence hesitant about reacting on the basis of a preliminary assessment of blame, may ask for some explanation. If acceptable accounts are given, blame may be removed. If the grievant is positive about the attribution of blame to the offender, she might demand an apology and a promise not to repeat the offense. If a promise is tendered, the perpetrator may be forgiven. The harmed person also may seek a remedy or restitution, and if it is given, there is a satisfactory (i.e., just) conclusion to the episode.

A final choice alternative available to a grievant is to directly punish the miscreant as a way of restoring justice. A rule of justice generally held by people is that the amount of suffering inflicted by a punishing action should be proportional to the amount of harm done by the blameworthy person. This is the familiar principle of lex talionis and is represented by the symbol of justice showing the balancing of two scales. The idea of getting even or exacting revenge captures the basic aim of retributive justice. Donnerstein and Hatfield (1982) have provided a reinterpretation of much of the laboratory research on aggression in terms of retribution for experienced inequities.

Intensity of punishment may also be affected by a desire to reform the harm-doer and to deter further offenses—both social control objectives. These additional objectives would cause the grievant to use more intense forms of punishment than if the only motive were to restore justice. An alleged harm-doer may not passively accept punishment, particularly if it is perceived as illegitimate or disproportionate, but may retaliate by punishing the grievant. The retaliation may further enrage the grievant, and escalation may occur.

SELF-PRESENTATION AND COERCION

Self-presentations typically take the form of noncoercive actions. However, the concern for asserting and defending public identities sometimes involves the use of coercion. It is necessary to specify the conditions under which these self-presentation concerns lead to coercive actions.

Assertive Self-Presentation

Most of the research on the relationship between self-presentation and coercion has focused on retaliation. It should be clear, however, that retaliation occurs after a first-attack, and it is important to understand how using coercion first is related to the acquisition of a desired identity. Toch (1980) argued that violent men frequently are concerned with projecting identities as strong, powerful, and courageous. He referred to "rep building" behavior, such as starting fights with total strangers for no apparent reason. These fights occur in front of audiences so the desired reputation can be publicized. For example, bullies typically choose to attack whipping boys on school grounds where audiences are available (Wachtel, 1973). Among many adolescent males and some men, particularly among those of lower socioeconomic status, there is a concern for a masculine identity collectively described as machismo (Lewis, 1961). A macho man may want to be viewed as aggressive, tough, dangerous, bad tempered, and as able to attract and control women. A macho identity serves to intimidate others and enhances power. This male concern for dominance may account for gender differences in violent behavior. Observation of quarrels among American children found that boys frequently used threats and physical force to attain their objectives, while girls more often used conflict resolution tactics (Miller, Danaher, & Forbes, 1986).

Rep building is strategic and trans-situational. Intimidation tactics are used for short term purposes, are situated, and are meant to inspire fear and submission by target persons (Jones & Pittman, 1982). Threats, insults, obscene gestures, staring, displays of weapons, and other forms of behavior help establish the actor as powerful and dangerous. Intimidation tactics may serve to enhance the effectiveness of threats and to deter others from engaging in coercive actions against the intimidator.

Another way to assert a desired identity is to compare self to others on dimensions where one is superior (Tajfel, 1978). This kind of downward comparison has been examined by Wills (1981), who distinguished between passive and active forms. Passive downward comparison occurs when the person points to a comparison but does nothing to affect the standings on the dimension of self or other. Active downward comparison occurs when the person acts to lower the position of others on a dimension. This process can involve the use of coercion. For example, Melburg and Tedeschi (1989) had a confederate perform better or equal to subjects on a set of anagrams. Subjects then had the opportunity to use shocks to evaluate the same or a different confederate on a different task. They found that subjects who suffered from comparison with a superior person gave more frequent shocks to indicate poor performance by either confederate. Thus, the desire to appear as at least as competent as the next person motivated subjects who performed comparatively more poorly than another person to use punitive means to enhance their identity.

Protective Self-Presentations

An individual values identities that facilitate or enhance the ability to influence other people. These identities have been referred to as power bases (French & Raven, 1959). Among such power bases are identities as an expert, as a legitimate authority, and as attractive (referred to as referent power). Control over rewards and punishments, and a reputation as a credible and trustworthy communicator also facilitate the effectiveness of influence attempts.

Power bases are identities, but they may also be viewed as resources that contribute to achieving interpersonal goals. Undermining these identities lessens the individual's ability to be successful in influencing others, and therefore interferes with goal attainment. Such a power loss is not confined to a single interaction but may have long term consequences. A person develops pride in possessing desirable social identities and will act to defend them, just as they defend themselves against physical attack or as they would defend their property and their loved ones. Just as a person would be motivated to defend his home and personal property against looters, there is strong concern to protect those identities that most crucially articulate the ability to get what one wants from others in social interactions.

People form grievances when their identities are attacked. However, unlike justice motivation, where the goal is to even the scales of justice, the goal of an identity dispute is to defeat the other person. The logic of an identity dispute is one of being "put down" or being "one up." An identity attack casts the target into a negative identity, making the target appears weak and ineffectual or perhaps morally disreputable. The target can nullify such aspersions on identities and can save face through a counterattack. Counterattacking shows strength, courage, competence, and moral fortitude. In other words, the person is motivated to maintain honor and not to allow others to act disrespectfully or disdainfully. However, a counterattack altercasts the other person into a negative identity, as possibly being weak and ineffective, and thus activating a desire to restore a positive identity by some strong action. This conflict spiral has been referred to by Goffman (1955) as a character contest. It sometimes takes highly ritualized forms, such as in the game of dozens or in duels and feuds.

The presence of audiences may heighten the experience of humiliation or shame from an identity attack, and increase the probability that the person will retaliate. Data from experiments and natural settings show that antagonists are more likely to retaliate when attacked in front of audiences (Brown, 1968; Felson, 1982). On the other hand, when the audience is believed to hold pacifistic values, subjects tend to exhibit less retaliation than when no audience is present (Borden, 1975). Effects of audiences on an antagonist's behavior also depend on whether the members of the audience attempt to mediate or exacerbate the conflict. There is evidence that at least one reason mediators are important is that they allow both parties to back down from a dispute without losing face (Pruitt & Johnson, 1970).

Perhaps the most reliable elictor of coercive actions are punitive verbal attacks by other people. Verbal abuse of a person is an almost effortless action and appears safer or less costly in terms of what the other person might do in response. Insults are the bullets of tongues, able to inflict emotional damage from a distance. Insults may be considered pedagogical tools, since they are frequently used to punish undesired behavior of others for the purpose of deterring or reducing that type of behavior in the future. In other words, insults are a form of coercive power. Insults attack identities of the target, and are associated with an experience of lowered power and moral worth. Perhaps all forms of punishment may be viewed as at least partial attacks on an individual's social identities, since there are implications of moral or social inferiority of the punished person.

A violation of rights, interference with opportunities, and constraints on freedoms may be experienced as harmful. The degree of legitimacy assigned to rights, the importance of opportunities, and the strength of constraints will be directly related to the amount of resentment experienced by the individual. According to Brown and Levinson (1987), the desire for autonomy is universal and threats to autonomy are perceived as attacks on identity. One way to react to such attacks is to resist the oppressor, and by coercive means if the costs of doing so are not too high. The motive of the oppressed person is to recover autonomy and hence one's honor.

Coercive actions undertaken with a justice motive are similar to, but not identical to, those performed to restore honor. There are at least two demonstrable differences between a motive to restore justice and a motive to restore honor. First, as has already been indicated, honor requires winning, whereas justice requires only an eye for an eye. In other words, responses to perceived injustice are proportionate to the provocation, but reactions to identity attacks are apt to be disproportionate. The involvement of social identities may explain why people punish wrong-doing directed at them more than wrong-doing directed at someone else. Second, grievances can be resolved and justice restored either by actions taken by the grievant against the offender or by someone else. Third parties, such as parents, courts, and supervisors, may exact justice by punishing or compelling restitution by a miscreant to the satisfaction of the injured party. However, persons motivated to restore honor prefer to carry out the punishment themselves, and prefer that the target knows who administered the punishment. This desire to pit one's own identities against that of the other person in a character contest explains the results obtained by Sermat (1967), who found that subjects were less likely to retaliate when harmed by a robot than by another person.

CONCLUSION

The social interactionist theory of coercive actions provides an integration of areas of research that have curiously remained semi-independent of each other throughout the past four decades. In this perspective, power and influence are central processes for explaining social actions. If it is further assumed that aggressive behavior consists of threats, punishments, and bodily force, and that these actions are carried out to achieve social goals, then aggression can be interpreted as alternative means of influencing others.

An explanation of aggressive behavior from a social interactionist viewpoint focuses on three motives for using aggression: for social control, for maintenance and restoration of justice, and to establish and defend identities. These motives are often elicited by situational factors, such as opportunities, unfair treatment, and disrespect by others. Individuals assess situations, make judgments, experience emotions, form some ideas about probabilities, costs, and gains, and then make decisions about how to act in the situation. Unlike traditional theories of aggression in which the individual is considered as reactive to attacks, stress, noxious stimuli, internal drives, instincts, hormones, and brain centers, the person in our theory is considered to be situated in a social context and her actions are explained by social processes. Coercive episodes often develop in a recursive manner, and do not consist only of the kind of attack–retaliation sequence assumed by most current theories of aggression

Social interactionist theory broadly incorporates cognitive processes, such as attributions of responsibility and blame, moral values, appraisals associated with particular emotions, evaluation of alternatives, formation of intentions and motives, and decision making. These cognitive processes occur within social contexts, often involving power differences between the interacting persons or where they are in conflict with one another. The implication of these social contexts are central to an explanation of why actors perform coercive actions.

The theoretical move away from intrapsychic explanations and toward a social explanation for aggressive actions also draws attention to the lack of a theory of social influence regarding the source of influence. Textbooks and the research literature show a strong bias in favor of examining the target of influence, and a general neglect of the source. When the source of influence is the focus of interest, it is usually referred to as leadership, self-presentation, prosocial behavior, and aggression, and not theoretically interpreted in terms of power and influence. While the present theory emphasizes the conditions under which an actor uses coercion, a more complete theory would examine other forms of influence, too.

REFERENCES

Averill, J. R. (1983). Studies on anger and aggression: Implications for theories of emotion. *American Psychologist, 38,* 1145–1160.

Bandura, A. (1973). *Aggression: A social learning analysis.* Englewood Cliffs, NJ: Prentice-Hall.

Berkowitz, L. (1989). The frustration-aggression hypothesis: An examination and reformulation. *Psychological Bulletin, 106*, 59–73.

Berkowitz, L. (1993). *Aggression: Its causes, consequences, and control*. New York: McGraw-Hill.

Bjorkqvist, K., Lagerspetz, K. M. J., & Kaukiainen, A. (1992). Do girls manipulate and boys fight?: Developmental trends in regard to direct and indirect aggression. *Aggressive Behavior, 18*, 117–127.

Boldizar, J. P., Perry, D. G., & Perry, L. C. (1989). Outcome values and aggression. *Child Development, 60*, 571–579.

Bond, M. H., & Tedeschi, J. T. (in press). Polishing the jade: A modest proposal for improving the study of social psychology across cultures. In D. Matsumoto (Ed.), *Handbook of culture and psychology*. New York: Oxford University Press.

Borden, R. J. (1975). Witnessed aggression: Influence of an observer's sex and values on aggressive responding. *Journal of Personality and Social Psychology, 31*, 567–573.

Briggs, J. L. (1970). *Never in anger: Portrait of an Eskimo family*. Cambridge, MA: Harvard University Press.

Brown, B. R. (1968). The effects of need to maintain face in interpersonal bargaining. *Journal of Experimental Social Psychology, 4*, 107–122.

Brown, P., & Levinson, S. C. (1987). *Politeness: Some universals in language usage*. New York: Cambridge University Press.

Buss, A. H. (1961). *The psychology of aggression*. New York: Wiley.

Chagnon, N. A. (1976). *Yanomamo, the fierce people*. New York: Holt, Rinehart and Winston.

Coleman, K. H. (1980). Conjugal violence: What 33 men report. *Journal of Marital and Family Therapy, 6*, 207–213.

Deutsch, M., & Krauss, R. M. (1960). The effect of threat upon interpersonal bargaining. *Journal of Abnormal and Social Psychology: 61*, 181–189.

Dollard, J., Doob, N., Miller, N. E., Mowrer, O. H., & Sears, R. R. (1939). *Frustration and aggression*. New Haven, CT: Yale University Press.

Donnerstein, E., & Hatfield, E. (1982). Aggression and inequity. In J. Greenberg & R. Cohen (Eds.), *Equity and justice in social behavior* (pp. 309–336). New York: Academic.

Eagly, A. H., & Steffen, V. J. (1986). Gender and aggressive behavior: A meta-analytic review of the social psychological literature. *Psychological Bulletin, 100*, 309–330.

Felson, R. B. (1982). Impression management and the escalation of aggression and violence. *Social Psychology Quarterly, 45*, 245–254.

Fischer, C. S. (1969). The effect of threats in an incomplete information game. *Sociometry, 32*, 301–314.

French, J. R. P., Jr., & Raven, B. (1959). The bases of social power. In D. Cartwright (Ed.), *Studies in social power* (pp. 221–256). Ann Arbor, MI: University of Michigan Press.

Geen, R. G. (1990). *Human aggression*. Pacific Grove, CA: Brooks/Cole.

Goffman, E. (1955). On face-work: An analysis of ritual elements in social interaction. *Psychiatry, 18*, 213–231.

Goldstein, P. J. (1981). Drugs and violent crime. In N. A. Weiner & M. A. Zahn (Eds.), *Violence: Patterns, causes, public policy*. San Diego, CA: Harcourt Brace Jovanovich.

Hornstein, H. A. (1965). The effects of different magnitudes of threat upon interpersonal bargaining. *Journal of Experimental Social Psychology, 1*, 282–293.

Jansen, M. A., and Meyers-Abel, J. (1981). Assertive training for battered women. A pilot program. *Social Work, 26*, 164–165.

Jones, E. E., & Pittman, T. S. (1982). Toward a general theory of strategic self-presentation. In J. Suls (Ed.), *Psychological perspectives on the self* (Vol. 1, pp. 189–213). Hillsdale, NJ: Lawrence Erlbaum.

Lewis, O. (1961). *The children of Sanchez: Autobiography of a Mexican family*. New York: Random House.

Maccoby, E. E., & Jacklin, C. N. (1974). *The psychology of sex differences*. Stanford, CA: Stanford University Press.

Melburg, V., & Tedeschi, J.T. (1989). Displaced aggression: Frustration or impression management? *European Journal of Social Psychology, 19*, 139–145.

Miller, P., Danaher, D., & Forbes, D. (1986). Sex-related strategies for coping with interpersonal conflict in children aged five and seven. *Developmental Psychology, 22*, 543–548.

Molm, L. D. (1988). The structure and use of power: A comparison of reward and punishment power. *Social Psychology Quarterly, 51*, 108–122.

Moyer, K. (1987). *Violence and aggression: A*

physiological perspective. New York: Paragon House.

Murdoch, P. (1967). Development of contractual norms in a dyad. *Journal of Personality and Social Psychology, 6*, 206–211.

Olweus, D. (1978). *Aggression in the schools: Bullies and whipping boys*. Washington, DC: Hemisphere.

Peirce, R. S., Pruitt, D. G., & Czaja, S. J. (1991). Complainant-respondent differences in procedural choice. Unpublished manuscript, State University of New York at Buffalo.

Perry, D. G., Perry, L. C., & Rasmussen, P. (1986). Cognitive social learning mediators of aggression. *Child Development, 57*, 700–711.

Pruitt, D. G., & Johnson, D. F. (1970). Mediation as an aid to face saving in negotiation. *Journal of Personality and Social Psychology, 14*, 239–246.

Pruitt, D. G., & Rubin, J. Z. (1986). *Social conflict: escalation, stalemate, and settlement*. New York: Random House.

Rule, B. G., & Nesdale, A. R. (1976). Moral judgments of aggressive behavior. In R. G. Geen & E. C. O'Neal (Eds.), *Perspectives on aggression*. New York: Academic.

Schönback, P. (1990). *Account episodes: The management or escalation of conflict*. New York: Cambridge University Press.

Schutz, A. (1967). *Phenomenology of the social world*. Evanston, IL: Northwestern University Press.

Sermat, V. (1967). The possibility of influencing the other's behavior and cooperation: Chicken vs. prisoner's dilemma. *Canadian Journal of Psychology, 21*, 204–219.

Tajfel, H. (1978). *Differentiation between social groups: Studies in the social psychology of intergroup relations*. New York: Academic.

Tedeschi, J. T. (1970). Threats and promises. In P. Swingle (Ed.), *The structure of conflict*. New York: Academic.

Tedeschi, J. T., Bonoma, T. V., & Lindskold, S. (1970). Threateners' reactions to prior announcement of behavioral compliance or defiance. *Behavioral Science, 13*, 131–139.

Tedeschi, J. T., & Felson, R. B. (1994). *Violence, aggression and coercive actions*. Washington, DC: American Psychological Association.

Tedeschi, J. T., Horai, J., Lindskold, S., & Faley, T. E. (1970). The effects of opportunity costs and target compliance on the behavior of a threatening source. *Journal of Experimental Social Psychology, 6*, 205–213.

Tedeschi, J. T., & Lindskold, S. (1976). *Social psychology: Interdependence, interaction, and influence*. New York: Wiley.

Tedeschi, J. T., Lindskold, S., & Rosenfeld, P. (1985). *Introduction to social psychology*. St. Paul, MN: West Publishing.

Tedeschi, J. T., Melburg, V., & Rosenfeld, P. (1981). Is the concept of aggression useful? In P. Brain & D. Benton (Eds.), *A multi-disciplinary approach to aggression research* (pp. 74–96). Elsevier North Holland, Biomedical Press.

Tedeschi, J. T., Schlenker, B. R., & Bonoma, T. V. (1973). *Conflict, power, and games*. Chicago: Aldine.

Tedeschi, J. T., Smith, R. B., III, & Brown, R. C., Jr. (1974). A reinterpretation of research on aggression. *Psychological Bulletin, 89*, 540–563.

Thibaut, J. (1968). The development of contractual norms in bargaining: Replication and variation. *Journal of Conflict Resolution, 12*, 102–112.

Thibaut, J., & Faucheux, C. (1965). The development of contractual norms in a bargaining situation under two types of stress. *Journal of Experimental Social Psychology, 1*, 89–102.

Toch, H. (1980). *Violent men: An inquiry into the psychology of violence*. Washington, DC: American Psychological Association.

Wachtel, P. L. (1973). Psychodynamics, behavior therapy, and the impeccable experimenter: An inquiry into the consistency of personality. *Journal of Abnormal Psychology, 83*, 324–334.

Weiner, B., Amirkan, J., Fokes, V. S., & Verette, J. (1987). An attributional analysis of excuse giving: Studies of a naive theory of emotion. *Journal of Personality and Social Psychology, 52*, 316–324.

White, R. K. (1968). *Nobody wanted war: Misperception in Vietnam and other wars*. Garden City, NY: Doubleday.

Wills, T. A. (1981). Downward comparison principles in social psychology. *Psychological Bulletin, 90*, 245–271.

Wilson, J. Q., & Herrnstein, R. J. (1985). *Crime and human nature*. New York: Simon & Schuster.

Zillman, D. (1983) Arousal and aggression. In R. G. Geen & E. I. Donnerstein (Eds.), *Aggression: Theoretical and empirical reviews*. (Vol. 1, pp. 75–101). New York: Academic.

PART II

THE ROLE OF COGNITIVE PROCESSES AND STRATEGIES IN SOCIAL INFLUENCE

Subtle Influences on Judgment and Behavior
Who is Most Susceptible?

RICHARD E. PETTY

Effects of Overt Head Movements on Attitudes
Effects of Cognitive Priming on Behavior
Effects of Mild Emotional States on Judgments, Attitudes,
    and Behavior
Are the Biasing Effects Under High Thought Conditions Inevitable?
Conclusion

*I*t is now quite clear from the work on attitudes and social cognition conducted over the past two decades, that people's judgments and behaviors can be influenced by the most seemingly innocuous and subtle manipulations. Thus, people express more favorable attitudes toward the economy after they have seen a happy rather than a sad movie (Forgas & Moylan, 1987); they agree more with a proposal to raise tuition when they hear it while nodding their heads in a vertical (yes) rather than a horizontal (no) manner (Wells & Petty, 1980); and they are more likely to interrupt somebody after they unscramble sentences with rude rather than polite content (Bargh, Chen, & Burrows, 1996). These and other effects appear to occur without a person's awareness (i.e., the effects are implicit). When people are attempting to be rational, they presumably would not want their judgments of the economy to be influ-

Address correspondence to: Richard E. Petty, Department of Psychology, Ohio State University, 1885 Neil Avenue Mall, Columbus, OH 43210-1222. E-mail: petty.1@osu.edu

enced by their current mood state, or their judgments of an important issue to be influenced by their head movements, or their social behavior to be influenced by an irrelevant cognitive task they have just completed.

This chapter is about the conditions under which these subtle effects are most likely to occur and *who* is most susceptible to these influences. A number of predictions are possible based on the available literature. One possibility is that these contaminating effects are likely to influence all people in all situations about equally because the mechanisms of influence are either automatic, or require relatively little cognitive effort. Another point of view is that these effects are most likely to operate when conditions reduce the likelihood of thinking because when people are carefully considering their judgments and actions, the impact of such subtle factors should be attenuated. Yet a third possibility, and the focus of this chapter, is that many such contaminating effects occur under the most thoughtful situations and for the most thoughtful people, because subtle contaminants can influence cognition without awareness, and the more cognitions one has, the more bias that can occur.[1]

This chapter focuses on some recent research we have been conducting on who is most susceptible to subtle contaminating variables, why they are susceptible, and whether or not these effects are inevitable. Research on three contaminants will be described: (1) effects of overt head movements on attitudes, (2) effects of cognitive primes on behavior, and (3) effects of mood state on judgments, attitudes, and behavior.

EFFECTS OF OVERT HEAD MOVEMENTS ON ATTITUDES

Background

One of our first studies of subtle influences on judgment concerned the effects of overt head movements on attitudes (Wells & Petty, 1980). We brought Ohio State University students into the lab and told them we were conducting a consumer study on headphones. The students listened to a presumed campus radio broadcast that began with music and led into an editorial about changing tuition at the students' university. The key manipulation in the study was whether the students had been instructed to move their heads from side to side (horizontal movements) or up and down (vertical movements) while listening to the tape. The participants were told that: "As scientists we were simulating movements people might make when using headphones." Following the broadcast,

---

1. Of course, as suggested by the Elaboration Likelihood Model (Petty & Cacioppo, 1986; Petty & Wegener, 1999), it also is possible that the same variables could have effects under high and low thinking conditions, though for different reasons (e.g., see Petty, Schumann, Richman, & Strathman, 1993). Our focus in this chapter is on the effects of subtle variables under high elaboration conditions as this is the less explored (and less obvious) mechanism.

participants rated the headphones, the music, and gave their opinions on what the appropriate tuition should be. The primary result was that the students' recommended tuition was more in accord with the one advocated in the message when they were engaged in vertical rather than horizontal head movements.

There are a number of possible explanations for this result. First a simple affective interpretation might say that head nodding induces some pleasant affect (or shaking induces some unpleasant affect) that becomes associated with the message (a classical conditioning effect). Wells and Petty (1980) did not favor this explanation because ratings of the headphones and the music were not influenced by the head movements, as might be expected from a simple affect transfer analysis. Rather, we favored a cognitive interpretation and suggested that vertical head movements were associated with and facilitated agreement, whereas horizontal head movements were associated with and facilitated disagreement. In essence, the head movements primed the concepts of agreement and disagreement. When agreement was primed, people agreed with the message, and when disagreement was primed, people disagreed with the message.

Recently, we have begun to explore another possibility based on the self-validation hypothesis (Petty, Briñol, & Tormala, 2000). This analysis also assumes that head movements prime the agreement and disagreement concepts, but that agreement/disagreement is associated with one's thoughts about the message rather than the message position. For clarity, imagine a person giving a speech who sees everyone in the audience moving their heads up and down in apparent agreement. This would presumably be quite comforting. The person would receive some external or social validation for what he or she was saying. On the other hand, if people in the audience were shaking their heads from side to side, the person would presumably lose confidence in what he or she said. The fact that people look to others as an indicator of the validity of what they are thinking or doing is a basic tenet of Festinger's (1954) social comparison theory (see also David & Turner, this volume; Turner, 1991). Furthermore, current research supports the view that confidence in one's beliefs can be affected by the opinions of others and plays an important role in social influence processes (e.g., see Hardin & Higgins, 1996; Stangor, Sechrist, & Jost, this volume).

If the opinions of others as expressed in their external head movements can plausibly provide some cues to the validity or invalidity of what a person is saying, could internal head movements (i.e., one's own head movements) provide a cue to the validity or invalidity of what a person is thinking—a self-validation effect? In the Wells and Petty (1980) study, one can't tease apart these explanations because the messages used were designed to contain very compelling arguments that elicited mostly favorable thoughts. Thus, if a "yes" head movement meant that "I agree with the message," more influence should result than a "no" head movement. But, if a yes movement meant that "I agree with my thoughts," a yes movement also should produce more agreement than no because the thoughts are favorable to the message and yes would mean that these favorable thoughts were correct or good (i.e., "I agree with my favorable thoughts," or "My favorable thoughts are valid"). But, what if a message elicited mostly negative thoughts because it contained weak and specious arguments (Petty, Wells, & Brock, 1976)? Here, the two explanations make opposite predictions. Once again, if a yes movement means that "I agree with the message," more influence should result than with a no movement. But if a yes movement means that "I agree with my thoughts," a yes movement should produce *less* agreement than a no movement because the person's thoughts are unfavorable to the message, and yes would mean that these unfavorable thoughts were correct or good (i.e., "I agree with my unfavorable thoughts" or "my unfavorable thoughts are valid"). If one's unfavorable thoughts to a message are perceived as valid, this would undermine the persuasiveness of the communication.

In sum, if head movements signal agreement or disagreement with the message, then it doesn't matter whether a person is thinking positive or negative thoughts—vertical head movements should always produce more agreement than horizontal movements. The same main effect prediction holds if head movements induce affect that either becomes associated with the message directly or biases people's thoughts (Petty, Schumann, Richman, & Strathman, 1993). On the other hand, if the head movements signal agreement or disagreement with one's own thoughts, then it matters quite a bit whether a person is generating mostly positive or negative thoughts during message exposure.

Testing the Self-Validation Hypothesis

To examine the self-validation possibility, we conducted an experiment where people were instructed to move their heads in a horizontal or vertical manner in conjunction with a message containing either strong or weak arguments (Briñol & Petty, 2000). The messages were pretested to elicit primarily favorable or unfavorable thoughts. The topic of the message was that students at the Autonomous University of Madrid should have to carry a mandatory ID card with them for security purposes—and participants were provided with arguments that were strong or weak (i.e., that in pretesting elicited primarily favorable or unfavorable thoughts in the absence of any head movements; see Petty & Cacioppo, 1986). The primary finding from this study was a Message Quality × Head Movement interaction (see Fig. 8.1). When the arguments were strong, yes (vertical) movements produced more agreement than no (horizontal) movements. This finding replicates the original Wells and Petty (1980) finding. In stark contrast, however, no movements actually led to more persuasion than yes movements when the message contained weak arguments and peoples' thoughts were largely unfavorable rather than favorable.

In a second study we examined whether this self-validation effect would occur mostly when the likelihood of thinking about the message was low or high. Our hypothesis was that the self-validation effect—which involves implicitly critiquing one's own thoughts—should be more likely to occur when the likelihood of thinking is high for two reasons. First, critiques of one's thoughts should

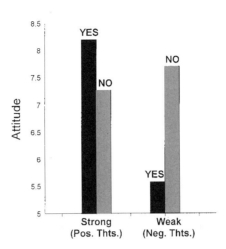

FIGURE 8.1. The effect of vertical (yes) and horizontal (no) head movements on attitudes following a strong or weak persuasive message (data from Briñol & Petty, 2000).

matter less if there were few thoughts to critique than if there were many. Second, the conditions that foster motivation and ability to think, also should foster people's motivation and ability to evaluate the thoughts that they have generated. That is, people should be more likely to care about evaluating their thoughts when the issue is personally relevant (Petty & Cacioppo, 1979) or they are held accountable for their judgments (Petty, Harkins, & Williams, 1980), and they should have greater ability to evaluate their thoughts when they have many rather than few cognitive resources available (Petty et al., 1976).

To examine this, we conducted a study that was basically the same as the first experiment except that we also varied the likelihood of thinking about the message. This was done with a combination of a motivational and an ability manipulation. In the low elaboration condition, the message was made to seem less important and it was also presented a bit faster over the headphones making it a little more difficult to process. As expected, a three-way interaction (Head movement × Argument Quality × Elaboration) emerged on the measure of attitude toward the focal issue. Under the high elaboration conditions, the results of Experiment 1 were replicated. That is, a significant two way interaction of Head Movements and Argument Quality was found. Under low elaboration conditions, no significant effects were obtained.

In a final study, in addition to assessing attitudes toward the focal issue, we also assessed individuals' thoughts and their confidence in their thoughts. This study replicated the attitude findings from the previous studies, and also showed that head movements have an effect on confidence in thoughts, but not in the nature (valence) of the thoughts themselves. Furthermore, confidence in one's thoughts mediated the effect of head movements on attitudes. Thus, contrary to the view that the effect of head movements would be universal, or confined to low thinking conditions, it was actually the most thoughtful conditions that led to an impact of head movements on attitudes.

EFFECTS OF COGNITIVE PRIMING ON BEHAVIOR

Background

Perhaps one of the most interesting contaminants of people's behavior, and one that has generated considerable recent research attention, is the effect of stereotype activation on action. In a series of studies, a number of researchers have examined the effects of activating stereotypes about one's own group or another group on behavior. The general result of this research is that activation of such stereotypes often leads people to behave in ways that are consistent with the activated stereotype (see Dijksterhuis, this volume; Wheeler & Petty, 2000). Thus, elderly people act more elderly (i.e., perform worse on a memory test) when a stereotype of the elderly is activated (Levy, 1996), but young people also act more elderly (e.g., walk slower) when an elderly stereotype is activated (Bargh, Chen, & Burrows, 1996). African Americans perform worse on a standardized achievement test when the African American stereotype is made salient (Steele & Aronson, 1995), but so, too, do White participants (Wheeler, Jarvis, & Petty, in press). Women perform worse on math tests when the female stereotype is activated, but so do men (Dijksterhuis & Cornielle, 1999). Stereotype activation not only leads to negative performance effects, but also can produce positive effects. Thus, if Dutch college students are primed with the stereotype of "soccer hooligan," they perform worse on a knowledge test, but if they are primed with "college professor," they do better (Dijksterhuis & van Knippenberg, 1998). If Asian women are primed with the female stereotype, they perform worse on a math test, but if they are primed with the Asian stereotype, they perform better (Shih, Pittinsky, & Ambady, 1999).

Thus, the effects of stereotype activation on behavior appear to be quite general—applying not only to members of the stereotyped group, but also to everybody else who is aware of the stereotype. This recent work on the behavioral effects of priming stereotypes builds on earlier research on trait or concept activation. In fact, a large number of studies in the social cognition literature going back to a study by Higgins, Rholes, and Jones in 1977, have demonstrated that the activation or priming of a particular concept in memory increases the likelihood that this concept will influence subsequent judgments and behaviors. For example, in one study (Carver, Ganellen, Froming, & Chambers, 1983), participants were primed with the concept of "hostility" by unscrambling sentences with hostile content. Participants in a control condition unscrambled sentences with neutral content. Following this priming procedure, individuals primed with hostile sentences chose higher shock levels to punish a confederate in a subsequent learning task than individuals primed with neutral sentences. In a similar vein, Herr (1986) found that people primed with hostile sentences behaved more competitively in a Prisoner's Dilemma game (see also Neuberg, 1988). But again, just as favorable stereotypes can lead to favorable behaviors, so too can priming favorable concepts or traits. For example, in one study (MaCrae & Johnston, 1998), college students unscrambled sentences with "helpful" words rather than "hostile" ones, and an increase in helping behavior was found. The students were more likely to help another person pick up some items that were dropped.

From the social psychological literature, it might appear as if the effects of subtle priming—whether of stereotypes or trait concepts—is pretty universal. But, if one considers the possible mechanisms by which subtle forms of priming might have their influence on behavior, one can reason that some people might be more susceptible to these effects than others. For example, it might be that thoughtful people would be less susceptible to these subtle effects than nonthoughtful people. This is because thoughtful people might be better able to override these relatively automatic effects with deliberative and controlled information processing. However, if these subtle effects occur outside of awareness, it is less likely that thoughtful people could override them, at least deliberately. Furthermore, if one thinks about the steps that might be involved in producing an effect of priming on behavior, there is reason to think that highly thoughtful people could be more susceptible to these effects.

Petty and Jarvis (1996) noted that in order for a primed category or stereotype to influence behavior, several steps may be involved to varying degrees. First, and most obviously, the relevant concepts must be activated from the memory store. That is, the concept of hostility, or beliefs associated with the elderly, need to be made accessible. Second, the activated concepts might influence or bias interpretations of the context in which behavior is to occur. That is, if hostility is primed, one's partner's actions might be interpreted as more hostile, or the situation might be interpreted as one in which aggression is appropriate. Or, if an Asian stereotype is primed, a testing situation might be interpreted as one in which achievement is expected, desirable, or more important, than if the female or African American stereotype is primed. Or, activation of the latter stereotypes might make the testing situation seem like one in which success is less possible, or likely, leading to effort withdrawal. That is, the prime can influence or bias the thoughts one has that are relevant to the behavioral context (much as affect can bias one's thoughts and interpretations; see Forgas, 1995; Petty et al., 1993). Third, in order for thoughts or judgments to influence behavior, the individual needs to act on any interpretations or judgments rendered. So, if one's partner seems hostile, should you actually give him or her more shock? Or if the situation seems like an achievement-oriented one, or one in which success is possible, should one actually exert more effort?

How would relatively thoughtful people respond at each of these stages compared to relatively unthoughtful people? First, some research suggests that thoughtful people have easier access to stored categories than unthoughtful people. For example, some research has suggested that people who have previously engaged in evaluative thought about an object or issue take less time to access their attitudes than people who have not (see Hermans & Eelen, in press; Petty & Jarvis, 1996; Smith, Haugtvedt, & Petty, 1994). It may be that chronically engaging in thought makes a wide variety of categories and beliefs more accessible. Thus, it might be easier to energize a wide variety of concepts for people who chronically like to think than for those who do not. The importance of this *accessibility stage* may be more important for some priming tasks than others. For example, it could be that accessibility differences would be more apparent for priming tasks such as unscrambling sentences. On the other hand, it could be that even subliminal manipulations have a greater impact on those who like to think because thinkers have a lower threshold for activation of a wide variety of concepts.

Second, if priming influences the thoughts that people have about information in the immediate context, the more thoughts you have in the context and about the context, the more bias that should be produced in the *interpretation stage*. As with the first stage, this second stage may be more influential for some priming tasks than others. For example, the teacher-learner paradigm used by Carver et al. (1983) and others seems especially likely to allow for interpretation because there are a number of trials with one's partner. But, even minimal situations typically provide some opportunity for interpretive thoughts prior to action.

Third, thoughtful people have been found to act in a manner that is more consistent with their judgments than nonthoughtful people (Cacioppo, Petty, Kao, & Rodriquez, 1986; see Petty, Haugtvedt, & Smith, 1995, for a review). So if two individuals think their partner is hostile, but one has been a bit more thoughtful in coming to this judgment, the thoughtful person would be more likely to act on this belief. There are a number of possible reasons for this difference in the *action stage*. For example, it might be that thoughtful people have more confidence in their judgments and thus are more willing to act on them. Or, as described previously, the judgments of thoughtful people might be more accessible making thoughtful people more able to act on their judgments.

Do Thoughtful People Show Enhanced or Reduced Behavioral Priming Effects?

In an initial study on behavioral priming, we wanted to examine the hypothesis that primed concepts would influence the overt behavior of thoughtful individuals more than nonthoughtful individuals. To divide our participants into those who were generally thoughtful or not, we used the need for cognition scale (Cacioppo & Petty, 1982). There are now a rather large number of studies that have validated this scale and shown its utility in distinguishing people who engage in thought in a wide variety of contexts from those who do not (see Cacioppo, Petty, Feinstein, & Jarvis, 1996, for a review). To examine the ability of priming to impact a consequential and personally relevant behavior, we provided each of our participants with one dollar in coins, and asked them to place a bet on a roulette wheel. Prior to the bet, the participants were subtly primed with the notions of winning or losing in presenting the game's instructions. Basically, the word "win" or "lose" was used multiple times in explaining the game (Petty, Strathman, & Bozzolo, 2000).

The roulette wheel was composed of one half black and one half red markers, which were arranged in such a way that the exact percentage of black and red, though actually 50-50, appeared ambiguous. Each participant was told that they could bet as much or as little as they wanted of their one dollar in favor of the ball landing on black. If the ball landed on black, they won an amount equal to what they bet (i.e., they won), but if the ball landed on red, they had to return the amount bet to the experimenter (i.e., they lost). Participants kept any money they won, as well as any portion of the dollar they did not bet.

Our critical hypothesis was that the betting behavior of thoughtful people would be more influenced by the prime than would the betting behavior of relatively unthoughtful people. First, the prime might be more likely to activate the concepts of winning or losing in thoughtful rather than nonthoughtful people. Second, as thoughtful people considered the roulette wheel before betting, the prime might influence their interpretation of the likelihood of winning (cf., Wegener, Petty, & Klein, 1994). Third, thoughtful people would be more likely to act on their interpretations of the situation.

Analysis of the amount bet clearly supported the primary hypothesis. That is, individuals high in need for cognition bet significantly more when they were primed with the notion of winning (i.e., $.80) rather than losing ($.55). In contrast, individuals low in need for cognition bet the same amount regardless of whether they were primed with winning (i.e., $.65) or losing ($.61). Thus, just as the effects of head nodding were more apparent under conditions of high rather than low thoughtfulness, the impact of a cognitive prime on behavior was more evident for individuals who chronically engage in thought than for those who do not.

EFFECTS OF MILD EMOTIONAL STATES ON JUDGMENTS, ATTITUDES, AND BEHAVIOR

Background

Of all the potential subtle contaminants on people's judgments, perhaps the most studied is a person's emotional state (see Forgas, 2001). One well replicated finding is that positive emotional states lead people to overestimate the likelihood of positive events relative to negative states, and negative states lead people to overestimate the likelihood of negative events relative to positive states (e.g., Johnson & Tversky, 1983; Mayer, Gaschke, Braverman, & Evans, 1992; Wegener et al., 1994). Recently, we have shown that the effect of emotional states on likelihood judgments is not just a valence effect, but also works for more specific emotions (DeSteno, Petty, Rucker, & Wegener, 2000). For example, within the negative emotions, making people angry increases the perceived likelihood of angering events compared to a sad state, whereas making people sad increases the perceived likelihood of sad events over an angry state.

According to the analysis of the effects of cognitive priming on behavior presented earlier, it also seems likely that thoughtful people would be more susceptible to the contaminating effects of emotional priming on their thoughts, and the actions that follow from them (Petty et al., 1993; see also Forgas, 1995). In one relevant study (Wegener et al., 1994) we presented happy or sad individuals with a persuasive message that was framed in a positive (e.g., if you agree with the advocacy good things will happen) or a negative (if you don't agree with the advocacy, bad things will happen) manner. Positive emotional states should increase the perceived likelihood of good things happening, and thereby increase the effectiveness of positively framed arguments. On the other hand, negative emotional states should increase the perceived likelihood of bad things happening, and thereby increase the effectiveness of negatively framed arguments (see Petty & Wegener, 1991). But, these effects should only occur for people who think about the message arguments, as it is only for these individuals that affective state will bias the perception of the arguments. In support of this reasoning, for individuals high in need for cognition, emotional state interacted with message framing to influence attitudes. When in a happy state, positively framed messages were more persuasive than negatively framed messages, but when in a sad state, negatively framed messages were more persuasive than positively framed messages (for a more complete analysis of the multiple effects of emotional states on persuasion, see Petty, DeSteno, & Rucker, 2000; Wegener & Petty, 1996).[2]

Effects of Specific Emotional States on Judgments

Recently, we have begun to examine the implications for persuasion of emotional manipulations that go beyond valence. For example, in one study, we compared the divergent negative emotional states of anger and sadness. In this research, individuals were first put in either a mild state of sadness or anger, and then exposed to a persuasive message that had message arguments framed in either a sad or in an angering manner (Petty, DeSteno, Rucker, & Wegener, 2000). In the sad emotional condition, participants read a depressing story about

---

2. According to the Elaboration Likelihood Model of persuasion (Petty & Cacioppo, 1986), emotional states can not only bias peoples' thoughts when the elaboration likelihood is high, but also can affect judgments by serving in other roles in other situations (e.g., influencing attitudes by a heuristic mechanism when the elaboration likelihood is low; affecting the amount of thinking when the elaboration likelihood is not constrained; see also Forgas, 1995; Schwarz, Bless, & Bohner, 1991). This multiple roles perspective is useful in accounting for a wide variety of variables such as majority and minority influence (e.g., see Martin & Hewstone, this volume) and "stealing thunder" effects (e.g., see Williams & Dolnik, this volume).

a natural disaster, and in the angering emotional condition, participants read a story about anti-American protests overseas (see DeSteno et al., 2000). Then, in the context of a second study, participants were exposed to a message that advocated an increase in the state sales tax. The sad message contained arguments pointing to consequences that pretest participants had rated as sad (e.g., "special needs infants remanded to the state will not receive adequate attention and care if the tax proposal is not implemented"), whereas the anger message contained arguments that pretest participants had rated as angering (e.g., "without a tax increase, the low number of state inspectors will mean that more individuals will wrongly take advantage of the health care system by submitting fraudulent claims"). After completing the critical attitude measures, participants completed the need for cognition scale (Cacioppo & Petty, 1982).

The overall results on the key attitude measure of support for the tax proposal revealed an Emotional State × Message Framing × Need for Cognition interaction. No significant effects were obtained for nonthoughtful individuals. On the other hand, for thoughtful individuals, emotional state biased judgments as predicted. That is, sad individuals were more persuaded by the sad than the angering message, but angered individuals were more persuaded by the angry than the sad message. Furthermore, these attitudinal effects were mediated by differences in the perceived likelihood of the consequences mentioned in the message.

To explore the behavioral implications of these attitudes, we asked participants to cast a vote for or against the tax increase. Here, the effect was even more dramatic. About 67% of the thoughtful individuals in the conditions where their emotions matched the message frame said they would vote for the tax increase, whereas only 26% of those whose emotions did not match the message frame said they would vote for the tax increase. In sum, like the effects of head movements and cognitive primes, the effect of emotional state on responses to persuasive communications was larger under conditions where thinking was most likely.

ARE THE BIASING EFFECTS UNDER HIGH THOUGHT CONDITIONS INEVITABLE?

Before addressing the effects of thought on the inevitability of bias, it is useful to consider what the literature suggests about the inevitability of bias in general. Perhaps most importantly, it is already apparent from the considerable prior research on category priming, that the biasing effects of primes can become attenuated and can even be reversed when the priming becomes blatant or obvious (i.e., is no longer subtle; e.g., see Higgins, 1996). But, there is relatively little work on differential susceptibility to these reversals. For some of the same reasons that thoughtful people and thoughtful situations might exacerbate the effects of subtle primes, thoughtful people and thoughtful situations should be more prone to a reverse bias when the priming becomes blatant, and people may want to avoid being influenced by an obvious biasing factor (Petty & Wegener, 1993; see Wegener & Petty, 1997; Wilson & Brekke, 1994, for reviews).

Emotional State and Judgment

First, consider the effects of mild emotional states on likelihood judgments. In the persuasion research by Petty, DeSteno, Rucker, and Wegener (2000) reviewed earlier, it was thoughtful people who were most influenced by the effects of emotional state on attitudes via the effect of emotion on likelihood judgments. That is, when sad, thoughtful people saw sad consequences as more likely, and thus were more persuaded by a message containing sad than angering arguments. But, when angered, thoughtful people saw angering consequences as more likely, and thus were more persuaded by a message containing angering than sad arguments.

In this research, the emotional induction was deliberately subtle and presented in a context divorced from the judgment context. What if the emotional induction was quite salient and obvious, and thus less likely to be divorced from the judgment context? To examine this, we conducted a study in which we did two things to make an emotional state blatant rather than subtle (DeSteno et al., 2000, Exp. 4). First, rather than reading a story about an external event, participants were asked to bring to mind a past instance in which they were sad, angry, or happy. Reading stories makes no explicit mention of the targeted emotion, whereas thinking about past instances of one's own emotions makes it very clear that emotions are being manipulated. If this didn't make it clear enough, however, participants also completed an emotions checklist right after the emotion manipulation and just before the judgment task.

For the judgment task, participants estimating the likelihood of various happy (e.g., "Of the 50,000 students currently enrolled at Ohio State, how many will receive an 'A' in a class central to their major this quarter?"), sad ("Of the 50,000 students currently enrolled at Ohio State, how many will experience the death of a loved one [e.g., close relative, close friend] within the next year?) and angry ("Of the 40,000 people who commute to work in downtown Columbus, how many will be late for a meeting today because they are stuck in traffic?") events. These items were presented in a random order on computer. Participants provided a numeric estimate for each question and all responses were standardized prior to analysis to eliminate any scaling differences. Responses of both high and low need for cognition individuals were examined.

The primary result was a Emotional State × Emotional Item × Need for Cognition interaction on estimates of frequency. The interaction was due to contrasting patterns for thoughtful and nonthoughtful people. Individuals low in need for cognition showed a congruency bias. By making emotional state salient, these individuals now revealed the bias that was absent when emotional state was manipulated more subtly and the likelihood judgments were embedded in a persuasive message. However, thoughtful people responded quite differently. These individuals showed a very clear reverse bias. For these individuals, when in a negative emotional state, positive events seemed more likely than negative ones, but when in a positive state, negative events seemed more likely than positive ones.

Behavioral Priming Effects

Before turning to an explanation of these reverse findings, let's return to the gambling paradigm described earlier. Recall that in one study (Petty, Strathman, & Bozzolo, 2000, Exp. 1), people were shown a roulette wheel in which there was actually about a 50% chance of winning. In the instructions for the game, participants were primed with the concept of winning or losing, and individuals high in need for cognition bet more when they were primed with winning than with losing. But, what would be the effect for thoughtful people if the priming was more blatant? Would we see the same type of attenuated or reversed effect that was observed with activating emotions in a blatant way? To examine this, we conducted another gambling study and examined the effectiveness of the win and lose primes with two different roulette wheels. Only high need for cognition individuals were recruited for participation (Petty et al., 2000, Exp. 2).

First, in addition to the ambiguous (50–50) roulette wheel, we used a wheel in which the likelihood of winning and losing was more obvious (i.e., 80–20). If the results of the initial gambling study were due to priming influencing interpretation of the roulette wheel (rather than a less interesting demand explanation), we would expect the priming manipulation to influence betting mostly when the roulette wheel was ambiguous. If the actual likelihood of winning was obvious, the priming effect should be reduced or eliminated. On the other hand, if the participants' responses were determined by a desire to fulfill the expectancies of the experimenter, or demand, the ambiguity of the roulette wheel would be expected to make less of a difference.

More importantly, though, the goal of this study was to examine the effect of a more blatant behavioral prime. So, in addition to including the subtle win prime used in our first gambling study, we also used a more blatant win prime that was designed to make the concept and expectation of winning very salient. To accomplish this, rather than simply using the word "win" in presenting the instructions for the game, in the blatant priming condition the experimenter explicitly indicated that she thought that participants would actually win the game. After the priming manipulation (subtle win, subtle lose, blatant win, no-prime), participants were shown either the 50-50 or the 80-20 wheel. As in the initial study, $1 in coins was distributed to participants, and they were asked to bet.

A significant 2 (Roulette Wheel) × 4 (priming condition) interaction emerged indicating that the priming manipulation had an impact on betting when the roulette wheel was ambiguous, but did not when the roulette wheel provided more confident information about the probability of winning. With the 80-20 wheel, participants simply bet more when the likelihood of winning was high regardless of priming condition. On the other hand, cell comparisons within the 50-50 roulette wheel condition showed that the subtle win prime participants produced higher bets than the subtle lose prime participants replicating the effect obtained in our first gambling study. The fact that the subtle win and lose primes had no effect with the 80-20 wheel helps to rule out the uninteresting interpretation that high need for cognition individuals were simply responding to an experimental demand implied by the subtle priming manipulation. If this was the case, they presumably would have responded when the roulette wheel was unambiguous as well. The most interesting and new finding is what happened with the blatant win prime. Just as we found when mood was highly salient, when the concept or idea of winning was very salient, high need for cognition participants showed a reverse bias. That is, they actually bet significantly less when there was a blatant win prime than when there was no priming.

Explaining Reverse Biases

What accounts for the reverse effects that we obtained with both emotion and concept priming when the priming was blatant? There are two likely explanations. The first explanation is theory-driven overcorrection. That is, if people think they are biased by mood or the experimental instructions, don't want to be, have an overestimate of the magnitude of bias, and have the resources to correct for the presumed bias, a reverse bias would result (see Petty & Wegener, 1993; Strack, 1992; Wegener & Petty, 1995, 1997; Wilson & Brekke, 1994). For example, a participant in the gambling study might reason that "the experimenter's suggestion that I will win might make me bet more than I should, so I should bet less to compensate." In the study of emotion and likelihood judgment, they might reason that "the anger manipulation is making traffic jams seem more likely than they really are, so I need to report a lower likelihood estimate to correct for this bias."

A second possibility is that when the emotional state or prime is quite obvious, it is used as a standard of comparison. That is, a blatantly activated concept or stereotype might be used as a standard against which alternatives are compared (e.g., Schwarz & Bless, 1992) or as an anchor to be evaluated (Wegener, Petty, Bedell, & Jarvis, in press). For example, a participant in the gambling study might think that, "It is not as likely that I'll win as the Experimenter implies (i.e., compared to the Experimenter's very positive perception of winning, I think winning is unlikely.)" Or, in the emotion and likelihood study, a person might reason, "Having many people get caught in a traffic jam is not as likely as my getting angry over a bad grade" (assuming that anger makes very angering events salient). Regardless of the precise mechanism by which these effects occur, it seems clear that blatant primes or emotions can lead to contrast effects especially among those who like to think.

CONCLUSION

Prior literature has made it clear that the blatancy of a prime can determine the extent to which assimilative or contrastive biases occur. It has been less appreciated that thoughtful people and thoughtful situations can produce greater biasing effects for both subtle and blatant primes. The current research demonstrates that thoughtful people can be more susceptible to a variety of subtle assimilative influences on their thoughts, judgments, and behavior than less thoughtful people. When the sources of influence become more blatant, however, thoughtful people can still be more biased, but the direction is reversed. It is useful to think of the subtly or blatancy of primes or other contextual influences as falling along a continuum. For individuals who are unlikely to be engaged in much thought (or in situations that engender little thought), there often will not be any bias produced by some contextual factor until the contextual factor becomes somewhat blatant and obvious. When there is a bias, the bias will tend to be in the direction of the biasing agent since corrections for the effects of biasing agents typically require relatively high amounts of cognitive effort. For very thoughtful individuals, on the other hand, a bias in the direction of the primed material occurs with very subtle priming, but can turn into a bias in the opposite direction when the prime becomes more blatant.

So ironically, it is the most thoughtful people who will sometimes show the most bias in their judgments and behaviors due to various irrelevant contextual variables. When the contextual biasing factor is subtle, thoughtful people are more likely to show a congruency or assimilation effect than unthoughtful people. The research presented here shows that when contextually primed material was subtle, thoughtful people showed greater bias of a "win" prime in their gambling behavior, and a greater effect of their head movements and emotional states on their attitudes than less thoughtful people. When the contextual biasing factor was blatant, however, thoughtful people were more likely to show a reverse (contrast) effect than were less thoughtful people. For thoughtful people, when an emotion manipulation was blatant, sad individuals judged sad events as significantly less likely than happy people, and when they were exposed to a blatant win prime, they bet significantly less money than a control group. Although no research has yet been conducted with a more blatant head movement manipulation, we suspect here too that if this manipulation was conducted in a very explicit rather than implicit manner (e.g., "nod your head in a yes manner as if you are in agreement"), thoughtful people would attempt an adjustment for this undue influence.

In sum, the current work stands as a corrective to those who have suggested or implied that the least thoughtful individuals should be most susceptible to assimilative biases whereas high thoughtful individuals are most susceptible to contrastive biases (e.g., Martin, Seta, & Crelia, 1990). The current research indicates that highly thoughtful people can be more susceptible to both assimilative and contrastive biases, and points to the blatancy or subtlety of the contextual manipulation as one crucial moderator of these effects. In a broader sense, and consistent with the objectives of this volume, this research suggests that social psychologists' past preoccupation with direct, impactful social influence processes was somewhat restrictive. As other contributions to this volume also illustrate, social influence processes operate on a number of subtle and not-so-subtle levels. To understand social influence fully, we need to pay attention to implicit cognitive processes of influence agents as well as influence recipients (see also chapters in this volume by Latané and Bourgeois, this volume; Schaller and Ng, this volume; Dijksterhuis, this volume; Williams & Dolnik, this volume; Mussweiler, this volume; Bless, Strack, & Walther, this volume). Consistent with the theme of this book, our work also suggests that understanding the various manifestations of how human beings influence each other and are influenced by each other is a core question for social psychology.

REFERENCES

Bargh, J. A, Chen, M., & Burows, L. (1996). Automaticity of social behavior: Direct effects of trait construct and stereotype activation on action. *Journal of Personality and Social Psychology, 71,* 230–244.

Briñol, P., & Petty, R. E. (2000). *Overt head movements and persuasion: A self-validation analysis.* Unpublished manuscript, Ohio State University, Columbus, OH.

Cacioppo, J. T., & Petty, R. E. (1982). The need for cognition. *Journal of Personality and Social Psychology, 42,* 116–131.

Cacioppo, J. T., Petty, R. E., Feinstein, J., & Jarvis, W. B. G. (1996). Dispositional differences in cognitive motivation: The life and times of individuals varying in need for cognition. *Psychological Bulletin, 119,* 197–253.

Cacioppo, J. T., Petty, R. E., Kao, C., & Rodriguez, R. (1986). Central and peripheral routes to persuasion: An individual difference perspective. *Journal of Personality and Social Psychology, 51,* 1032–1043.

Carver, C. S., Ganellen, R. J., Froming, W. J., & Chambers, W. (1983). Modeling: An analysis in terms of category accessibility. *Journal of Experimental Social Psychology, 19,* 403–421.

DeSteno, D., Petty, R. E., Rucker, D., & Wegener, D. T. (2000). Beyond valence in the perception of likelihood: The role of emotion specificity. *Journal of Personality and Social Psychology, 78,* 397–416

Dijksterhuis, A., & Cornielle, (1999). Unpublished manuscript. University of Nijmegen, Nijmengen, Netherlands.

Dijksterhuis, A., & van Knippenberg, A. (1998) The relation between perception and behavior, or how to win a game of Trivial Pursuit. *Journal of Personality and Social Psychology, 74,* 865–877.

Festinger, L. (1954). A theory of social comparison processes. *Human Relations, 7,* 117–140.

Forgas, J. P. (1995). Mood and judgment: The affect-infusion model (AIM). *Psychological Bulletin, 117,* 39–66.

Forgas, J. (Ed.). (2001). *Handbook of affect and social cognition.* Mahwah, NJ: Erlbaum.

Forgas, J. P., & Moylan, S. (1987). After the movies: The effects of mood on social judgments. *Personality and Social Psychology Bulletin, 13,* 467–477.

Hardin, C., & Higgins, E. T. (1996). Shared reality: How social verification makes the subjective objective. In R. M. Sorrentino & E. T. Higgins (Eds.), *Handbook of motivation and cognition: Foundations of social behavior* (pp. 2–84). New York: Guilford.

Hermans, D., & Eelen, P. (in press). A time analysis of the affective priming effect. *Cognition and Emotion.*

Herr, P. M. (1986). Consequences of priming: Judgment and behavior. *Journal of Personality and Social Psychology, 51,* 1106–1115.

Higgins, E. T. (1996). Knowledge activation: Accessibility, applicability, and salience. In E. T. Higgins & A. Kruglanski (Eds.) *Social psychology: Handbook of basic principles* (pp. 133–168). New York: Guilford.

Higgins, E. T., Rholes, W. S., & Jones, C. R. (1977). Category accessibility and impression formation. *Journal of Experimental Social Psychology*, *13*, 141–154.

Johnson, E., & Tversky, A. (1983). Affect, generalization, and the perception of risk. *Journal of Personality and Social Psychology, 45*, 20–31.

Levy, B. (1996). Improving memory in old age through implicit self-stereotyping. *Journal of Personality and Social Psychology, 71*, 1092–1107.

MaCrae, C. N., & Johnston, L. (1998) Help, I need somebody: Automatic action and inaction. *Social Cognition*, *16*, 400–417.

Martin, L. L., Seta, J. J., & Crelia, R. A. (1990). Assimilation and contrast as a function of people's willingness and ability to expend effort in forming an impression. *Journal of Personality and Social Psychology*, *59*, 27–37.

Mayer, J., Gaschke, Y., Braverman, D., & Evans, T. (1992). Mood-congruent judgment is a general effect. *Journal of Personality and Social Psychology*, *63*, 119–132.

Neuberg, S. L. (1988). Behavioral implications of information presented outside of conscious awareness: The effect of subliminal presentation of trait information on behavior in the prisoner's dilemma game. *Social Cognition*, *6*, 207–230.

Petty, R. E., Briñol, P., & Tormala, Z. (2000). *Self-validation and persuasion: The role of confidence in one's own cognitive responses.* Unpublished manuscript, Ohio State University, Columbus, OH.

Petty, R. E., & Cacioppo, J. T. (1979). Issue involvement can increase or decrease persuasion by enhancing message-relevant cognitive responses. *Journal of Personality and Social Psychology*, *37*, 1915–1926.

Petty, R. E., & Cacioppo, J. T. (1986). The Elaboration Likelihood Model of persuasion. In L. Berkowitz (Ed.), *Advances in experimental social psychology* (Vol. 19, pp. 123–205). New York: Academic.

Petty, R. E., DeSteno, D., & Rucker, D. (in press). The role of affect in attitude change. In J. Forgas (Ed.), *Handbook of affect and social cognition* (pp. 212–233). Mahwah, NJ: Erlbaum.

Petty, R. E., DeSteno, D., Rucker, D., & Wegener, D. (2000). Unpublished raw data. Department of psychology, Ohio State University, Columbus, OH.

Petty, R. E., Harkins, S. G., & Williams, K, D. (1980). The effects of group diffusion of cognitive effort on attitudes: An information processing view. *Journal of Personality and Social Psychology*, *38*, 81–92.

Petty, R. E., Haugtevdt, C., & Smith, S. M. (1995). Elaboration as a determinant of attitude strength: Creating attitudes that are persistent, resistant, and predictive of behavior. In R. E. Petty & J. A. Krosnick (Eds.), *Attitude strength: Antecedents and consequences* (pp. 93–130). Mahwah, NJ: Erlbaum.

Petty, R. E., & Jarvis, W. B. G. (1996). An individual differences perspective on assessing cognitive processes. In N. Schwarz & S. Sudman (Eds.), *Answering questions: Methodology for determining cognitive and communicative processes in survey research* (pp. 221–257). San Francisco: Jossey-Bass.

Petty, R. E., Schumann, D. M., Richman, S., & Strathman, A. J. (1993). Positive mood and persuasion: Different roles for affect under high and low elaboration conditions. *Journal of Personality and Social Psychology*, *64*, 5–20.

Petty, R. E., Strathman, A. J., & Bozzolo, A. (2000). Unpublished raw data. Department of psychology, Ohio State University, Columbus, OH.

Petty, R. E., & Wegener, D. T. (1991). Thought systems, argument quality, and persuasion. In R. S. Wyer & T. K. Srull (Eds.), *Advances in social cognition* (Vol. 4, pp. 147–161). Hillsdale, NJ: Erlbaum.

Petty, R. E., & Wegener, D. T. (1993). Flexible correction processes in social judgment: Correcting for context induced contrast. *Journal of Experimental Social Psychology*, *29*, 137–165.

Petty, R. E., & Wegener, D. T. (1999). The Elaboration Likelihood Model: Current status and controversies. In S. Chaiken & Y. Trope (Eds.), *Dual process theories in social psychology* (pp. 41–72). New York: Guilford.

Petty, R. E., Wells, G. L., & Brock, T. C. (1976). Distraction can enhance or reduce yielding to propaganda: Thought disruption versus effort justification. *Journal of Personality and Social Psychology, 34,* 874–884.

Schwarz, N., & Bless, H. (1992). Constructing reality and its alternatives: An inclusion/exclusion model of assimilation and contrast effects in social judgment. In L. L. Martin & A. Tesser (Eds.), *The construction of social judgments* (pp. 217–245). Hillsdale, NJ: Erlbaum.

Schwarz, N., Bless, H., & Bohner, G. (1991). Mood and persuasion: Affective states influence the processing of persuasive communications. In M. P. Zanna (Ed.), *Advances in experimental social psychology* (Vol. 24, pp. 161–201). San Diego, CA: Academic.

Shih, M., Pittinsky, T. L., & Ambady, N. (1999). Stereotype susceptibility: Identity salience and shifts in quantitative performance. *Psychological Science, 10,* 80–83.

Smith, S. M., Haugtvedt, C. P., & Petty, R. E. (1994). Need for cognition and the effects of repeated expression on attitude accessibility and extremity. *Advances in Consumer Research, 21,* 234-237.

Steele, C. M., & Aronson, J. (1995) Stereotype threat and the intellectual test performance of African-Americans. *Journal of Personality and Social Psychology, 69,* 797–811.

Strack, F. (1992). The different routes to social judgments: Experiential versus informational based strategies. In L. L. Martin & A. Tesser (Eds.), *The construction of social judgments* (pp. 249–275). Hillsdale, NJ: Erlbaum.

Turner, J. C. (1991). *Social influence.* London: Open University Press.

Wegener, D. T., & Petty, R. E. (1995). Flexible correction processes in social judgment: The role of naive theories in corrections for perceived bias. *Journal of Personality and Social Psychology, 68,* 36–51.

Wegener, D. T., & Petty, R. E. (1996). Effects of mood on persuasion processes: Enhancing, reducing, and biasing scrutiny of attitude-relevant information. In L. L. Martin & A. Tesser (Eds.). *Striving and feeling: Interactions between goals and affect* (pp. 329–362). Mahwah, NJ: Erlbaum.

Wegener, D. T., & Petty, R. E. (1997). The flexible correction model: The role of naive theories of bias in bias correction. In M. P. Zanna (Ed.), *Advances in experimental social psychology* (Vol., 29, pp. 141–208). San Diego, CA: Academic Press.

Wegener, D. T., Petty, R. E., Bedell, B., & Jarvis, W. B. G. (in press). Implications of attitude change theories for numerical anchoring: Anchor plausibility and the limits of anchor effectiveness. *Journal of Experimental Social Psychology.*

Wegener, D. T., Petty, R. E., & Klein, D. (1994). Effects of mood on high elaboration attitude change: The mediating role of likelihood judgments. *European Journal of Social Psychology, 23,* 25–44.

Wells, G. L., & Petty, R. E. (1980). The effects of overt head movements on persuasion: Compatibility and incompatibility of responses. *Basic and Applied Social Psychology, 1,* 219–230.

Wheeler, S. C., Jarvis, W. B. G., & Petty, R. E. (in press). Think unto others . . . : The self-destructive impact of negative racial stereotypes. *Journal of Experimental Social Psychology.*

Wheeler, S. C., & Petty, R. E. (2000). *The effects of stereotype activation on behavior: A review of possible mechanisms.* Unpublished manuscript. Ohio State University, Columbus, OH.

Wilson, T. D., & Brekke, N. (1994). Mental contamination and mental correction: Unwanted influences on judgments and evaluations, *Psychological Bulletin, 116,* 117–142.

9

On Being Moody but Influential
The Role of Affect in Social Influence Strategies

JOSEPH P. FORGAS

What is the role of affect in the way people select and execute various social influence strategies? Are happy or sad persons better at producing persuasive arguments? Does a happy mood predispose us to use more cooperative, lenient strategies when trying to influence others? Although affect obviously plays an important role in most aspects of interpersonal behavior (Forgas, 2001; Zajonc, 1980, 2000), the influence of moods on social

This work was supported by a Special Investigator award from the Australian Research Council, and the Research Prize by the Alexander von Humboldt Foundation to Joseph P. Forgas. The contribution of Joseph Ciarrochi, Stephanie Moylan, Patrick Vargas, and Joan Webb to this project is gratefully acknowledged.

    Address all correspondence to: Joseph P. Forgas, School of Psychology, University of New South Wales, Sydney 2052, Australia; E-mail jp.forgas@unsw.edu.au

influence strategies received relatively little attention in the past. This chapter argues that affective states play a significant role in the way various social influence strategies are planned and executed. A number of empirical studies demonstrating this link also are reviewed. In particular, three sets of experiments are described, demonstrating that low-intensity moods significantly impact on (1) the quality of persuasive arguments produced, (2) the use of, and responses to, requests, and (3) preferred negotiating strategies. Further, it is argued that these effects are largely moderated by the kind of information processing strategies people adopt when thinking about and planning their social influence strategies. A comprehensive theory relevant to these effects, the Affect Infusion Model also is described (Forgas, 1995a).

CONCEPTUAL BACKGROUND

The study of social influence processes has always been a core area of social psychology, and some of our most exciting and important research findings come from this field. It is all the more surprising, then, that few attempts have been made to explore the role that affective states and moods play in the way social influence strategies are planned, used, and responded to. Whether one considers research on conformity, obedience, bystander effects, or attitude change, few studies have explicitly looked at the role of affect in these phenomena (for some notable exceptions, see Petty, DeSteno, & Rucker, in press; Harmon-Jones, 2001).

Yet understanding how human beings use and respond to social influence is one of the key questions for psychology. Social living is only possible because we possess an elaborate capacity to employ and respond to complex social influence strategies. Modern industrial societies place greater pressures on us as we try to coordinate our behaviors and achieve our interpersonal objectives than has been the case in earlier times. Most of our social interactions now involve strangers and superficially known others. As a result, the frequently subconscious and automatic task of interpreting other people, and planning our interpersonal strategies has become far more complex and demanding (Goffman, 1972; Heider, 1958). Effectively using and responding to social influence thus requires ever-more sophisticated and elaborate cognitive processes.

The evidence reviewed here suggests that it is the very complexity and indeterminacy of many social encounters that enables affect to play a role in how people use, interpret, and respond to social influence. The principle appears to be that the more complex and ambiguous a social situation, the more likely that people will need to draw on their preexisting knowledge and engage in open, constructive thinking in order to plan and enact appropriate influence strategies. A number of theories as well as empirical studies now predict that such open, elaborate processing strategies are more likely to influenced by affective states (Forgas, 1995a, 2000, 2001).

How can we account for the relative absence of research on the role of affect in social influence processes? The lack of interest in this issue is all the more surprising if we consider that most people are intuitively aware that their feelings have a profound influence on their thoughts, judgments, and behaviors. Also philosophers and writers have also long been fascinated by the complex influence of affect on interpersonal relations. Many of these theorists saw affect as a dangerous, invasive force that tends to subvert rational thinking, and impairs the effective use of power and influence (Machiavelli, 1961). Within psychology, Freud's psychodynamic theories played a key role in emphasizing the dangerous, invasive character of affective impulses, suggesting that controlling affective states requires considerable countervailing psychological resources.

However, this view has been challenged during the last few decades as a result of important advances in neuroanatomy, psychophysiology, and social cognition research. Recent evidence suggests that affect is often a necessary and useful component of adequately responding to difficult social situations (Adolphs & Damasio, 2001; Damasio, 1994; Ito & Cacioppo, 2001). Unfortunately, a precise understanding of the mechanisms responsible for these effects has been slow to emerge. It was only during the last two decades that empirical research on the role of affect in social behaviors has been in the ascendancy. Most of what we now know about the role of affect in social thinking and behavior has been discovered since the early 1980s. A key objective of contemporary research, and this chapter in particular, is to consider how, when, and why affective states influence interpersonal behavior and influence strategies. As a first step, some of the early research and theories illustrating affective influences on social behaviors are reviewed. A recent multiprocess theory, the Affect Infusion Model ([AIM], Forgas, 1995a) is outlined as a comprehensive account of how, when, and why affective states will or will not impact on social influence processes. The second half of the chapter presents empirical evidence demonstrating the role of affect in a variety of social influence processes.

BACKGROUND RESEARCH ON AFFECT AND SOCIAL INFLUENCE

In the early 1980s, psychologists such as Zajonc (1980, 2000) argued that affective reactions often constitute the primary and dominant influence on dealing with social situations, and function as an independent and often dominant force in determining people's social strategies and responses. According to this view, affect is not just one of the three faculties of the human mind—and a relatively neglected one at that—but one of the primary forces driving most interpersonal behaviors. Several lines of evidence seem to support such a view. Affective reactions certainly seem to play a primary role in determining how people evaluate everyday social situations (Forgas, 1979, 1982), and how they categorize social stimuli (Niedenthal & Halberstadt, 2000).

In one early study, Razran (1940) found that affect had a significant mood-congruent effect on how people responded to social influence attempts such as persuasion: Those in a good mood responded more positively than those in a bad mood. In another experiment testing psychoanalytic predictions, Feshbach and Singer (1957) predicted that attempts to suppress affect should increase the 'pressure' for affect to infuse unrelated behaviors and judgments. As expected, participants fearing electric shocks were more likely to see "another person as fearful and anxious" (p. 286), and this effect was greater when participants were instructed to suppress their fear. Feshbach and Singer (1957) argued that "suppression of fear facilitates the tendency to project fear onto another social object" (p. 286).

Conditioning researchers, such as Byrne and Clore (1970) suggested that it is incidental associations between affective states and other stimuli that significantly influence how we respond to people. For example, the positive or negative moods elicited by pleasant or aversive environments could be readily associated with a person encountered in that environment, producing more or less positive evaluative responses to the person (Gouaux, 1971; Griffitt, 1970). Unfortunately, neither the psychoanalytic nor conditioning theories could offer a convincing explanation of exactly how, why, and when affect infusion occurs. It was not until the emergence of cognitive information processing theories in recent years that we gained a better understanding of the psychological mechanisms that link affect, cognition, and interpersonal behaviors involving social influence.

Contemporary Explanations Linking Affect and Interpersonal Behavior

Two theories linking affect to judgments have received empirical support. The affect-as-information model (Schwarz & Clore, 1988) argues that people sometimes directly use their prevailing affective state as information in inferring their responses to social situations. The alternative affect priming theory predicts that affect will influence the outcome of social judgments and behaviors through selectively priming and making more accessible affect-related constructs (Bower, 1981; Bower & Forgas, in press).

According to the affect-as-information theory, when responding to a social situation, "rather than computing a judgment on the basis of recalled features of a target, individuals may . . . ask themselves: 'How do I feel about it?' . . . and . . . in doing so, they may mistake feelings due to a preexisting state as a reaction to the target" (Schwarz, 1990, p. 529). Thus, affective states influence attitudes and behaviors because of an inferential error: People may misread their prevailing affective states and may misattribute it to an unrelated person or situation, as long as the cause of the affective state is not salient at the time. This strategy is most likely when people lack sufficient interest, motivation, or resources to compute a more elaborate response. Most situations involving social influence are likely to involve some degree of inferential processing, even if the thinking is often automatic and subconscious. We need a complementary theory, such as the affect priming model, to explain affect infusion and mood congruence in such more elaborately processed situations. (Throughout this chapter, we will use the term 'affect infusion' to denote the process, and 'affect congruence' or 'mood congruence' to denote the outcome of such processes.)

The affect priming theory proposed by Bower (1981) suggests that all representations about the social world, including affective states, are integrally linked within an associative network of memory. The experience of an affective state should thus automatically prime associated ideas and memories, and these are more likely to be used in constructive social and interpersonal tasks (e.g., Bower, 1981; Clark & Isen, 1982; Forgas & Bower, 1987; Isen, 1984, 1987). However, affect priming is not a universal phenomenon (Eich & Macauley, 2000; Forgas, 1995a). It is most likely when actors face a complex and demanding social situation that requires open, constructive processing that facilitates the incidental use of affectively primed information (Fiedler, 1991, 2000; Forgas, 1995a; Sedikides, 1995). Recent integrative theories such as the Affect Infusion Model (Forgas, 1995a) argue that the nature and extent of affective influences on social behavior largely depends on the kind of information processing strategy people employ.

Affect and Information Processing Strategies

It turns out that affect may not only influence the content of cognition and thus subsequent behaviors, but may also impact on the *process* of cognition, that is, how people deal with social information (Clark & Isen, 1982; Fiedler & Forgas, 1988). Generally, people in a positive affective state tend to use less effortful and more superficial processing strategies, reach decisions more quickly, use less information, avoid demanding, systematic thinking, and are more confident about their responses. In contrast, negative affect frequently triggers a more effortful, systematic, analytic, and vigilant processing style (Clark & Isen, 1982; Isen, 1984, 1987; Schwarz, 1990). However, positive affect also can produce distinct processing advantages. People in a positive mood often adopt more creative, open, constructive, and inclusive thinking styles, and show greater cognitive and behavioral flexibility (Bless, 2000; Fiedler, 2000). These effects probably reflect the evolutionary role of positive and negative affect in triggering different processing styles (Higgins, 2001). Feeling good promotes a more assimilative, schema-based, top-down processing style, while negative affect produces a more accommodative, bottom-up, and externally-focussed processing strategy (Bless, 2000; Fiedler, 2000; Higgins, 2001). These mood effects on thinking should have significant implications for the way people exercise and respond to social influence, such as persuasive arguments, requests, or negotiations, as the research reviewed in this chapter suggests.

The Affect Infusion Model (AIM).   Affect thus has a complex influence on both the content, and the process of the way people interpret social situations and plan strategic interpersonal behaviors (Forgas, 2000, in press-a). A comprehensive theory of these effects should specify the circumstances that promote or inhibit affect congruence, and also should define the processing conditions that lead to affect priming, or affect-as-information processes. The AIM (Forgas, 1995a; 2001) accomplished this by predicting that affect infusion should only occur in circumstances that promote an open, constructive processing style (Fiedler, 1991; Forgas, 1992b, 1995b). Constructive processing may be defined as those cognitive tasks that involve the active elaboration and transformation of the available stimulus information, require the activation and use of previous knowledge structures, and result in the creation of new knowledge from the combination of stored information and new stimulus details. The AIM has been adequately described elsewhere; only a brief overview is included here (Forgas, 1992a, 1995a, 2001, in press).

The AIM identifies four alternative processing strategies people may use when responding to a social situation: *direct access, motivated, heuristic,* and substantive processing. These four strategies differ in terms of two basic dimensions: the degree of cognitive effort exerted in seeking a solution, and the degree of openness of the information search strategy (actively seeking and using new information to construct a response). The combination of these two processing dimensions, quantity (effort), and quality (openness) produces four distinct processing styles: (1) substantive processing (high effort/open), (2) motivated processing (high effort/closed), (3) heuristic processing (low effort/open, constructive), and (4) direct access processing (low effort/closed). Affect infusion is most likely when a constructive strategy is used, such as substantive or heuristic processing, as these strategies are most likely to require the use of novel information. In contrast, affect infusion is unlikely when a task calls for highly directed and predetermined motivated or direct access processing (see also Fiedler, 1990, 1991).

The direct access strategy involves the direct retrieval of a preexisting response, and is most likely when the task is highly familiar, and when no strong cognitive, affective, situational, or motivational cues call for more elaborate processing. Producing such a preformed response requires no constructive processing so affect infusion should not occur. The motivated processing strategy involves highly selective and targeted thinking that is dominated by a particular motivational objective. This strategy also precludes open information search, and should be impervious to affect infusion (Clark & Isen, 1982). However, motivated processing may also produce a reversal of mood congruence effects (Berkowitz, Jaffee, Jo, & Troccoli, 2000; Forgas, 1991; Forgas & Fiedler, 1996).

In contrast, both heuristic and substantive processing require constructive thinking and thus may facilitate affect infusion. Heuristic processing is most likely when the task is simple, familiar, and of little personal relevance, and when cognitive capacity is limited, there are no motivational pressures for more detailed processing, and there are no 'direct access' responses to fall back on. Heuristic processing can produce affect infusion when people rely on the 'how do I feel about it' heuristics to produce a response (Clore, Gasper, & Garvin, in press; Schwarz & Clore, 1988). In most realistic influence situations people will actually need to engage in substantive processing that requires them to rely on their preexisting memory-based knowledge to produce a response (although this processing may often be subconscious; see this volume, chapters by Cialdini, Dijsksterhuis, Petty, and Ng for some relevant examples). Substantive processing is likely when the task is demanding, atypical, complex, novel, or personally relevant, and when there are no direct access responses available, and no clear motivational goals to guide processing. The AIM makes the interesting and counterintuitive prediction that affect infusion (and mood congruence) should be greater when more extensive processing is required to deal with a more complex, demanding, or novel task (Fiedler & Stroehm, 1986; Forgas, 1992b; 1993; 1995b; 1998a,b; Forgas & Bower, 1987).

The AIM also specifies how features of the task, the person, and the situation influence processing choices, and recognizes that affect itself can influence processing choices (for details, see Forgas, 1995a). The two key predictions of the AIM when applied to social influence phenomena are that (1) positive and negative moods should influence the effectiveness of influence strategies because these moods recruit different thinking styles that are more or less attuned to situational information; and (2) there should be an absence of affect infusion when direct access or motivated processing is used, and a presence of affect infusion during heuristic and substantive processing. The implications of this model have now been tested in a number of experiments, as the next section summarizes.

AFFECT AND SOCIAL INFLUENCE STRATEGIES: THE EMPIRICAL EVIDENCE

Feeling Good and Being Persuasive? Affect and Persuasive Communication

As the previous review suggests, positive affect often promotes a more top-down, schema-driven processing style, while negative mood recruits a more bottom-up strategy that pays more attention to the available stimulus information (Bless, 2000; Fiedler, 2000). These effects can have important consequences. For example, judgmental mistakes such as the fundamental attribution error tend to be reduced when people experience negative affect (Forgas, 1998c). This seems to occur because aversive mood makes people pay greater attention to situational information and process their responses in a more careful, piecemeal fashion. It may be that negative affect also has a corresponding beneficial influence on the production of some social influence strategies that require attention to situational details, such as the generation of higher quality persuasive messages.

What role does mood play in the production of persuasive messages? Language is perhaps the most ubiquitous and flexible medium of social influence (see also Ng, this volume; Williams & Dolnik, this volume), allowing almost unlimited scope for creating more or less direct persuasive strategies. There has been extensive research on affective influences on the way persuasive messages are received (Petty, DeSteno, & Rucker, in press; Petty, this volume). However, very little is known about the complementary question: What is the role of affect in the way persuasive messages are produced and used? One possible reason is that the psychology of how persuasive messages are received is of greater practical importance in marketing and advertising than understanding the psychology of message production. Affective influences on message production are of less interest to professional persuaders than are the mental processes of the intended recipients. However, amateur persuaders—and this includes all of us—must produce their persuasive strategies on-line, and be responsive to the feedback they receive from their interlocutors.

Several recent experiments looked at this question. In the first study, 59 volunteer students participants were induced into positive or negative mood by watching short videotapes, described as part of a separate experiment. The happy tape showed excerpts from a popular comedy series, and the sad film dealt with death from cancer. After the mood induction, participants were asked to persuade an acquaintance either to support, or reject two propositions: that student fees should be increased, and that Aboriginal land rights should be extended in Australia. On both of these issues the majority of students had a preferred view (against fees, and for land rights). Each participant produced persuasive arguments on both topics, arguing the popular position on one issue and the unpopular position on the other. Persuasive arguments were written down and were subsequently rated by two trained judges who achieved an inter-rater reliability of .86 on three 10-point scales (argument quality, persuasiveness, and positive-negative valence). As the quality and persuasiveness measures were strongly correlated ($r = .78$), these two measures were combined.

The mood induction was highly effective; those in the happy and sad conditions rated their mood as substantially different. Mood also had a strong influence on argument quality. Those in a negative mood produced significantly higher quality and more persuasive arguments than did those in a happy mood. Issue popularity had no main or interactive effect on argument quality; thus, sad mood increased the quality of arguments irrespective of the issues argued or the popularity of the position taken. An analysis of variance of the second dependent variable, argument valence, showed that there was a nonsignificant trend towards a mood-congruent pattern, as happy persons tended to produce more positive, and sad persons produced more negative, arguments.

These results showed that negative mood improved, and positive mood impaired the quality of persuasive arguments produced. In a second, follow-up experiment we used a similar procedure and included a neutral mood condition. Immediately after the video mood induction, participants produced persuasive arguments for or against Australia becoming a republic, and for or against a right-wing party, the One Nation party. The majority of students were against the One Nation party, and supported the republic. Students argued the popular position on one issue and the unpopular position on the other issue. The arguments produced were again rated on three characteristics using ten-point ratings scales by raters who achieved an inter-rater reliability of .91 (persuasive-ness/argument quality; valence [positive-negative], and self-relevance). The to-tal number of arguments (quantity) also was recorded.

The mood induction was again highly effective. Several theoretically inter-esting effects also emerged. There were more arguments produced when advo-cating a popular position, and these arguments were higher in quality and more self-referential than in the unpopular condition. However, the arguments pro-posed for the unpopular position were more positive in valence, as if students tried to produce more positive statements to compensate for the unpopularity of the position they were advocating. Of greater interest is that mood again had a highly significant influence on argument quality. Students in a sad mood pro-duced arguments that were rated as higher in quality and more persuasive than arguments produced by happy students, with an intermediate performance by the neutral group (Fig. 9.1).

This is an interesting finding, and confirms that even minor changes in mood induced by viewing a videotape can have a significant impact on the qual-ity and likely effectiveness of the persuasive messages produced. This result is consistent with theoretical predictions derived from the AIM and other theo-ries (Bless, 2000; Fiedler, 2000; Forgas, 1995a) that predict that negative mood should promote a more careful, systematic processing style more attuned to the requirements of a particular situation. We might expect, for example, that people in a negative mood would be better at tailoring their persuasive messages to particular audiences than people in a good mood. Such a mood-induced pro-cessing dichotomy was further supported by the finding that happy participants produced markedly more self-relevant and personal arguments than did sad participants (Fig. 9.1). This is what one would expect according to recent affect/cognition theories that predict that positive affect should promote a less situationally focused and more schematic processing style (Bless, 2000; Fiedler, 2000). Such arguments appear to be more personal and self-relevant, but also less effective and persuasive, as we have found here.

Finally, there also was some evidence for a significant mood congruency effect in argumentation (Fig. 9.1). Participants in a positive mood produced more arguments with a positive affective tone than did subjects in a negative mood, a mood-congruent pattern also found in other studies (Bower & Forgas, 2001; Forgas, 1992a, 1993, 1995b; Forgas & Bower, 1987). This experiment thus confirmed that affect can have a significant influence on the quality of social influence strategies such as persuasive arguments. The absence of an interaction between mood and issue popularity suggests that the psychological mechanisms responsible for these outcomes are likely to be quite robust.

In the next, third study, the same procedure was repeated but this time we used a different mood induction method to establish that the phenomenon can be obtained irrespective of the particular mood induction used. An autobio-graphical method was used, asking participants to recall and write down posi-tive or negative episodes from the past, before performing the persuasive argu-mentation task. Results in this third study largely mirrored the findings obtained

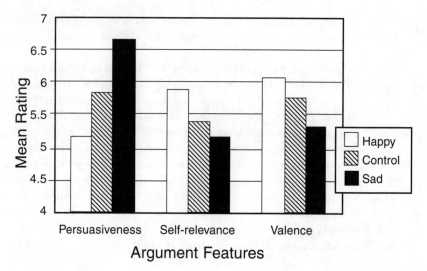

FIGURE 9.1. Affective influences on the production of persuasive messages: People in a negative mood produce more persuasive and higher quality messages; but a positive mood increases the rated originality and creativity of persuasive messages. There also is a tendency for people to rely on more mood-congruent arguments when formulating persuasive communication (unpublished data).

in the two earlier experiments, and are not described in detail here. They help to establish however that the pattern of results obtained in the first study is robust and replicable.

Although these experiments produced consistent results, they also suffer from some shortcomings. The arguments were produced in a hypothetical situation and there was no real social interaction. Participants also did not receive any feedback as is often the case in real-life interactions. To deal with these issues, in Experiment 4 participants interacted with a 'partner' through a computer keyboard as if exchanging emails, and produced their persuasive arguments using this medium. In fact, the computer was preprogrammed to 'respond' to persuasive messages in standard ways indicating agreement or disagreement. The AIM also predicts that strong motivational pressures should produce motivated processing and thus reduce affective influences. To test this, Experiment 4 also manipulated the motivation to be persuasive, by offering some participants a significant reward (the chance to win highly desired movie passes). Finally, Experiment 4 also used a different, false feedback mood induction procedure. In a 'spatial-numerical test,' participants performed a series of size, shape, and frequency estimation tasks, and received manipulated feedback about their good or bad performance to induce positive or negative mood (see Forgas, 1998c).

After the mood induction, participants were told that the communication task involved trying to persuade another student to volunteer for an unrelated subsequent experiment. Half the participants were promised a substantial reward (movie passes). The interaction was described as part of a 'mediated communication exercise' carried out through the computer keyboard with the other subject seated in a neighboring room in order to "reduce interference from unwanted variables such as physical appearance." Participants also were told that the procedure required that their partner could only use a very limited range of standard sentences in responding to their messages, and were not allowed to write anything else. The 'allowed' messages were in fact programmed into the computer, typed one letter at the time to simulate a human partner, and communicated increasingly positive, accepting or increasingly negative, rejecting reactions to the participant's persuasive messages (see Table 9.1 for a summary of these responses). All students readily accepted this explanation.

The instructions stated that in trying to persuade the other student to volunteer for the experiment, participants should start by writing three persuasive arguments, wait for a response, and then write one argument at a time and wait for the response. In fact, each participant was allowed to produce eight arguments in total before the procedure was terminated. The eight arguments were divided into three categories: the initial three arguments, before any feedback was received, the middle two arguments, and the final three arguments. Responses from the 'partner' were either accepting, indicating increasing persuasion, or rejecting, indicating increasing rejection (Table 9.1). Two raters blind to the manipulations rated each argument for quality, complexity, persuasiveness, originality, and valence and achieved an inter-rater reliability of .82 or higher on each of these measures.

The mood induction was highly successful. There also was significant overall mood main effect on argument quality. The negative mood group generated higher quality arguments than the neutral group who in turn did better than the positive group. Further analyses evaluated the effects of mood on argument originality while controlling for argument quality. We also looked at the effect

TABLE 9.1. Positive, Encouraging or Negative, Discouraging
Feedback Sentences

Trial	Encouraging condition	Discouraging condition
1	I am not sure whether or not I like or agree with what you are saying.	I am not sure whether or not I like or agree with what you are saying
2	I somewhat like and agree with what you are saying	I somewhat dislike and disagree with what you are saying
3	I somewhat like and agree with what you are saying	I somewhat dislike and disagree with what you are saying
4	I like and agree with what you are saying	I dislike and disagree with what you are saying.
5	I like and agree with what you are saying	I dislike and disagree with what you are saying.
6	OK, I know I'm not supposed to say this, but I have decided to do the study	OK, I know I'm not supposed to say this, but I have decided not tot do the study

of mood on quality while controlling for originality. The analysis of covariance again revealed a strong mood effect on the quality of arguments; however, originality was a significant covariate. This mood effect was further qualified by a clear interaction with the reward condition. Mood had a greater effect on argument quality in the low reward condition than the high reward condition.

In the low reward condition the negative mood group produced higher quality arguments than the neutral mood group, who in turn produced higher quality arguments than the positive group. None of the groups were significantly different in the high reward condition. This finding confirms a key prediction of the AIM, that mood effects on information processing—and subsequent social influence strategies—are strongest in the absence of motivated processing, such as the existence of a strong reward to perform well. Negative mood improved argument quality, but only when there was no external reward. The provision of a reward eliminated mood effects on argument quality by imposing a strong external influence on how the task was approached, and thereby overriding more subtle internal mood effects.

An analysis of argument originality while controlling for argument quality also showed a significant mood main effect, again qualified by a clear interaction between mood and reward. Mood had a marked effect on argument originality only in the low, but not the high reward condition. Those in a negative mood group produced fewer original arguments than the neutral mood group and the neutral mood group produced less original arguments that the positive mood group. This result is consistent with theoretical predictions suggesting that positive affect promotes a more creative, flexible, and internally focused processing style—hence greater argument originality—even though the overall quality and persuasiveness of arguments was higher in negative mood.

These experiments thus provide convergent evidence that slight changes in incidental mood can produce profound differences in the quality and effectiveness of the persuasive arguments people produce as part of their social influence strategies. The robustness of these mood effects is confirmed by the fact that similar results were obtained in both hypothetical situations and in realistic interactions, with a variety of attitude topics, using a range of different mood induction procedures, and irrespective of the popularity and social desirability of the position argued. The fourth experiment also showed that mood effects on argument quality can be reduced when a strong external motivation is provided to participants. Experiment four also found that even though negative mood produced higher quality and more persuasive arguments, positive mood had a beneficial effect on the originality and creativity of the arguments.

These results make sense in terms of our theoretical predictions, and the implications of the AIM in particular. This is just what we would expect if negative mood led to a more careful, situationally focused and bottom-up information processing style. This kind of processing can produce more persuasive and higher quality—although less creative and original—verbal arguments in social influence tasks. Other influence strategies, such as the use of direct verbal requests, can also be influenced by mood as the next section shows.

AFFECTIVE INFLUENCES ON THE USE OF REQUESTS

In addition to influencing the quality of persuasive arguments, affect can also have a mood-congruent, informational effect on compliance-gaining strategies such as the formulation of requests. Requesting—asking a person to do something for us—is almost always a difficult and complex interpersonal task (Gibbs, 1985). People must phrase their request with great care so as to maximize the likelihood of compliance (by being more direct), without risking giving offense (by not being too direct; see also Knowles, Butler, & Linn, this volume). Requesting thus involves inherent ambiguity and conflict and typically requires some degree of constructive, substantive processing. We expected that positive mood should selectively prime positive associations and thus produce a more confident, direct requesting style, and negative mood should lead to more cautious, polite requests.

In one study mood was induced by asking participants to recall and think about happy or sad autobiographical episodes (Forgas, 1999a, Exp. 1). Next, participants were asked to select more or less polite request forms they would use in an easy, and in a difficult request situation. As predicted, happy participants preferred more direct, impolite requests, while sad persons selected cautious, indirect, polite request alternatives. As predicted by the AIM, mood effects on requesting were stronger when the request situation was more difficult, and thus required more substantive processing. In a follow-up experiment, happy or sad participants were asked to produce their own open-ended requests, which were subsequently rated for politeness and elaboration (Forgas, 1999a, Exp. 2). Again, those in a positive mood produced requests that were rated as more direct, impolite and less elaborate than the requests used by individuals in a negative mood. These mood effects also were greater when the request situation was more difficult and problematic. In a further study participants (who were feeling happy or sad after watching videotapes) selected from more or less polite requests the alternatives they would prefer to use in a variety of realistic social situations (Forgas, 1999b, Exp. 1). We found that affective influences on request preferences were greatest on decisions about using direct, impolite, and unconventional requests that most clearly violate cultural conventions of politeness, and should recruit the most substantive, elaborate processing strategies. In all of these instances, more substantive processing recruited by more difficult request situations actually increased the extent of mood effects.

In order to establish the external validity of this phenomenon, a further experiment used unobtrusive methods to test how affect influences naturally produced requests (Forgas, 1999b, Exp. 2). After viewing happy or sad films, in an apparently impromptu development the experimenter asked participants to get a file from a neighboring office while the next stage was being set up. All participants agreed. The words used in requesting the file were recorded by a concealed tape recorder in the neighboring office, and the requests were subsequently analyzed for politeness and other qualities. We found a strong affective influence on these requests. Negative mood resulted in requests that were

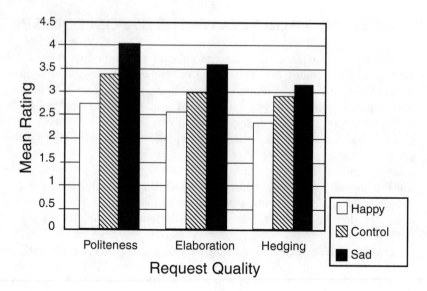

FIGURE 9.2. Mood effects on the level of politeness, elaboration, and hedging in naturally produced requests: Positive mood produces less polite, less elaborate, and less hedging requests in a naturalistic situation (data based on Forgas, 1999b).

rated as more polite, elaborate, hedging, and indirect; positive mood in turn produced less polite, less elaborate, and less hedging and more direct requests (Fig. 9.2). Those in a negative mood also were more hesitant, and delayed making their requests much longer than did control, or happy persons.

In order to assess processing styles while producing requests, participants' recall memory for the exact words used also was assessed. Greater recall accuracy—indicating more elaborate and detailed processing—was positively and significantly related to the degree of mood effects on request preferences. This finding supports the prediction based on the AIM that affect infusion should be greater when more elaborate, substantive processing is used. These results confirm that affect plays a critical role in social influence behaviors, with negative mood producing higher quality persuasive arguments, but more cautious, hesitant, polite, and hedging interpersonal behaviors.

THE ROLE OF AFFECT IN PERCEIVING SOCIAL SITUATIONS AND RESPONDING TO SOCIAL INFLUENCE

Affective influences on active influence strategies are not the whole story, however. Affect has an even more pervasive impact on how influence situations are interpreted, and ultimately, responded to. As the perception and interpretation of social behaviors is a highly constructive task, affect priming should influence how various social acts are evaluated. This principle was confirmed in a study assessing the role of affect in how social behaviors are perceived and interpreted (Forgas, Bower, & Krantz, 1984). Positive or negative moods were induced using a hypnotic mood induction procedure. Participants then watched a videotape of their own social interactions with a partner from the previous day. Happy people identified far more positive, skilled behaviors and fewer negative, unskilled behaviors both in themselves and in their partners than did sad subjects. Objective raters who viewed the same encounters showed no such distortions.

These findings show that changes in mood state can have a disproportionate influence on how people perceive social influence situations. Observed behaviors require inferential processing and interpretation to be understood (Heider, 1958). The mind-set that observers bring to the task—influenced by their affective state and their affectively primed thoughts and associations—is thus likely to have a significant impact. As this study suggests, even simple, relatively unambiguous behaviors such as a smile or a nod that may appear 'friendly' when the observer is in a good mood may well be judged as 'awkward' or 'condescending' when the observer experiences negative affect.

Other studies also evaluated the influence of affect on how people deal with interpersonal conflicts (Forgas, 1994). In these experiments, partners were induced to feel good or bad, and then made judgments about their preferred social influence strategies in various real-life relationship conflicts. Negative affect produced a more critical and pessimistic approach to conflicts; positive affect in turn resulted in more optimistic and lenient responses. These mood effects were significantly greater when the conflicts were more complex and involved rather than simple and routine. As serious conflicts require more elaborate, substantive processing the likelihood of affect infusion also is greater (Forgas, 1995a). The more constructively we need to think to respond to a social situation, the more likely that affectively primed thoughts and ideas will influence our reactions.

Ultimately affect may influence not only compliance gaining strategies of influence agents, such as the quality of requests and persuasive messages, but also how people respond to real-life influence attempts, such as receiving an unexpected request (Forgas, 1998b). Responding to such approaches requires a rapid behavioral reaction based on the constructive cognitive processing of the situation that may be highly mood sensitive. In a study done in a university library, affect was induced by leaving mood-induction folders containing pretested pictures (or text) designed to induce positive or negative mood on some unoccupied library desks. Arriving students were surreptitiously observed to ensure that they fully exposed themselves to the mood induction (almost everybody did). Soon afterwards, they were approached by another student (in fact, a confederate) and received an unexpected polite or impolite request for several sheets of paper needed to complete an essay. Their responses were noted. A short time later, a second confederate explained that the request was in fact staged, and asked participants to evaluate the request and the requester, and their recall of the request. There was a clear mood-congruent pattern: Negative mood resulted in a more critical, negative attitude to the request and the requester and less compliance than did positive mood. These mood effects were greater when the request was impolite rather than polite, presumably because impolite, unconventional requests are likely to require more elaborate and substantive processing. This explanation was confirmed by better recall memory for these impolite messages later on. Routine, polite requests in turn were processed less substantively, were less influenced by mood, and also were remembered less well later on.

AFFECT INFUSION IN PLANNED STRATEGIC ENCOUNTERS

Affective states might play a particularly important role in elaborately planned influence strategies that people use in complex negotiating encounters (Forgas, 1998a). We tested this by first giving participants positive, negative, or neutral feedback about their performance on a verbal test to induce mood. Participants then engaged in an informal, interpersonal, and a formal, intergroup negotiating task with other individuals or groups in what they thought was a separate experiment. Those in a positive mood formulated more optimistic, cooperative, and integrative action plans, actually behaved less competitively, were more willing to use integrative strategies such as making deals, and as a result proved to be more successful at this task (Fig. 9.3). Why do these effects occur? An

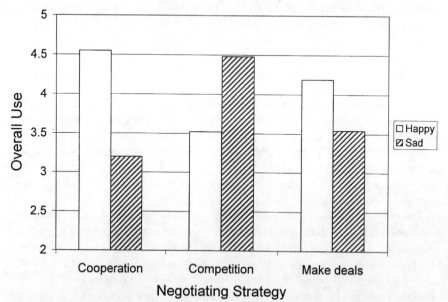

FIGURE 9.3. The effects of mood on bargaining and negotiation strategies: Positive mood increases cooperation and the willingness to make deals, and negative mood increases competitive strategies both in interpersonal, and intergroup negotiation (data based on Forgas, 1998a).

unpredictable social encounter such as a negotiation requires open, constructive processing in order to formulate bargaining plans. Negotiators must go beyond the information given and rely on their thoughts and memories to construct a strategy. Affect can selectively prime affect-congruent thoughts and associations, and these ideas in turn influence the formulation of their attitudes, plans, and behaviors.

We found that affect infusion also was moderated by individual differences between negotiators. People who had high scores on measures such as machiavellism and need for approval were less influenced by mood than were low scorers on these measures. As implied by the AIM, affect infusion was constrained for high-scoring individuals who habitually approach interpersonal tasks such as a bargaining encounter from a highly motivated, predetermined perspective. It seems that individual differences that predict the motivated processing of social information—such as self-esteem, social anxiety, and the like—tend to significantly moderate affective influences on social cognition and behavior (Ciarocchi & Forgas, 1999, in press; Rusting, 1998; 2001).

Overall, these results show that affect has a significant influence not only on people's constructive interpretation of social situations, but also on their subsequent strategic interpersonal behaviors. These findings also confirm that the role of affect in social influence strategies is highly process dependent: Affect infusion is increased or reduced depending on just how much open, constructive processing is used to deal with a more or less demanding interpersonal task, and how motivated people are to engage in the task.

CONCLUSION

It seems that mild everyday moods can have a significant effect on how people interpret social situations, and how they use and respond to social influence attempts. These experiments found that feeling good or feeling bad has a marked effect on the quality and originality of the persuasive messages produced, the directness of requests, and the cooperativeness of bargaining strategies. Different information processing strategies play a key role in explaining these effects, as suggested by the AIM (Forgas, 1995a). In general, more extensive, substantive processing recruited by more difficult interpersonal tasks enhanced mood-congruity effects (Forgas, 1992b; 1994; 1995b). In contrast, affect infusion is absent when a task could be performed using a simple direct access strategy, or a highly motivated strategy. In these conditions, there is less of opportunity for affectively primed thoughts to influence the outcome (Fiedler, 1991; Forgas, 1995a).

Several of these experiments also demonstrated that affect infusion into social influence processes occurs not only in the laboratory, but also in many real-life situations. Even dealing with relationship conflicts can be subject to significant mood-congruent bias (Forgas, 1994). Consistent with the arguments of this book, the evidence reviewed here clearly suggests that a full understand-

164 SOCIAL INFLUENCE

ing of how social influence strategies operate requires careful attention to the cognitive processes of influence agents, as well as recipients. Obviously a great deal more research is needed before we can fully understand the multiple influences that affect has on social judgments and strategic interpersonal behaviors; hopefully this chapter will stimulate further interest in this fascinating and rapidly developing area of inquiry.

REFERENCES

Adolphs, R., & Damasio, A. (2001). The interaction of affect and cognition: A neurobiological perspective. In J. P. Forgas (Ed.). *The handbook of affect and social cognition* (pp. 27–50). Mahwah, NJ: Erlbaum.

Allport, G. W. (1954). *The nature of prejudice*. Reading, MA: Addison-Wesley.

Berkowitz, L., Jaffee, S., Jo, E., & Troccoli, B. T. (2000). On the correction of feeling-induced judgmental biases. In J. P. Forgas (Ed.), *Feeling and thinking: The role of affect in social cognition* (pp. 131–152). New York: Cambridge University Press.

Bless, H. (2000). The interplay of affect and cognition: The mediating role of general knowledge structures. In: J. P. Forgas (Ed.), *Feeling and thinking: The role of affect in social cognition* (pp. 201–222). New York: Cambridge University Press.

Bower, G. H. (1981). Mood and memory. *American Psychologist, 36*, 129–148.

Bower, G. H., & Forgas, J. P. (2001). Mood and Social Memory. In J. P. Forgas (Ed.), *The handbook of affect and social cognition*. Mahwah, NJ: Erlbaum.

Byrne, D., & Clore, G. L. (1970). A reinforcement model of evaluation responses. *Personality: An International Journal, 1*, 103–128.

Ciarrochi, J. V., & Forgas, J. P. (1999). On being tense yet tolerant: The paradoxical effects of trait anxiety and aversive mood on intergroup judgments. *Group dynamics: Theory, research and practice, 3*, 227–238.

Ciarrochi, J. V., & Forgas, J. P. (in press). The pleasure of possessions: Affect and consumer judgments. *European Journal of Social Psychology*.

Clark, M. S., & Isen, A. M. (1982). Towards understanding the relationship between feeling states and social behavior. In A. H. Hastorf & A. M. Isen (Eds.), *Cognitive so-cial psychology* (pp. 73–108). New York: Elsevier-North Holland.

Clore, G. L., Gasper, K. & Garvin, E. (2001). Affect as information. In J. P. Forgas (Ed.), *The handbook of affect and social cognition* (pp. 121–145). Mahwah, N J: Erlbaum.

Damasio, A. R. (1994). *Descartes' error*. New York: Grosste/Putnam.

Eich, E., & Macauley, D. (2000). Fundamental factors in mood-dependent memory. In J. P. Forgas (Ed.), *Feeling and thinking: The role of affect in social cognition* (pp. 109–130). New York: Cambridge University Press.

Feshbach, S., & Singer, R. D. (1957). The effects of fear arousal and suppression of fear upon social perception. *Journal of Abnormal and Social Psychology, 55*, 283–288.

Fiedler, K. (1990). Mood-dependent selectivity in social cognition. In W. Stroebe & M. Hewstone (Eds.), *European review of social psychology* (Vol. 1, pp. 1–32). New York: Wiley.

Fiedler, K. (1991). On the task, the measures and the mood in research on affect and social cognition. In J. P. Forgas (Ed.), *Emotion and social judgments* (pp. 83–104). Oxford, England: Pergamon.

Fiedler, K. (2000). Towards an integrative account of affect and cognition phenomena using the BIAS computer algorithm. In J. P. Forgas (Ed.), *Feeling and thinking: The role of affect in social cognition*. New York: Cambridge University Press.

Fiedler, K., & Forgas, J. P. (1988) (Eds.). *Affect, cognition, and social behavior: New evidence and integrative attempts* (pp. 44–62). Toronto: Hogrefe.

Fiedler, K., & Stroehm, W. (1986). What kind of mood influences what kind of memory: The role of arousal and information structure. *Memory and Cognition, 14,* 181–188.

Forgas, J. P. (1979). *Social episodes: The study of interaction routines.* London: Academic.

Forgas, J .P. (1982). Episode cognition: Internal representations of interaction routines. In L. Berkowitz (Ed.) *Advances in Experimental Social Psychology* (Vol. 15, pp. 59–101). New York: Academic.

Forgas, J. P. (1991). Mood effects on partner choice: Role of affect in social decisions. *Journal of Personality and Social Psychology, 61,* 708–720.

Forgas, J. P. (1992a). Affect in social judgments and decisions: A multi-process model. In M. Zanna (Ed.), *Advances in experimental social psychology* (Vol. 25, pp. 227–275). New York: Academic.

Forgas, J. P. (1992b). On bad mood and peculiar people: Affect and person typicality in impression formation. *Journal of Personality and Social Psychology, 62,* 863–875.

Forgas, J. P. (1993). On making sense of odd couples: Mood effects on the perception of mismatched relationships. *Personality and Social Psychology Bulletin, 19,* 59–71.

Forgas, J. P. (1994). Sad and guilty? Affective influences on the explanation of conflict episodes. *Journal of Personality and Social Psychology, 66,* 56–68.

Forgas, J. P. (1995a). Mood and judgment: The affect infusion model (AIM). *Psychological Bulletin, 117*(1), 39–66.

Forgas, J. P. (1995b). Strange couples: Mood effects on judgments and memory about prototypical and atypical targets. *Personality and Social Psychology Bulletin, 21,* 747–765.

Forgas, J. P. (1998a). On feeling good and getting your way: Mood effects on negotiation strategies and outcomes. *Journal of Personality and Social Psychology, 74,* 565–577.

Forgas, J. P. (1998b). Asking nicely? Mood effects on responding to more or less polite requests. *Personality and Social Psychology Bulletin, 24,* 173–185.

Forgas, J. P. (1998c). Happy and mistaken? Mood effects on the fundamental attribution error. *Journal of Personality and Social Psychology, 75,* 318–331.

Forgas, J. P. (1999a). On feeling good and being rude: Affective influences on language use and request formulations. *Journal of Personality and Social Psychology, 76,* 928–939

Forgas, J. P. (1999b). Feeling and speaking:

Mood effects on verbal communication strategies. *Personality and Social Psychology Bulletin, 25,* 850–863.

Forgas, J. P. (Ed.). (2000). *Feeling and thinking: The role of affect in social cognition.* New York: Cambridge University Press.

Forgas, J. P. (Ed.). (2001). *The handbook of affect and social cognition* (pp. 293–319). Mahwah, NJ: Erlbaum.

Forgas, J. P. (in press). Feeling and doing: Mood effects on interpersonal behaviors. *Psychological Inquiry.*

Forgas, J. P., & Bower, G. H. (1987). Mood effects on person perception judgements. *Journal of Personality and Social Psychology, 53,* 53–60.

Forgas, J. P., Bower, G. H., & Krantz, S. (1984). The influence of mood on perceptions of social interactions. *Journal of Experimental Social Psychology, 20,* 497–513.

Forgas, J. P., Bower, G. H., & Moylan, S. J. (1990). Praise or blame? Affective influences on attributions for achievement. *Journal of Personality and Social Psychology, 59,* 809–818.

Forgas, J. P., & Fiedler, K. (1996). Us and them: Mood effects on intergroup discrimination. *Journal of Personality and Social Psychology, 70,* 36–52.

Gibbs, R. (1985). Situational conventions and requests. In J. P. Forgas (Ed.), *Language and social situations* (pp. 97–113). New York: Springer.

Goffman, E. (1972). *Frame analysis.* London: Penguin.

Gouaux, C. (1971). Induced affective states and interpersonal attraction. *Journal of Personality and Social Psychology, 20,* 37–43.

Griffitt, W. (1970). Environmental effects on interpersonal behavior: Ambient effective temperature and attraction. *Journal of Personality and Social Psychology, 15,* 240–244.

Harmon-Jones, E. (2001). The role of affect in cognitive dissonance processes. In J. P. Forgas (Ed.), *The handbook of affect and social cognition,* (237–256). Mahwah, NJ: Erlbaum.

Heider, F. (1958). *The psychology of interpersonal relations.* New York: Wiley.

Higgins, E. T. (2001). Promotion and prevention experiences: Relating emotions to non-emotional motivational states. In Forgas, J. P. (Ed.), *The handbook of affect and social cognition.* Mahwah, NJ: Erlbaum.

Isen, A. M. (1984). Towards understanding the role of affect in cognition. In R. S. Wyer & T. K. Srull (Eds.), *Handbook of social cognition* (Vol. 3, pp. 179–236). Hillsdale, NJ: Erlbaum.

Isen, A. M. (1987). Positive affect, cognitive processes and social behaviour. In L. Berkowitz (Ed.), *Advances in experimental social psychology* (Vol. 20, pp. 203–253). New York: Academic.

Ito, T. & Cacioppo, J. (2001). Affect and attitudes: A social neuroscience approach. In J. P. Forgas (Ed.). *The handbook of affect and social cognition.* Mahwah, NJ: Erlbaum.

Machiavelli, N. (1961). *The prince.* London: Penguin.

Niedenthal, P., & Halberstadt, J. (2000). Grounding categories in emotional response. In J. P. Forgas (Ed.), *Feeling and thinking: The role of affect in social cognition* (pp. 357–386). New York: Cambridge University Press.

Petty, R. E., DeSteno, D., & Rucker, D. (2001). The role of affect in attitude change. In J. P. Forgas (Ed.), *The handbook of affect and social cognition.* Mahwah, NJ: Erlbaum.

Razran, G. H. S. (1940). Conditioned response changes in rating and appraising sociopolitical slogans. *Psychological Bulletin, 37,* 481–491.

Rusting, C. L. (1998). Personality, mood, and cognitive processing of emotional informa-tion: Three conceptual frameworks. *Psychological Bulletin, 124(2),* 165–196.

Rusting, C. (2001). Personality as a mediator of affective influences on social cognition. In J. P. Forgas (Ed.), *The handbook of affect and social cognition.* Mahwah, NJ: Erlbaum.

Schwarz, N. (1990). Feelings as information: Informational and motivational functions of affective states. In E. T. Higgins & R. Sorrentino (Eds.), *Handbook of motivation and cognition: Foundations of social behaviour* (Vol. 2, pp. 527–561). New York: Guilford.

Schwarz, N., & Clore, G. L. (1988). How do I feel about it? The informative function of affective states. In K. Fiedler & J. P. Forgas (Eds.), *Affect, cognition, and social behavior* (pp. 44–62). Toronto, Canada: Hogrefe.

Sedikides, C. (1995). Central and peripheral self-conceptions are differentially influenced by mood: Tests of the differential sensitivity hypothesis. *Journal of Personality and Social Psychology, 69(4),* 759–777.

Zajonc, R. B. (1980). Feeling and thinking: Preferences need no inferences. *American Psychologist, 35,* 151–175.

Zajonc, R. B. (2000). Feeling and thinking: Closing the debate over the independence of affect. In J. P. Forgas (Ed.), *Feeling and thinking: The role of affect in social cognition* (pp. 31–58). New York: Cambridge University Press.

10

Memory as a Target of Social Influence?

Memory Distortions as a Function of Social Influence and Metacognitive Knowledge

HERBERT BLESS
FRITZ STRACK
EVA WALTHER

The idea that individuals' attitudes and behaviors are susceptible to social influence reflects widely shared common sense. Numerous research findings also have been presented that underscore this notion (see Eagly & Chaiken, 1993; Petty & Cacioppo, 1981). After all in everyday life, we are the

Address correspondence to: Herbert Bless, Mikrosoziologie und Sozialpsychologie, Fakultät für Sozialwissenschaften, Universität Mannheim, D-68131 Mannheim, Germany; E-mail: hbless@sowi.uni.mannheim.de

target as well as the initiator of attempts to change other's attitudes and behaviors (Cialdini, this volume). In contrast to the widely accepted idea that our attitudes and behaviors are prone to social influence, the idea that our memory could be influenced by others appears as a rather disturbing thought. Could it really be possible that we believe we remember something simply because others have talked us into that—or is this phenomena restricted to science fiction novels and movies? Social psychology textbooks seem to imply the latter and often restrict the definition of social influence to an effort on the part of one person to change behaviors or attitudes[1] of others (e.g., Baron & Byrne, 1994). The idea that individuals´ memory can be influenced by others is rarely mentioned.

Interestingly, the idea that our memory reports can be altered by others has a long tradition in the area of eyewitness testimony (cf. Loftus, 1979). This research has addressed various mechanisms that increase the likelihood of memory distortions, for example, hypnosis, dream interpretation, leading questions, or misleading feedback. Different models have been proposed to account for the impact of these mechanisms. However, in general, these explanations give little attention to the social aspect of memory distortions. Instead, they focus primarily on the idea that individuals cannot correctly discriminate whether memory traces result from a particular event "X" or from some other source of information (Johnson & Hasher, 1987; Loftus & Hoffman, 1989; Loftus, Miller, & Burns, 1978). In this regard, the origin of the other source of information is largely neglected (for one of a few exceptions see Betz, Skowronski, & Ostrom, 1996).

With the present approach we are taking an explicit social psychological perspective—one that holds a conceptualization of memory that emphasizes, similar to attitudes, the *constructive* aspect of recall and recognition, and attributes an important role to inferences and judgments. Building on Festinger's (1954) social comparison theory we assume that individuals tend to rely on information that is implicitly or explicitly provided by others when they feel uncertain about their own attitudes, values, and behaviors. We extend this idea to memory and specify conditions that increase or decrease individuals' uncertainty about their memory. In the remainder of this chapter, we first outline our general assumption and then report experimental research demonstrating that information provided indirectly and directly by others systematically influences individuals' memory performance.

APPLYING SOCIAL COMPARISON TO MEMORY

In accordance with the general notion of Festinger's (1954) social comparison theory, we assume that individuals are particularly susceptible to social influ-

---

1. Given Schachter and Singer's (1962) work on emotions, it seems legitimate to add emotions to this list, although emotions are hardly found in the "social influence" chapters in Social Psychology textbooks.

ence if they are not confident in their own judgments of the situation. In order to reduce their uncertainty, individuals will then rely on information that is, intentionally or unintentionally, subtly or obviously, provided by others. Shifting these considerations from attitudes, beliefs, or behaviors to memory, the belief that an event has occurred can be treated like an attitude that a person may hold. Social influence on memory should then be most likely to occur when individuals lack confidence in their memorial beliefs.

The first question emerging from such a perspective pertains to how individuals can possibly fail to be confident about their memory. If they have to decide whether an event has occurred, individuals' uncertainty may result from the fact that the mere absence of a memory trace by itself is not always diagnostic. Imagine, for example, a person being asked whether yesterday she saw a blue Volkswagen parked in front of her house. This situation parallels experimental settings in which participants working on a recognition test have to decide whether a specific stimulus has been previously presented. Let us assume that the individual does not have a recollective experience of a blue Volkswagen, or in the laboratory setting, that the participant does not find a memory trace for the stimulus in question. This absence of a memory trace may have at least two different implications. First, it may reflect that the stimulus has not been presented, or second, that the stimulus has been presented but its presentation cannot be remembered. Given this deficient diagnosticity of the absence of a memory trace, additional inferences become necessary. These inferences may either increase or decrease individuals' confidence that the absence of a memory trace does, in fact, imply the nonoccurrence of the event. Applying Festinger's (1954) theorizing to memory, we generally assume that when people are not confident that the absence of a memory trace implies the absence of a stimulus, they tend to rely on other people to determine whether the stimulus had been presented.

Similar considerations can be applied to the presence of a memory trace which may either imply that the event has actually occurred or, alternatively, that the memory trace is due to influences independent of the event. In particular, individuals may confuse the source of their memory trace, and falsely attribute the memory trace to the occurrence of the event rather than to postevent information, imagining the event, or other types of source confusions (for a systematic treatment of this issue, see Johnson & Hasher, 1987). If individuals are aware of alternative sources for their recollection, they may be more or less confident that their recollection of an event implies its occurrence. Individuals' uncertainty again opens up the field for social influence. Specifically, we assume that the less confident an individual is that the presence of a recollection experience implies that the stimulus had actually been presented, the more the individual will be susceptible to social influence (Johnson, Hashtroudi, & Lindsay, 1993). In the remainder of this chapter we focus on the ambivalence of the absence rather than of the presence of a memory trace. We assume, however, that the same principles operate in both situations.

INCREASING AND DECREASING UNCERTAINTY
BY METACOGNITIVE KNOWLEDGE

According to the above considerations individuals´ memory is susceptible to social influence if individuals are not confident that the absence of a recollective experience implies the nonoccurrence of an event (and if individuals are not confident about the origin of this recollective experience). The next step from such a perspective is to identify variables that increase or decrease individuals' confidence in their memory experiences, and to test whether social influence on memory is a function of these variables.

Elsewhere we have discussed the potential impact of a number of variables (see Bless & Strack, 1998), thereby addressing features of the stimulus in question, encoding conditions, retrieval conditions, person attributes, and the impact of individuals' subjective theories about memory processes. The central assumption of our analyses holds that these variables influence individuals' metacognitive knowledge about the memorability of an event and that individuals can apply this knowledge (e.g., Brewer & Treyens, 1981) to determine the implication of a missing recollective experience. For example, individuals usually assume a salient event as more likely to be remembered than nonsalient event, they assume less memorability if the event was encoded under suboptimal conditions, or if they consider themselves as a person who generally has a poor memory for the event in question (see Bless & Strack [1998] for a more extended discussion). Note, that for the following discussion it is the individuals´ subjective beliefs about the memorability that plays a central role which may or may not overlap with the objective memorability itself.

If metacognitive knowledge implies that an event in question should be remembered, individuals should be confident that the lack of a recollective experience provides a sound basis to infer the nonoccurrence of the event. In contrast, metacognitive knowledge also may imply that an event is not remembered. In this case, individuals should feel less confident about the implications of the lack of a recollective experience. Individuals will then need to apply alternative inferential strategies and we assume that the reliance on information provided by others constitutes one alternative strategy. According to these considerations, individuals' uncertainty about the interpretation of the absence of a recollective experience should make them more susceptible to social influence.

EXPERIMENT 1: THE MODERATING ROLE
OF ITEM SALIENCE

Whether or not the lack of a recollective experience is sufficient to infer the nonoccurrence of an event often may depend on whether the event is perceptually or categorically distinct. As first demonstrated by Von Restorff (1933), individuals are more likely to recall items that are distinct from other items in a learning list rather than nondistinct items (for other examples see Detterman &

Ellis, 1972). If individuals are aware that such salient items are more likely to elicit a recollective experience than nonsalient items, the salience of an event should influence their confidence regarding whether or not the absence of a recollective experience implies nonoccurrence.

Specifically, if the item is held to be highly memorable, individuals should be very confident that the absence of a recollective experience implies nonoccurrence. In this case, individuals are unlikely to rely on information provided by others, and should therefore be minimally susceptible to social influence. Individuals face a different situation, however, if they cannot remember an event and have no reason to believe that the event in question is particularly memorable. In this case, they remain uncertain as to whether the absence of a recollective experience is due to the nonoccurrence of the event or to a failure of remembering the event. We assume that under these circumstances, individuals will engage in an alternative inferential strategy. Because one such strategy could be the reliance on information provided by others, individuals in this situation should be more susceptible to social influence.

Strack and Bless (1994) investigated these considerations by employing a recognition paradigm in which the salience of the items and different degrees of social influence were manipulated. Specifically, participants were presented with 34 black-and-white slides, photographed in a similar fashion that depicted different objects. To manipulate low versus high salience within participants, we presented 30 photographs of tools (e.g., hammer, screwdriver, silverware, or kitchen utensils), and, dispersed among these tools, four photographs of nontools, each of which belonged to a unique category (e.g., bouquet of flowers, shoe, book). It was assumed that the four nontools would be salient in contrast to the remaining objects (see Taylor & Fiske, 1978; Von Restorff, 1933). All slides were presented long enough to be easily recognized (ca. 1.04 sec).

After a short break, participants were provided with a booklet containing a recognition task. Specifically, participants were asked whether or not they had seen a specific object on the slides that had previously been projected. Participants responded with respect to four different types of objects: (1) salient distractor items (i.e., nontools not previously projected), (2) nonsalient distractors (i.e., tools not previously projected), (3) salient targets (i.e., nontools previously projected), and (4) nonsalient targets (i.e., tools previously projected).

To manipulate social influence we used an experimental paradigm introduced by Loftus (1975), in which participants are provided with information by others by subtly introduced presuppositions. Building on previous research, we assumed that questions with a definite article (e.g. "Did you see *the* hammer?") implicitly presupposed that this item had, in fact, been presented. In contrast, no presupposition is implied if the same question is asked using the indefinite article (e.g. "Did you see *a* hammer?"). This manipulation typically resulted in more affirmative responses when the definite article was employed, even if the target had not been presented (for an overview see Loftus, 1979). According to these considerations, for some participants the wording of the question employed the definite article, whereas for the remaining participants the wording of the question employed the indefinite article. We assumed that the differential impact of the definite versus the indefinite article on participants' recognition judgments would reflect the degree of social influence operating in a recognition situation. Note that this argument implies that the impact of the linguistic form is not due to differential memory distortions (e.g., Loftus & Hoffman, 1989). In line with other theorizing (Dodd & Bradshaw, 1980; Smith & Ellsworth, 1987), the argument implies that more complex inferences are involved that may, for example, be determined by characteristics of the communicator (e.g., his or her credibility or expertise).

The results of this study (Strack & Bless, 1994, Exp. 1; see Fig. 10.1) revealed that the recognition of targets was almost perfect under all conditions. Whether the item was salient or not, whether the definite or the indefinite article was used, far more than 90% of the old stimuli were correctly recognized. Thus, social influence in form of a presupposition had little impact on targets independent of their salience.

More important with respect to the lack of a recollective experience, however, are the results obtained for the distractor items. As these items had not been presented, participants were unlikely to have a recollective experience for their presentation. As can be seen in Figure 10.1, for nonsalient distractors, the use of the definite article led to a significantly higher proportion of "yes" responses (38.5%) than the use of the indefinite article (18%), whereas the type of article had no effect for salient distractors. As can be seen there were absolutely no false alarms for salient distractors.

In sum, these findings suggest that individuals' recognition responses were

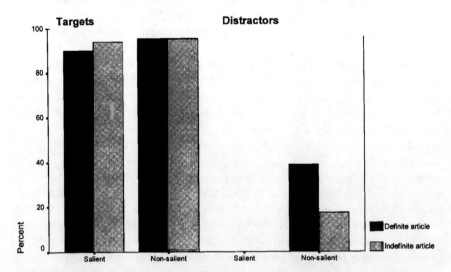

FIGURE 10.1. Recognition (percentage of "Yes" responses) for targets and distractors as a function of item salience and presupposition (data from Strack & Bless, 1994, Experiment 1).

subject to social influence, and that this influence was mediated by individuals' confidence in the implications of their recollective experiences. In accordance with our assumptions, the impact of the presupposition conveyed by the linguistic cue affected the recognition of nonsalient but not of salient items. Given the high subjective memorability of salient items, participants could presumably be very confident that the absence of a recollective experience for these items implied nonoccurrence. As a consequence of their confidence, they refrained from applying alternative inference strategies that implied the reliance on information linguistically provided by others. In contrast, given the low subjective memorability of nonsalient items, participants were presumably less confident that the absence of a recollective experience for these items implied actual nonoccurrence. As a consequence of this uncertainty, participants were more likely to apply alternative inference strategies, and relied on information linguistically provided by others.

EXPERIMENT 2: SUBOPTIMAL ENCODING CONDITIONS AS A FACILITATOR OF SOCIAL INFLUENCE

According to our general considerations, variables that increase or decrease individuals' perception of memorability moderate the impact of social influence on memory performance. Whereas some factors, such as salience, may increase perceived memorability, other factors decrease perceived memorability. One prominent variable in this respect is the amount of elaboration during encoding. After all, individuals are well aware that insufficient elaboration during encoding can be the cause of a lack of recollective experiences (e.g., Craik & Lockart, 1972). If so, individuals should be less confident in their lack of recollective experiences if they perceive the encoding situations as suboptimal. In turn, the decreased confidence should increase the susceptibility to social influence.

We tested this assumption by modifying the paradigm described above. In particular, we created conditions under which participants did not have enough time to elaborate on some of the presented items (Strack & Bless, 1994, Exp. 2). For this purpose, we presented ten targets for only .04 seconds in the suboptimal subthreshold condition, followed by immediate masking (making recognition virtually impossible). In the super-threshold condition we presented 10 targets for 2.04 seconds (making it virtually impossible *not* to recognize them). Very importantly, these ten targets were *not* included in the later recognition set.

As for Experiment 1, the recognition of targets was again almost perfect under all conditions. Regardless of whether the item was salient or not, whether the definite or the indefinite article was used, or whether some other stimuli were presented suboptimally, far more than 90% of the old stimuli were correctly recognized. Again these results suggest that when participants had a clear recollection of the presentation of the stimulus, they were not susceptible to social influence.

As can be seen in Figure 10.2, a different picture emerges for the distractor

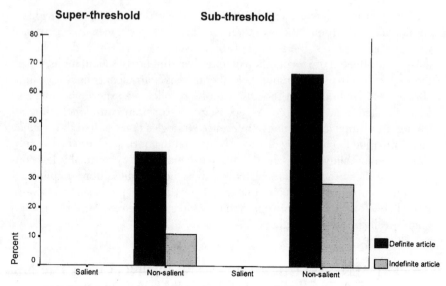

FIGURE 10.2. Recognition for distractors as a function of item salience, presupposition, and perceived encoding conditions (data from Strack & Bless, 1994, Experiment 2).

items. The use of the definite versus indefinite articles had no effect on salient distractors, causing not even one false alarm. For nonsalient distractors, in contrast, the use of the definite article led overall to a significantly higher proportion of "yes" responses (52%) than the use of the indefinite article (21%) reflecting social influence. Most important, the difference between the use of the definite and indefinite articles was more pronounced in the suboptimal condition than in the super-threshold condition. Presenting some items suboptimally presumably reduced participants' confidence that the lack of a recollective experience necessarily implied nonoccurrence, because they could attribute this lack to the impoverished presentation. As a consequence, participants were more likely to rely on alternative strategies which made them more susceptible to social influence in form of the presupposition.[2] Note that these conclusions are

---

2. These conclusions are additionally supported by an examination of participants' confidence in the correctness of their provided answers. After each recognition response, participants were asked to indicate how confident they were about the correctness of their response. As hypothesized, participants were significantly more confident in rejecting salient than nonsalient distractors. Moreover, participants' confidence was lower if the short exposure time suggested the possibility that the trace was weakened. Confidence was not affected by these conditions when the test stimuli were targets, presumably reflecting that participants had a clear recollection of the presentation of the stimulus, which in turn made them less susceptible to social influence.

based primarily on the results obtained for the distractors. As these distractors were never presented, their encoding was in fact not influenced by the threshold manipulation. The important variable is therefore not a suboptimal encoding but whether individuals *perceive* the encoding condition to be suboptimal and consider it a potential cause for the absence of a memory trace.

The perception of insufficient elaboration during encoding may, of course, have numerous origins. According to our assumptions, we should obtain similar effects for other variables that individuals perceive as potential causes for suboptimal encoding. For example, we may expect social influence to be stronger if individuals believe that they encoded the information in question under distraction, under time pressure, while they were simultaneously working on other tasks, day dreaming, or ruminating. Moreover, individuals may assume that some emotional states, for example fatigue or anxiety, decrease encoding elaboration.

EXPERIMENT 3: THE EFFECTS OF GROUP SIZE AND DISSENTERS

So far, by discussing the role of salience and suboptimal encoding conditions, we have addressed variables that open or close the gate for social influence on memory (see Bless & Strack, 1998, for a more extended discussion of other variables). After having speculated about the antecedents of social influence on memory, we now address aspects of how the influential information is provided. It is no surprise that important determinants of the social influence process pertain to how individuals provide information to others, whether they are in a majority or minority (Martin & Hewstone, this volume), how many people provide information and how many exchanges there are in total (Latané & Bourgeois, this volume), and the match between features of the communication and features of the target recipient (Schaller, this volume). In general, we argue that under the specified conditions, any information that individuals perceive as relevant may have the potential to influence individuals' memory judgments. According to this assumption, presuppositions as applied in the reported studies are, of course, not the only vehicles for social influence. It seems therefore quite straightforward to investigate the potential of classic social influence variables to impact individuals' memory judgments.

Classic research on social influence suggests that individuals can be strongly influenced by the perception of others' behavior or of the expressions of their attitudes. Given our considerations we can then derive that individuals' memory reports are influenced by their perception of other individuals' reports about the presence or the absence of an event or item. This impact should, however, be restricted to situations in which the memorability of the item is considered low because under these conditions individuals are uncertain about the implication of the absence of a recollective experience. Moreover, in line with prior research, we expected that the more other persons claim to have seen an item, the stronger the social influence (see Gerad, Wilhelmy, & Connolly, 1968; Latané & Wolf, 1981). This assumption is, however, qualified by the negatively accelerated relationship between group size and social influence.

In order to test these considerations, participants were exposed to a similar set of stimuli used in Experiments 1 and 2. After a filler task, participants were provided with a recognition test. At this time, participants learned that the recognition test contained answers given by other participants who had already taken part in the study. To cover this manipulation, the experimenter informed participants that all answers are given on a scanable questionnaire for economical reasons, and as a consequence they would see answers provided by prior participants. Participants were explicitly told to ignore the answers of prior participants. Depending on the experimental condition, either no, five, or ten bogus participants had already given their answers on the answer sheet.

As in Experiment 1 and 2, no effects were obtained for targets; that is, we observed a very high percentage of correct identifications in this case. Moreover, again replicating prior findings, individuals' responses toward salient distractor items were unaffected by the ostensible answers of other participants. With respect to our hypothesis, the most relevant results came from the analyses of the nonsalient distractors. Given the low memorability of these items, participants should be influenced by the bogus answers of other participants. Participants should judge a never presented nonsalient distractor item as presented when the five or ten other participants had ostensibly indicated that this item had been presented.

The results presented in the left part of Figure 10.3 support this hypothesis. As can be seen, participants in the control condition (42.5%) were less likely to judge the nonsalient distractors as presented than participants exposed to the answers of five other participants who claimed the presentation of these items (51.5%). This effect of the social influence variable was even more pronounced (57%) when the answers of ten rather than five other persons were provided. These findings converge with the results reported above. Again we observed a significant impact of the information provided by other individuals, and this effect was restricted to conditions when the memorability of the items in question was low.

Traditional research in the area of social influence suggests at least two different mechanisms why individuals can be strongly influenced by the perception of others' behavior (see Deutsch & Gerad, 1955). First, others may exert a motivational influence to comply with the majority due to conformity. This form of social influence is mostly restricted to judgments and behaviors that are expressed publicly (Asch, 1951, 1952). Second, social influence may take the form of informational influence when individuals feel uncertain about their own attitudes (Festinger, 1954). To reduce uncertainty, individuals will rely on information provided by others and this will become apparent both in individuals' public and private convictions. As outlined above, our assumptions are built on this latter idea of the informative influence. Given that in the reported studies

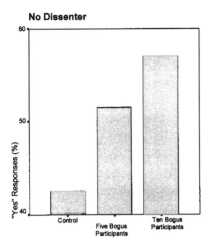 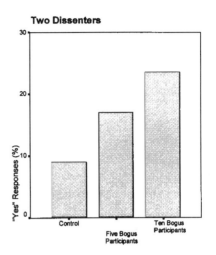

FIGURE 10.3. Mean percentage of "Yes" responses to nonsalient distractor items as a function of group size and dissenter.

the presuppositions were introduced rather subtly, and given that individuals' responses were given privately, the results are consistent with this notion.

To further explore this assumption, we created conditions in which the answers of the bogus participants did not unanimously reflect the presence of a nonsalient distractor item but in which the answers of two dissenters (correctly) indicated the absence of these items. We assumed that the observed effect should be eliminated by the two dissenters if it was due to motivational influence (Asch, 1952). If the effect was due to an informational influence, we expected the effect to be potentially reduced but not eliminated. Given these considerations, the results presented in the right part of Figure 10.3 suggest an *informational* rather than a *motivational* form of social influence. Even in the presence of dissenting answers, participants' responses were still strongly influenced by the majority of bogus participants' answers. Interestingly, the two dissenters were more likely to reduce the social influence when they were embedded in a group of five rather than a group of ten bogus participants.

The differential percentages of "yes" responses in the control group reflect different base rates for the different items; that is, different stimuli were used for targets and distractors in the dissenter versus no-dissenter conditions. Note, however, that these differences cannot account for the obtained effects. It should also be noted, that in the present study we additionally manipulated the sub- versus super-threshold presentation as in Experiment 2. The obtained results for this factor are very consistent with the findings of Experiment 2. For reasons of presentation, the results are collapsed across this factor (for a full presentation of the findings and a more extended description of the cover story and discussion see Walther, Bless, Strack, Rackstraw, & Wagner, 2000).

Interestingly, the obtained findings converge with research by Kassin and Kiechel (1996). In their studies, participants were accused of having hit a "forbidden" key while working on the computer, which caused serious consequences. Although participants had in fact not hit the key, they admitted to having performed this action. They were most likely to do so when a supposed witness claimed to have seen the action (in our case when other participants claimed the occurrence of the event). Converging with the results of Experiment 2, Kassin and Kiechel (1996) report that impairing encoding conditions (e.g., by increasing the speed the participants needed to work on the computer) increased yielding to the (false) accusation. As our present framework, the authors emphasize (1) the absence of a clear memory of the event and (2) information provided by others as the major factors for these false memory reports.

EXPERIMENT 4: NORMATIVE VERSUS INFORMATIVE INFLUENCE

The findings presented so far suggest that the observed social influence on memory results less from a desire not to deviate from the group norm than from a social comparison process that provides the person with information about reality (Festinger, 1954). Experiment 4 was designed to demonstrate the reliability of the findings of Experiment 3 and to further support our hypothesis of an informational, rather than a normative, influence. In general, we employed a similar design as in Experiment 3. We presented participants with a set of stimuli on the computer, similar to the stimuli in Experiments 1, 2, and 3. After a filler task, participants were provided with a recognition test. The test again comprised targets, distractors, and salient and nonsalient items. We additionally varied the instructions participants received prior to their working on the recognition test (after the encoding of the target stimuli). Participants in the normative influence condition learned that a group discussion with all other participants would take place at the end of the session. This instruction emphasized particularly the impression one participant makes on other participants, and was designed to stress the normative aspect. If the obtained social influence on memory was due to a normative social influence the effect should be more pronounced the more this aspect is present in the situation. In the informative influence condition, we stressed the importance of correct answers on the recognition test and that the best participants would receive an extra reward. Finally, a neutral group received no further instructions. All these participants were exposed to other participants' ostensible responses. In addition, we ran a control group that was not exposed to other participants' answers and that did not receive any additional instructions. Participants were sitting in different cubicles of the computer room and were now told that due to some computer problem, the experimenter had to use an older version of the program—and unfortunately they would therefore see other participants' responses which they were told to ignore.

Again, and as predicted we obtained no effect of the presence or absence of the bogus participants' responses for the salient items, irrespective of being targets or distractors. Similarly, no effects were obtained for the nonsalient targets. Again of most interest are the results for the nonsalient distractor items. As predicted, we observed a significant impact of the bogus participants' ostensible answers. Participants were more likely to falsely report that they had seen a distractor item in the presentation after they had observed other participants indicating the presence of these items. The different instructional sets had little impact on the degree of participants yielding to the social influence: 36% of responses (falsely) implied the presence of a nonsalient distractor item in the control group (no information about other participants' responses), 54% of the responses in the neutral group (other participants' responses but no additional instruction), 53% of the responses in the informative influence condition, and 46% of the responses in the normative influence condition. Most important, increasing the normative aspect of the situation by the instructional set did not increase participants' yielding to the social influence. In fact, in this condition, yielding was least pronounced, although the difference to the neutral group and the normative influence condition did not reach conventional levels of significance.[3] Although it is always difficult to interpret nonsignificant differences, these results, on the one hand, seem to suggest that the observed impact of bogus participants' responses were not primarily mediated by normative social influence. On the other hand, it could be argued that normative and informative influences may be less distinguishable, both on an empirical and on a conceptual level than implied by Deutsch and Gerad (see David & Turner, this volume).

CONCLUSION

In sum, the present findings strongly suggest that social influence is not restricted to individuals' attitudes and behaviors but that individuals' memory performance can be very susceptible to social influence. Whereas in social psychology this idea has been rather neglected, research in other domains has investigated how information provided by others may increase the likelihood of memory distortions, particularly in the area of eyewitness testimony (Loftus, 1979). Most of theses approaches focus primarily on the idea that individuals cannot correctly discriminate whether memory traces result from a particular event or from some other source of information (Johnson & Hasher, 1987; Loftus & Hoffman, 1989; Loftus, Miller, & Burns, 1978). In contrast, our own account

---

3. As in Experiment 3, we additionally manipulated the presence or absence of dissenters. The obtained results for this factor are completely consistent with the findings of Experiment 3. A full presentation of these findings would be beyond the scope of the present chapter (for a full presentation of the findings and additional analyses, see Walther, Bless, Strack, Rackstraw, & Wagner, 2000).

emphasizes the social and constructive aspect underlying social influence on memory.

In general, we assume that the absence of a memory trace for itself is not diagnostic with respect to whether an event in question has occurred or not. On the one hand, the absence of a recollective experience may reflect that the event did not occur; on the other hand, it may reflect that the event did occur but that the individual cannot remember it. As a result, individuals may feel uncertain about the implication if they do not have a recollective experience. In accordance with Festinger's (1954) social comparison theory we argue that individuals can reduce this uncertainty by relying on information that is directly or indirectly provided by others. The reported studies address the two aspects that emerge from such a perspective. First, we have addressed the role of metacognitive processes about the memorability of an item that increase or decrease individuals' uncertainty, and second we have addressed different aspects of how information is provided by others.

In line with our assumptions, social influence on memory was a function of the judged memorability of the item in question. Across all four studies, we observed no effect on salient items. In the case of salient items, the absence of a recollective experience is highly diagnostic and implies the nonoccurrence of an event: "If this event had occurred, I would surely remember it." As a consequence, individuals were less likely to rely on information provided by others—independent of whether this information was provided in the form of presuppositions (Exp. 1 and 2) or in the form of responses by other individuals (Exp. 3 and 4). Whereas salience presumably increased the perceived memorability, suboptimal encoding conditions decreased the perceived memorability, which in turn increased the impact of the information provided by others (Exp. 2). In many cases, individuals' assumptions about the memorability may be correct—after all, memory performance is, in fact, better for salient items and it is usually impaired when the information is not processed in depth due to suboptimal encoding conditions (for overview see Baddeley, 1990). One may easily add numerous variables such as self-reference (e.g., Klein & Kihlstrom, 1986), mood-congruity (e.g., Bower, 1981; Forgas, 1992; Forgas & Bower, 1987, 1995), and so forth. For our argument, however, it is not important whether individuals' assumptions about memory processes match actual effects. Individuals only have to believe that their memory is affected by a specific variable. It may therefore be sufficient to make individuals believe that a certain variable influences their memory performance (Förster & Strack, 1998).

The present theorizing holds that when individuals feel uncertain about the implications of the absence of a recollective experience, any information that individuals perceive as relevant may have the potential to influence individuals' memory judgments. The presented results support this hypothesis by providing evidence that indirectly provided information in the form of presuppositions (Exp. 1 and 2) as well as directly provided information in the form of other individuals' responses (Exp. 3 and 4) can alter individuals memory reports. In particular the latter two studies strongly emphasize the social nature of this influence.

Although the conclusion that the observed findings are due to an informational rather than a normative influence (see Insko, Smith, Alicke, Wade, & Taylor, 1985) may need further examination, several aspects of the presented findings support the former rather than the latter alternative. First, we did not observe an overall tendency to yield to social influence as might have been expected on the basis of a normative influence. In fact, the effects were very specific and were not observed when individuals responded to salient items. Second, in the reported studies participants gave their responses not publicly, which again reduces the likelihood that the observed effects are due to normative influence. Moreover, increasing the normative aspect of the situation decreased, rather than increased the impact of other individuals' responses on memory performance (Exp. 4).

Looking ahead, several aspects may deserve attention by future research. First, whereas the present chapter focuses on the absence of a memory trace, similar hypotheses can be derived for situations in which a memory trace is present. In this case, individuals need to determine whether the recollective experience was caused by the actual occurrence of the event or by subsequent information (Loftus, 1975), or by merely imagining the event (Johnson & Raye, 1981). If individuals are aware of these alternatives, they may be hesitant to use the presence of a recollective experience to inform that the event occurred. Then, the same principle discussed for the absence of a memory trace may apply for the presence of a memory trace: The less confident an individual is that his or her recollection implies a specified occurrence, the more the individual ought to rely on information by others. Second, accepting the provided framework as a research heuristic, future research can examine other prominent variables of social influence. For example, it would be interesting to investigate (1) the social status of the person providing the external information, (2) the recipients' and the communicators' affective states (see Forgas, this volume), or (3) individuals' subjective theories about cognitive processes (Strack & Mussweiler, this volume).

Independent of the exact outcome of these future investigations, we believe that the present approach could provide a fruitful framework for investigating social influence on memory. It directs attention to a—at least within social psychology—widely neglected area. Moreover, it allows researchers to derive a number of new and testable hypotheses. Finally and perhaps most importantly, the present approach emphasizes the role of inferences and judgments in the domain of memory—an aspect that has so far received less attention than deserved.

REFERENCES

Asch, S. E. (1951). Effects of group pressure upon the modification and distortion of judgements. In H. Guetzkow (Ed.), *Groups, leadership and men* (pp. 177–190). Pittsburgh, PA: Carnegie Press.

Asch, S. E. (1952). *Social psychology.* New York: Prentice-Hall.

Baddeley, A. D. (1990). *Human memory: Theory and practice.* Boston: Allyn and Bacon.

Baron, R. B., & Byrne, D. (1994). *Social psychology. Understanding human interaction* (7th ed). Boston: Allyn and Bacon.

Betz, A. L., Skowronski, J. J., & Ostrom, T. M. Baron, R. B., & Byrne, D. (1994). *Social psychology. Understanding human interaction* (1996). Shared realities: Social influence on stimulus memory. *Social Cognition, 2,* 113–140.

Bless, H., & Strack, F. (1998). Social influence on memory: Evidence and speculations. In V. Yzerbyt, G. Lories, & B. Dardenne (Eds.), *Metacognition: Cognitive and social dimensions* (pp. 90–106). London: Sage.

Bower, G. H. (1981). Mood and memory. *American Psychologist, 36,* 129–148.

Brewer, W. F., & Treyens, J. C. (1981). Role of schemata in memory for places. *Cognitive Psychology, 13,* 207–230.

Craik, F. I. M., & Lockhart, R. S. (1972). Levels of processing: A framework for memory research. *Journal of Verbal Learning and Verbal Behavior, 11,* 671–684.

Dettermann, D. K., & Ellis, N. R. (1972). Determinants of induced amnesia in short-term memory. *Journal of Experimental Psychology, 95,* 308–316.

Deutsch, M., & Gerard, H. B. (1955). A study of normative and informative social influence upon individual judgement. *Journal of Abnormal and Social Psychology, 51,* 629–636.

Dodd, D. H., & Bradshaw, J. M. (1980). Leading questions and memory: Pragmatic constraints. *Journal of Verbal Learning and Verbal Behavior, 19,* 695–704.

Eagly, A. H., & Chaiken, S. (1993). *The psychology of attitudes.* Fort Worth, TX: Harcourt Brace Jovanowich.

Festinger, L. (1954). A theory of social comparison processes. *Human relations, 7,* 117–140.

Forgas, J. P. (1992). Affect in social judgments and decisions: A multi-process model. In M. P. Zanna (Ed.), *Advances in Experimental Social Psychology* (Vol. 25, pp. 227–275). San Diego, CA: Academic.

Forgas, J. P. & Bower, G. H. (1987). Mood effects on person-perception judgments. *Journal of Personality and Social Psychology, 53,* 53–60.

Förster, J., & Strack, F. (1998). Subjective theories about encoding may influence recognition. Judgmental regulation in human memory. *Social Cognition, 16,* 78–92 .

Gerard, H. B., Wilhelmy, R. A., & Conolley, E. S. (1968). Conformity and group size. *Journal of Personality and Social Psychology, 8,* 79–82.

Insko, C. A., Smith, R. H., Alicke, M. D., Wade, J., & Taylor, S. (1985). Conformity and group size: The concern with being right and the concern with being liked. *Personality and Social Psychology Bulletin, 11,* 41–50.

Johnson, M. K., & Hasher, L. (1987). Human learning and memory. *Annual Review of Psychology, 38,* 631–686.

Johnson, M. K., & Hashtroudi, S., & Lindsay, D. S. (1993). Source monitoring. *Psychological Bulletin, 114,* 3–28.

Johnson, M. K., & Raye, C. L. (1981). Reality monitoring. *Psychological Review, 88,* 67–85.

Kassin, S. M., & Kiechel, K. L. (1996). The social psychology of false confessions: Compliance internalization, and confabulation. *Psychological Science, 7,* 125–128.

Klein, S. B., & Kihlstrom, J. F. (1986). Elaboration, organisation and the self-reference effect in memory. *Journal of Experimental Psychology: General, 115,* 26–38.

Latané, B., & Wolf, S. (1981). The social impact of majorities and minorities. *Psychological Review, 88,* 439–453.

Loftus, E. F. (1975). Leading questions and the eyewitness report. *Cognitive Psychology, 7,* 560–572.

Loftus, E. F. (1979). *Eyewitness testimony.* Cambridge, MA: Harvard University.

Loftus, E. F., & Hoffman, H. G. (1989). Misinformation and memory: The creation of new memories. *Journal of Experimental Psychology: General, 118,* 100–104.

Loftus, E. F., Miller, D. G., & Burns, H. J (1978). Semantic integration of verbal information into a visual memory. *Journal of Experimental Psychology: Human Learning and Memory, 4,* 19–31.

Petty, R. E., & Cacioppo, J. T. (1981). *Attitudes and persuasion: Classic and contemporary approaches.* Dubuque, IA: Brown.

Schachter, S., & Singer, J. E. (1962). Cognitive, social and physiological determinants of emotional state. *Psychological Review, 69,* 379–399.

Smith, V .L., & Ellsworth, P. C. (1987). The

social psychology of eyewitness accuracy: Misleading questions and communicator expertise. *Journal of Applied Psychology, 72,* 294–300.

Strack, F., & Bless, H. (1994). Memory for nonoccurrence: Metacognitive and presuppositional strategies. *Journal of Memory and Language, 33,* 207–217.

Taylor, S. E., & Fiske, S. T. (1978). Salience, attention, and attribution: Top-of-the-head phenomena. In L. Berkowitz (Ed.), *Advances in experimental social psychology* (Vol. 11, pp. 249–288). New York: Academic.

Walther, E., Bless, H. Strack, F., Rackstraw, P., & Wagner, D. (2000). *"I remember what you are saying–or do I?" The influence of metacognitive knowledge, group size, and uncertainty on memory distortions.* Manuscript submitted for publication.

Von Restorff, H. (1933). Über die Wirkung von Bereichsbildungen im Spurenfeld. *Psychologische Forschung, 18,* 299–342.

11

Influencing through the Power of Language

SIK HUNG NG

*L*et me introduce the main theme of the present chapter through Allport's (1954) definition of social psychology. According to this widely cited definition, social psychology is "an attempt to understand and explain how the thought, feeling, and behaviour of individuals are influenced by the actual, imagined, or implied presence of other human beings" (p. 5). There are three interesting points about Allport's conception of social psychology that are relevant here. First, it finds a home for social psychology in the science of social influence. Second, Allport describes social influence in an open-ended way without the restrictions of directionality and intentionality. This point is important because much of social influence observed in the laboratory is unintentional and untraceable directly to particular agents or particular acts. For example, coaction effects are unlikely to be perceived as intentional, and influence leading to bystander apathy can hardly be traced directly to a particular 'influencer.' In the world outside the laboratory, influence is even more diffused and more anonymously exercised. The culmination of those two points is that social influence is a privileged and potentially a very broad topic in social psychology. To

Address correspondence to Sik Hung Ng, School of Psychology, Victoria University of Wellington, P.O. Box 6000, Wellington, New Zealand. E-mail address: sikhung.ng@vuw.ac.nz

185

put it more strongly, Allport's definition implies that social psychology is effectively the science of social influence (see, for example, Jones, 1985).

Third, and most relevant of all for present purposes, Allport wrote about influence in the passive voice from the point of view of the recipient of influence. (He could have worded it using the active voice from the viewpoint of the influencer.) This target or influencee perspective, as we shall see below, converges with some of the most influential theories in social psychology. Reflecting (or perhaps influenced by) this perspective, a great deal of contemporary research has little to do with the active process of influencing and much more to do with the outcomes at the end of the process. Furthermore the analysis of outcome is mostly pitched at the level of individuals, exactly as Allport has envisaged. By comparison, little attention has been paid to group-level outcomes such as the development of hierarchical structures in real groups.

The present chapter is guided by the simple idea that social influence comprises, at the very least, influencing and its effects on the influencee (the target). Integrating these two core components and relating them to contextual variables (e.g., third parties) is a goal to which I aspire but not the one that I will attempt here. Instead, my present goal is more limited. I first review a selection of the literature to show that current research is influencee-oriented, and while it has made considerable progress on this, the research carries the double biases of overlooking both influencing and group-level outcomes. To address the first of the two biases, I outline a framework for analysing three levels of influencing in general. Following from this, I cross to the topic of language use, first to show its relevance to influencing by summarizing five major links between language use and power. I then map the levels of influencing onto three of those links, namely, the use of language to create influence, to depoliticize influence attempts, and to make routine a dominance relationship. In the final part of the paper, which addresses group-level outcomes, I focus on the "use of language to create influence" link and discuss two theoretical models for understanding how verbal interaction may establish an influence hierarchy in group and intergroup contexts. Experimental results suggest that the language-as-a-resource model holds true in both contexts, but that social identity processes also are involved in the intergroup context. I conclude with the speculation that influencing is at the heart of the formation of real groups which, unlike psychological groups, involve social interactions and have structures, not just as a cognition in the head.

INFLUENCING AND ITS EFFECTS ON THE INFLUENCEE

Numerous studies have been carried out on social influence since Triplett's (1898) early experiment on the topic. No fewer than 24 types of influence have been identified in a recent review (Levy, Collins, & Nail, 1999). Various taxonomies have been proposed concerning the power bases of influencing (e.g., French & Raven, 1959; Raven, 1992), the relational-cognitive bases of accepting influence (e.g., Deutsch & Gerard, 1955; Kelman, 1958), as well as influence tactics and their underlying psychological principles (e.g., Cialdini, 1993). The field of study itself also has been reviewed extensively (e.g., Cialdini & Trost, 1998) and reinterpreted in a most insightful way (e.g., Moscovici, 1976; Turner, 1991; see also Cialdini, David, & Turner, and Latané & Bourgeois, this volume). All these studies indicate the richness and vitality of the topic of social influence, just as Allport has envisaged.

One of the early insights of social psychology, exemplified by field theory and social exchange theory, is the recognition that a power-wielder is only as influential as the influencee (the target) and his or her allies will permit (see review by Ng, 1980). In field theoretical terms, a power-wielder achieves influence only when he or she induces sufficient force to overcome the influencee's resistance (see also Knowles, Butler, & Linn, this volume). An influencee's resistance, in turn, is often embedded in group norms as much as in individual personality, cognitions, or emotions. Thus to influence an individual, the influencing party often has to influence the group as a whole. In a similar vein, social exchange theory traces control (by power-wielders) to influencee's dependence. A power-wielder's control over the influencee is possible because of the latter's total dependence; behavior control is possible because of contingency dependence, and contact control is reliant on relational dependence. The last-named dependence, together with the allied concept of comparison level for alternatives, highlight the role played by third parties in what may appear at first sight to be a strictly dyadic affair. For example, in close relationships, the grip of one partner on the other will loosen when an attractive third party appears and becomes accessible.

Field theory and social exchange theory are general theoretical systems not confined exclusively to social influence. We now turn to theories that are specifically formulated to account for influence. Here, we find that some of the most significant and certainly the most widely cited theories are also influencee-oriented. For example, the theory of normative and informational social influence (Deutsch & Gerard, 1955) proposes that an individual is influenced by others because of his or her dependence on them. Thus, dependence on others for social approval gives rise to normative social influence. People who accept influence in order to satisfy this social-relational motivation (to avoid social rejection, to maintain solidarity, to become accepted as part of a group) are likely to comply outwardly without genuine private consent or conversion. They also would engage in only shallow cognitive processing without much attention to message contents, argument merit, and so forth. On the other hand, dependence on others as a guide to social reality would lead to informational social influence. People who accept influence out of this cognitive motivation (to reduce uncertainty, to maintain confidence, to validate private beliefs against a consensual group norm) are likely to engage in elaborate cognitive processing and undergo more genuine change. Kelman's (1958) compliance-identification-internalization trichotomy is similarly influencee-oriented, even though the underlying mechanisms are different in both number and details from Deutsch and Gerard's (1955) dual-process theory.

The demarcation between the normative and the informational has set the tone for a great deal of research on social influence (for a schematic review, see Hogg, 1992). Within this dualism, informational social influence is the clear winner. Its ascendancy is due partly to the belief that it alone tackles the 'real' thing about influence (genuine internal change rather than superficial outward compliance). Another reason is its fit with prevailing cultural values. By describing men and women as thinking and meaning-making individuals even amidst external pressure, it safeguards the Western ideal of rugged individualism that values self-bounded independence over social connectedness. Normative processes, by contrast, lack both qualities. As Kerr (1992) has pointed out in another context, although norms are viewed as important, they appear to be obvious enough and are deemed to be theoretically uninteresting factors (to theorists in Western individualistic cultures). The end result is that normative processes are marginalized in research (Mackie & Smith, 1998; Ng, 1980).

Influencee-oriented theories and research have succeeded in illuminating the processes of being influenced. Attempts have also been made to bridge the exaggerated demarcation between normative and informational processes, some with considerable success (see Mackie & Wright, in press; Turner, 1991; and the chapter by David & Turner in the present volume). However, the focus on influencees carries the risk of losing sight of the influencing party. An indication of the dwindling interest in influencing can be discerned from the ascent of social cognition and social identity theories during the last two decades, especially their application to social influence. Which aspects of social influence have received the most attention? If one uses the heuristic-systematic model (Chaiken, 1987), the elaboration likelihood model (Petty & Cacioppo, 1986), and self-categorization theory (Turner, 1991) as exemplars, one would find that social influence has been reduced or short-circuited to information-processing or to group-mediated acceptance of influence, all about and from the point of view of the *influencee.* This is not to devalue the exercises (they are clearly insightful and superior to both Deutsch and Gerard's [1955] and Kelman's [1958] models), or to deny the fact that they take into account the social context to varying degrees, only that they are overwhelmingly influencee-oriented and do not look at the process of *doing* the influencing.

But just as it is important to understand the processes of accepting (or resisting, opposing) influence (see Knowles, Butler, & Linn, this volume), it is also necessary to know the processes of influencing, and this is true for two reasons. First, influencing is necessary for a proper understanding of influence as a whole. Second, influencing is an area of considerable importance in its own right. For example, why and how do leaders become corrupt? How do group members negotiate an influence hierarchy from scratch? How do people learn to influence (to persuade, to cheat, etc.) as they grow up, and what are the contextual influences on their influencing strategies (see also Forgas, and Williams & Dolnik, this volume)? What roles does language play? How may all of these, and many more, vary (or remain invariant) across cultures?

For the reasons above, research on influencing has a definite role to play. A useful framework for looking at influencing, derived from the literature on power (see Ng, 1980), is to distinguish three levels of influencing on the bases of immediacy, directness, and conflict of interests or disagreement. At the first level, A, an influencing party (professors, minorities, Hitler, mass media, internet, etc.), may influence person B directly face-to-face and immediately for effect. At the second level of influencing, which is less immediate and direct than the first level, A may prepare the agenda, so to speak, by mobilizing relevant social values and institutional practices to limit discussion to only 'safe' issues, close off unwanted courses of action, remove potential allies from the influencee, and so on. These two levels of influencing contain an irreducible residue of conflict of interests or disagreements, and both involve the active overcoming of resistance or the reinforcing of dependence.

At the third level, and most subtle of all because of the apparent absence of conflict of interests or disagreements, A may plant an idea in B's mind, shape B's wants, and so forth such that, over time, B comes to think, feel, and act in the way A wants to but under the false consciousness of autonomy and owner-ship. This third-level influencing may reproduce itself. For example, children who have been brought up (influenced) by their parents to behave the way the parents want may re-enact third-level influencing on their own children. The generational reproduction of influencing, of course, may continue over succes-sive generations. Three things then emerge. First, a culture (or tradition, ideol-ogy) will develop. Second, this culture becomes dissociated (forgotten in the mind of later generations) from its initial source. Third, it becomes self-per-petuating. I think B. F. Skinner (1976) was trying to engineer this kind of cul-ture in his novel *Walden Two*. In a remarkable simulation experiment, Jacob and Campbell (1961) set up and perpetuated a micro-culture through several generations of participants in the laboratory. Many of the pragmatic strategies used by influence agents such as advertising, sales, and marketing professionals also aim to achieve such third level, internalized influence (see also Cialdini, this volume). However, such attempts often fail because of the wariness of an increasingly skeptical population.

In social psychology, the types of influencing that have attracted attention from researchers are mainly first-level influencing. This level of influencing has been found to arise from who the influencing parties (agents) are, what they possess, and how they act. Agents who are ingroup or reference group mem-bers would be in a position to exert influence over those who identify with them. The same applies to experts, legitimate authorities, and attractive and trustworthy communicators. These are commonly known as 'source' factors in classical communication/persuasion paradigms. Influencing will also flow from what agents possess in relation to what influencees want (e.g., wealth, informa-tion) or dread (e.g., punishment). French and Raven (1959) summarized the source and possession factors under various bases of power. Note that power is not, and should not be, confined to coercion although there is a tendency among some social psychologists to equate power with coercion or dominance (e.g., Moscovici, 1976). Agents without power can still influence if they act (verbally and nonverbally) in particular ways. For example, minorities can influence by organizing and patterning their collective behavior in a 'synchronically' and 'diachronically' consistent style (e.g., Moscovici, 1976). A door-knocking sales agent can win over a customer by adopting persuasive tactics such as 'a foot in the door' (e.g., Cialdini, 1993; see also Cialdini, this volume). Or agents may use various deception devices (e.g., Robinson, 1996). Note that 'act' factors, unlike 'source' and 'possession' factors, are not person-specific and can be used by the majority and the powerful as much as by the minority and the powerless. More generally, 'act' factors are at play wherever and whenever influence has to be negotiated on the spot. (See also chapters in this volume, by Cialdini, Latané, & Bourgeois, Tedeschi, and Williams & Dolnik.)

The concentration of social psychological research on first-level influencing may be due in part to researchers' preference for measurable, often transient, influence outcomes that are expected to emerge promptly after a direct influence attempt. This methodological bias (or favoritism) inevitably limits the study of influencing to only those that are relatively direct, immediate, and involving conflict of interests or disagreements. Another reason for the prominence of first-level influencing research is that the reward system in social psychology, at least in recent decades, tends to favor theory-testing over description and has done little to promote labor-intensive studies of influencing that involve sequential interaction over longer periods of time.

Both reasons are justifiable in themselves, and I do not wish to undervalue the progress made through research on first-level influencing. Historically such research has provided a wealth of data and discoveries of interesting phenomena that are counterintuitive and often socially relevant. Examples would include social facilitation, conformity/compliance, social norm formation, obedience to authority, minority influence, group polarization, and social loafing. Those data and discoveries in turn have stimulated theoretical research on processes of change. There are also concepts (e.g., ecological control by Cartwright, 1965), theoretical models (e.g., Raven's [1992] power/interaction model of interpersonal influence) and participant observations (e.g., Cialdini, 1993) that can provide the needed bridge between first- and higher-level influencing. Nonetheless the fact remains that research on influencing in social psychology is narrowly focused. This book thus has a particularly important role to play in refocussing the field, and calling attention to the many direct and indirect ways that influence processes operate.

To broaden the focus, it would be useful to attend to influencing at the higher levels. As well, it would be useful to connect influencing to power and language, which brings me to the second part of this chapter.

LINKS BETWEEN POWER AND LANGUAGE: THE BIG FIVE

Compared to the topic of social influence, language was traditionally at the periphery of social psychology and has only recently gained more attention.

The importance of language to social psychology lies in its use: Humans are uniquely equipped biologically and culturally to use language for a variety of expressive, communicative, and strategic purposes. This pragmatic approach to language, with its focus on the use of language rather than on language comprehension or abstract linguistic principles (e.g., syntax), was pioneered in speech act theory (e.g., Austin, 1962; Grice, 1975) and conversation analysis (e.g., Sacks, Schegloff, & Jefferson, 1974). Recognition of its relevance to social psychology through the early works of Brown, Harré, Robinson, and Giles (see Clark, 1985), together with social psychological studies of the 'message' factor in persuasion, have set the stage for the study of language use to shift from the periphery toward the core of social psychology. The shift in recent years has been accelerated by a number of developments associated with discursive psychology, the linguistic category model, social representations, and communication (see review by Krauss & Chiu, 1998).

There are five major links between power and language (Ng & Bradac, 1993). Two of them can be grouped under 'power *behind* language.' That is, language can (1) reveal and (2) reflect the power that lies behind it, but has no power of its own. When a robber intimidates, "Look, I gotta loaded gun here, give me the money or I'll shoot!" she is using language to reveal her coercive power base and to communicate her intention—"I want your money." She is not using language to create power, even though she would be using it in such a way as to convince her target that she is really dangerous, determined, and morally unrestrained. Language also is a symbol of and reflects the power or status of the community of speakers who use that language. This allows a speaker to invoke the power behind that language by deliberately using a high status language to invite deference or submission. For example, an Arab priest may summon a commoner in classical (high status) instead of vernacular (low status) Arabic. In revealing and reflecting power, language is used as a passive conduit or enhancer of power but has no power of its own.

On the other hand, individuals or group members can use language (3) to create influence, (4) to depoliticize their influence attempts, and (5) to make an existing dominance relationship routine so it seems natural. These three language-power links, that constitute the 'power *of* language,' represent the different levels of influencing introduced earlier on.

Language is a symbolic resource that can be used on its own to influence and control other people, or conversely, to reduce one's dependence on others. To the extent that the outcome is successful, language creates influence (first-level influencing). Concurrent with the use of language to influence, speakers may cover it up through lying, obfuscated speech, masked communication, and so on (Ng & Bradac, 1993; Robinson, 1996). Or they may, before influencing, use preparatory devices to set the stage for influencing (Raven, 1992). When either or both of these happen, language functions to depoliticize the exercise of power. Depoliticization will take the study of influencing beyond the first level to the second and possibly also the third level. Finally, as language is a repository of dominance relationships, its vocabulary and prescribed ways of communicating are biased in favor of the dominant party. Collusion by both parties in the use of a biased language will reproduce the dominance and, over time, routinize dominance by making it accepted as a part of the natural, un-questioned order of things. In this sense, routinization is third-level influenc-ing. Examples can be found in sexual (Crawford, 1995), racial (van Dijk, 1987), and ageist (Nussbaum, Hummert, Williams, & Harwood, 1996) relations.

Elsewhere my coauthors and I have discussed the five power-language links at some length (Ng, 1996; Ng & Bradac, 1993; Reid & Ng, 1999). For the present chapter, I will focus on the use of language to create influence in group and intergroup contexts.

USING LANGUAGE TO CREATE INFLUENCE: GROUP AND INTERGROUP PROCESSES

One of the cleanest paradigms for demonstrating the power of language to cre-ate influence is the 'message' factor in classical communication/persuasion re-search. One-sided versus two-sided arguments, fear arousal versus no fear arousal, strong versus weak arguments, and so forth, have been found to pro-duce varying degrees of influence, sometimes as main effects, but more often as interaction effects involving 'recipient' and/or 'source' factors. The so called powerful and powerless speech is another such paradigm, with numerous stud-ies showing the effects of speech style (e.g., speech rate, hesitancy, linguistic markers of polite speech) and oratorical devices (e.g., two-part contrast, posi-tion taking, three-part list). Other paradigms include speech evaluation and the linguistic category model, which show, respectively, the effects of high- versus low-status accents and of different categories of verbs. Another example of the use of language to create power is illustrated in the chapters by Forgas, and by Williams and Dolnik (this volume).

Studies conducted under those paradigms use a variety of measures to index influence, such as attitude change, consumer choice, impression forma-tion, applause, and causal attribution. Depending on the research question, measures of influence may be taken from individuals or groups (e.g., joint group decisions) but none to my knowledge has dealt with *group structure* or struc-tural change. This situation echoes Allport's (1935) individualistic conception of social psychology alluded to earlier. More than that, even in studies involving groups, most are really just about individuals in (minimal) groups. The neglect of group structure is a lacuna that needs addressing. Another lacuna is the rarity of studies that actually observe verbal interaction in groups rather than just manipulate aspects of language use as 'independent' variables.

How do group members sort themselves out into high and low influence members? Can one track hierarchical formation to prior verbal interactions? If yes, what aspects of language use are responsible for creating hierarchy? What might this tell us about the social psychological processes of influencing, and how might those processes differ (or remain the same) from group to intergroup contexts? At the end of the day, what can we learn from this about the formation of real groups, as distinct from psychological groups?

Some of the answers have already been given by Bales (1956) in his pioneering research on small groups. In newly formed groups made up of unacquainted persons of similar background, Bales (1956) found that power differentiation within the group corresponded to the differential distribution of talk among group members. Those who talked more were more likely to emerge as leaders and be acknowledged as such. The power of speaking turns, more so than utterance content (which was the focus of Bales' early work), was explained in economic or resource terms:

> When one member speaks, it takes time and attention from all other members of the group, some of whom may want to speak themselves. To take up time speaking in a small group is to exercise power over the other members for at least the duration of the time taken, regardless of the content. . . . Within the small group the time taken by a given member in a given session is practically a direct index of the amount of power he has attempted to exercise in that period. (Bales, 1970, pp. 76–77.)

To replicate and extend Bales' finding, my associates and I carried out a series of studies. In the first study, Brooke and Ng (1986) assembled groups made up of about four unacquainted university students, and asked them to view a video about a controversial topic and then to discuss issues depicted in the video. At the end of the discussion, group members rated each other on several social evaluation measures (e.g., social attractiveness and social dynamism). They also ranked their own as well as each other's influence during the discussion. In all six groups studied, the influence hierarchy passed the concordance test for consensus, and was positively validated by the social evaluation measures. As such, the influence rankings were accepted as a measure of the emergent hierarchy of influence among group members. We transcribed the discussions for detailed analyses and found, in support of Bales (1970), a positive relationship between rate of speaking turns and influence ranking. Contrasting this positive finding, stylistic features formerly thought to be responsible for powerful and powerless speech (e.g., hedges, polite markers) were unrelated to influence ranking.

Two further studies, again using consensual influence hierarchy formation as the criterion variable, replicated the effect of speaking turns (Ng, Bell, & Brooke, 1993; Ng, Brooke, & Dunne, 1995). They also discovered, counterintuitively, that turns obtained by interruption were as strong as, or even stronger than, turns obtained by noninterruption means in predicting influence. (See Ng, 1996, for an explanation of this finding and other mechanisms of conversational influence.)

In a major development of our research, we tested if turns would continue to function as a resource for influencing in an intergroup context. Three pro- and three anti-capital punishment adherents were assembled for each of eight interactive intergroup discussions to discuss capital punishment (Reid & Ng,

2000). Ingroup influence hierarchy (rankings of and by the three individuals who had the same view towards capital punishment) corresponded highly with relative turns, confirming previous results. The same high correspondence was found for outgroup hierarchy (rankings of procapital punishment members by anti people, and vice versa), thus extending previous results. Both ingroup and outgroup hierarchies were widely consensual.

Those results and others (e.g., Hollander, 1985; Mullen, Salas, & Driskell, 1989) clearly indicate that the process of conversational interaction, in this case, gaining speaking turns, is important for understanding influencing in both group and intergroup contexts.

The intergroup experiment by Reid and Ng (2000) also examined how the intergroup context might mediate turn-taking. Self-categorization theory suggests that "prototypicality" would be a strong contextual variable (Turner, 1991). Applying this idea to verbal interaction, we reasoned that success at gaining turns would depend on the degree of fit between utterance and group prototype. Utterances are prototypical if they are normatively consistent with the speaker's ingroup position; in this way, they embody the ingroup identity vis-à-vis the outgroup (cf. Oakes, Turner, & Haslam, 1991). Speakers who encode their utterances prototypically might be in a particularly strong position to gain turns.

We coded the content of a turn for "prototypicality." If the utterance was normatively consistent with the speaker's ingroup position, the turn was coded as prototypical. The excerpt of conversation below illustrates two prototypical turns. At turn 1, a procapital punishment speaker tried to defend her ingroup's position by differentiating it from the practice of the legal system. Her utterance was interrupted by an anti-capital punishment speaker, who argued that as capital punishment would not work in practice it should not be implemented. This argument was considered to be normatively consistent with the anti position (and in opposition to the pro position). Hence it was coded as prototypical of the speaker's ingroup. By the same token, the pro speaker's utterance was prototypical of her own ingroup.

> Pro: Well eh that is that is the legal system that's not behind what the principle supports [that principle is you do]
>
> Anti: [so is it] saying that in theory it's ok but in practice it's never going to work out so why implement it
>
> (Reid & Ng, 2000, p. 90)

Within a turn, if the utterance was inconsistent with the ingroup position (that is, consistent with the *outgroup* position), it was coded as anti-prototypical; and if it was neutral to both the ingroup and outgroup position, it was coded as nonprototypical. As might be expected, there were very few anti-prototypical turns and these were dropped from further consideration.

Since overall turns were highly correlated with interruption turns, only the latter was used for analyses. (See above for an example of an interruption turn, namely, the anti-speaker's turn.) The results were, first, that prototypical utterances led to more successful than unsuccessful interruptions, whereas nonprototypical utterances showed the reverse. Second, interruptions worded in prototypical utterances were longer and more highly correlated with influence ranking than those worded in nonprototypical utterances. This pattern of results suggests an interactionally negotiated process that is grounded in the intergroup context. Speakers who use prototypical utterances help to define and delineate group identities. For this they will be granted speaking rights and hence the ability to gain turns. For the same reason, listeners will be extraordinarily attentive and this allows longer turns to develop. More turns and longer turns then channel conversational resources to those speakers, thus putting them in a strong position to exercise influence. In this way, speakers and listeners interactively and jointly transform a psychological group into a real group that has an agreed influence hierarchy.

The picture painted above is tentative and more research is needed to firm up the empirical base and to strengthen the chain of argument. For what it is worth, it opens up a way of interrelating language use and social identity in the common framework of influencing. The latter (influencing), is the real stuff that real groups are made out of.

CONCLUSION

To conclude this chapter let us return to the general issue of the relationships between social influence and social psychology. When Allport (1954) found a home for social psychology in social influence, that home, as we have seen, was primarily for the study of *being influenced* rather than with *influencing*. Furthermore, the home provided accommodation mainly for *interpersonal* influence, and little else for influences in *group* or *intergroup* contexts. Recent works, particularly those of Moscovici (1976) and Turner (1991), have broadened the two limitations respectively. But regrettably, precious little research has dealt with both limitations at the same time; and as a result, research on influencing in group and intergroup contexts remains conspicuously undeveloped.

In addressing the lacuna above, the present chapter has focussed on processes of verbal interaction and language use that underlie the formation of influence hierarchies within groups in intra- and intergroup contexts. Admittedly the findings in support of the resource hypothesis and self-categorization theory are limited to a narrow phase of group development, and much remains to be done with regard to the higher and more subtle levels of influencing outlined earlier. To a certain extent, subtle influencing overlaps with the 'indirect' processes referred to throughout the present volume; but in addition, it highlights the importance of a multi-disciplinary perspective to influencing that would include, at a minimum, political sociology and media studies on top of social psychology.

Finally, we should not lose sight of what the study of social influence is for.

From an academic point of view, it is first and foremost for the advancement of knowledge. As Moscovici (1976, pp. 6–7) has so eloquently stated, "It is my contention that influence is the central process of social psychology, upon which all the other processes depend. As such, it could serve as the principle which could integrate all the facts and all the theories of social psychologists. Without recognition of this, there can be no progress in theoretical and empirical knowledge." We may be sceptical of Moscovici's contention, but we ought to admire his vision of the wider picture. From yet another point of view, the study of social influence, especially if and when this is grounded in a multi-disciplinary perspective, ought to be linked with *social change*. Indeed the very title of Moscovici's (1976) book is precisely that: *Social influence and social change*. If as social psychologists we have lost sight of this critically important linkage, perhaps it is because we have never taken the linkage seriously enough while all this time the world around us has changed!

REFERENCES

Allport, G. W. (1954). The historical background of modern social psychology. In G. Lindzey (Ed.), *Handbook of social psychology* (vol. 1, pp 3–56). Reading, MA: Addison-Wesley.

Austin, J. (1962). *How to do things with words*. Oxford, England: Oxford University Press.

Bales, R. F. (1956). Task status and likeability as a function of talking and listening in decision making groups. In L. D. White (Ed.), *The state of social sciences* (pp. 148–161). Chicago, IL: University of Chicago Press.

Bales, R. F. (1970). *Personality and interpersonal behaviour*. New York: Holt, Reinhart, and Winston.

Brooke, M. E., & Ng, S. H. (1986). Language and social influence in small conversational groups. *Journal of Language and Social Psychology, 5*, 201–210.

Cartwright, D. (1965). Influence, leadership, control. In J. G. March (Ed.), *Handbook of organisations* (pp. 1–47). Chicago: Rand McNally.

Chaiken, S. (1987). The heuristic model of persuasion. In M. P. Zanna, J. M. Olson, & C. P. Herman (Eds.), *Social influence: The Ontario symposium* (Vol. 5, pp. 3–39). Hillsdale, NJ: Erlbaum.

Cialdini, R. B. (1993). *Influence: The psychology of persuasion*. New York: Quill.

Cialdini, R. B., & Trost, M .R. (1998). Social influence: Social norms, conformity, and compliance. In D. T. Gilbert, S. T. Fiske, & G. Lindzey (Eds.), *The handbook of social psychology* (4th ed., pp. 151–192). New York: McGraw-Hill.

Clark, H. H. (1985). Language use and language users. In G. Lindzey & A. Aronson (Eds.), *The handbook of social psychology* (3rd ed., pp. 179–231). New York: Harper & Row.

Crawford, M. (1995). *Talking difference: On gender and language*. London: Sage.

Deutsch, M., & Gerard, H. B. (1955. A study of normative an informational social influences upon individual judgment. *Journal of Abnormal and Social Psychology, 51*, 629–636.

French, J. R. P., Jr., & Raven, B. H. (1959). The bases of social power. In D. Cartwright (Ed.), *Studies in social power* (pp. 150–167). Ann Arbor, MI: Institute for Social Research.

Grice, H. P. (1975). Logic and conversation. In P. Cole & I. L. Morgan (Eds.), *Syntax and semantics. Vol. 3: Speech acts* (pp. 41-58). New York: Academic.

Hogg, M. A. (1992). *The social psychology of group cohesiveness: From attraction to social identity*. New York: Harvester Wheatsheaf.

Hollander, E. P. (1985). Leadership and power. In G. Lindzey & E. Aronson (Eds.), *Handbook of social psychology* (3rd. ed., pp. 485–537). New York: Random House.

Jacob, R. C., & Campbell, D. T. (1961). The perpetuation of an arbitrary tradition through several generations of a laboratory micro-culture. *Journal of Abnormal and Social Psychology, 62*, 649–658.

Jones, E. E. (1985). Major developments in social psychology during the past five decades. In G. Lindzey & E. Aronson (Eds.), *The handbook of social psychology* (3rd ed., Vol. 1, pp. 47–107). New York: Random House.

Kelman, H. C. (1958). Compliance, identification, and internalization: Three processes of attitude change. *Journal of Conflict Resolution, 2*, 51–60.

Kerr, N. L. (1992). Norms in social dilemmas. In D. A. Schroeder (Ed.) *Social dilemmas: Perspectives on individuals and groups* (pp. 31–48). Westport, CT: Praeger.

Krauss, R. M., & Chiu. C. Y. (1998). Language and social behaviour. In D. Gilbert, S. Fiske, & G. Lindzey (Eds.), *Handbook of social psychology* (4th ed., pp. 41–88). New York: Guilford.

Levy, D. A., Collins, B. E., & Nail, P. R. (1999). A new model of interpersonal influence characteristics. *Journal of Social Behavior and Personality, 13*, 715–733.

Mackie, D. M., & Smith, E. R. (1998). Intergroup relations: Insights from a theoretically integrative approach. *Psychological Review, 105*, 499–529.

Mackie, D. M., & Wright, C. L. (in press). Social influence in an intergroup context. In C. Insko & R. Brown (Eds.), *European Review of Social Psychology*. London: Blackwell.

Moscovici, S. (1976). *Social influence and social change*. London: Academic.

Mullen, B., Salas, E., & Driskell, J. E. (1989). Salience, motivation, and artifact as contributions to the relation between participation rate and leadership. *Journal of Experimental Social Psychology, 25*, 545–559.

Ng, S. H. (1980). *The social psychology of power*. London: Academic Press.

Ng, S. H. (1996). Power: An essay in honour of Henri Tajfel. In W. P. Robinson (Ed.), *Social identity: The developing legacy of Henri Tajfel* (pp. 191–215). Oxford, England: Butterworth & Heinemann.

Ng, S. H., Bell, D., & Brooke, M. (1993). Gaining turns and achieving high influence ranking in small conversational groups. *British Journal of Social Psychology, 32*, 265–275.

Ng, S. H., & Bradac, J. J. (1993). *Power in language: Verbal communication and social influence*. Newbury Park, CA: Sage.

Ng, S. H., Brooke, M., & Dunne, M. (1995). Interruption and influence in discussion groups. *Journal of Language and Social Psychology, 14*, 369–381.

Nussbaum, J. F., Hummert, M. L., Williams, A., & Harwood, J. (1996). Communication and older adults. In B. R. Burleson (Ed.), *Communication yearbook* (Vol. 19, pp. 1–47). Thousand Oaks, CA: Sage.

Oakes, P. J., Turner, J. C., & Haslam, S. A. (1991). Perceiving people as group members: The role of fit in the salience of social categorization. *British Journal of Social Psychology, 30*, 125–144.

Petty, R. E., & Cacioppo, J. (1986). The Elaboration Likelihood Model of persuasion. In L. Berkowitz (Ed.), *Advances in experimental social psychology* (Vol. 19, pp. 123–205). New York: Academic.

Raven, B. H. (1992). A power/interaction model of interpersonal influence: French and Raven thirty years later. *Journal of Social Behavior and Personality, 7*, 217–244.

Reid, S. A., & Ng, S. H. (1999). Language, power and intergroup relations. *Journal of Social Issues, 55*, 119–139.

Reid, S. A., & Ng, S. H. (2000). Conversation as a resource for influence: Evidence for prototypical arguments and social identification processes. *European Journal of Social Psychology, 30*, 83–100.

Robinson, W. P. (1996). *Deceit, delusion, and detection*. London: Sage.

Sacks, H., Schegloff, E., & Jefferson, G. (1974). A simplest systematics for the organization of turn-taking for conversation. *Language, 50*, 696-735.

Sherif, M. (1962). Intergroup relations and leadership: Introductory statement. In M. Sherif (Ed.), *Intergroup relations and leadership* (pp. 3–21). New York: John Wiley.

Skinner, B. F. (1976). *Walden two*, rev. ed. New York: Macmillan.

Triplett, N. (1898). The dynamogenic factors in pacemaking and competition. *American Journal of Psychology, 9*, 507–533.

Turner, J. C. (1991). *Social influence*. Pacific Grove, CA: Brooks/Cole.

van Dijk, T. A. (1987). *Communicating racism: Ethnic prejudice in thought and talk*. London: Sage.

12

Resisting Influence
Judgmental Correction
and its Goals

FRITZ STRACK
THOMAS MUSSWEILER

*I*n the course of its history, research on "social influence" has shifted its focus from behavior to attitudes and beliefs. For a certain period of time, the
domain of "social influence" was predominantly concerned with the "mere
presence" of others as a central determinant of a target's behavior. As a facilita-
tor of achievement in both athletic (Triplett, 1898) and mental (Moede, 1920)
tasks, the physical attendance of nonparticipating individuals was considered to
be sufficient to account for observed improvements. However, when experimental findings revealed a more mixed pattern of effects, more attention was
directed toward the underlying psychological mechanisms (Zajonc, 1965).

In contrast, in the domain of judgment, "social influence" was always associated with specific psychological mechanisms that were seen as either motivational or informational in nature (e.g., Deutsch & Gerard, 1955). The need for

Address correspondence to: Fritz Strack, Psychologie II, Universität Würzburg,
Röntgenring 10, 97070 Würzburg, Germany. E-mail: strack@psychologie.uni-
wuerzburg.de

199

an inclusion of underlying mechanisms is most apparent in the domain of "persuasion" and "attitude change." While researchers in the Yale Attitude Change Program (e.g., Hovland, Janis, & Kelley, 1953) conceived of attitudinal influence as a special type of learning that could be understood by identifying the situational and personal determinants, this doctrine was soon considered to be incapable of explaining many of the phenomena that had been described.

This deficit was most apparent for the so-called "sleeper effect" (Kelman & Hovland, 1953) which qualified the conditions under which the success of a social (in this case "attitudinal") influence depended on whether the communicator (or the source) was endowed with credibility (see Hovland & Weiss, 1951). In particular, the "sleeper effect" postulated that the handicap of low credibility would gradually dissolve as a function of the time that went by. This result gave rise to speculations about divergent mental dynamics elicited by the message and its source, namely that information about the source would be lost much sooner than the content of the message.

Whereas the phenomenon was on the table, the cognitive processes had not been sufficiently understood until much later when cognitive social psychologists studied the mechanisms of priming, in particular the conditions under which this procedure was effectively operating or not (e.g., Higgins, Rholes, & Jones, 1977; Srull & Wyer, 1979; Wyer & Srull, 1981). It came as a surprise that this type of cognitive influence was particularly effective if the information was presented in a subliminal fashion (Bargh & Pietromonaco, 1982). This finding also sheds some light on the sleeper effect if one assumes that the lesser effectiveness of the supraliminal priming is due to people's awareness of episodic characteristics of the priming. Following this logic suggests that if an individual's attention is directed toward the characteristics of the source, the impact of the source and its characteristics will be increased. Interestingly, first evidence was again obtained in a study on the sleeper effect: If after the long delay, people had been reminded of the source and its low credibility, the agreement with the message was again diminished (Kelman & Hovland, 1953).

Within the priming paradigm, Strack, Schwarz, Bless, Kübler, and Wänke (1993) had subtly reminded participants of the priming episode before they had to evaluate ambiguous behaviors of a target person. As a consequence, the judgmental assimilation toward the primed stimulus was reversed (see Fig. 12.1) which suggests that people modify or correct their judgments when they are aware of an influence.

There are at least two cognitive mechanisms by which correction may be achieved (e.g., Strack, 1992; Strack & Hannover, 1996). In particular, decontamination (see Wilson & Brekke, 1994) may occur either by a recomputation of the judgment or by an adjustment of the response. Specifically, people may try to recompute their judgment by disregarding contaminated information. This type of correction requires that the purified judgment can be based on information that is not contaminated. For example, jurors who have been instructed to disregard an inadmissible piece of information may base their verdict on other aspects of the evidence. Alternatively, judges may compensate for

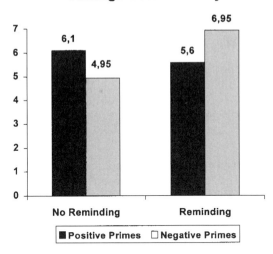

FIGURE 12.1. Ratings of likeability as a function of prime valence and being reminded of the priming event. More positive numbers represent more positive evaluations. Adapted from Strack et al. (1993).

a presumed influence by adjusting their response. Whereas this strategy does not demand a search for uncontaminated information, it requires a notion about the direction of the influence. For example, if a person wants to assess the correct temperature of water by using the elicited thermal sensation on her skin, she is well advised to adjust her judgment for the influence of a previous exposure to a hot or cold fluid. However, it is not enough to be aware of the influence. In addition, the person must possess some intuitive knowledge or beliefs about the likely impact of the previous exposure on her subsequent temperature sensations (see Förster & Strack, 1998).

A domain in which the decontamination of judgments found a particular interest is that of stereotypes. Because stereotypes are considered to be overgeneralizing or even wrong and certainly politically unacceptable (Brigham, 1971), people are often motivated to purge their judgments from these influences. In fact, it has been argued that people whose judgments are not stereotyped differ from their stereotyped counterparts not in less stereotyped knowledge structures but in their willingness to avoid stereotyped judgments (Devine, 1989).

This seems to indicate the fact that the desire to purge one's judgments from stereotyped influences may be fueled by at least two motives. First, people may want to be politically correct and fair in their judgment of others. As Plant and Devine (1998) have demonstrated, the motivation to be unprejudiced is an important factor in suppressing a stereotype. Second, people may want to be factually correct and avoid the costs that are associated with faulty decisions.

There is reason to assume that these two goals go along with the two correctional strategies. That is, people whose primary goal is to be fair are more likely to compensate the presumed influence of the stereotype by adjusting their response in the opposite direction. As most stereotypes have evaluatively negative implications, a greater positivity may be a reasonable adjustment by default. However, as most stereotypes also include at least some positive characteristics (e.g., "athletic" and "musical" in the African American case), judges may use their more specific knowledge about the stereotype to counteract its influence. The goal of factual correctness, in contrast, may induce people to recompute their judgment on the basis of new and presumably uncontaminated information.

While there exists a considerable number of studies in which the operation of adjustment was convincingly demonstrated (e.g., Wegener & Petty, 1997), there is little research on recomputation and no research in which the two strategies are juxtaposed and explored as a function of different correctional goals.

In the next part of this chapter, we attempt such an endeavor and report three studies in which people are asked to form an impression of a target person while they are asked to avoid stereotypic influences. In the first experiment, it will be demonstrated that people's knowledge of a stereotype does, in fact, guide the adjustment of their response. In the second study, judges may choose between adjusting and recomputing. In the third experiment, different correctional goals were induced to identify preferences for adjustment versus recomputation.

EXPERIMENT 1:
CORRECTION WITHOUT NEW INFORMATION

The purpose of the first experiment was to demonstrate the theory-based nature of correctional adjustments. In particular, we assume that to compensate for a presumed influence, people must have some knowledge about the stereotype in question. It was predicted that instructions to avoid being influenced by the gender of the target person should decrease the likelihood of ascribing characteristics that are typical for the gender stereotype. In a similar vein, it is possible that characteristics that are untypical for the gender stereotype will be more likely to be attributed to the target person.

Because all studies are similar in procedure, we describe the first experiment in detail, whereas for the remaining studies we only note procedural deviations when they occur.

Participants received a short résumé of a fictitious applicant, a short statement that a colleague had prepared about her or him, and two questionnaires pertaining to these materials. For half of the participants, the applicant was female ("Mrs. Christiane Müller"), for the other half he was male ("Mr. Christian Müller"). Neither the résumé nor the statement had direct implications for the two critical dimensions.

The first questionnaire participants received was meant to support the cover story and assessed participants' evaluation of peripheral qualities of the materials such as the elaborateness of the résumé. The second questionnaire assessed participants' impression of the applicant on 14 dimensions. Instructions pointed out that the purpose of this questionnaire was to find out whether the presented materials allow their reader to develop a personal impression of the applicant. Moreover, half of the participants were instructed to ensure that their judgment about the applicant was not influenced by her or his gender ("Please do not let the applicants' gender influence your judgment"). Judgments were given on 9-point rating scales ranging from "little" to "very," while the order of the dimensions was kept the same for all participants. The critical dimensions were chosen so that strong gender stereotypes existed for two of them. Pretesting had revealed that on the first dimension ("technically skilled"), men were typically seen as more competent than women, whereas the opposite was true for the second ("empathy"). No clear gender stereotypes existed for the remaining 12 dimensions (e.g., motivated, tolerant, environmentally concerned, etc.).

Figure 12.2 depicts the results summarized as the difference between the two critical traits, which always contributed to the index. Specifically, participants' scores on the "technically skilled" dimension were subtracted from their scores on the "empathy" dimension. As a consequence, more positive scores indicate a higher consistency of the judgment with the female stereotype. The results provide support for the gender-specific applicability of the two traits. That is, when participants had to generate their judgment without correction instructions, the trait ratings of the female applicant were more in line with the female than those for the male applicant. This pattern, however, was reversed if

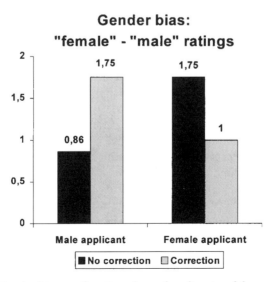

FIGURE 12.2. Gender bias as a function of sex of applicant and for correction. More positive numbers represent more female trait ascriptions.

judges were asked to avoid being influenced by the gender of the applicant. Specifically, judgments of the male applicant were more in line with the female stereotype than those for the female target.

These results suggest that in the absence of additional uncontaminated information, people's knowledge of the gender stereotype is used to counteract a presumed influence. Specifically, on dimensions that are most closely related to the stereotype, the pattern of ascriptions was reversed such that more of the typically male characteristic was attributed to the female target and more of the typically female characteristic to the male applicant. This compensation corresponded with the actual influence of the stereotype. This suggests that participants tried to adjust for the assumed influence of the stereotype.

EXPERIMENT 2: CORRECTION WITH AND WITHOUT NEW INFORMATION

Whereas in Study 1 such an adjustment of one's responses was the only way to reach one's correctional goal, the question arises how an alternative correctional option may affect the judgments. In particular, one might ask how the possibility to recompute may influence the judgments. Is there a preference for one strategy over the other? The second experiment was designed to examine this question. To do so, half of the participants were given the chance to consider additional information to avoid a potential influence of the target's gender on their judgments. To assess the impact of the new pieces of information, the information was constructed such that they were evaluatively consistent with the implications of the gender stereotype. That is, when participants were asked to correct their judgments, stereotype-inconsistent judgments were diagnostic of adjustments whereas stereotype-consistent judgments indicated recomputations.

The résumé and the questionnaires were similar to Experiment 1. In contrast to the first study, however, the applicant was always female ("Angela Müller"). Moreover, in addition to the résumé and the statement by a colleague, half of the participants received a booklet with 50 short episodes about the target. Ten of these episodes had clear negative implications for the stereotypic male dimension "technical skills" (e.g. "Two weeks ago Angela was pretty helpless, when her printer wouldn't stop printing out pages and pages of data. She was unable to interrupt the process and still uses the resulting stack of paper for notes") and ten had clear positive implications for the stereotypic female dimension "empathetic" (e.g. "I like talking with Angela over lunch break. She listens attentively and usually has good advice when I've got something on my mind."). Thus, the implications of these 20 episodes were consistent with the general stereotype of women being empathetic but technically unskilled. The remaining 30 episodes had no implications for the two critical dimensions (e.g. "In the summer time Angela likes to work with her window wide open. She also has a lot of plants in her office.").

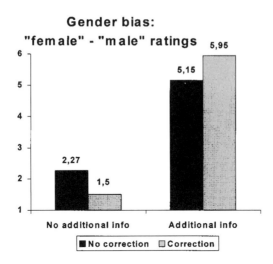

**Gender bias:
"female" - "male" ratings**

FIGURE 12.3. Gender bias as a function of correction instructions and the availability of additional information. More positive numbers represent more female trait ascriptions.

As can be seen from Figure 12.3, when no additional information was available, participants who were instructed not to be influenced by her gender judged the female target person to be more technically skilled and less empathetic than participants who did not receive these instructions. This finding replicates the results of Experiment 1. However, when additional information was available, this pattern was reversed. Here, lower ratings for Angela's technical skills and higher ratings for her empathic skills were given in the correction condition.

These results replicate the findings of the previous study. Specifically, participants who had no opportunity to include additional information adjusted their response on the basis of the presumed influence of the stereotype. However, if there was a possibility to use additional information to decontaminate their judgments, this information was used. When the appropriate information is available, the present results suggest a preference for recomputation.

However, such a conclusion may be misleading because the preference for one particular type of correction may depend on a particular correctional goal. For example, a person with a strong concern about being prejudiced may try to deviate from the contents of the stereotype. As stereotypes are predominantly negative in their evaluative content (Brigham, 1971), a simple decontamination may consist of changing the judgment into a more positive direction (Wyer & Budesheim, 1987; Wyer & Unverzagt, 1985). If the person knows the specific contents of a stereotype, a potential influence may be counteracted by adjusting the response on the relevant dimensions. This strategy, however, does not necessarily increase the accuracy of the judgment because there is no guarantee that the particular target does not possess a characteristic that is included in the stereotype but instead possesses features that the stereotype excludes, as our previous results seem to suggest. Therefore, if a person is primarily concerned about the accuracy of the judgment, focusing on individuating information about the target may be a more adequate means for improving the judgment. That is, instead of using stereotypes to simplify the judgment under suboptimal conditions (Bodenhausen & Lichtenstein, 1987), people may focus on individuating information when they are motivated to increase accuracy.

To examine these possibilities, we varied people's correctional goals in our final study. In particular, participants were either asked to be *fair* and avoid being influenced by the gender of the target person. Alternatively, they were asked to be as *accurate* as possible in their judgment. It was expected that the fairness goal would lead to adjustment whereas the accuracy goal would lead to an increased use of the individuating information.

EXPERIMENT 3: CORRECTION IN PURSUIT OF DIFFERENT CORRECTIONAL GOALS

In contrast to the preceding study, all participants received additional information about the female target person ("Angela M."). Specifically, in addition to the résumé and the previous statement about the applicant, each participant received a booklet containing short descriptions of 50 episodes about Angela. The stereotypic male dimension was identical to the preceding studies ("technical skills"). However, the stereotypic female dimension was changed and had mild positive implications for the two related dimensions of social competence and empathy (e.g. "Angela is very sensitive to bad vibrations among her colleagues. Usually she manages to loosen up tensions with a funny remark." "Angela wants to have children. She is certainly going to be a good mother."). Based on pretesting, these were the two dimensions with the strongest positive stereotype for women.

To induce different correctional goals, the correction instructions were changed. In the "accuracy" instructions, participants were told to be as accurate as possible in their judgment. In the "fairness" instructions, however, they were told to be as fair as possible and to make sure that their judgment was not influenced by Angela's gender. Two thirds of the participants received one of the two correction instructions and one third received no correction instruction at all.

The mean ratings for the stereotypic male dimension and the stereotypic female dimension are depicted in Figure 12.4, in which ratings of social competence and empathy were combined to an index score. As is apparent from the means, the combined ratings under no correction instructions are lower (i.e., relatively less consistent with the female stereotype) than under the accuracy instruction but higher than under the fairness instruction.

These findings clearly suggest that the choice of a correctional strategy depends on the goal that is pursued in the judgment situation. That is, when participants were asked to be fair, they actually used their knowledge of the

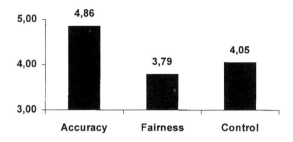

FIGURE 12.4. Gender bias as a function of correctional goals. More positive numbers represent more female trait ascriptions.

stereotype to compensate for its influence. In contrast, when they tried to be accurate, they used the additional information that was available to them.

GENERAL DISCUSSION

These findings suggest that people may strategically counteract the influence of information on their judgments. While previous studies have focussed on the awareness of the influence, like in studies of the sleeper effect and more recent priming experiments, the present findings highlight the fact that people pursue epistemic or social goals when they try to decontaminate their judgments (see also Kruglanski, 1996). Of course, the two goals we have mentioned here, accuracy and fairness, do not exhaust the list and must certainly be supplemented by others, like the goal to restore one's freedom of choice, as proposed in reactance theory (Brehm, 1966).

The present findings suggest that to understand how people try to liberate themselves from unwanted influence, we need to understand what exactly they want to accomplish.

However, the present data—along with many other findings—indicate that judges' attempts to resist an unwanted influence do not necessarily eliminate bias. Rather, they may bias the judgment in the opposite direction, such that under correction instructions in Study 1, the male target was assigned more female characteristics than the female target, and vice versa. Going beyond the present results, such a boomerang effect may result from both ways of implementing correctional goals. Specifically, judges who focus on new evidence have to identify information that qualifies as uncontaminated. Such a categorization, however, may be based on inferences that use the valence of the information as a cue. That is, people may select information that is inconsistent with the value attached to the stereotype. As a result, the informational basis for the judgment may be more inconsistent with the stereotype if people engage in a recomputation than if the stereotype is not activated at all.

Similarly, judges who correct by adjusting their response on the scale seem to overestimate the influence of the stereotype. As a consequence, they adjust too much and produce contrast effects. This suggests that even if people know that and they are—and how they are—influenced by a stereotype, they have faulty assessments about the strength of the presumed influence. Consequences of such erroneous self-knowledge have been identified by Nisbett and Wilson (1977) who found that the causal determinants of a person's own behavior are often misidentified. The fact that people's beliefs about the influences on their own mental functioning may determine the solution of basic psychological tasks like memory has been demonstrated in our own work (e.g., Strack & Bless, 1994; see also Bless, Strack, & Walther, this volume). We found that the induced belief about a better memorability of words that had a high versus low (and vice versa) probability of occurrence influenced their willingness to reject distracters in a recognition tasks (see Strack & Förster, 1998). Presumably, this was the case because on the basis of this self-knowledge, participants inferred that they would have remembered the particular word, had it been presented. Of course, the accuracy of the final judgment depends on the correctness of the self-knowledge that serves as a basis. That is, the more accurate people's knowledge about their own psychological functioning, the more accurate their memory performance. Although in the domain of attitudinal judgments, "accuracy" must be understood in relation to a control condition, it can be assumed that the same principle applies. That is, the more accurate the knowledge about the direction and strength of an influence the more accurate the resulting judgment. However, it should be noted that people are more prone to be affected by knowledge that they believe to reflect idiosyncratic aspects of their behavior than by knowledge about baseline characteristics (Strack & Förster, 1998). Thus, to know one's own proneness to certain judgmental biases seems to elicit stronger corrective responses than to be informed about the average effect of a particular determinant.

The present findings have another interesting implication. If a correction through adjustment requires knowledge of the stereotype, then the stereotype must be activated each time the correction takes place. As a consequence, the content of the stereotype will be subsequently more accessible and may influence judgment and behavior in situations when people are not aware of being influenced. Research on rebound effects as a consequence of suppressing a stereotype (e.g. Macrae, Bodenhausen, Milne, & Jetten, 1998) highlights this ironic possibility.

CONCLUSION

The present line of research implies that many influence attempts operate on an automatic level and lie outside of target's awareness (Cialdini, 1993; this volume). Under such circumstances, resistance cannot be made contingent on the experience of being influenced. Rather, it requires a regulative intervention that is based on knowledge about potential determinants, about the direction of their effects, and about their potency. In addition, the regulation of social judgments may be based on knowledge about one's own psychological functioning (Strack & Förster, 1998). The underlying principle that self-knowledge serves as a basis for acquiring knowledge about the world also may be applied to the regulation of stereotyped judgments. For example, a person may not only know the content of a stereotype but also may be aware of the circumstances under which the stereotype is most likely to affect judgments and behaviors. Thus, this person may decide to postpone a response if she or he knows that an immediate reaction may prejudiced and unfair.

While it is often difficult to identify prejudiced *attitudes* by asking explicit questions (e.g., Plant & Devine, 1998), prejudiced *behavior* can be easily observed under conditions that prevent people from regulating their behavior. Such circumstances were created by Doob and Gross (1968) in a natural setting in which the experimenter's car would temporarily block the traffic at an intersection after the light had changed to green. The incident of honking by the next driver, its latency, and its duration were used as measures of aggression. This paradigm was used not only to study various determinants of aggression (like heat or the presence of violent cues) but also to investigate the role of stereotypes. For example, Deaux (1971) found that female drivers were more likely to be honked at than male drivers. In a related extension of the Doob and Gross paradigm, Forgas (1976) varied the nationality of the blocking car and assessed other drivers' reactions in different European countries. Specifically, the experimenter's car either displayed German or Australian insignia (flag and national identification code) in the rear window and blocked intersections in France, Spain, Italy, and Germany. It was assumed that the generally more negative German national stereotype would facilitate hostile honking behavior, compared to the rather nondescript Australian stereotype. As predicted, in countries other than Germany, blocked drivers were faster at using their horn if the driver of the blocking was presumably a German rather than an Australian.

More recently, results of a procedure developed by Greenwald, McGhee, & Schwartz (1998) suggest that impulsive behavioral responses in the domain of stereotypes or even attitudes in general may be dissociated from people's deliberate evaluations. Specifically, in their Implicit Association Test (IAT), participants are trained to emit a particular response (e.g., to hit a key with their right or left hand) to indicate the predetermined valence of a stimulus (e.g., a baby for a positive and a traffic accident for a negative valence). Thereby, an association between the response and a valence is being established. The second task requires participants to categorize stimuli on a dimension that includes a valence in an implicit fashion. For example, people have to indicate if the person depicted in a photo is Black or White. If it is the case that the racial stereotype as it is represented in the person entails an evaluative component, the categorization will be facilitated if the response is already associated with same valence. As a result, people will be faster in categorizing a person as Black if the same motor response was previously activated to classify objects as "negative" (Greenwald et al., 1998; for a German application of the IAT, see Neumann et al., 1998). Moreover, IAT responses have been found to activate subcortical brain mechanisms that are typically involved in immediate affective reactions while the "explicit" expression of racial attitudes did not elicit such reactions (Phelps et al., 2000). This finding is consistent with results by Fazio, Jackson, Dunton, & Williams (1995) who found no correlation between the explicit Modern Racism Scale and implicit evaluative priming.

These results describe some limits of resisting the influence of stereotypes. Specifically, a behavioral reaction that is compatible with the valence of the stereotype is difficult to regulate if the person is not aware of the role of the stereotype in eliciting the behavior. Of course, this should be most likely to be the case under conditions that prevent such self-reflection. However, there is hope that even such behavioral manifestations of stereotypes may be altered under the appropriate interventions. For example, yet unpublished work by Mitchell, Nosek, and Banaji (cited in Banaji, in press) suggests that different construals of the attitude object may influence IAT responses. Kawakami, Dovidio, Moll, Hermsen, and Russin (2000) have found that training the negation of stereotypic associations practicing incompatible responses may also break the preexisting associations.

In summary, it seems that resisting unwanted influences in social judgment is more complex than one would assume. In a situation that affords self-reflection, the goal to decontaminate a judgment may be achieved if one knows the contaminating influence, and its direction and strength because judgments may be recomputed or adjusted. However, if behavioral responses are immediately associated (either through experimental or preexperimental learning) with the valence of a stereotype, simply pursuing the goal of mental decontamination is not sufficient. Rather, the underlying mechanisms must be broken up. However, to succeed in this endeavor, more knowledge about the dynamics of implicit attitudes and stereotypes is warranted (see Banaji, in press).

REFERENCES

Banaji, M. R. (in press). Implicit attitudes can be measured. In H. L. Roediger III, J. S. Nairne, I. Neath, & A. Surprenant (Eds.), *The nature of remembering: Essays in honor of Robert G. Crowder*. New York: American Psychological Association.

Bargh, J. A., & Pietromonaco, P. (1982). Automatic information processing and social perception: The influence of trait information presented outside of conscious awareness on impression formation. *Journal of Personality and Social Psychology, 43*, 437–449.

Bodenhausen, G. V., & Lichtenstein, M.

(1987). Social stereotypes and information-processing strategies: The impact of task complexity. *Journal of Personality and Social Psychology, 52*, 871–880.

Brehm, J. W. (1966). *A theory of psychological reactance*. New York: Academic.

Brigham, J. C. (1971). Ethnic stereotypes. *Psychological Bulletin, 76*, 15–33.

Cialdini, R. B. (1993). *Influence. Science and practice* (3rd ed.). New York: HarperCollins.

Deaux, K. K. (1971). Honking at the intersection: A replication and extension. *Journal of Social Psychology, 84*, 159–160.

Deutsch, M., & Gerard, H. B. (1955). A study of normative and informational influence upon individual judgment. *Journal of Abnormal and Social Psychology*, *51*, 629–636.

Devine, P. G. (1989). Stereotypes and prejudice: Their automatic and controlled components. *Journal of Personality and Social Psychology*, *56*, 5–18.

Doob, A. N., & Gross, A. E. (1968). Status of frustrator as an inhibitor of horn-honking responses. *Journal of Social Psychology*, *76*, 213–218.

Fazio, R. H., Jackson, J. R., Dunton, B. C., & Williams, C. J. (1995). Variability in automatic activation as an unobtrisive measure of racial attitudes: A bona fide pipeline? *Journal of Personality and Social Psychology*, *69*, 1013–1027.

Forgas, J. P. (1976). An unobtrusive study of reactions to national stereotypes in four European countries. *Journal of Social Psychology*, *99*, 37–42.

Förster, J., & Strack, F. (1998). Subjective theories about encoding may influence recognition. Judgmental regulation in human memory. *Social Cognition*, *16*, 78–92.

Greenwald, A. G., McGhee, D. E., & Schwartz, J. L. K. (1998). Measuring individual differences in implicit cognition: The implicit association test. *Journal of Personality and Social Psychology*, *74*, 1464–1480.

Higgins, E. T., Rholes, W. S., & Jones, C. R. (1977). Category accessibility and impression formation. *Journal of Experimental Social Psychology*, *13*, 141–154.

Hovland, C. I., Janis, I. L., & Kelley, H. H. (1953). *Communication and persuasion: Psychological studies of opinion change.* New Haven, CT: Yale University Press.

Hovland, C. I., & Weiss, W. (1951). The influence of source credibility on communication effectiveness. *Public Opinion Quarterly*, *15*, 635–650.

Kawakami, K., Dovidio, J. F., Moll, J., Hermsen, S., & Russin, A. (2000). Just say no (to stereotyping): Effects of training in the negation of stereotypic associations on stereotype activation. *Journal of Personality and Social Psychology*, *78*, 871–888.

Kelman, H. C., & Hovland, C. I. (1953). "Reinstatement" of the communicator in delayed measurement of opinion change. *Journal of Abnormal and Social Psychology*, *48*, 327–335.

Kruglanski, A. W. (1996). Goals as knowledge structures. In P. M. Gollwitzer & J. A. Bargh (Eds.), *The psychology of action: Linking cognition and motivation to behavior* (pp. 599–618). New York: Guilford.

Macrae, C. N., Bodenhausen, G. V., Milne, A. B., & Jetten, J. (1998). Out of mind but back in sight: Stereotypes on the rebound. *Journal of Personality and Social Psychology*, *67*, 808–817.

Moede, W. (1920). *Experimentelle massenpsychologie. Beiträge zur experimentalpsychologie die gruppe.* Leipzig, Germany: Hirzel.

Neumann, R., Ebert, M., Gabel, B., Gülsdorff, J., Kranich, H., Lauterbach, C., & Wiedl, K. (1998). Vorurteile zwischen bayern und Norddeutschen: Die Anwendung einer neuen methode zur erfassung evaluativer assoziationen in vorurteilen. *Zeitschrift für Experimentelle Psychologie*, *45*, 99–108.

Nisbett, R. E., & Wilson, T. D. (1977). Telling more than we can know: Verbal reports on mental processes. *Psychological Review*, *84*, 231–259.

Phelps, E., A., O'Connor, K. J., Cunningham, W. A., Funayama, E. S., Gatenby, J. C., Gatenby, Gore, J. C., & Banaji, M. R. (2000). Performance on indirect measures of race evaluation predicts amygdala activation. *Journal of Cognitive Neuroscience, 12,* 729–738.

Plant, E. A., & Devine, P. G. (1998). Internal and external motivation to respond without prejudice. *Journal of Personality and Social Psychology*, *75*, 811–832.

Srull, T. K., & Wyer, R. S. (1979). The role of category accessibility in the interpretation of information about persons: Some determinants and implications. *Journal of Personality and Social Psychology*, *37*, 1660–1672.

Strack, F. (1992). The different routes to social judgments: Experiential vs. informational strategies. In L. L. Martin & A. Tesser (Eds.), *The construction of social judgment* (pp. 249–275). Hillsdale, NJ: Erlbaum.

Strack, F., & Bless, H. (1994). Memory for nonoccurrences: Metacognitive and presuppositional strategies. *Journal of Memory and Language*, *33*, 203–217.

Strack, F., & Förster, J. (1998). Self-reflection and recognition: The role of metacognitive knowledge in the attribution of recollective experience. *Review of Personality and Social Psychology*, *2*, 111–123.

Strack, F., & Hannover, B. (1996). Awareness of influence as a precondition for implementing correctional goals. In P. M. Gollwitzer & J. A. Bargh (Eds.), *The psychology of action: Linking cognition and motivation to behavior* (pp. 579–596). New York: Guilford.

Strack, F., Schwarz, N., Bless, H., Kübler, A., & Wänke, M. (1993). Awareness of the influence as a determinant of assimilation vs. contrast. *European Journal of Experimental Social Psychology, 23,* 53–62.

Triplett, N. (1898). The dynamogenic factors in pace making and competition. *American Journal of Psychology, 9,* 507–533.

Wegener, D. T., & Petty, R. E. (1997). The flexible correction model: The role of naive theories of bias in bias correction. In M. P. Zanna (Ed.), *Advances in experimental social psychology* (Vol. 29, pp. 141-208). San Diego, CA: Academic.

Wilson, T. D., & Brekke, N. (1994). Mental contamination and mental correction: Unwanted influences on judgments and evaluations. *Psychological Bulletin, 116,* 117–142.

Wyer, R. S., & Budesheim, T. L. (1987). Person memory and judgments: The impact of information that one is told to disregard. *Journal of Personality and Social Psychology, 53,* 14–29.

Wyer, R. S., & Srull, T. K. (1981). Category accessibility: Some theoretical and empirical issues concerning the processing of social stimulus information. In E. T. Higgins, C. P. Herman, & M. P. Zanna (Eds.), *Social cognition: The Ontario Symposium* (Vol. 1, pp. 161–197). Hillsdale, NJ: Erlbaum.

Wyer, R. S., & Unverzagt, W. H. (1985). The effects of instructions to disregard information on its subsequent recall and use in making judgments. *Journal of Personality and Social Psychology, 48,* 533–549.

Zajonc, R. B. (1965). Social facilitation. *Science, 149,* 269–274.

13

Revealing the Worst First
Stealing Thunder
as a Social Influence Strategy

KIPLING D. WILLIAMS
LARA DOLNIK

Should Stealing Thunder Work?
First Empirical Investigations
The Generality of the Stealing Thunder Tactic
Boundary Conditions and Possible Explanations
Stealing Thunder and the Central and Peripheral Routes
    to Persuasion
Conclusion

As the contributions to this book clearly indicate, social influence includes a far greater variety of interpersonal strategies than social psychologists traditionally assumed. Many of these influence strategies are indirect, subtle, and even perplexing (see chapters by Butler, Linn, David & Turner, Forgas, Knowles, and Spears, Postmes, Lea, & Watt). For instance, could it ever be an adaptive influence strategy to reveal negative or damaging information about ourselves? In this chapter we argue that the answer is frequently in the affirmative.

Imagine a bustling courtroom, filled with people. The jury has been sworn in. Their task in the coming weeks will be to determine the guilt or innocence of a man who allegedly placed a job advertisement in search of a part-time secretary, agreed to meet a young woman for an interview at a local diner, then

Address for correspondence: Kipling D. Williams, Department of Psychology, Macquarie University, Sydney, NSW, 2109, Australia. E-mail: kip@psy.mq.edu.au

drove her to a quarry and stabbed her several times with a large knife until she died. The defense attorney rises to give his opening statement. Opening statements are a critical part of the persuasion process for attorneys: The jury is attentive, and this is the attorney's first opportunity to present his client's story to the people who will ultimately make a decision about which story they believe. Conditions are optimal for social influence; at the beginning of a trial, jurors are freshly motivated to process information and they should be more open-minded than at any other time in the trial. Now would be the time to create a favorable impression toward the defendant. The defense attorney begins his opening statement. "Ladies and gentlemen, let's begin by looking at my client. He's ugly and he's scary looking." To the observers (20 of whom happened to be observing the case as part of their psychology and law class), this was not quite what they had expected to hear from the defense attorney. It was even more surprising that the defense attorney chose to present this negative information about his own client at the first opportunity he had when, surely, he wanted to present his client in the best possible light. What was the attorney doing? Was he giving up on the case already?

Cialdini (this volume) argues that social psychologists would benefit from observing the results of years of social-evolutionary selection processes accrued through trial-and-error methods used by social influence professionals. Here we were observing a social influence professional in his own arena: the courtroom. Yet, instead of creating a positive impression about his client, the defense attorney was doing just the opposite. Did he know something social psychologists did not know?

In fact, the defense attorney was using a dissuasion tactic that Williams, Bourgeois, and Croyle (1993) subsequently referred to as "stealing thunder" (see also McElhaney, 1987). In the context of our current research focus, stealing thunder involves revealing incriminating evidence about oneself (or one's client) before someone else reveals it. The aim of stealing thunder is to minimize the damage of the incriminating evidence. The scenario described above was not an isolated incident. Stealing thunder was abundant on both sides of the table in the O. J. Simpson trial. It is so common that it is not unusual to observe its use in such authoritative legal programs as *Ally McBeal*, *The Practice*, and *Law & Order*. Authors of texts on trial technique recommend this tactic. The strategy behind it involves ascertaining whether the weaknesses in the case are likely to be revealed by the opposition, and if so, divulging the information first. As Mauet (a leading author of trial technique texts) warns, "If you don't [divulge the information], your opponent will, with twice the impact." (Mauet, 1992, pp. 47–48; see also, Bergman, 1979; Keeton, 1973; McElhaney, 1987; Stuesser, 1993). Moreover, when Williams et al. (1993) asked attorneys whether they would use this tactic, every attorney claimed that there were no circumstances in which they would *not* use it.

This chapter focuses on the story that research has to tell (so far) about stealing thunder. We do this in a number of stages. First we consider what the social influence literature would lead us to expect from such a tactic. Then, we examine the early empirical evidence: In a controlled simulated court context, could we demonstrate the effectiveness of stealing thunder? Next, we test whether the tactic generalizes to other social influence domains, such as politics and interpersonal relations. In the last section, we examine the boundary conditions and social influence processes that may explain the effect. Finally we discuss directions for future research.

SHOULD STEALING THUNDER WORK?

Unlike many social influence tactics, empirical investigation of the effects of stealing thunder has a relatively short history. This may be because most social psychological theories would predict that stealing thunder should *not* work. Indeed, stealing thunder should backfire for several reasons.

First, it creates a negative schema of the defendant (Asch, 1946; McKelvie, 1990). Bringing up damaging information early in the trial may create a negative early impression of the defendant that biases jurors' perception of the remaining evidence against the defendant's case. There is considerable research and theory in social psychology that supports the benefits of creating an early positive impression (Kelley, 1950; Widmeyer & Loy, 1988). Positive first impressions have been shown to be especially effective in simulated courtroom contexts (Pyszczynski & Wrightsman, 1981).

Second, stealing thunder may be expected to be ineffective because it increases the salience and hence the availability of negative information about the defendant (Cacioppo & Petty, 1979). Because stealing thunder in a courtroom context constitutes being exposed to the negative information twice (once from the stealing side, and once again by the opposing side), jurors should be more likely to remember this information and, consequently, be negatively influenced by it.

Third, by admitting the negative information, all doubts as to the veracity of that information should evaporate, leaving the juror no option but to incorporate the evidence as factual. Indeed, research has shown that when an individual speaks against his or her self-interest, message recipients are more likely to believe the information (Wood & Eagly, 1981).

What reasons, then, can we assemble from social psychology that would predict its effectiveness? First, speaking against one's self-interest is one way to be seen as more credible (Eagly, Wood, & Chaiken, 1978). Audiences may not be able to imagine why an individual (or his or her attorney) would reveal negative and incriminating information, and may be left with the only plausible conclusion—this is an honest person. People might be more forgiving of someone's discretions if they feel closer to the person or think that the individual is being sincere, honest, and forthright with them. Indeed, the legal system provides tangible rewards to defendants who honestly admit to their crimes

In some respects, this is similar to Aron, Melinat, Aron, Vallone, and Bator (1997) research on self-disclosure which involved participants being paired with unfamiliar others. People who were paired with partners who disclosed personal information reported feeling closer to their partner than those who engaged in small talk. However, there are some obvious differences between thinking that potentially damaging information has been revealed to you personally and seeing someone reveal the information to the world at large.

The second reason that stealing thunder may work is that perhaps it is not the act of stealing thunder, per se, but what can be done with the thunder when it is stolen. Because thunder stealers are first to reveal the potentially damaging information, they have the opportunity to put a positive or discounting spin on it. They can frame the thunder in a way that diminishes its importance or makes it seem negligible or irrelevant to the decision at hand. Indeed, the legal advocacy expert Mauet seems to regard this explanation as the operative one, when he states "the key is to mention the weakness without emphasis and to present it in the least damaging light" (1992, p. 48). Similarly, McGuire's (1964) inoculation theory suggests that providing message recipients with a weakened version of the opposing position makes them resistant to its influence later.

Third, when only the opposing side brings up the negative information, the audience might surmise that one side was withholding the information from them. We know that when information is perceived to be scarce or secret it is regarded as being more valuable, and hence more influential (Brock, 1968; Cialdini, 1993). If both sides in a trial reveal the negative information, it may be perceived as being less scarce, and consequently, less valuable and important. In other words, "old news is no news."

Finally, audience members may be faced with a conundrum that they can only solve by diminishing the revelation's importance or changing its meaning. They may be reacting to the stolen thunder as though they were thinking, "I am listening to a defense attorney and he seems to be saying something damaging about his client, but this can't be right. Perhaps it really isn't that bad after all: what do I think this information *really* says about the defendant?" This explanation is consistent with Asch's (1940, 1948) proposition that message recipients will change the meaning of the message in accordance with what they know about the message source. It is also generally consistent with Pennington and Hastie's (1986, 1988, 1992) story model of juror information processing. This model suggests that jurors understand and organize information in narrative form. They do this fairly early on in a trial so that where the story has gaps, jurors fill those gaps with their own narrative-consistent interpretations of the information (ForsterLee, Horowitz, & Bourgeois, 1993).

Before we examine further the possible reasons why stealing thunder should or should not work, we summarize the early research that set out to test the effectiveness of the tactic in controlled conditions.

FIRST EMPIRICAL INVESTIGATIONS

Williams et al. (1993) conducted the first experimental investigation of the stealing thunder tactic. They conducted two experiments; the first examined its use in a criminal case in which the defendant's prior convictions constituted the negative piece of information to be used as the thunder. The second tested the tactic in a civil case, in which the negative information was an expert witness's willingness to testify on either side of an issue. In both experiments, participants heard or read one of three versions of a trial. The three conditions for the criminal (and civil) case were: (1) No Thunder, in which the negative information about the defendant (or expert witness) was absent from the presentation; (2) Thunder, in which the prosecutor (or defense) introduced the negative information about the defendant (expert witness); and (3) Stolen Thunder, in which the defendant's (expert witness's) attorney brought up the negative information prior to the prosecutor (plaintiff) doing so.

The results of the criminal trial used in Study 1 indicated, first, that thunder was indeed damaging when compared to no thunder. Mock jurors were more likely to indicate higher probabilities of guilt when the prosecutor extracted the defendant's prior convictions compared to when there was no mention of his prior convictions. More importantly, compared to the thunder condition, stealing thunder resulted in significantly lower probabilities of guilt. For the civil trial used in Study 2, thunder was again demonstrated to be damaging when compared with no thunder. When the defense attorney extracted from the plaintiff's expert witness that he had indeed testified to the exact opposite opinion just a week before, mock jurors found the expert less credible and were more likely to find in favor of the defendant. When the plaintiff's attorney stole the defense's thunder, mock jurors found the expert more credible, and were more likely to find for the plaintiff; even more so than for the no thunder condition.

The results of both experiments indicated that consistent with trial advocacy experts' beliefs, stealing thunder minimized the impact of the negative information on participants' verdicts. But is the tactic limited to the courtroom context?

THE GENERALITY OF THE STEALING THUNDER TACTIC

Adopting the paradigm used by Williams et al. (1993), subsequent research has addressed whether stealing thunder also can be effective in reducing the impact of damaging information outside of legal contexts. So far, two other domains of social influence have been examined: interpersonal relations and political contexts.

Stealing Thunder in Interpersonal Relations

In her honors thesis, Kathy Zablocki (1996) looked at the effectiveness of stealing thunder on the early stages of dating. Zablocki was interested in whether males who were waiting for an experiment with an attractive female (who was actually an experimental confederate) would agree to join the female for coffee after the experiment. From other research indicating that males are quite willing to agree to female pick-up lines (Clark & Hatfield, 1989) the answer to this question would seem to be fairly obvious. But there was a catch. In two of the three conditions, the males found out that she had genital herpes. While waiting for the experiment to begin, the attractive female chatted pleasantly with the unsuspecting male. During this 5-minute interchange, the males were exposed either to no information regarding the herpes (no thunder), witnessed a prescription for genital herpes with a pamphlet about the disease fall out of her purse as she left for the restroom (thunder), or prior to witnessing the purse's contents spill, were told by the female that she had herpes (stealing thunder). After she returned, she asked the male to join her for coffee, and recorded his response.

In the no thunder condition, 60% of the males agreed to join her for coffee. When they saw the herpes-related contents spill out of her purse, only 50% agreed. But, when she stole thunder by telling them about her herpes prior to the contents spilling, 70% agreed to join her. Because the number of participants in this experiment was limited, there were no significant differences between the conditions. But the results do suggest that stealing thunder also could be an effective strategy in interpersonal relations, although clearly more evidence is needed to establish the generality of the tactic in this domain.

Stealing Thunder in Politics

The political domain is another in which stealing thunder could possibly prove useful. Can politicians who are involved in some sort of scandal steal thunder? We do not need to think long before we can come up with a variety of instances in which politicians have been involved in scandals. We would be more hard-pressed, however, to recall instances in which the politician involved was the first to reveal the scandal. Todd Baldwin (1992) for his honors thesis, and Sherri Ondrus (1994) for her master's and Ph.D. (1998) theses at the University of Toledo, examined two questions related to such a possibility. First, compared to when an investigative reporter leaked the scandalous information, would participants be more or less likely to indicate they would vote for the candidate when he stole thunder? Second, would reporters indicate more or less willingness to pursue the story of the scandal if the candidate stole thunder?

To answer these questions, participants read ostensible *USA Today* newspaper articles that described a candidate, James Miller, who was running for reelection. Using the three-condition stealing thunder paradigm as before, participants were randomly assigned to one of three sets of stories. In the first, there was no mention of a scandal of any sort; in the second, an investigative reporter revealed the scandal; and in the third, the candidate himself revealed the scandal. After reading the stories, participants were asked how much they liked the candidate and how likely it would be that they would vote for him. When the candidate stole thunder it increased participants' liking and voting willingness, almost to the level of no thunder.

These results were replicated by Ondrus (Ondrus & Williams, 1995) using slightly different experimental procedures and with different thunder. Participants listened to a series of radio reports about a candidate who was known for his outspoken views in condemnation of "dead-beat Dads"—fathers who, after divorce, did not pay their child support. In the thunder and stealing thunder conditions, participants heard that the candidate himself had failed to pay child support for several years. This information was either revealed by an investigative reporter (thunder), or by the candidate himself (stolen thunder). Again, there was a no thunder condition in which the candidate was not involved in any wrongdoing. The same pattern of results emerged: Stealing thunder diminished the negative impact observed in the thunder condition.

It was not only voters who were dissuaded from forming negative impressions by the stealing thunder tactic. Actual reporters, journalism students, and psychology students playing the role of reporters were exposed to the three conditions, this time when the thunder dealt with the candidate's false report of being a war-hero. The actual reporters indicated that they would be less interested in pursuing the story when the candidate stole thunder than when they had uncovered the information themselves. Furthermore, the journalism students and role-playing journalists wrote shorter, less condemning stories about the political candidate when he stole thunder than when it had been revealed by another source (Ondrus & Williams, 1996, 1998).

On the whole, these empirical investigations into the generality of stealing thunder's effectiveness suggest that stealing thunder can be used successfully to reduce the impact of damaging information in a variety of contexts. We now turn our attention to examining the boundary conditions and social influence processes that may explain the effect.

BOUNDARY CONDITIONS AND POSSIBLE EXPLANATIONS

This section of our chapter focuses specifically on the empirical evidence that informs us about the conditions under which stealing thunder does and does not reduce the impact of damaging information. Understanding these boundary conditions will enable us to develop hypotheses to explain the underlying processes on which the tactic operates. In particular, we discuss how the empirical evidence fits with classic dual processing models of persuasion (e.g., Elaboration Likelihood Model, see also Petty, this volume).

We have already presented evidence to suggest that stealing thunder is an effective method of reducing the impact of damaging information in a variety of different contexts. But our research also has focused on trying to determine when it will not work. This research has involved manipulating aspects of the thunder information (such as the timing of stolen thunder, the seriousness of the thunder, and whether stealing thunder depends on the stealer putting a positive spin on the incriminating information); characteristics of the stealer (for example his or her race); characteristics of message recipients (such as their motivation and ability to process the information); and strategies that the opposition could use to counter the effects of stealing thunder (such as ignoring the information, or warning jurors that the stealer is manipulating them). We also have investigated what happens to the effectiveness of stealing thunder when message recipients anticipate group deliberation. We now proceed to examine empirical evidence for each of these potential boundary conditions, and discuss their theoretical implications.

The Nature of the Thunder Information

Does the effectiveness of stealing thunder depend on timing? In the civil courtroom case examined in Study 2, Williams et al. (1993) asked whether it mattered if the thunder was stolen either early or relatively late in the trial information (but prior to the thunder in both cases). According to theories of impression formation, worse impressions about the witness should be formed if the message recipients were provided the damaging information earlier rather than later in the process. Early negative information should set up a negative schema, from which all further information is distorted in such a way as to fit that negative schema. They found, however, that stealing thunder was equally effective irrespective of when the thunder was stolen.

More recently, we tested additional conditions that suggest that while early versus late presentation may not have an impact on the effectiveness of stealing thunder, the timing of the disclosure with respect to the prosecution's disclosure (i.e., the thunder) does. In particular, Dolnik and Williams (2000a) examined whether stealing thunder would still reduce the impact of damaging information if the defendant revealed the information *after* the prosecution had brought it up. Of course, acknowledging the thunder only after the opposition has brought it up is not really "stealing thunder." Nevertheless, this question must be asked because the standard three condition paradigm (i.e., no thunder, thunder, stolen thunder) leaves open the possibility that the effect is not resting upon whether or not the thunder is stolen, but rather that it is simply acknowledged by the side that it can damage. Thus, in this study we employed four conditions: no thunder, thunder, stolen thunder (revealed prior to the opposition's discussion of the thunder), and acknowledged thunder (acknowledged after the opposition first revealed it). We found that stealing thunder was once again effective, but acknowledged thunder was not (and was no different than thunder).

To what extent does the effectiveness of stealing thunder depend upon the nature of the thunder? Although stealing thunder seems to be effective in a number of different contexts, we might think that if the thunder information was extremely damaging, not even stealing thunder would reduce the impact it has on the message recipients.

In Baldwin and Williams's (1993) examination of stealing thunder in a political context, they manipulated the severity of thunder by revealing that the candidate had either bounced a series of checks (relatively minor thunder), or had housed stolen drugs in a drug smuggling operation (relatively severe thunder). The results indicated that stealing thunder reduced the impact of the damaging information regardless of how serious it was.

Although Baldwin and Williams (1993) were unable to find a thunder severity limit, it seemed implausible to us that stealing thunder would work for all types of thunder. So, in a simulated courtroom context, we manipulated how closely linked the thunder information was to the crime charged. In a case involving negligent homicide resulting from reckless driving, we manipulated the thunder information such that for some participants, the driver admitted that he had consumed two 6-packs of beer (a distal cause), whereas for other participants it was that the defendant admitted veering into the oncoming lane (a proximal cause). Much to our surprise, stealing thunder was still successful in significantly reducing the impact of the damaging information, even when the thunder was the key piece of evidence in the case.

We are not claiming that we have at this point exhausted all possible extremes for how severe or proximal the thunder is. It is probable that it will be of little help for a defendant to say, "I killed her" prior to the prosecution revealing this information. Clearly, more research is needed to determine how negative the thunder has to be before stealing it is no longer effective.

Does the effectiveness of stealing thunder depend upon the stealer putting a positive spin on the damaging information?

Mauet (1992) believed that the reason stealing thunder worked was because it allowed the stealer to put a positive or discounting spin on the thunder. To the extent that creating such a spin is necessary for stealing thunder to work, then the effectiveness of stealing thunder is not so surprising and is generally consistent with schema or first impression explanations offered in the social psychological literature. By diminishing the relevance or harmfulness of the thunder, the stealer can create a positive self- (or client) image, and also inoculate (McGuire, 1964) or forearm message recipients with counterarguments to resist the opposition's discussion of the damaging information. The early studies left the door open as to whether framing or spin was operating. Williams et al. (1993) used what they called "minimal framing" when stealing thunder. For example, when the defendant had previously been found guilty of a similar crime (Study 1), the defense attorney downplayed its significance by noting that it was not to be considered evidence of culpability. The judge reiterated this argument during jury instructions. When the medical expert in Study 2 told the court that he had given expert opinion with contrary conclusions one week earlier, he also explained that as an expert he could testify for both sides of the argument.

In order to test whether framing or spin was a necessary condition for stealing thunder to be effective, Dolnik and Williams (2000a; Study 1) used a four-condition paradigm (no thunder, thunder, stolen thunder with framing, and stolen thunder without framing). The defendant was being tried for dangerous driving that had caused a death, and the thunder information was that he had been drinking alcohol prior to the automobile accident. The framing used in this study was that when asked if he had been drinking prior to driving, he admitted he had, but said that it was not enough to affect his driving. As expected, when the defendant stole thunder and framed it in a self-serving manner, he was perceived to be more credible than when he did not employ framing. Contrary to the expectations held by schema theorists and legal professionals, however, stealing thunder without framing was *most* successful in reducing the impact of the damaging information. In this condition, credibility did not mediate the verdict. For the dichotomous guilt measure, stealing thunder without framing resulted in significantly fewer guilty verdicts than the thunder condition, whereas stealing thunder with framing did not differ from either thunder or stolen thunder without framing. However, the results for mean probability of guilt scores showed that both stealing thunder conditions were successful in reducing the impact of damaging information, with no difference resulting between stolen thunder with framing and stolen thunder without framing.

The conclusion to be drawn here is not that framing is ineffective; indeed, more compelling examples of framing could be quite effective, perhaps especially when combined with contrition or regret. But that was not our question; we wanted to know whether framing was essential for stealing thunder to work, and it was not. This suggests that stealing thunder is not merely a method for creating a positive twist on potentially damaging information, thereby instantiating a positive schema. It also suggests that credibility per se, is not the only driving force behind stealing thunder's effectiveness.

Characteristics of the Thunder Stealer and Recipients

Does stealing thunder work for everyone who uses it?   Another potential boundary condition may be the characteristics of the thunder stealer. Is it possible that stealing thunder does not work equally for all people? And if not, why not? One such message source characteristic that may interact with the success of stealing thunder is race. Research by White and Harkins (1994) and Petty, Flemming, and White (1999), indicated that the race attributed to the source of a persuasive message reliably affected not only the message's persuasiveness, but also the depth of processing that message recipients engaged in. Specifically, Caucasian participants were more likely to scrutinize the strengths and weaknesses of a message if it was attributed to a Black, rather than a White individual. They also were less persuaded overall by messages attributed to Blacks. This effect did not generalize across all alternative races; Asian sources, for instance, did not produce hyperscrutiny. The reasoning behind this effect is still debatable, but it may stem from some form of biased processing as a result of modern prejudice or stereotype incongruency. Nevertheless, the effect does suggest that varying the race of the thunder stealer may produce radically different consequences. If Black sources are put under additional scrutiny, then perhaps stealing thunder will boomerang. If message recipients are motivated to find fault, then an early admission of wrongdoing might allow them to create the negative schema that is suggested in the persuasion literature.

In an experiment assessing mock voter's impression of a political candidate, White and Williams (1998; Study 1) examined the effects of that candidate's race in a 3 (no thunder, thunder, stolen thunder) × 2 (White candidate, Black candidate) design. Caucasian participants read an ostensible newspaper article about a candidate running for Senate. Although there was no mention of the candidate's race in the article, a picture of a middle-aged Black or White man was contained within the article. The thunder information in this scenario was that the candidate was on the "Dead-beat Dads" list because he had not paid the required child support allowance to his ex-wife.

The results of this study showed that stealing thunder was successful for the White candidate; but that its use boomeranged when employed by the Black candidate. That is, when the Black candidate revealed the damaging information himself, participants indicated that they would be *less* likely to vote for him than when a reporter divulged the information. This pattern of results suggests that the tactic of stealing thunder may not always work, and in fact, may be counterproductive in certain instances. It also suggests other possible processes by which stealing thunder might operate.

First, these results may indicate that if participants are more likely to scrutinize the message, stealing thunder will not work. This explanation implies that the act of stealing thunder may be relied upon as a heuristic or peripheral cue that allows message recipients to arrive at a decision without engaging in effortful processing. A second possibility, which assumes that the White participants held negative attitudes toward Blacks, is that stealing thunder only works for individuals who are not already disliked by message recipients. A third possibility, which assumes that not paying child support is stereotypic of Black males, suggests that stealing thunder might not work when the thunder information is congruent with source attributes; that is, if the thunder information is consistent with stereotypes that message recipients hold for the individual employing the tactic, then the tactic will not work. Further research will be necessary to determine the underlying mechanisms behind the processing of stealing thunder that variations in race of the tactic user have uncovered.

Does stealing thunder work for all message recipients?   Research focusing on the attributes of the message recipients has examined their ability or motivation to process the message. Ondrus and Williams (1995) investigated stealing thunder in the political domain. They employed the three standard presentation conditions of damaging information (i.e., no thunder, thunder, stolen thunder) in the form of a radio news presentation. While listening to this broadcast, participants either completed a high demand cognitive task (to limit their ability to process the information in the news broadcast) or a low demand cognitive task. Results indicated that stealing thunder was more effective when participants were not cognitively busy. This suggests that stealing thunder is more effective when participants are able to meaningfully process the information presented to them. This result also is contrary to the explanation that stealing thunder operates as purely a peripheral cue. If that were the case, then stealing thunder in the present study should have been more effective when message recipients were cognitively busy, because it is in this condition that peripheral cues are most relied upon.

The second experiment focused on message recipients' motivation to process the information they were presented with. White and Williams (1998; Study 2) employed the no thunder, thunder, and stolen thunder conditions, and monitored whether participants were engaging in central or peripheral processing by measuring their levels of Need for Cognition (NFC), a personality variable that indicates an individual's tendency to engage in and enjoy thinking, (Cacioppo, Petty, & Kao, 1984). Low NFC individuals are generally less likely than high NFC individuals to carefully attend to and process message arguments.

White and Williams's (1998; Study 2) held constant the race of the message source—he was always White. Results showed that although stealing thunder was an effective strategy for the low NFC participants, it "boomeranged" for the high NFC participants. In contrast to Ondrus and Williams's (1995) findings, White and Williams's (1998) results once again appear to support the notion that stealing thunder is used as a peripheral cue because it is more effective when message recipients do *not* process the information carefully.

Strategies to Counteract the Effectiveness of Stealing Thunder

Another way in which to uncover boundary conditions is to examine whether there are strategic methods that the opposition could use to undo the effects of stealing thunder. Dolnik and Williams (2000a; Study 2) addressed the effects of two possible responses that the opposing attorney could use when the opposition steals thunder. One option open to the opponent is simply ignoring the damaging evidence. This may give message recipients the impression that by stealing thunder the defendant has given them relevant information and they will use it accordingly. If message scarcity (or it's flip-side, "old news is no news") has any merit, then by ignoring the thunder the attorney does not make the damaging information excessively available by mentioning it again. Another option open to the opponent is to point out to message recipients that a social influence tactic had been used on them to manipulate their attitudes. Other research has shown that being forewarned is forearmed (Petty & Cacioppo, 1977, 1979)—that is, being told ahead of time that someone is trying to persuade them will prevent message recipients from being persuaded. But the countertactic we are testing here would suggest the sufficiency of any warning; even one given after a tactic has been used.

Dolnik and Williams (2000a; Study 2) added two new conditions to the original stealing thunder paradigm that were consistent with these ideas: stolen thunder—not repeated and stolen thunder—tactic revealed. The results for the repetition manipulation demonstrated that not repeating the negative information once it had been stolen was no different from repeating it; stealing

thunder effectively reduced the impact of the negative information in both stealing thunder conditions. This result also diminished the plausibility of the "old
news is no news" hypothesis. For participants in the stolen thunder—tactic revealed condition, stealing thunder was no longer effective. This condition resulted in a significantly higher percentage of guilty verdicts and higher probability of guilt scores than the stolen thunder condition, and was no different
from the thunder condition. Thus, this particular boundary condition is one
that opponents have control over—they can opt to reveal the tactic and undermine stealing thunder's effectiveness.

The Effectiveness of Stealing Thunder on Individuals Anticipating Group Deliberation

The question of whether the effects of stealing thunder will survive traditional
group processes is of theoretical as well as practical interest (especially in the
context of jury decision-making). Studies have not examined whether, once stealing thunder has been employed, its success will survive when mock jurors anticipate having to reach a unanimous verdict through group deliberation. Research by Petty, Harkins, and Williams (1980) has shown that when individuals
anticipate that their attitudes will be pooled with the attitudes of other individuals to form a single group opinion, they are less likely to engage in careful
processing. They explained this reduction in cognitive effort as a consequence
of social loafing: people are less motivated and engage in less effortful behavior
when they believe their contributions will be combined with others (see Karau
& Williams, 1993, for a review of social loafing). If stealing thunder works better when message scrutiny is reduced (as shown by White and Williams, 1998),
then stealing thunder should be even more effective when individuals anticipate pooling their attitudes with others, as would be the case during deliberation. On the other hand, Kaplan and Miller (1978) have argued that many individual-level effects in mock juror research will wash out when extended to group
deliberation. The first step in group deliberation, we argue, is the anticipation
of group decision making. Our results (Dolnik & Williams, 2000b) indicated
that even for participants who believed that they were going to participate in
group deliberations, stealing thunder was effective. Oddly, however, for participants who anticipated group deliberation, the thunder condition (which was
anti-defendant) was no more likely to result in guilty verdicts than in the no
thunder condition. In this experiment, stealing thunder resulted in lower guilt
ratings than either the no thunder or the thunder conditions. Clearly, more
research is needed to explain these results.

Theoretical Implications of the Boundary Conditions

We have offered and tested several possible explanations of the boundary conditions and stealing thunder. These included framing (i.e., putting the negative
information in its best light and downplaying its significance; see Kassin, Reddy,

& Tulloch, 1990); counterargument formation (i.e., warning of the upcoming damaging testimony to give message recipients the opportunity to form counterarguments to fend against it; see Cialdini, Petty, & Cacioppo, 1981); old news is no news (i.e., information that is too available loses its value; see Brock, 1968; Brock & Brannon, 1992); and credibility (i.e., if a person introduces information against their own best interests they appear more credible and are therefore more persuasive; see Eagly, Wood, & Chaiken, 1978). Framing has been shown to be an unnecessary condition, the old news is no news appears to be ruled out, and credibility in some cases increased with stealing thunder and led to favorable responses. But our results also indicated that although the thunder stealer was considered more credible when he framed the negative information, the tactic was actually more effective when he did not frame the evidence.

We also have proposed that stealing thunder may cause message recipients to change the meaning of the thunder information, or perhaps even to change the related information within the case. That is, presenting negative information about oneself might force message recipients to make sense of the information in a way that makes it consistent with what they would expect to hear from a defendant (Asch, 1948; see David & Turner, this volume). According to this view, message recipients must contend cognitively with an apparent contradiction: The source of the message is revealing something that he or she should not be revealing. One way to cope with this contradiction is to reevaluate (e.g., by changing the meaning of) the revealed information so that it becomes consistent with their expectations about what the source should have said. In Study 2 (Dolnik & Williams, 2000a), we included measures that provided initial evidence for this proposition.

To assess change of meaning, we asked questions about how participants perceived the defendant and how they interpreted the evidence presented. Our results indicated that participants in the stolen thunder condition interpreted the thunder information as being less serious and less damaging to the defendant's case than participants in the thunder condition. This effect not only emerged for the thunder information, but also for other evidence given in the trial transcript. For instance, mock jurors in the stolen thunder condition regarded the evidence that the defendant veered onto the wrong side of the road prior to the accident as less convincing and damaging, and at the same time, regarded the defendant's character witness's testimony as more convincing and important. Of course, these mock juror assessments could be verdict-driven rather (i.e., made post-hoc to justify their verdict) rather than tactic-driven, so follow-up research is needed to determine if, when, and how jurors regard the evidence as it is being given. We are currently tapping into mock jurors' real-time assessments of the evidence as they are exposed to it as one approach to test the change of meaning hypothesis.

The interesting aspect of the change of meaning hypothesis is that it suggests an active, engaged message processor rather than a passive, heuristic-prone message recipient. Yet, some of our other studies are more consistent with stealing thunder operating through peripheral or heuristic processing. We now review our available evidence as it pertains to whether stealing thunder engages active and deep message processing, or whether it operates as a heuristic cue to persuasion. We rely on one dual processing theory—Petty and Cacioppo's (1986) Elaboration Likelihood Model (ELM)—to guide our analysis.

STEALING THUNDER AND THE CENTRAL AND PERIPHERAL ROUTES TO PERSUASION

According to the ELM, persuasion can occur through central or peripheral route processing. Central route processing occurs when individuals are able and motivated to elaborate on the arguments in the message. If the elaborations are predominantly favorable to the message, then persuasion will occur, but if they are largely unfavorable, the persuasive attempt will boomerang. Persuasion through the central route has been shown to be more durable and resistant to change (Haugtvedt & Petty, 1992), but in order for persuasion to go through this route, message recipients must be both able and motivated to process the message. When either motivation or ability are lacking, then message recipients are more likely to utilize peripheral route processing. Persuasion through this route occurs when individuals are not attending to the validity of the arguments presented, but rather to other (i.e., peripheral) cues that are associated with message quality, (e.g., source credibility, message length, and confidence in presentation).

The research findings thus far do not tell a uniform story that stealing thunder operates through any single route to persuasion. Some of the results are consistent with peripheral route processing. Source credibility can be a peripheral cue, and Williams et al. (1993) found that stealing thunder increased source credibility, which in turn increased the favorability of the verdicts. Likewise, White and Williams (1998) found that message recipients who were most likely to engage in message elaboration (i.e., either those reading about Black candidates or those with high NFC scores) were least likely to be dissuaded by the negative revelation when the thunder was stolen. Finally, when participants anticipated group deliberation stealing thunder was effective. Anticipation of group deliberation should reduce message processing, hence these results were consistent with peripheral route processing.

On the other hand, Dolnik and Williams (2000a) found that whereas credibility and favorable verdicts increased when a defendant stole thunder and framed it in a discounting manner, stealing thunder without framing (and without increasing credibility) worked even better. Furthermore, our most recent evidence is consistent with the argument that considerable message processing is taking place, such that mock jurors change the meaning of not only the thunder evidence, but other evidence as well.

To muddy the waters even further, we (Dolnik & Williams, 2000a, b) have consistently found that NFC was not a reliable predictor for stealing thunder's effectiveness. This would suggest that processing depth is either unrelated to stealing thunder's effectiveness, or that for some people stealing thunder works through the peripheral route whereas for others it works through the central route, or that both routes are operating for all message recipients.

Thus, the sum total of the evidence to date covers all possible routes: peripheral, central, neither, or both, but within any study, some routes appear to be less viable than others. The question we are left with seems to be, Under what conditions does stealing thunder operate through peripheral route processing, and under what conditions does it operate through central route processing?

Perhaps we should be looking to single-process theories of persuasion (see for example, Self-Categorization Theory, David & Turner, this volume) to see whether they offer more insight to the process underlying the effectiveness of stealing thunder. For example, it could be that stealing thunder works for sources toward whom message recipients are favorably predisposed, or at least are not unfavorably disposed.

CONCLUSION

Stealing thunder has been shown to be an effective method of minimizing the impact of damaging information in a variety of different contexts. There seems to be more than one underlying process that accounts for its effectiveness, and it is our objective to investigate further which processes are viable and under which conditions. There are several possibilities also suggested by the other chapters in this volume. For example, we may consider the role that imagination plays (see Cialdini, this volume) as a means to explain why stealing thunder works without framing. When no explanation is provided, it is possible that participants are forced to make sense of the information by imagining what sort of scenarios would cause the message source to reveal it to others. Perhaps, along the lines of the change of meaning hypothesis, when participants are encouraged to use their imagination, they will be more likely to create a context in which the thunder information is really not damaging.

Perhaps stealing thunder surprises message participants, disrupting their normal schema-driven assessments (see Knowles, Butler, & Linn, this volume). As Knowles et al. have shown through a series of clever manipulations, simply changing the wording of simple requests to be unexpected by making them slightly nonsensical is sufficient to increase compliance. Perhaps to some extent it is the unexpected nature of such an admission that accounts for increased compliance with the revealer's desires. The psychological preparation that message recipients go through in anticipation of a hard-sell might be disrupted when suddenly faced with a self-incriminating admission, leaving the target of social influence susceptible to other weapons of influence (Cialdini, 1993). Could stealing thunder be another means of presenting a story in an unexpected way, thus increasing compliance with the stealer's intent?

Another explanation is that stealing thunder works because the defendant is presenting counterstereotypic information to participants, that forces them to reinterpret the thunder information in a more positive light or recategorize the source's identity. Given the data obtained so far, this explanation relies upon the assumption that it is counternormative for a person with whom we are ill acquainted to reveal self-incriminating information. This assumption seems particularly pertinent in a criminal courtroom context in which previous research suggests that we expect the defendant to exhibit the negative traits associated with criminal behavior. Moreover, this approach suggests that when the thunder information is stereotypically consistent with what participants believe about the source, stealing thunder should boomerang. We are currently examining this possibility in both legal and employment interview contexts, by manipulating thunder that is either stereotypically consistent or stereotypically inconsistent with expectations of the source.

Finally, future studies in the legal domain should address whether the effects of stealing thunder are generalizable from *juror* decision-making to *jury* decision-making. Will the stealing thunder tactic survive group processes? As the number of decision makers increases, there is an increased likelihood that someone in the group will interpret stealing thunder as a confession or as a manipulative tactic. On the other hand, if stealing thunder deprives juries of their investigative role by handing them the answer on a plate, perhaps they are motivated to develop new roles, such as determining whether the law is just or fair, that could lead to jury nullification (Horowitz, 1985).

At present, we are impressed by the robustness of the stealing thunder tactic. If negative information is likely to surface, something as simple as an early admission of a wrong-doing, without any framing or spin, appears to be sufficient to disarm message recipients enough to make favorable decisions toward the thunder stealer. In the broader context, our research suggests that both motivational (i.e., need for consistency, as suggested by the change of meaning hypothesis) and cognitive (i.e., message elaboration, use of stereotypes) processes play a potential important role when social influence operates through a method of *dissuasion*; that is, when we attempt to influence people to *not* consider something that might otherwise be influential. The evidence we described here complements the arguments presented by several other chapters (e.g., Knowles, Butler, & Linn, Bless, Strack, & Walther, Ng) that social influence phenomena include a rich variety of direct and indirect mechanisms. We hope that the stealing thunder strategy we explored will stimulate further research into this intriguing example of social influence, and at the same time, will help to expand and redefine the scope of social influence research consistent with the objectives of this volume.

REFERENCES

Aron, A., Melinat, E., Aron, E. N., Vallone, R. D., & Bator, R. J. (1997). The experimental generation of interpersonal closeness: A procedure and some preliminary findings. *Personality and Social Psychology Bulletin, 23,* 363–377.

Asch, S. E. (1940). Studies in the principles of judgments and attitudes II: Determination of judgments by group and ego standards. *Journal of Social Psychology, 12,* 433 -465.

Asch, S. E. (1946). Forming impressions of personality. *Journal of Abnormal and Social Psychology, 41,* 258 -290.

Asch, S. E. (1948). The doctrine of suggestion, prestige, and imitation in social psychology. *Psychological Review, 55,* 250 -276.

Baldwin, T. (1992). *Stealing thunder in a political campaign: Blame management through honesty.* Unpublished Manuscript. University of Toledo.

Baldwin, T., & Williams, K. D. (1993, May). *Stealing thunder in a political campaign: Blame management through honesty.* Presented at the Midwestern Psychological Association, Chicago.

Bergman, P. (1979). *Trial advocacy in a nutshell.* St Paul, MN: West.

Brock, T. C. (1968). Implications of commodity theory for value change. In A. G. Greenwald, T. C. Brock, & T. M. Ostrom (Eds.), *Psychological foundations of attitudes* (pp. 243–275). New York: Academic.

Brock, T. C., & Brannon, L. A. (1992). Liberalization of commodity theory. *Basic Applied Social Psychology, 13,* 135–144.

Cacioppo, J. T., & Petty, R. E. (1979). Effects of message repetition and position on cognitive response, recall, and persuasion. *Journal of Personality and Social Psychology, 37,* 97–109.

Cacioppo, J. T., Petty, R. E., & Kao, D. F. (1984). The efficient assessment of need for cognition. *Journal of Personality Assessment, 48,* 306–307.

Cialdini, R. B. (1993). *Influence: Science and practice* (3rd ed.). New York: HarperCollins.

Cialdini, R. B., Petty, R. E., & Cacioppo, J. T. (1981). Attitude and attitude change. *Annual Review of Psychology, 32,* 357–404.

Clark, R. D., & Hatfield, E. (1989). Gender differences in receptivity to sexual offers. *Journal of Psychology & Human Sexuality, 21,* 39-55.

Dolnik, L., & Williams, K. D. (2000a). *Revealing the worst first: When does stealing thunder reduce the impact of damaging evidence?* Unpublished Manuscript. University of New South Wales.

Dolnik, L., & Williams, K. D. (2000b). *The effects of anticipated group deliberation on stealing thunder.* Unpublished manuscript. University of New South Wales.

Eagly, A. H., Wood, W., & Chaiken, S. (1978). Causal inferences about communicators and their effect on opinion change. *Journal of Personality and Social Psychology, 36,* 424–435.

ForsterLee, L., Horowitz, I. A., & Bourgeois, M. J. (1993). Juror competence in civil trials: The effects of preinstruction and evidence technicality. *Journal of Applied Psychology, 78,* 14–21.

Haugtvedt, C. P., & Petty, R. E. (1992). Personality and persuasion: Need for cognition moderates the persistence and resistance of attitude changes. *Journal of Personality and Social Psychology, 36,* 308–319.

Horowitz, I. A. (1985). The effect of jury nullification instruction on verdicts and jury functioning in criminal trials. *Journal Law & Human Behavior, 9,* 25–36.

Kaplan, M. F., & Miller, L. E. (1978). Reducing the effect of juror bias. *Journal of Personality and Social Psychology, 36,* 1443–1455.

Karau, S. J., & Williams, K. D. (1993). Social loafing: A meta-analytic review and theoretical integration. *Journal of Personality and Social Psychology, 65,* 681–706.

Kassin, S. M., Reddy, M. E., & Tulloch, W. F. (1990). Juror interpretation of ambiguous evidence: The need for cognition, presentation order, and persuasion. *Law and Human Behavior, 14,* 43–56.

Keeton, R. (1973). *Trial tactics and methods.* Boston, MA: Little, Brown.

Kelley, H. H. (1950). The warm-cold variable in first impressions of persons. *Journal of Personality, 18,* 431–439.

Mavet, T. A. (1992). *Fundamentals of trial techniques* (3rd ed.). Boston: Little, Brown.

McElhaney, J. W. (1987). Stealing their thunder. *Litigation, 13,* 59–60, 68.

McGuire, W. J. (1964). Inducing resistance to persuasion: Some contemporary approaches. In L. Berkowitz (Ed.), *Advances in experimental and social psychology* (Vol. 1, pp. 192–229). New York: Academic.

McKelvie, S. J. (1990). The Asch primacy effect. Robust but not infallible. *Journal of Social Behavior and Personality, 5,* 135–150.

Ondrus, S. A. (1994). *Stealing thunder by a political candidate: A test of control or peripheral processing.* Unpublished Master's Thesis. University of Toledo, OH.

Ondrus, S. A. (1998). *Scooping the press: Re-*

ducing newspaper coverage of political scandal by stealing thunder. Unpublished Doctoral Dissertation, University of Toledo, OH.

Ondrus, S. A., & Williams, K. D. (May, 1995). *Effects of stealing thunder by a political candidate: Admit or deny?* Paper presented at Midwestern Psychological Association, Chicago.

Ondrus, S. A., & Williams, K. D. (1996, May). *Effects of stealing thunder by a candidate on media dissemination of scandal.* Presented at the Midwestern Psychological Association, Chicago.

Ondrus, S. A., & Williams, K. (1998, July). *Effects of stealing thunder by a politician on newspaper coverage of political scandal.* Presented at the 21st Annual meeting of the International Society of Political Psychology, Montreal, Canada.

Pennington, N., & Hastie, R. (1986). Evidence evaluation in complex decision making. *Journal of Personality and Social Psychology, 51,* 242–258.

Pennington, N., & Hastie, R. (1988). Explanation-based decision making: The effects of memory structure on judgment. *Journal of Experimental Psychology: Learning, Memory, and Cognition, 14,* 521–533.

Pennington, N., & Hastie, R. (1992). Explaining evidence: Tests of the story model for juror decision making. *Journal of Personality and Social Psychology, 62,* 189–206.

Petty, R. E., & Cacioppo, J. T. (1977). Forewarning, cognitive responding, and resistance to persuasion. *Journal of Personality and Social Psychology, 35,* 645–655.

Petty, R. E., & Cacioppo, J. T. (1979). Effects of forewarning of persuasive intent and involvement on cognitive responses and persuasion. *Personality and Social Psychology Bulletin, 5,* 173–176.

Petty, R. E., Flemming, M. A., & White, P. H. (1999). Stigmatized sources and persuasion: Prejudice as a determinant of argument scrutiny. *Journal of Personality and Social Psychology, 76,* 19–34.

Petty, R. E., Harkins, S. G., & Williams, K. D. (1980). The effects of diffusion of cognitive effort on attitudes: An information processing view. *Journal of Personality and Social Psychology, 38,* 81–92.

Pyszczynski, R. A., & Wrightsman, L. S. (1981). The effects of opening statements on mock jurors' verdicts in a simulated criminal trial. *Journal of Applied Social Psychology, 11,* 301–313.

Stuesser, L. (1993). *An introduction to advocacy.* Vancouver, British Columbia: LBC Information Services.

White, P. H., & Harkins, S. G. (1994). Race of source effects in the Elaboration Likelihood Model. *Journal of Personality and Social Psychology, 67,* 790–807.

White, P., & Williams, K. D. (1998, August). *Does stealing thunder always work?: Black candidates beware!* Presented at the American Psychological Association Annual Convention, San Francisco, CA

Widmeyer, W. N., & Loy, J. W. (1988). When you're hot, you're hot! Warm-cold effects in first impressions of persons and teaching effectiveness. *Journal of Educational Psychology, 60,* 89–99.

Williams, K. D., Bourgeois, M. J., & Croyle, R. T. (1993). The effects of stealing thunder in criminal and civil trials. *Law and Human Behavior, 17,* 597–609.

Wood, W., & Eagly, A. H. (1981). Stages in analysis of persuasive messages: The role of causal attributions and message comprehension. *Journal of Personality and Social Psychology, 40,* 246–259.

Zablocki, K. (1996). *Stealing thunder about having a sexually-transmitted disease.* Unpublished Honor's Thesis. University of Toledo, OH.

PART III

SOCIAL INFLUENCE AND GROUP BEHAVIOR

14

Social Influence and Intergroup Beliefs
The Role of Perceived Social Consensus

CHARLES STANGOR
GRETCHEN B. SECHRIST
JOHN T. JOST

A guiding principle in the field of social psychology has been the powerful influence that other people exert on our beliefs, attitudes, and behaviors. Although research examples illustrating the influence others have on one's attitudes and behaviors in general are relatively numerous, the influence of other people's beliefs on intergroup attitudes and behaviors (stereotypes, prejudice, and discrimination) has not received a great deal of focused theoretical or empirical attention. The present chapter therefore addresses the potential impact of social influence on intergroup beliefs and behaviors.

Address correspondence to: Charles Stangor, Department of Psychology, University of Maryland, College Park, MD 20742, USA. E-mail: stangor@psyc.umd.edu

STEREOTYPING AND CONSENSUS

Stereotypes are developed and changed as a result of information that comes from indirect sources such as parents, peers, and the media, and through direct contact with members of social outgroups. Although both direct and indirect sources are generally acknowledged as determinants of stereotyping and prejudice, most models of stereotype formation (cf. Eagly & Kite, 1987; Hamilton & Gifford, 1976) and stereotype change (Hewstone & Brown, 1986; Rothbart & John, 1992; Stephan, 1985), as well as current reviews of the stereotyping and prejudice literature (Brewer & Brown, 1998; Fiske, 1998; Hamilton & Sherman, 1994), have primarily addressed the influence of direct intergroup contact.

According to intergroup contact approaches, intergroup beliefs are the result of interactions with outgroup members. It has been proposed that stereotypes develop through direct (but frequently biased) observation of the behaviors of members of different social groups (Eagly & Kite, 1987; Hamilton & Gifford, 1976), and from observing the behaviors of others in the media (e.g. Ruscher, in press). In support of these approaches, research has demonstrated that stereotypes are sensitive to the actual characteristics of social groups (e.g. Weber & Crocker, 1983), and that intergroup contact is successful in changing perceptions of social groups under certain conditions, especially if intergroup cooperation and a successful goal relevant to both groups are present.

There are, however, difficulties with assuming that intergroup attitudes are formed and changed primarily through direct contact with members of the outgroup. For one, research has demonstrated that stereotypes and prejudice can be developed about groups with which the individual has had very little, or even no, direct contact (Maio, Esses, & Bell, 1994), and that there is frequently only a very low correlation between amount of contact with a group and attitudes toward the group (Katz & Braly, 1933). Research also indicates that stereotypes are by and large difficult to change through exposure to individual exemplars who disconfirm existing beliefs (Hewstone & Brown, 1986; Rothbart & John, 1985). This is partly because it is difficult to create positive intergroup interactions, and partly because, even when contact leads to a change in attitudes toward individual group members, attitudes toward the group as a whole frequently do not follow.

A second way that stereotypes may be developed and changed is as a result of communication and sharing of beliefs among the members of a given social group or culture. Indeed, many conceptual definitions of stereotypes include the requirement that they be consensually shared (e.g. Gardner, 1994; Jost & Banaji, 1994; Schaller & Conway, 1999, in press; Stangor & Lange, 1994; Stangor & Schaller, 1996; Tajfel, 1982), and social stereotypes have their negative impact on members of stigmatized groups precisely because virtually all members of the culture hold similar beliefs about them. Thus, if stereotypes and prejudice are shared by members of social groups, it seems reasonable to expect that they are developed and changed in part through processes of social influence in general and through group norms in particular.

Past social psychological research suggests that attitude change that arises in conjunction with the beliefs of ingroup members is strong and long-lasting (Festinger, 1954; Lewin, 1952; Orive, 1988a,b). Therefore, it is worth considering the potential that stereotypes and prejudice are the result, at least in good part, of perceptions of ingroup norms, in addition to any potential learning that occurs through direct intergroup contact. Consider, for instance, a college student who studies in an exchange program in a foreign country. According to direct approaches, this student is likely to change his or her opinion regarding the host country and its citizens as a result of his or her experiences abroad. If the experience is primarily positive, then attitudes should become more positive; if the experience is primarily negative, then attitudes should become more negative.

But most exchange students do not travel alone. Indeed, because they are likely to live together, take classes together, and attend common events, the student is likely to interact as much or more with other members of his or her own nationality, as with members of the host country during the sojourn. These colleagues—members of the ingroup—serve not only as sources of information about the host country and its members, by relating their daily experiences with them, but also as a source of validation and potential distortion for the individual's opinions. Because exchange students frequently have plenty of contact with other ingroup members, it is probably safe to say that attitude change in such situations is as much a function of ingroup as of outgroup interaction.

Thus, knowledge about the beliefs of other ingroup members should have an important influence on stereotyping and prejudice, such that individuals' intergroup beliefs develop and change as a function of their perceptions of the beliefs of relevant others. Discovering that members of one's own group are favorable toward an outgroup should lead to positive beliefs, whereas learning that members of one's own group are unfavorable toward an outgroup should lead to negative beliefs.

THEORIES OF SOCIAL INFLUENCE

At least three theories concerning the impact of our perceptions of others' beliefs on our own beliefs are relevant to our analysis. These theories represent informational, identification, and cultural approaches, respectively.

Informational Approaches

According to Festinger's (1950) approach to social influence, "an opinion, a belief, an attitude is 'correct,' 'valid,' and 'proper' to the extent that it is anchored in a group of people with similar beliefs, opinions and attitudes" (pp. 272–273). Festinger considered the process of consensual validation to occur when the awareness of sharing beliefs with others validates those beliefs. Furthermore, according to Festinger's (1954) theory of social comparison, people have a need to actively evaluate and compare their opinions in order to establish a sense of validity or correctness in their own beliefs. When objective or physical means of evaluation are unavailable, people turn to similar others or ingroup members to have their opinions validated or to assess the correctness of their beliefs.

Hardin and Higgins (1996) have recently reviewed the literature relating to consensual validation and argued that individuals grasp reality through interaction with and verification of others, and that people need validation from others to develop their own view of reality. According to Hardin and Higgins (1996), people attempt to establish a shared reality, and come to know the self and their world through shared perceptions. Thus, whenever an individual is faced with uncertainty, he or she turns to others for information and validation. According to the analyses of Festinger, Hardin, and Higgins, it is the need to feel certainty or confidence in one's beliefs that drives social influence. The awareness of the beliefs of others serves the functions of reducing uncertainty and acquiring knowledge about one's social world.

Identification Approaches

Social identity and self-categorization theories (e.g. Haslam et al., 1996; Tajfel & Turner, 1979; Turner, 1987) also suggest that attitudes and beliefs are developed and changed through processes of social validation by others and have emphasized the importance of identification as a mechanism underlying this influence. According to these theories, when an individual defines him- or herself as a member of a group that he or she considers important (identifies with), the individual is motivated to agree (share beliefs) with this ingroup (Turner, 1991). Identifying with the group that provides consensus information is an essential aspect of social influence according to social identity and self-categorization theories. Thus, people are expected to change their beliefs to the extent that they identify with members of the ingroup.

Social identity and self-categorization theories suggest that social validation by others occurs such that people change their beliefs because they desire identification or affiliation with other ingroup members (Deutsch & Gerard, 1955). In this case, changes in attitudes, beliefs, and behaviors occur to the extent that the relationship with the person or group is an integral aspect of the person's self-concept (e.g., Kelman, 1961). Social identity and self-categorization theories emphasize the significance of social groups in defining personal identities, proposing that individuals are strongly motivated to share beliefs with other members of the ingroup (Abrams & Hogg, 1988; Turner, 1991). Thus, information about the beliefs of others may be effective in changing opinions largely because of needs to identify and affiliate with other people.

Consistent with social identity and self-categorization theories, research has demonstrated that people are more susceptible to attitude change attempts when the information is provided by ingroup members with whom they identify, as compared to outgroup members (Martin, 1988; van Knippenberg & Wilke,

1988). In addition, research has shown that individuals, in becoming prototypical ingroup members or in adopting their group memberships as integral parts of their self-concepts, tend to become more extreme in their attitudes and to change their attitudes to be consistent with a valued or salient ingroup (Abrams & Hogg, 1988; Haslam et al., 1996; Kelman, 1961; Newcomb, 1943, 1963; Turner, 1987, 1991).

Cultural Approaches

A final approach to conceptualizing the influence of shared beliefs is a cultural one. Bar-Tal (1998) has outlined a general model of the implications of being aware that beliefs are shared with others. According to his model, there are two important mediating factors involved in the awareness of sharing beliefs: confidence in the beliefs and a sense of similarity to those people who share the beliefs. According to Bar-Tal, individuals feel more confident in their beliefs when they know the beliefs are shared by ingroup members. Drawing on the theories of Festinger (1950, 1954), Bar-Tal's model indicates that being aware that beliefs are shared validates the beliefs, and thus increases the confidence with which the beliefs are held. Bar-Tal also proposes that the knowledge that beliefs are shared with others increases the sense of similarity to those who share the beliefs. The sharing of beliefs is one of the bases of perceiving oneself as similar to others and may serve to strengthen one's perceptions of similarity, which in turn serves to maintain effective group functioning (Bar-Tal, 2000; Cartwright & Zander, 1968).

Furthermore, Bar-Tal's (2000) model proposes that increases in belief confidence and a sense of similarity can influence individual and societal outcomes. Consequences of sharing beliefs with others include resistance to persuasion, increases in satisfaction and self-esteem, and enhanced group decision-making. In addition, the model suggests that the awareness of sharing beliefs produces increased liking for, identification with, perceived homogeneity of, and cohesiveness of group members who share the beliefs. Bar-Tal's model also suggests several antecedents to the awareness of sharing beliefs, such as factors related to the beliefs (number, relevance, and centrality of the beliefs), society members (individual characteristics), society (type of society and cohesiveness), and the situation or context (e.g., external threat).

In short, then, theories regarding the potential for stereotype changes as a result of social influence have focused on either informational principles involving the construction of reality, motivational principles involving identification, or cultural principles involved in perceptions of similarity and sharing. These mechanisms are not mutually exclusive—any or all of them may be operating to influence beliefs. In the following sections we review research, both from our lab as well as from the work of others, that has investigated the impact of perceived consensus on expressed stereotyping and prejudice and wherever possible, we consider evidence pertaining to the mechanisms underlying these effects, although these mechanisms are often very difficult to disentangle.

EMPIRICAL RESEARCH

Several existing studies support the notion that intergroup beliefs result from perceiving the opinions of other ingroup members, and at least some of these studies are informative about underlying mechanisms. For example, Blanchard, Crandall, Brigham, and Vaughn (1994) found that hearing another student from one's own university condemn racism increased participants expressed anti-racist opinions and hearing someone condone racism reduced anti-racist expressions, in comparison to a control condition in which no information about others' opinions was provided. In addition, these results occurred regardless of whether participants' responses were spoken publicly (in the presence of the person making the comment and the experimenter) or written privately on a questionnaire and sealed in an envelope, suggesting that informational internalization did occur.

In another relevant study, Wittenbrink and Henly (1996, Exp. 3) gave high and low prejudiced White participants—as determined on the basis of scores on McConahay, Hardee, and Batts' (1981) Modern Racism Scale—the expectation that other individuals believed that African Americans had either a large proportion or small proportion of negative characteristics. Participants then completed the Modern Racism Scale again. Results indicated that highly prejudiced participants expressed more favorable attitudes toward African Americans after they had been provided with positive, as opposed to negative, feedback about the beliefs of others, but initially low prejudiced individuals did not show any change as a result of the opinion feedback.

Haslam et al. (1996) asked participants to make estimates about the percentage of members of a given ingroup (Australians) and a given outgroup (Americans) that possess certain characteristics. Participants then were provided with information that other people, either ingroup members or prejudiced outgroup members, were in agreement or disagreement with the participants' original beliefs, or participants were given no information about the beliefs of other people. Haslam et al. found that people changed their stereotypes of national groups so that they were more similar to the beliefs allegedly held by members of a desirable ingroup (other unprejudiced students at one's college), and they changed their stereotypes away from the beliefs allegedly held by an undesirable outgroup (prejudiced people).

Other researchers have focused particularly on the contents of ingroup communication in producing stereotype development and change. According to Schaller and Conway (1999; see Schaller, this volume) interpersonal communication has an important influence on the contents of stereotypes. The contents of interpersonal communications may be influenced by individuals' goals and motives. For example, Ruscher and colleagues (Ruscher & Duval, 1998; Ruscher, Hammer, & Hammer, 1996) have found that when given a consensus motivation, such as being asked to achieve consensus and to think as a team, dyads focus their conversation around stereotype-consistent information. When a negative stereotype is revealed about a target person, dyads talk about the stereotype and focus on information to support the stereotype in forming impressions of that person. The dyads want to find things they agree upon and want to be liked by each other, so they use negative stereotypes as a means of achieving similarity and consensus. The consensus of the stereotype is validating, so it increases attraction and makes stereotypes harder to change.

RESEARCH FROM OUR LAB

We (Sechrist & Stangor, in press; Sechrist, Stangor, & Jost, 1998; Stangor, Sechrist, & Jost, in press) have conducted a number of studies designed to study the influence of consensus information on intergroup beliefs and behavior, and to understand the potential variables mediating this influence.

Influence of Consensus Information on Intergroup Beliefs

Stangor, Sechrist, and Jost (in press) conducted three experiments designed to assess the impact of perceived consensus on expressed stereotyping and prejudice. In each case, the research concerned the stereotypes and attitudes that European American college students hold about African Americans. In our first experiment, European American students initially provided their own racial beliefs and then estimated fellow students' beliefs about eight positive and eight negative stereotypes about African Americans. At a second experimental session, held one week after the first, we then provided them with (false) information indicating that, according to our research, the students at the university were actually either more or less favorable in their evaluation of African Americans than the participants had originally estimated. We created this feedback idiographically, by adding or subtracting an average of 20 percentage points from each participant's own initial estimates of the beliefs of others. Then, after receiving the false feedback, and as part of a supposed computer malfunction, participants were asked to rate their stereotypes of African Americans again. The results demonstrated that perceptions of the beliefs of others can significantly change racial stereotypes. Students who received feedback indicating that other students held more favorable stereotypes than they originally estimated expressed more positive and fewer negative stereotypes after the feedback than before it. On the other hand, participants who received feedback indicating that others held more unfavorable stereotypes than they originally estimated subsequently expressed more negative, but not fewer positive, stereotypes.

Our second experiment was designed to demonstrate that the effects of perceived consensus would be stronger for students who were exposed to information about the opinions of ingroup rather than outgroup members, that feedback about stereotypes would generalize to perceptions of other racial attitudes toward the group, and that the changes would occur on a nonreactive measure. Using the same general procedure as in Experiment 1, participants first estimated the stereotypes held by other ingroup members, and then were given information indicating that other students held more favorable stereotypes about African Americans than they had originally estimated.[1] Furthermore, this information supposedly described either the beliefs of other students from the students' own college or the beliefs of students from a different college. At a later session held about one week later and in an entirely unrelated context, the participants were asked to indicate their attitudes toward African Americans on a feeling thermometer. Results indicated that participants reported significantly more favorable attitudes toward African Americans when the positive consensus information they had received supposedly described members of their ingroup, as compared with members of an outgroup.

In a third experiment, rather than providing information indicating that their beliefs about others were more positive or more negative than was actually the case, we instead provided participants with information that their beliefs were either shared or were not shared by other students at their university. Specifically, after indicating their own stereotypes about African Americans, participants were told that, based on the findings of prior research, either 81% or 19% of other students at their university shared these beliefs. At this point, participants were given allegedly "objective" information about the actual traits possessed by African Americans as an attempt to change their beliefs. This "objective feedback" was created to be more positive than the participant's initial beliefs by adding (for positive traits) and subtracting (for negative traits) an average of 25% from percentages the participants estimated in their initial ratings. The dependent measure was the amount of stereotype change in the direction of this new information. All participants expressed more positive and fewer negative stereotypes after receiving the (positive) "objective" information. However, participants who had been given information that others shared their beliefs (high perceived consensus) showed less opinion change, on both positive and negative stereotypes, in comparison with participants who were given information that others did not share their beliefs (low perceived consensus). Thus, the agreement of others appeared to bolster racial stereotypes and to make them resistant to "objective" evidence.

Influence of Perceived Consensus on Behavior and Cognitive Accessibility

In subsequent research, Sechrist and Stangor (in press) explored the extent to which perceived consensus influenced both behavior and the cognitive accessibility of group beliefs. In Experiment 1, European American participants were selected to be either high or low in prejudice toward African Americans, based on prior responses to the Katz and Hass (1988) Pro-Black Scale. The partici-

---

1. In this and in subsequent experiments we did not provide feedback indicating that others were more negative than originally estimated. We did this for ethical reasons—to avoid making the beliefs of our participants more unfavorable.

pants completed this measure again at the lab and were told that either 81% or 19% of other college students shared their beliefs on this measure. At this point, and supposedly while ostensibly waiting for the experiment to continue, the students were asked to wait in a hallway that contained a bank of seven chairs; an African American confederate was sitting in the chair at one end. Behavior was measured unobtrusively in terms of the number of chairs left between the participant's chosen seat and the confederate. We found that high prejudice participants sat farther away from the confederate than did low prejudice participants. Moreover, as predicted, this difference was significantly greater for participants in the high consensus condition than for participants in the low consensus condition. Furthermore, the correlation between expressed attitudes (on the Pro-Black Scale) and behavior (seating distance) was significantly greater for participants in the high (versus low) consensus condition. Thus, perceived consensus appears to increase attitude-behavior consistency in the domain of racial relations.

According to current models, stereotypes represent the beliefs that are mentally associated with category labels in memory (Dovidio, Evans, & Tyler, 1986; Kunda & Thagard, 1996; Stangor & Lange, 1994; Wittenbrink, Judd, & Park, 1997), and thus which come to mind when the category is activated. On the basis of such models, we predicted in Experiment 2 that learning that one's stereotypes are shared with others would alter the mental representation of those beliefs such that they would become more closely associated with the category label in memory, and thus be more quickly activated upon exposure to the relevant category label.

European American participants first estimated the percentage of African Americans whom they believed possessed each of 18 stereotypical traits, as in our prior studies. Then, again as in our prior studies, participants received information that either 81% or 19% of other students at their university agreed with their judgments. Participants then completed an apparently unrelated task, conducted by a different experimenter. This was a lexical-decision task in which they were presented with a series of letter strings that were either words or nonwords, and they were asked to indicate as quickly and as accurately as possible if the string was or was not a word. The words in this task included the traits of African Americans from the initial questionnaire as well as nonwords. Unbeknownst to the participants, however, preceding the presentation of each letter string a prime was presented for 15 ms. The prime preceding the mask was either the word "black," or a neutral prime "xxxxx."

Participants who learned that their stereotypes of African Americans were shared with others (high perceived consensus) were significantly faster at identifying those same stereotypes as words after the "black" primes than after the "xxxxx" primes, but this difference did not occur for participants who had learned that their stereotypes were not shared with others. Thus, as expected, stereotypes that are perceived as shared are more cognitively accessible, in the sense that they come to mind quickly on exposure to the category label, and thus facilitate their identification as words.

The Mediating Roles of Confidence and Identification

Taken as a whole, then, the results of our research programs and those of others demonstrate that perceiving that others share or do not share stereotypes and prejudice exerts a strong influence on subsequent stereotyping and prejudice. Furthermore, these effects appear to represent real attitude change (acceptance) because the change has been shown to occur on unobtrusive behaviors and judgments, and even on reaction time measures in which the primes were subliminal. In subsequent research, we have collected evidence concerning the mediation of these effects.

Confidence. According to informational approaches, as well as the cultural model of Bar-Tal (2000), individuals accept the beliefs of others in order to validate their own beliefs. One prediction that can be derived from this perspective is that people should express more confidence in beliefs that they perceive to be shared with others (Baron et al., 1996; Orive, 1988a). Supporting this hypothesis, Sechrist, Stangor, and Jost (1998, Exp. 1) first had European American participants indicate their stereotypes about African Americans and then indicate their confidence in those beliefs. Then, using our standard idiographic procedure, participants received information indicating that other stu-

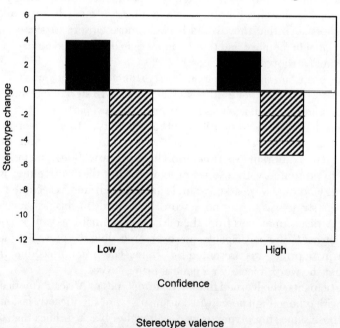

FIGURE 14.1. Change in positive and negative stereotypes (Time 2 minus Time 1) after receiving positive "objective" information as a function of initial confidence (Data based on Sechrist et al., 1998, Exp. 1).

dents at their university held more positive and fewer negative stereotypes than they had originally estimated and then again indicated their own stereotypes. As shown in Figure 14.1, although all participants expressed more positive and fewer negative stereotypes after receiving this (positive) information, the extent of change was significantly greater for participants who initially reported having low confidence in their stereotypes than it was for participants who initially reported having high confidence in their stereotypes (as determined via median split on the initial confidence scores).

Using a procedure similar to that employed in our prior research, Sechrist et al. (1998, Exp. 2) first asked participants about their beliefs toward African Americans, and then provided them with either high (81% agreement), low (19% agreement), or no consensus information about the beliefs of others (the participants in this control group only reviewed their own prior responses). Following an attempt to change their beliefs by providing ostensibly favorable "objective" information about the actual traits possessed by African Americans, research participants again rated their beliefs and their confidence in them. As shown in Figure 14.2, participants in the low consensus condition experienced a decrease in confidence over time, whereas participants in the high consensus condition experienced an increase in confidence over time. Participants in the

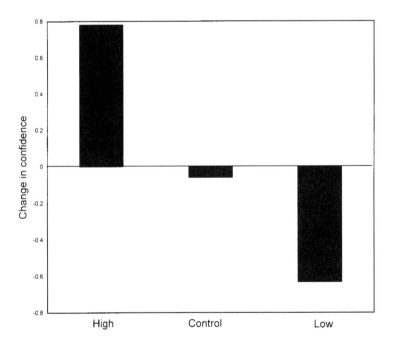

FIGURE 14.2. Change in confidence (Time 2 minus Time 1) as a function of perceived consensus (Data based on Sechrist et al., 1998, Exp. 2).

control condition exhibited no change in their degree of confidence in their beliefs over time ($M = -.06$).

Taken together, the results of these experiments confirm our expectation that the impact of consensus information on intergroup beliefs is mediated in part by changes in the confidence with which those beliefs are held.

Identification. According to social identity and self-categorization theories, when an individual defines him- or herself as a member of a group, the individual is motivated to agree (share beliefs) with this ingroup. We conducted two experiments to examine the role of group identification in consensus-based stereotype change. In Sechrist et al. (1998, Exp. 3), participants were preselected to be high versus low in identification with their university, based on their responses to a scale assessing this attitude (Brown, Condor, Mathews, Wade, & Williams, 1986). Using our standard procedure, participants expressed their stereotypes toward African Americans and then were provided with consensus information that was more favorable than their original estimates. As shown in Figure 14.3, results demonstrated that both high and low identifiers changed their beliefs in the direction of the consensus information on both positive and negative stereotypes—there were no interactions between identification and stereotype change.

Finally, Sechrist et al. (1998, Exp. 4) provided University of Maryland students with positive consensus information about the stereotypes of African

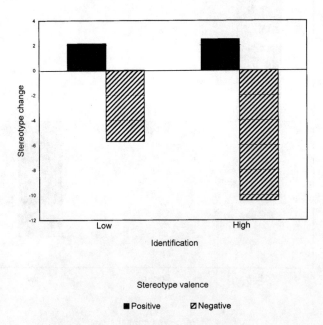

Figure 14.3. Change in positive and negative stereotypes as a function of measured identification with the ingroup (Data based on Sechrist et al., 1998, Exp. 3).

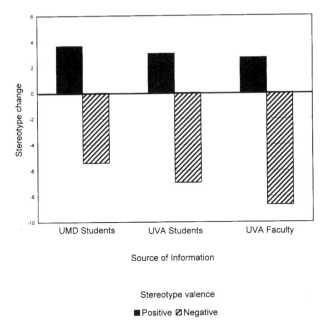

FIGURE 14.4. Change in positive and negative stereotypes as a function of source of information (Data based on Sechrist et al., 1998, Exp. 4).

Americans held by other University of Maryland students, University of Virginia students (a competitive outgroup), and University of Virginia faculty members (a source with which the students were not expected to highly identify). Except for its source, the consensus feedback was identical in all three conditions. Not surprisingly, the students identified substantially more highly with their own reference group (Maryland students, $M = 7.05$) than with either University of Virginia students ($M = 6.11$) or University of Virginia faculty ($M = 6.00$). As shown in Figure 14.4, although all participants expressed more positive and fewer negative stereotypes after learning the consensus information, no differences in the influence of consensus information among conditions were found. All participants changed their beliefs in the direction of the consensus information, regardless of the source of the information—there were no interactions between the source variable and stereotype change.

CONCLUSION

The present chapter has summarized existing research demonstrating the influence of consensus information on intergroup beliefs and behavior. The research demonstrates that perceptions of the beliefs of others influence one's own stereotypes and prejudices, such that beliefs are changed to be more similar to those of others, are held with greater confidence, are more cognitively accessible, and are more likely to influence behavior when they are consensually shared than when they are not. The research from our lab has consistently found that the presentation of information regarding the beliefs of others has strong effects upon individuals. The change is long-lasting; we have found that it lasts for up to two weeks. And the change is real in the sense that it is observed on nonreactive measures, including unobtrusive measures of seating distance, measures assessed in a different experimental context, and responses to stereotypes following subliminal primes.

In terms of underlying mechanisms, our research to date provides evidence for an informational function of perceived consensus. Individuals express more confidence in their beliefs if they are validated by others, and individuals who are less confident show more belief change toward the opinions of others. However, our research has not yet demonstrated that it is necessary for participants to identify with the groups that provide the source of the information. Indeed, in none of our studies has the manipulation or measurement of identification been found to influence the extent of stereotype change, and change was even found in students as the result of exposure to the opinions of faculty members at a different university (with whom they were unlikely to identify). Thus, we temporarily conclude that it is not a prerequisite that individuals identify with the group providing the consensus information in order to be influenced by that information, although it is possible that identification does play some role.

It is our belief that a full understanding of stereotype development and change must take into consideration the importance of perceptions of shared beliefs. Stereotypes and prejudice are likely to be developed and changed in large part through contact with ingroup, rather than outgroup, members. As children play they are likely to talk about their stereotypes and share them with each other, and this communication likely creates and reinforces tolerant or intolerant beliefs. As employers make hiring and personnel decisions that either benefit or harm members of racial minorities, they are influenced in large part by the prevailing cultural norms of their organization—whether these norms are for tolerance or intolerance. Political leaders also express relatively tolerant or intolerant values and beliefs, and these become part of the cultural fabric of society. In short, people hold their stereotypes in large part because they perceive (accurately or inaccurately) that others do, too.

In addition to contributing to an understanding of the genesis and application of intergroup beliefs, our program of research also suggests possible interventions to reduce negative intergroup attitudes. Most generally, our approach suggests that belief change does not only come from contact with members of outgroups. Indeed, many of the most intractable contemporary intergroup conflicts occur between groups that have plenty of contact with each other. If racial stereotypes persist in large part because people assume that negative intergroup beliefs are socially shared by others, then the potential for undermining these negative beliefs through the presentation of consensus feedback is a promising intervention. If unfavorable beliefs are the result of ingroup norms, changing prejudice involves changing those norms. This might involve being exposed to the beliefs of another person or other persons with more favorable attitudes, for instance by having low prejudiced persons discuss their views with persons who are higher in prejudice. Such exchanges of information, if set in a context in which low prejudice is the more socially desirable viewpoint, could be effective in improving attitudes.

Changing beliefs, especially negative stereotypes, by providing consensus information need not involve providing people with false information about the beliefs of other people, as we have done in our experiments. To the extent that pluralistic ignorance exists around issues of stereotypes and prejudice, providing people with information about the actual beliefs of other people or the actual reality of the social norms could be effective. For example, within colleges, universities, companies, clubs, and so on, the actual beliefs of individuals could be assessed, and information about the beliefs of others could be subsequently provided. In many cases, it is likely that the true beliefs of others will be more favorable than individuals originally estimated, and thus provide accurate information about the prevalence of beliefs within the culture that may be expected to produce change in the favorable direction.

Interventions also might focus on children and early adolescents, by providing them with information about the favorable beliefs that others have about different social outgroups. Children and adolescents spend more of their time interacting with peers, in comparison to parents and other adults, and peers have a significant influence on trivial matters, such as clothes and music, as well as important attitudes and behaviors (Berndt, 1992; 1996; Csikszentmihalyi & Larson, 1984). For example, studies have found that peers influence adolescents' use of tobacco, alcohol, and marijuana (Chassin, Presson, Montello, Sherman, & McGrew, 1986), sexual behavior (Berndt & Savin-Williams, 1993), and attitudes toward school and achievement (Epstein, 1983).

What all of this points to is that social influence processes permeate virtually every aspect of thought and behavior in children and adults. We are thoroughly influenced, often without being aware of it, by the opinions of others, regardless of whether or not we are perceiving those opinions accurately. The optimistic message that comes from our research program is that perceived consensus and social influence processes can be used to undermine stereotyping and prejudice. Because unfavorable attitudes toward outgroups are maintained in part by the assumption that these attitudes are widely shared, they are open to revision on the basis of new information about the degree of consensus surrounding these attitudes. By removing the consensual backing from attitudes about outgroups, it may be possible over time to unravel the basis for shared reality, upon which systems of stereotyping and prejudice ultimately depend.

REFERENCES

Abrams, D., & Hogg, M. A. (1988). Comments on motivational status of self-esteem in social identity and intergroup discrimination. *European Journal of Social Psychology, 18*, 317–334.

Baron, R. S., Hoppe, S. I., Kao, C. F., Brunsman, B., Linneweh, B., & Rogers, D. (1996). Social corroboration and opinion extremity. *Journal of Experimental Social psychology, 32*, 537–560.

Bar-Tal, D. (2000). *Shared beliefs in a society*. Thousand Oaks, CA: Sage.

Berndt, T. J. (1992). Friendship and friends' influence in adolescence. *Current directions in psychological science, 1*, 156–159.

Berndt, T. J. (1996). Friendships in adolescence. In N. Vanzetti & S. Duck (Eds.), A lifetime of relationships (pp. 181–212). Pacific Grove, CA: Brooks.

Berndt, T. J., & Savin-Williams, R. C. (1993). Peer relations and friendships. In P. H. Tolan & B. J. Cohler (Eds.), *Handbook of clinical research and practice with adolescents* (pp. 203–219). New York: Wiley & Sons.

Blanchard, F. A., Crandall, C. S., Brigham, J. C., & Vaughn, L. A. (1994). Condemning and condoning racism: A social context approach to interracial settings. *Journal of Applied Psychology, 79*, 993–997.

Brewer, M. & Brown, R. (1998). Intergroup relations. In S. Fiske, D. Gilbert & G. Lindzey (Eds.), *Handbook of social psychology* (vol. 2, pp. 554–594). Boston: McGraw-Hill.

Brown, R. J., Condor, S., Mathews, A., Wade, G., & Williams, J. (1986). Explaining intergroup differentiation in an industrial organization. *Journal of Occupational Psychology, 59*, 273–286.

Cartwright, D., & Zander, A. (1968). *Group dynamics*. New York: Harper Row.

Chassin, L., Presson, C. C., Montello, D., Sherman, S. J., & McGrew, J. (1986). Changes in peer and parent influence during adolescence: Longitudinal versus cross-sectional perspectives on smoking initiation. *Developmental Psychology, 22*, 327–334.

Csikszentmihalyi, M., & Larson, R. (1984). *Being adolescent*. New York: Basic Books.

Deutsch, M., & Gerard, H. B. (1955). A study of normative and informational social influences upon individual judgment. *Journal of Abnormal and Social Psychology, 51*, 629–636.

Dovidio, J., Evans, N., & Tyler, R. (1986). Racial stereotypes: The contents of their cognitive representations. *Journal of Experimental Social Psychology, 22*, 22–37.

Eagly, A. H., & Kite, M. E. (1987). Are stereotypes of nationalities applied to both women and men? *Journal of Personality and Social Psychology, 53*, 451–462.

Epstein, J. L. (1983). The influence of friends on achievement and affective outcomes. In J. L. Epstein & N. Karweit (Eds.), *Friends in school: Patterns of selection and influence in secondary schools* (pp. 177–200). New York: Academic.

Festinger, L. (1950). Informal social communication. *Psychological Review, 57*, 271–282.

Festinger, L. (1954). A theory of social comparison processes. *Human Relations, 7*, 117–140.

Fiske, S. T. (1998). Stereotyping, Prejudice and Discrimination. In S. Fiske, D. Gilbert, & G. Lindzey (Eds.) *Handbook of social psychology* (vol. 2, pp. 357–414). Boston: McGraw-Hill.

Gardner, R. C. (1994). Stereotypes as consensual beliefs. In M. P. Zanna & J. M. Olson (Eds.), *The psychology of prejudice: The Ontario Symposium* (Vol. 7, pp. 1–31). Hillsdale, NJ: Lawrence Erlbaum.

Hamilton, D. L., & Gifford, R. K. (1976). Illusory correlation in interpersonal perception: A cognitive basis of stereotypic judgments. *Journal of Experimental Social Psychology, 12*, 392–407.

Hamilton, D. L., & Sherman, J. W. (1994). Stereotypes. In R. S. Wyer & T. K. Srull (Eds.), *Handbook of social cognition* (Vol. 2, pp. 1–68). Hillsdale, NJ: Erlbaum.

Hardin, C., & Higgins, T. (1996). Shared reality: How social verification makes the subjective objective. In R. M. Sorrentino & E. T. Higgins (Eds.), *Handbook of motivation and cognition: Foundations of social behavior* (pp. 28–84). New York: Guilford.

Haslam, S. A., Oakes, P. J., McGarty, C., Turner, J. C., Reynolds, K. J., & Eggins, R. A. (1996). Stereotyping and social influence: The mediation of stereotype applicability and sharedness by the views of in-group and out-group members. *British Journal of Social Psychology, 35*, 369–397.

Hewstone, M., & Brown, R. (1986). *Contact and conflict in intergroup encounters*. London: Basil Blackwell.

Jost, J. T., & Banaji, M. R. (1994). The role of stereotyping in system-justification and the production of false consciousness. *British Journal of Social Psychology, 33*, 1–27.

Katz, D., & Braly, K. W. (1933). Racial stereotypes of one hundred college students. *Journal of Abnormal and Social Psychology, 28*, 280–290.

Katz, I., & Hass, R. G. (1988). Racial ambivalence and American value conflict: Correlational and priming studies of dual cognitive structures. *Journal of Personality and Social Psychology, 55*, 893–905.

Kelman, H. C. (1961). Processes of opinion change. *Public Opinion Quarterly, 25*, 57–78.

Kunda, Z., & Thagard, P. (1996). Forming impressions from stereotypes, traits and behaviors: A parallel constraint satisfaction theory. *Psychological Review, 103*, 284–308.

Lewin, K. (1952). Group decision and social change. In G. E. Swanson, T. M. Newcomb, & E. L. Hartley (Eds.), *Readings in social psychology* (pp. 197–211). New York: Henry Holt & Company.

Maio, G. R., Esses, V. M., & Bell., D. W. (1994). The formation of attitudes toward new immigrant groups. *Journal of Applied Social Psychology, 24*, 1762–1776.

Martin, R. (1988). Minority influence and "trivial" social categorization. *European Journal of Social Psychology, 18*, 465–470.

McConahay, J. B., Hardee, B. B., & Batts, V. (1981). Has racism declined? It depends upon who's asking and what is asked. *Journal of Conflict Resolution, 25*, 563–579.

Newcomb, T. M. (1943). *Personality and social change: Attitude formation in a student community*. New York: Dryden.

Newcomb, T. M. (1963). Persistence and regression of changed attitudes: Long range studies. *Journal of Social Issues, 19*, 3–14.

Orive, R. (1988a). Group consensus, action immediacy, and opinion confidence. *Personality and Social Psychology Bulletin, 14*, 573–577.

Orive, R. (1988b). Social projection and social comparison of opinions. *Journal of Personality and Social Psychology, 54*, 953–964.

Rothbart, M., & John, O. P. (1985). Social categorization and behavioral episodes: A cognitive analysis of the effects of intergroup contact. *Journal of Social Issues, 41*, 81–104.

Rothbart, M. & John, O. (1992). Intergroup relations and stereotype change: A social-cognitive analysis and some longitudinal findings. In P. M. Sniderman & P. E. Tetlock (Eds.), *Prejudice, politics and race in America* (pp. 32–59). Stanford: Stanford University Press.

Ruscher, J. B. (in press). *Prejudiced communication*. New York: Guilford.

Ruscher, J. B., & Duval, L. L. (1998). Multiple communicators with unique target information transmit less stereotypical impressions. *Journal of Personality and Social Psychology, 74*, 329–344.

Ruscher, J. B., Hammer, E. Y., & Hammer, E. D. (1996). Forming shared impressions through conversation: An adaptation of the continuum model. *Personality and Social Psychology Bulletin, 7*, 705–720.

Schaller, M., & Conway, L. G. (1999). Influence of impression-management goals on the emerging contents of group stereotypes: Support for a social-evolutionary process. *Personality and Social Psychology Bulletin, 25*, 819–833.

Schaller, M., & Conway, L. G. (in press). From cognition to culture: The origins of stereotypes that really matter. In G. Moskowitz (Ed.), *Future directions in social cognition*. Hillsdale, NJ: Erlbaum.

Sechrist, G. B., & Stangor, C. (in press). The influence of consensus information on intergroup beliefs and behavior. Manuscript submitted for publication. *Journal of Personality and Social Psychology*.

Sechrist, G. B., Stangor, C., & Jost, J. T. (1998). *Confidence and identification as mediators of perceived consensus*. Unpublished data, University of Maryland.

Stangor, C., & Lange, J. (1994). Mental representations of social groups: Advances in conceptualizing stereotypes and stereotyping. *Advances in Experimental Social Psychology, 26*, 367–416.

Stangor, C., & Schaller, M. (1996). Stereotypes as individual and collective representations. In C. N. Macrae, C. Stangor, & M. Hewstone (Eds.), *Stereotypes and stereotyping* (pp. 3–40). New York: Guilford.

Stangor, C., Sechrist, G. B., & Jost, J. T. (in press). Changing racial beliefs by providing consensus information. *Personality and Social Psychology Bulletin*.

Stephan, W. G. (1985). Intergroup relations. In G. Lindzey & E. Aronson (Eds.), *The handbook of social psychology*. New York: Random House.

Tajfel, H. (1982). Social psychology of intergroup relations. *Annual Review of Psychology, 33,* 1–39.

Tajfel, H., & Turner, J. C. (1979). An integrative theory of intergroup conflict. In W. G. Austin & S. Worchel (Eds.), *The social psychology of intergroup relations* (pp. 33–48). Monterey, CA: Brooks/Cole.

Turner, J. C. (1987). *Rediscovering the social group: A self-categorization theory*. Oxford, England: Basil Blackwell.

Turner, J. C. (1991). *Social influence*. Pacific Grove, CA: Brooks Cole.

Weber, R., & Crocker, J. (1983). Cognitive processes in the revision of stereotypic beliefs. *Journal of Personality and Social Psychology, 45,* 961–977.

Wittenbrink, B., & Henly, J. R. (1996). Creating social reality: Informational social influence and content of stereotypic beliefs. *Personality and Social Psychology Bulletin, 22,* 598–610.

Wittenbrink, B., Judd, C., & Park, B. (1997). Evidence for racial prejudice at the implicit level and its relationship with questionnaire measures. *Journal of Personality and Social Psychology, 72,* 262–274.

van Knippenberg, A., & Wilke, H. (1988). Social categorization and attitude change. *European Journal of Social Psychology, 18,* 395–406.

15

Attitudes, Behavior, and Social Context
The Role of Norms and Group Membership in Social Influence Processes

DEBORAH J. TERRY
MICHAEL A. HOGG

*A*ttitude researchers have focused much of their attention on attitude-behavior relations and attitude change (see Eagly & Chaiken, 1993). Despite the fact that attitude research is central to the realm of social psychology, the role of social influence in attitude-behavior relations and persuasion has received less attention. For the most part, an individualistic perspective has been taken—attitudes are regarded as part of people's personal belief structures. As a consequence, most research on attitude-behavior rela-

Address for Correspondence: Deborah Terry, School of Psychology, University of Queensland, Brisbane QLD 4072. E-mail: deborah@psy.uq.edu.au

tions and attitude change has been conducted at this same level of abstraction. Indeed, the dominant tendency in the attitude change and persuasion literature has been to treat persuasive communication and social influence in groups as separate areas of research inquiry. Nevertheless, on the basis of social identity theory (Hogg & Abrams, 1988; Tajfel & Turner, 1979; Turner, 1982) and self-categorization theory (Turner, 1985; Turner, Hogg, Oakes, Reicher, & Wetherell, 1987; see also David & Turner, this volume; Spears, Postmes, Lea, & Watt, this volume), a strong theoretical case can be made for the view that attitude change and persuasion cannot be well understood without reference to the wider social context of group memberships. Attitudes themselves can be regarded as social products to the extent that they are likely to be influenced by the norms and perceived expectations of groups to which people belong. Furthermore, norms of behaviorally-relevant social groups are likely to influence people's willingness to engage in attitudinally-consistent behavior—to do so may help to validate their group membership.

In the present chapter, we focus on attitude-behavior consistency, and propose that both the attitudinal congruency of ingroup norms and the salience of the group membership influence the extent to which people behave in accord with their attitudes. Our assertion that attitude-behavior consistency cannot be understood without reference to the wider social context of group memberships is supported with the discussion of the results of our recent research in three areas. In addition to demonstrating support for the proposed effects of socionormative influences (i.e., ingroup norms) on the extent to which people behave in accordance with their attitudes, the results of our recent research indicate that such effects are independent of the corresponding effects of attitude accessibility (a central sociocognitive mechanism proposed to explain variation in attitude-behavior consistency; see Fazio, 1986, 1989; Fazio, Powell, & Herr, 1983), and that ingroup norms influence attitude-behavior relations under both spontaneous and deliberative decision-making conditions (cf. Fazio, 1990b). Furthermore, we present evidence that indicates that such norms are relevant to an understanding of the link between prejudiced attitudes and discriminatory behavior.

SOCIAL IDENTITY/SELF-CATEGORIZATION THEORIES AND ATTITUDE-BEHAVIOR RELATIONS

Traditionally, research on the role of norms in attitude-behavior relations has been conducted from the perspective of the theories of reasoned action (Fishbein & Ajzen, 1975) and planned behavior (Ajzen, 1991; see Terry, Gallois, & McCamish, 1993, for an overview of these theories). Both theories consider behavioral intentions to be the most proximal determinant of behavior. Intentions, in turn, are proposed to be influenced not only by people's attitudes toward the behavior, but also by the subjective norm, defined as people's perception of social pressure from significant others to perform the behavior. Research has, however, found only weak support for the proposed role of subjective norms. For instance, Ajzen (1991) found that in more than half of the 19 extant tests of the theory of planned behavior, the norm-intention link was nonsignificant (for similar results, see e.g., Godin, 1993). In light of consistent evidence linking intentions to attitudes and perceived behavioral control (proposed in the theory of planned behavior as a predictor of intention), Ajzen concluded that personal factors are more influential in the prediction of intentions than social factors.

Terry and Hogg (1996; Terry, Hogg, & Duck, 1999; Terry, Hogg, & White, 2000) challenged this conclusion, suggesting that the lack of stronger support for the proposed role of subjective norms may reflect limitations in Fishbein and Ajzen's (1975) conceptual treatment of this construct. Specifically, Fishbein and Ajzen did not conceptualize norms in line with the wider social psychological literature on social influence—that is, as the accepted or implied rules that specify how people should behave—and conceived of norms as being additive across significant others rather than being linked to specific behaviorally relevant reference groups. Furthermore, Terry and Hogg reviewed evidence suggesting that norms may moderate the effects of attitudes on intentions (the contingent consistency hypothesis; see e.g., Grube & Morgan, 1990), and noted that evidence of a link between normative beliefs (i.e., the beliefs proposed to underlie the subjective norm) and attitudes questions the assumption made in the theories of reasoned action and planned behavior that the normative and attitudinal components of the models are cognitively independent (Liska, 1984). Rather than playing down the role of norms and group influence, we have suggested that a reconceptualization of the normative component of these theories in line with recent social psychological models of group influence, specifically social identity theory (Tajfel & Turner, 1979; Turner, 1982; also Hogg & Abrams, 1988) and self-categorization theory (Turner et al., 1987; see also David & Turner, this volume; Spears, Postmes, Lea, & Watt, this volume), may help to preserve a central role for norms in the study of attitude-behavior relations.

Social identity theory is a general theory of group processes and intergroup relations, that distinguishes group phenomena from interpersonal phenomena. When people define themselves in terms of a self-inclusive social category (e.g., a sex, class, team) two processes come into play: (1) categorization, which means that differences between ingroup and outgroup and similarities among ingroup members (including self) on stereotypical dimensions are perceptually accentuated; and (2) self-enhancement which, because the self-concept is defined in terms of group membership, means that people will seek to favor the ingroup. Recently, Turner et al. (1987) extended social identity theory to focus more specifically on the role of the categorization process—self-categorization theory. Derived from social identity and self-categorization theories is a model of social influence in groups, called referent informational influence (Turner, 1982; see also Turner, 1991), that is underpinned by the cognitive process of self-categorization. According to this process, when a social identity is salient, people use available, and usually shared, social comparative information to construct a context-specific group norm—a group prototype. The group prototype describes and prescribes beliefs, attitudes, feelings, and behaviors that optimally minimize ingroup differences and maximize intergroup differences (the principle of metacontrast). As well as underpinning the construction of an ingroup prototype, the process of self-categorization assimilates self to the prototype (depersonalization) and thus transforms self: Self-perception, beliefs, feelings, and behaviors are now defined in terms of the group prototype rather than in terms of the unique characteristics of the self.

On the basis of the sociocognitive processes of categorization and depersonalization, a clear case can be made for the role of group norms in attitude-behavior relations. Self-categorization as a member of a contextually salient group means that the self is defined in terms of the ingroup prototype. If the prototype embodies an attitudinally-congruent group norm, then assimilation of self to the prototype means that a person's behavior will be brought in line with his or her attitude, presumably because the fact that the attitude is normative—and hence group-defining—renders the attitude accessible. According to Fazio (1986), the critical factor for attitude-behavior congruency is the cognitive accessibility of the attitude; highly accessible attitudes are proposed to guide behavior through the mediating process of selective perception of the situation. We take this analysis further, and argue that ingroup members adhere behaviorally to a normatively-supported, and hence accessible, attitude because to do so serves to reduce uncertainty about the appropriateness of a given course of action (Hogg, 2000; Hogg & Mullin, 1999) and at the same time validates both the self-concept and the member's status as a group member. In contrast, when an attitude is not normative, attitude-behavior correspondence should be reduced not only because the attitude is relatively inaccessible, but also because it has not been legitimized by a salient group membership.

From a social identity/self-categorization perspective, the lack of evidence linking norms to intentions is not surprising, given the fact that subjective norms are not tied to specific group memberships. We argue that the norms of a group that are relevant to the behavior will influence behavior, but that the extent to which the group membership is a salient basis for self-definition also needs to be taken into account. Furthermore, the social identity/self-categorization perspective is in line with the contingent consistency hypothesis, which, as noted, states that people are more likely to behave in accordance with their attitudes if the normative climate supports the attitude. We go one step further in arguing that norms should increase the correspondence between attitudes and behavior to the extent that the attitude is normative—that is, the norm and attitude are congruent—for a self-inclusive ingroup, and the social identity is a salient component of a person's self-definition. In two tests of the theory of planned behavior, Terry and Hogg (1996) found that the perceived norms of the reference group of friends and peers influenced intentions to engage in regular exercise and sun-protective behavior, but only for those who identified strongly with the group, a pattern of results that was replicated in a study of community residents' recycling behavior (Terry, Hogg, & White, 1999).

In the present chapter, we describe the results of a number of experiments designed to examine—in a more controlled setting—the effects of group norms and salience of the group membership on attitude-behavior consistency. In addition to providing a further examination of the role of ingroup norms in attitude-behavior relations, two sets of studies have been concerned explicitly with the interplay between the effects of socionormative and sociocognitive factors on attitude-behavior consistency. First, we describe the results of a number of experiments designed to examine the effects of group norms, salience of the group membership, and attitude accessibility on attitude-behavior consistency. Second, we consider the effects of group norms and group salience as a function of the mode of behavioral decision-making. A more recent direction that our recent research has taken is to focus on the role that ingroup norms play in the link between intergroup attitudes and discriminatory behavioral tendencies. This research is described at the conclusion of the chapter.

GROUP NORMS, GROUP SALIENCE, AND ATTITUDE ACCESSIBILITY

In addition to the field research cited above, we have conducted a number of experiments designed to examine the effects of ingroup norms and salience of group membership on attitude-behavior relations. From a social identity/self-categorization theory perspective, the central prediction tested in this research was that attitude-behavior consistency would be enhanced when people were exposed to an ingroup norm that was attitudinally-congruent, but only if the group membership was a salient basis for self-conception. On the basis that high levels of group identification indicate that the group membership is likely to be—in an enduring sense at least—a salient basis for self-definition, measures of identification can be used to examine the moderating influence of group salience on the relationship between ingroup norms and attitude-behavior consistency. However, a stronger test of this moderating influence is to manipulate group salience experimentally, such that the group is an important and salient basis for self-conception for some participants, but only a latent category, and hence not a basis for self-definition, for others.

To examine the interplay between social identity and social cognitive variables in attitude-behavior relations, we also focused on the role of attitude accessibility. According to Fazio and colleagues (e.g., Fazio, 1986, 1989; Fazio et al., 1983), the extent of attitude-behavior consistency is determined primarily by the cognitive accessibility of the attitude or, in other words, the salience of the attitude in memory. Highly accessible attitudes are proposed to guide subsequent behavior through the mediating process of selective perception (Fazio, 1986; see also Jamieson & Zanna, 1989), which means that the perception of the attitude object is influenced by the activated attitude and, which in turn, means that the behavioral response is attitudinally-congruent. There is evidence that attitude accessibility can be experimentally manipulated by asking participants to express repeatedly the relevant attitude (e.g., Downing, Judd, & Brauer,

1992; Powell & Fazio, 1984). Fazio (1986) also has argued that some attitudes are more chronically accessible than others—for instance, when attitudes are formed on the basis of direct experience with the attitude object or when people are confident in their attitude. Typically, attitude accessibility is assessed in terms of response latencies to attitudinal questions—the faster people give their response, the more accessible the attitude (e.g., Downing et al., 1992; Fazio, 1990a). In a large body of research, Fazio and colleagues have demonstrated that the more accessible the attitude is, the greater the likelihood that it will influence behavior (e.g., Fazio, Powell, & Williams, 1989; Fazio & Williams, 1986; Houston & Fazio, 1989; see also Bassili, 1995). This evidence has been obtained, irrespective of whether attitude accessibility is experimentally manipulated or whether an attitude is assessed as being chronically more accessible.

Although the mechanism by which normative attitudes guide behavior is thought to be one of increased accessibility of the attitude, simply making the attitude itself accessible (e.g., by having participants repeatedly express their attitude) should have weaker effects than the attitude-behavior consistency that follows from exposing participants to an attitudinally-congruent ingroup norm. Ingroup norms make the corresponding attitude accessible (if it is attitudinally congruent), but there are strong motivational reasons why group members would want to behave in accord with their normatively-supported and accessible attitude. To do so serves to reduce people's uncertainty in terms of the appropriateness of the attitude and to engender a sense of meaning about the social world. Behaving in accordance with a normative attitude also validates the self-concept and the person's status as a group member. Thus, the cognitive activation of a group prototype makes an attitude that concurs with the group prototype accessible, and the motivational processes that underpin group behavior (self-enhancement [Tajfel & Turner, 1979] and uncertainty reduction [Hogg, 2001; Hogg & Mullin, 1999]) provide the prescriptive impetus to translate an attitude into a behavioral response. Thus, it was expected that: (1) both attitude accessibility and ingroup norms would influence attitude-behavior consistency, and (2) the effects of attitude accessibility on attitude-behavior relations would be independent of the effects due to ingroup norms. In other words, it was proposed that the effects of ingroup normative support on attitude-behavior consistency should not be a result of simply making an attitude more cognitively accessible.

The first experiment (White, Hogg, & Terry, in press, Exp. 1) focused on students' attitudes towards comprehensive exams. In this experiment, ingroup salience (low vs. high) and the attitudinal congruency of the ingroup norms (congruent vs. incongruent) were manipulated. Attitude accessibility was assessed in terms of attitude confidence. To manipulate ingroup salience, participants ($N = 160$) were either asked to describe themselves as an individual person and to list attributes that made them unique as an individual (low salience), or to describe themselves as a University of Queensland (UQ) student and to list their similarities with other such students (high salience; see Hogg & Hardie, 1991). Participants then viewed bargraphs showing the percentage of opposition to three issues (including the target issue) from students at UQ (ingroup) and from students at a rival university (outgroup). The graphs either indicated that the ingroup was strongly opposed to comprehensive exams and the rival campus supported them or vice versa.

As expected, participants exposed to an attitudinally-congruent (rather than an incongruent) ingroup norm behaved more consistently with their initial attitude on two measures of behavior (signing a relevant letter and signing a petition); however, contrary to predictions, these effects did not vary as a function of ingroup salience. There also was evidence that on the measure of willingness to sign the petition, attitude confidence was associated positively with attitude-behavior correspondence. As expected, this effect was independent of, and weaker, than the effect due to norm congruency.

A second experiment was conducted in which attitude accessibility was manipulated and the salience manipulation was strengthened (see White et al., in press, Exp. 2). The target issue was "separate bicycle lanes on roads" which was linked to gender identity. Under conditions of high or low gender salience, participants ($N = 167$) were exposed to attitude-congruent or attitude-incongruent ingroup normative support (contrasted with an opposing outgroup norm). Attitude accessibility was manipulated using the repeated expression method. As expected, there was evidence that participants exposed to norm congruent information were more likely to engage in attitudinally-congruent behavior (in relation to willingness to donate time) under conditions of high rather than low group salience. When exposed to norm-incongruent information, there was a tendency for attitude-behavior consistency to be most marked when the group membership was not made salient. This is consistent with the prediction that ingroup normative information has the least impact on attitude-behavior consistency when the group membership is not a salient basis for self-conception. On two binary behavioral measures (responses to a state transport ballot and willingness to sign a petition), there was evidence that participants were more likely to behave in accordance with their initial attitudes when (1) they received ingroup normative support, and (2) when they were in the high attitude accessibility condition. Once again, the effects of attitude accessibility were weaker than those observed for norm congruency.

Although providing some support for the predicted effects of ingroup norms, the first two studies were limited in that an attitudinally-incongruent ingroup norm was always accompanied by an attitudinally-incongruent outgroup norm. Thus, it was unclear whether the effects of ingroup norms were a consequence of the fact that an explicit intergroup contrast was drawn between ingroup norms and the norms of a relevant outgroup. To examine this possibility, an additional experiment (White, Terry, & Hogg, 2000) was conducted in which ingroup norm congruency (congruent vs. incongruent) and outgroup norm congruency (congruent vs. incongruent) were independently manipulated. Ingroup salience was held constant at high levels, and attitude accessibility was measured in terms of attitude confidence. As in the previous studies, attitude accessibility was associated with stronger attitude-behavior consistency. Independent of the influence of attitude accessibility, information about ingroup norms (rather than outgroup norms) had significant and stronger effects on attitude-behavior consistency. These results provide further evidence that ingroups exert more influence than outgroups (see Wilder, 1990), and also question the necessity for ingroup normative information to be accompanied by contrasting outgroup information for ingroup norms to influence attitude-behavior consistency. There may be a similarity between the effects of ingroup norms on attitude-behavior consistency and group polarization (e.g., Turner, 1985; Wetherell, 1987), where there does not appear to be a need to have an explicit outgroup for ingroup polarization to occur (see Hogg & Abrams, 1988).

Taken together, the results of these experiments provide strong support for the expectation that participants will be more likely to engage in attitudinally-congruent behavior when they receive normative support for their attitude from a relevant reference ingroup. In the second experiment, where the manipulation of group salience was more successful than in the first experiment, we also found some evidence that, as expected, the effect of ingroup normative support was stronger under high than low group salience conditions. In each of the experiments, there was support for Fazio's (1986) prediction that greater attitude accessibility is associated with stronger attitude-behavior consistency. The fact that accessibility did not interact with group salience or normative support accords with the expectation that social identity and cognitive accessibility processes have independent effects on attitude-behavior consistency. People do appear to behave in accordance with their attitudes if those attitudes are cognitively accessible, but quite independently, and to a stronger extent, they also bring their behavior in line with their attitudes when there is normative support for these attitudes, presumably because there are strong motivational reasons for ingroup members to behave in accord with normatively-supported attitudes.

GROUP NORMS, GROUP SALIENCE, AND MODE OF BEHAVIORAL DECISION-MAKING

In a second body of experimental research examining the effects of social identity and social cognitive factors on attitude-behavior consistency, we manipulated (in addition to the attitudinal-congruence of the ingroup norm) the mode of behavioral decision-making. In a similar vein to dual process models of attitude change (i.e., elaboration likelihood model [Petty & Cacioppo, 1986] and heuristic-systematic model [Chaiken, Liberman, & Eagly, 1989]), Fazio (1990b) distinguished two different processes through which attitudes can influence behavior: a spontaneous, theory-driven process, and a deliberative, data-driven process. In his MODE model (Motivation and Opportunity as DEterminants of mode of behavioral decision-making), Fazio hypothesized that under conditions that favor peripheral route processing of persuasive messages (i.e., low motivation and low ability [see Petty & Cacioppo, 1986]), links between attitudes and behavior arise as a consequence of spontaneous processing, rather than as a consequence of deliberative or reasoned processing. Specifically, when participants are making behavioral decisions via the spontaneous route, attitudes—to the extent to which they are cognitively accessible—guide behavior through the mediating process of selective perception of the situation (Fazio, 1990b; see also Jamieson & Zanna, 1989). Under deliberative processing, behavioral decisions are made in accord with the mechanism that underpins the theories of reasoned action and planned behavior—namely, as a consequence of effortful consideration of the available information, including the consequences of performing the behavior, the perceived expectations of others, and perceptions of behavioral control. Previous research has provided some support for the general predictions of the MODE model (Sanbonmatsu & Fazio, 1990; Schuette & Fazio, 1995).

Although Fazio (1990b) acknowledged that norms may influence behavioral decision-making under spontaneous processing, systematic consideration of a number of different factors, including norms, in the formation of a behavioral decision is restricted to the realm of deliberative processing. Thus, according to the MODE model, the effects of norms should be more marked under deliberative than spontaneous behavioral decision-making. In contrast, on the basis of social identity/self-categorization theory, we would predict that, irrespective of mode of behavioral decision-making, ingroup norms should influence attitude-behavior consistency. Under both processing routes, group norms should be a central and important guide to behavioral responses for group members. However, because people for whom the group membership is a salient basis for self-conception are motivated to consider self-relevant group norms carefully (see Mackie, Worth, & Ascunsion, 1990; also Forgas & Fiedler, 1996), the effect of norms under deliberative decision-making conditions should be most marked for participants for whom the group membership is highly salient or self-relevant. When the group membership is only a latent category, the effect of the normative information should be relatively weak, because the opportunity to make the behavioral decision systematically means that the normative information is likely to be rejected because of the low personal relevance of the group membership. Thus, we anticipated that the effects of ingroup norms would be most marked under conditions of deliberative decision-making when the group membership was a salient basis for self-definition.

In a preliminary study of the effects of ingroup norms and mode of behavioral decision-making on attitude-behavior consistency, we conducted a study of career choice in psychology (Terry, Hogg, & McKimmie, 2000, Exp. 1). After indicating their preferred career choice (attitude), participants received norm-consistent (ingroup members supported their career preference), norm-inconsistent (ingroup members supported another career preference), or no-norm (no clear norm for ingroup members) information. Then we then manipulated mode of behavioral decision-making using a manipulation that was designed to increase participants' motivation to make the behavioral decision deliberatively. The main dependent variable was whether participants chose to attend an information session that was consistent with their initial preferred career choice. As expected, irrespective of the mode of behavioral decision-making, attitude-behavior consistency was strongest when participants were exposed to an attitudinally-congruent ingroup norm. Thus, under both types of decision-making, ingroup norms clearly had an impact on attitude-behavior consistency.

To examine the interplay among manipulations of ingroup norms, group salience, and mode of behavioral decision-making on attitude-behavior consistency, a second experiment was conducted using a mock jury paradigm (Terry, Hogg, & McKimmie, 2000, Exp. 2), a paradigm that has been widely used in a range of different areas of social psychology (e.g., Davis, 1986; Davis, Stasson, Ono, & Zimmerman, 1988; Kaplan & Miller, 1978; MacCoun & Kerr, 1988; Stasser & Davis, 1977). Student participants were divided into jury groups under high or low group salience conditions, indicated their initial attitudes to a number of crimes—including the focal crime of computer hacking—and were exposed to ingroup normative information, which was congruent or incongruent with their initial attitude. They then read case notes relating to an alleged occurrence of computer hacking, and they were required to make individual decisions about guilt and punishment (behavior) under restricted or liberal time constraints (manipulation of spontaneous vs. deliberate mode of behavioral decision-making). The principal dependent variable was the extent of attitude-behavior *in*consistency.

On the absolute measure of attitude-behavior inconsistency, there was a significant main effect for norm congruency. As predicted, individuals in the norm incongruent condition displayed greater attitude-behavior inconsistency than participants in the norm congruent condition. Further analyses revealed that in the norm incongruent condition, attitude-behavior inconsistency, for the most part, reflected movement towards the pole represented by the group norm; of the participants whose behavioral recommendation was inconsistent with their initial attitude, 80% moved in the direction of the group norm. To assess the relative importance of norms and attitudes in the prediction of the behavioral recommendation, multiple regression analyses were conducted with behavior as the criterion. Participants' perceived level of appropriate punishment (attitude) and perceived ingroup norm were predictors. Analyses were performed separately for high and low salience participants; however, because there were no effects of mode of decision-making in the previous analyses, participants in the two conditions were considered together. In line with the theoretical basis for this research, norms were predictive of behavior only when group membership was highly salient.

Because there was evidence that the manipulation of group salience did not have a strong effect on perceived identification with the group, a second set of analyses was performed where identification (rather than the manipulated salience variable) was used as an independent variable. These analyses revealed that for participants who did not identify strongly with the group (i.e., it was not a salient basis for self-definition), norm congruency did not have a significant effect on attitude-behavior inconsistency. In contrast, participants who identified strongly with the group were influenced by the group norm. Those who received an incongruent group norm displayed greater attitude-behavior inconsistency compared to those who received a congruent norm. Among the norm incongruent participants, there was further evidence that movement towards the group norm was greatest for the high identifiers. Furthermore, norms were predictive of behavior only when individuals strongly identified with the group.

In support of the central hypothesis, the extent of attitude-behavior consistency was influenced by the attitudinal congruence of normative information. On the measure of attitude-behavior inconsistency, there was evidence that an incongruent group norm induced greater behavioral deviance from a previously expressed attitude than exposure to a congruent group norm; moreover, further analyses revealed that the attitude-behavior consistency in the norm incongruent condition, for the most part, reflected movement towards the group norm. As expected, there also was some evidence that the influence of norms on the behavioral recommendation tended to be greatest when the group was a salient basis for self-definition—particularly when assessed in terms of strength of group identification; however, there was no evidence that the latter effects were most marked under deliberative decision-making conditions.

The results of the research on the effects of ingroup norms, group salience, and mode of behavioral decision-making not only further support the proposed role of normative factors in the prediction of attitude-behavior consistency, but also provide some insight into the interplay between social identity and sociocognitive factors in this context. Contrary to Fazio's (1990b) MODE model, the results of the two experiments indicated that, irrespective of the cognitive conditions under which a behavioral decision is made, ingroup norms impact on attitude-behavior consistency (cf. Wellen, Hogg, & Terry, 1998). The same results were obtained across two different types of manipulation—a motivational and an ability-based manipulation of decision-making. Although in the jury decision-making study there was some evidence that the effects of norms were more marked for those who identified strongly with the group, there was no evidence that this was restricted to conditions designed to engender deliberative decision-making. Thus, there was no evidence that the effects of norms—even when the group membership was a salient basis for self-conception—varied as a function of mode of behavioral decision-making. This pattern of results is contrary to the MODE model (Fazio, 1990b), that suggests that information, such as ingroup norms, should receive more careful consideration and hence should have more impact under deliberative than spontaneous decision-making conditions.

INTERGROUP ATTITUDES, INGROUP NORMS, AND DISCRIMINATORY BEHAVIOR

Although the proposed social identity/self-categorization perspective on the role of social influence in attitude-behavior relations has received some support in relation to nonsocial attitudes, its utility in the more socially-relevant domain of intergroup attitudes has yet to be examined. Moreover, beyond an examination of the proposed moderating roles of group salience and strength of group identification, other factors that may influence the strength of the effects of ingroup norms have received little research attention. In the context of intergroup attitudes, the extent to which such attitudes are expressed in discriminatory behavior should be increased for those people motivated to attain a positive social identity. Thus, people's beliefs about the nature of relations between their own group and relevant outgroups should moderate the impact of group norms on attitude-behavior consistency, a perspective that specifically articulates the sociocognitive focus of self-categorization theory with the broader macro-social emphasis of social identity theory (Tajfel & Turner, 1979; also Ellemers, 1993; Hogg & Abrams, 1988; Tajfel, 1974). Although dominant groups are constantly striving to maintain their superior position, stronger status protection responses should be elicited when group members perceive that this position is insecure. Thus, it is proposed that an insecure social identity will strengthen the likelihood that dominant group members will behaviorally express their attitudes towards minority groups. Under unstable conditions, the status hierarchy might change or be weakened, which is likely to engender feelings of threat among members of the dominant group. Thus, for dominant group members, attitude-behavior consistency should be influenced by the attitudinal congruence of the ingroup norms, particularly when they perceive that their high status position is under threat.

To test this prediction, a study of participants with promulticulturalism attitudes (Terry, Hogg, Blackwood, & Johnson, 2000) was undertaken. In this study, normative information attributed to Australian students that was either congruent or incongruent with participants' attitudes towards multiculturalism was presented under conditions of either high or low salience of national identity. In addition, the moderating effect of the perception of economic group-status threat was examined. Based on social identity/self-categorization theory, it was proposed that the effects of the group norm would be more marked for the participants in the high contextual salience condition than for those in the low contextual salience condition. It was further proposed that the effect of group norms on participants in the high salience condition would be most marked for those who perceived high levels of economic group-status threat.

Participants in the study were Anglo-Australian first-year psychology students who participated in the study for partial course credit. A total of 197 students participated in the study; however, only data from those participants ($N = 168$) who indicated that they were promulticulturalism at Time 1 and who participated in the study at both Times 1 and 2 were included in the analysis. In the premanipulation session (Time 1), participants completed the first questionnaire that, in addition to demographic items, included 12 items that were designed to tap into perceptions of the extent to which the national economic climate was under threat (e.g., "Relative to the costs of living, I feel that Australian wages have declined over the last ten years"). A single-item measure of overall support for multiculturalism (on a 9-point scale) was also obtained at Time 1. This measure was used to compute the amount of attitude change across the course of the study.

One week after the premanipulation questionnaire was completed, participants returned for the experimental session. Participants in the high contextual salience condition watched a video made up of advertisements that had been designed to elicit nationalist sentiment. For participants in the low salience condition, the video was made up of advertisements selected to match the pace and mood of the high salience video but not to elicit national identity. Following the salience manipulation, participants were provided with normative information that was either attitudinally-congruent (80% of Australian students supported multiculturalism) or attitudinally-incongruent (80% of Australian students opposed multiculturalism). The normative information was presented in two forms: five statements from a representative sample of Australian students and summary data of students' attitudes to multiculturalism, ostensibly obtained from a recent survey of Australian students.

The participants were then introduced to the dependent variables measuring behavioral support for multiculturalism. Three items were used to assess willingness (behavioral intentions) to support multiculturalism. Embedded with similar items on environmental protection and homosexuality, participants were asked to indicate their willingness to engage in three behaviors opposing multiculturalism (responses on these items were recoded to reflect support for multiculturalism). Based on research that has suggested that prejudice may be manifested in the withholding of behavioral support (e.g., Devine, 1989), an additional item was designed to tap covert expressions of racism. It required participants to indicate the order in which they would support seven motions (including one supporting an anti-racism campaign) being placed on the agenda for the National Union of Students' Conference. The behavioral support item was scored in terms of whether the motion was placed in the top three for placement on the agenda (high support) or in the lower four (low support). To assess changes in attitude towards multiculturalism from Time 1 to Time 2, participants were again asked to respond to the item used at Time 1 to assess overall support for multiculturalism.

Initial analyses indicated that the experimental manipulations of contextual salience and norm congruency were successful. The focal analyses revealed no main or interactive effects of norm congruency or contextual group salience on behavioral support. On willingness to engage in attitudinally-congruent behavior, there was a significant Norm × Salience interaction. For participants in the high salience condition, there was a significant effect for norm congruency. As expected, participants presented with attitudinally-congruent normative information (promulticulturalism) displayed a greater willingness to engage in behavior consistent with their attitudes than those presented with attitude-incongruent norms. The willingness of participants in the low salience condition to behave in accordance with their attitudes was unaffected by the presentation of normative information. On the attitude change measure, there was a significant main effect of norm-congruency with participants exposed to the attitudinally-incongruent normative information (anti-multiculturalism) exhibiting a greater shift towards opposition to multiculturalism compared to those exposed to the attitudinally-congruent normative information. Although the latter effect was not dependent on the contextual salience of national identity, there was some evidence that it was most marked for those who identified strongly, in an enduring sense, as an Australian (a measure of this variable was also obtained at Time 1).

On the measure of willingness to engage in attitudinally-congruent (promulticulturalism) behavior, there was a significant main effect for threat with less willingness to engage in attitudinally-congruent behavior among those who perceived high economic group-status threat. This main effect was qualified by a significant Threat × Norm × Salience interaction. When participants perceived high levels of economic group-status threat and contextual group salience was high, there was a significant effect of group norms: Willingness to engage in attitude-consistent behavior was weaker for those exposed to an incongruent group norm than for those exposed to a congruent group norm. When high levels of group-status threat were perceived but contextual salience was low, the effect of ingroup norms was not significant. A similar pattern of results was obtained on the measure of (positive) change in attitude to multiculturalism from Time 1 to Time 2. Specifically, there was a significant shift in attitudes in the direction of the attitudinally-incongruent norm—that is, attitudes towards multiculturalism became less positive—among the participants who perceived high levels of economic group-status threat and for whom the national identity was contextually salient, a pattern of results not observed for the participants in the low salience condition who perceived high group-status threat. On the measure of behavioral support (support for an anti-racism campaign), there was some evidence that the effect of the attitude-incongruent (anti-multiculturalism) normative information was influenced by perceptions of economic group-status threat. Participants who perceived high levels of group-status threat were more likely than low threat participants to oppose an anti-racism campaign when presented with the attitude-incongruent norm.

Taken together, the results of this study provide support for the assertion that people are more likely to behave in accordance with their intergroup attitudes if the attitude is normative for (i.e., it is supported by) a salient reference group. Ingroup norms for multiculturalism influenced willingness to engage in promulticulturalism behaviors but only when the relevant identity was contextually salient. This pattern of results was essentially mirrored on the measure of attitude change across the course of the study. The results of the study, thus, indicate that the nature of the normative environment is an important factor in determining whether people behaviorally express their intergroup attitudes. The role of group influence has received relatively little theoretical and empirical interest in recent research on prejudice and discrimination (cf. Jetten, Spears, & Manstead, 1996). Yet, phenomena such as the relatively sudden increase in the behavioral expression of prejudiced attitudes are difficult to explain without acknowledging the role that the broader normative climate plays in providing support for people to bring their intergroup behavioral intentions and responses in line with their intergroup attitudes.

As expected, there was evidence that the effects of group norms were most marked for those who perceived high levels of group-status threat. When ethnocentric attitudes are normative for a self-inclusive and salient ingroup, the extent to which such attitudes are expressed in discriminatory behavior should be increased for those people motivated to attain a positive social identity. Thus, stronger status protection responses should be elicited when group members perceive that this position is insecure, a prediction that was supported. Future research on the interplay among prejudiced attitudes, group norms, and discriminatory behavior should seek to, more explicitly, address the predictions that can be derived from the macro-social emphasis of social identity theory by examining the effects of the factors that should underpin perceptions of status threat among dominant group members. These factors include the stability of the intergroup structure, the permeability of intergroup boundaries, and perceptions of the legitimacy of their status position (Tajfel, & Turner, 1979; see also Ellemers, 1993; Hogg & Abrams, 1988).

CONCLUSION

Taken together, the results of the research reviewed in this chapter furnish support for the proposed reconceptualization of the role of norms in attitude-behavior relations along the lines suggested by social identity/self-categorization theories. The results of the research provide clear evidence for the central prediction that the attitudinal-congruence of an ingroup norm will influence attitude-behavior consistency. In a range of attitudinal contexts, participants were more likely to behave in accordance with their attitude when exposed to an attitudinally-congruent ingroup norm than when exposed to an incongruent norm. The evidence for a main effect of norm congruency on attitude-behavior consistency is in line with social identity and self-categorization theories—exposure to an attitudinally-congruent group norm should strengthen attitude-behavior consistency because it validates the attitudinally-congruent behavior as appropriate for group members. The second pattern of results that supports our theoretical perspective is the evidence that the extent to which the group membership that defines the norm is a salient basis for self-conception moderates the influence of ingroup norms.

In addition to the consistent findings observed for ingroup norms, the experimental research reported in this chapter demonstrates, quite clearly, that the effects of norm congruency are independent of attitude accessibility and are not dependent on mode of behavioral decision-making. These results, at a general level, accord with a social identity/self-categorization perspective, although we expected that salient ingroup norms would be most influential under conditions that engender deliberative consideration of the normative information. The attitude change literature (see e.g., Mackie & Queller, 2000) has provided some support for the latter prediction, which suggests that the ability to deliberatively process ingroup information may be particularly relevant when group members are exposed to persuasive messages.

In conclusion, the present results are important, in that they reflect clear support for the prediction that norm congruency influences the strength of attitude-behavior consistency. Such results should serve to maintain an important and central role for social influence in attitude-behavior relations—a role that has been questioned by recent commentators (e.g., Ajzen, 1991)—along the lines suggested by social identity and self-categorization theories. As such, they open the way for further research to take a more fine-grained look at the role that group membership and group norms play in this context. In particular, the results indicate the importance of taking into account the broader normative climate in any account of the conditions under which people will behaviorally express their prejudiced intergroup attitudes. Such results have the potential to reinvigorate research on the role of socionormative factors in the study of prejudice and discrimination, and in this way help to account for recent increases in the expression of xenophobic and ethnocentric attitudes.

REFERENCES

Ajzen, I. (1991). The theory of planned behavior. *Organizational Behavior and Human Decision Processes, 50,* 179–211.

Bassili, J. N. (1995). Response latency and the accessibility of voting intentions: What contributes to accessibility and how it affects vote choice. *Personality and Social Psychology Bulletin, 21,* 686–695.

Chaiken, S., Liberman, A., & Eagly, A. H. (1989). Heuristic and systematic processing within and beyond the persuasion context. In J. S. Uleman & J. A. Bargh (Eds.), *Unintended thought* (pp. 212–252). New York: Guilford.

Davis, J. H., Stasson, M. F., Ono, K., & Zimmerman, S. (1988). Effects of straw polls on group decision making: Sequential voting pattern, timing, and local majorities. *Journal of Personality and Social Psychology, 55*(6), 918–926.

Davis, R. W. (1986). Pretrial publicity, the timing of the trial, and mock jurors' decision processes. *Journal of Applied Social Psychology, 16*(7), 590–607.

Devine, P. (1989). Stereotypes and prejudice: Their automatic and controlled components. *Journal of Personality and Social Psychology, 56,* 5–18.

Downing, J. W., Judd, C. M., & Brauer, M. (1992). Effects of repeated expressions on attitude extremity. *Journal of Personality and Social Psychology, 63,* 17–29.

Eagly, A. H., & Chaiken, S. (1993). *The psychology of attitudes*. Fort Worth, TX: Harcourt Brace Jovanovich.

Ellemers, N. (1993). The influence of sociostructural variables on identity management. *European Review of Social Psychology, 4,* 27–57.

Fazio, R. H. (1986). How do attitudes guide behavior? In R. M. Sorrentino & E. T. Higgins (Eds.), *The handbook of motivation and cognition: Foundations of social behavior* (pp. 204–243). New York: Guilford.

Fazio, R. H. (1989). On the power and functionality of attitudes: The role of attitude accessibility. In A. R. Pratkanis, S. J. Breckler, & A. G. Greenwald (Eds.), *Attitude structure and function* (pp. 153–179). Hillsdale, NJ: Lawrence Erlbaum.

Fazio, R. H. (1990a). A practical guide to the use of response latency in social psychological research. In M. S. Clark (Ed.), *Review of personality and social psychology: Vol. 11. Research methods in personality and social psychology* (pp. 74–97). Newbury Park, CA: Sage.

Fazio, R. H. (1990b). Multiple processes by which attitudes guide behavior: The MODE model as an integrative framework. In M. P. Zanna (Ed.), *Advances in experimental psychology* (Vol. 23, pp. 75–109). San Diego: Academic.

Fazio, R. H., Powell, M. C., & Herr, P. M. (1983). Toward a process model of the attitude-behavior relation: Accessing one's attitude upon mere observation of the attitude object. *Journal of Personality and Social Psychology, 44*, 723–735.

Fazio, R. H., Powell, M. C., & Williams, C. J. (1989). The role of attitude accessibility in the attitude-to-behavior process. *Journal of Consumer Research, 16*, 280–288.

Fazio, R. H., & Williams, C. J. (1986). Attitude accessibility as a moderator of the attitude-perception and attitude-behavior relations: An investigation of the 1984 presidential election. *Journal of Personality and Social Psychology, 51*, 505–514.

Fishbein, M., & Ajzen, I. (1975). *Belief, attitude, intention, and behavior: An introduction to theory and research.* Reading, MA: Addison-Wesley.

Forgas, J. P., & Fiedler, K. (1996). Us and them: Mood effects on intergroup discrimination. *Journal of Personality and Social Psychology, 70*(1), 28–40.

Godin, G. (1993). The theories of reasoned action and planned behavior: Overview of findings, emerging research problems and usefulness for exercise promotion. *Journal of Applied Sport Psychology, 5*, 141–157.

Grube, J. W., & Morgan, M. (1990). Attitude-social support interactions: Contingent consistency effects in the prediction of adolescent smoking, drinking, and drug use. *Social Psychology Quarterly, 53*, 329–339.

Grube, J. W., Morgan, M., & McGree, S. T. (1986). Attitudes and normative beliefs as predictors of smoking intentions and behaviors: A test of three models. *British Journal of Social Psychology, 25*, 81–93.

Hogg, M. A. (2000). Subjective uncertainty reduction through self-categorization: A motivational theory of social identity processes. *European Review of Social Psychology, 11*, 223–255.

Hogg, M. A., & Abrams, D. (1988). *Social identifications: A social psychology of intergroup relations and group processes.* London: Routledge.

Hogg, M. A., & Hardie, E. A. (1991). Social attraction, personal attraction, and self-categorization: A field study. *Personality and Social Psychology Bulletin, 17*, 175–180.

Hogg, M. A., & Mullin, B-A. (1999). Joining groups to reduce uncertainty: Subjective uncertainty reduction and group identification. In D. Abrams & M. A. Hogg (Eds.), *Social identity and social cognition* (pp. 249–279). Oxford, England: Blackwell.

Houston, D. A., & Fazio, R. H. (1989). Biased processing as a function of attitude accessibility: Making objective judgments subjectively. *Social Cognition, 7*, 51–66.

Jamieson, D. W., & Zanna, M. P. (1989). Need for structure in attitude formation and persuasion. In A. R. Pratkanis, S. J. Breckler, & A. G. Greenwald (Eds.), *Attitude structure and function* (pp. 383–406). Hillsdale, NJ: Erlbaum.

Jetten, J., Spears, R., & Manstead, A. S. R. (1996). Intergroup norms and intergroup discrimination: Distinctive self-categorization and social identity effects. *Journal of Personality and Social Psychology, 71*, 1222–1233.

Kaplan, M. F., & Miller, L. E. (1978). Reducing the effects of juror bias. *Journal of Personality and Social Psychology, 36*, 1443–1455.

Liska, A. (1984). A critical examination of the causal structure of the Fishbein and Ajzen attitude-behavior model. *Social Psychology Quarterly, 47*, 61–74.

MacCoun, R. J., & Kerr, N. L. (1988). Asymmetric influence on mock jury deliberation: Jurors' bias for leniency. *Journal of Personality and Social Psychology, 54*, 21–33.

Mackie, D. M., & Queller, S. (2000). The impact of group membership on persuasion: revisiting "Who says what to whom with what effect?" In D. J. Terry & M. A. Hogg (Eds.), *Attitudes, behavior, and social context: The role of norms and group membership* (pp. 135–155). Hillsdale, NJ: Erlbaum.

Mackie, D. M., Worth, L. T., & Ascunsion, A. G. (1990). Processing of persuasive in-group messages. *Journal of Personality and Social Psychology, 58*, 812–822.

Petty, R. E., & Cacioppo, J. T. (1986). The elaboration likelihood model of persuasion. *Advances in Experimental Social Psychology, 19*, 123–205.

Powell, M. C., & Fazio, R. H. (1984). Attitude

accessibility as a function of repeated attitudinal expression. *Personality and Social Psychology Bulletin, 10,* 139–148.

Sanbonmatsu, D. M., & Fazio, R. H. (1990). The role of attitudes in memory-based decision-making. *Journal of Personality and Social Psychology, 59,* 614–622.

Schuette, R. A., & Fazio, R. H. (1995). Attitude accessibility and motivation as determinants of biased processing: A test of the MODE model. *Personality and Social Psychology, 21,* 704–710.

Stasser, G., & Davis, J. H. (1977). Opinion change during group discussion. *Personality and Social Psychology Bulletin, 3,* 252–256.

Tajfel, H. (1974). Social identity and intergroup behavior. *Social Science Information, 13,* 65–93.

Tajfel, H., & Turner, J. C. (1979). An integrative theory of intergroup conflict. In W. G. Austin & S. Worchel (Eds.), *The social psychology of intergroup relations* (pp. 33–47). Monterey, CA: Brooks-Cole.

Terry, D. J., Gallois, C., & McCamish, M. (1993). The theory of reasoned action and health behavior. In D. J. Terry, C. Gallois, & M. McCamish (Eds.), *The theory of reasoned action: Its application to AIDS-preventive behavior* (pp. 1–27). Oxford, England: Pergamon.

Terry, D. J., & Hogg, M. A. (1996). Group norms and the attitude-behavior relationship. A role for group identification. *Personality and Social Psychology Bulletin, 22,* 776–793.

Terry, D. J., Hogg, M. A., Blackwood, L., & Johnson, D. (2000) *Prejudiced attitudes, group norms, and discriminatory behavior.* Manuscript submitted for publication.

Terry, D. J., Hogg, M. A., & Duck, J. (1999). Group membership, social identity, and attitudes. In D. A. Abrams & M. A. Hogg (Eds.), *Social identity and social cognition* (pp. 280–314) Oxford, England: Blackwell.

Terry, D. J., Hogg, M. A., & White, K. A. (2000). Group norms, social identity, and attitude-behavior relations. In D. J. Terry & M.A. Hogg (Eds.), *Attitudes, behavior, and social context: The role of norms and group membership* (pp. 67–94). Hillsdale, NJ: Erlbaum.

Terry, D. J., & Hogg, M. A, & McKimmie, B.

M. (2000). Group salience, norm congruency, and mode of behavioral decision-making: The effect of group norms on attitude-behavior relations. *British Journal of Social Psychology, 39,* 337–361.

Terry, D. J., Hogg, M. A., & White, K. M. (1999). The theory of planned behavior: Self-identity, social identity, and group norms. *British Journal of Social Psychology, 38,* 225–244.

Turner, J. C. (1982). Towards a cognitive redefinition of the social group. In H. Tajfel (Ed.), *Social identity and intergroup relations* (pp. 15–40). Cambridge, England: Cambridge University Press.

Turner, J. C. (1985). Social categorization and the self-concept: A social cognitive theory of group behavior. In E. J. Lawler (Ed.), *Advances in group processes: Theory and research* (Vol. 2, pp. 77–122). Greenwich, CT: JAI.

Turner, J. C. (1991). *Social influence.* Milton Keynes, England: Open University Press.

Turner, J. C., Hogg, M. A., Oakes, P. J., Reicher, S. D., & Wetherell, M. S. (1987). *Rediscovering the social group: A self-categorization theory.* Oxford, England: Basil Blackwell.

Wellen, J. M., Hogg, M. A., & Terry, D. J. (1998). Group norms and attitude-behavior consistency: The role of group salience and mood. *Group Dynamics: Theory, Research, and Practice, 2,* 48–56.

Wetherell, M. (1987). Social identity and group polarisation. In J. C. Turner, M. A. Hogg, P. J. Oakes, S. D. Reicher, & M. Wetherell (Eds.), *Rediscovering the social group: A self-categorization theory* (pp. 142–170). Oxford, England: Blackwell.

White, K. M., Hogg, M. A., & Terry, D. J. (in press) Attitude-behavior relations: The role of ingroup norms and attitude accessibility. *Basic and Applied Social Psychology.*

White, K. M., Terry, D. J., & Hogg, M. A. (2000). *The role of normative support in attitude-behavior correspondence and attitude change: Ingroup versus outgroup norms.* Manuscript submitted for publication.

Wilder, D. A. (1990). Some determinants of the persuasive power of ingroups and outgroups: Organization of information and attribution of independence. *Journal of Personality and Social Psychology, 59,* 1202–1213.

16

Social Influence Effects on Task Performance
The Ascendancy of Social Evaluation Over Self-Evaluation

STEPHEN G. HARKINS

*I*n the current chapter, we examine the effects of social influence on task performance. More specifically, we present a line of research in which we have compared the efficacy of the potential for social evaluation, a source of social influence, against the potency of the potential for self-evaluation in motivating task performance.

Self-evaluation processes play a central role in theorizing in the social psychological literature. For example, the self-evaluation process has been the direct focus of some research (e.g., Higgins, Strauman, & Klein, 1986; Masters & Keil, 1987) and has also been incorporated in numerous theories (e.g., Bandura's [1986] theory of self-efficacy; Deci & Ryan's [1985] theory of self-determination; Greenwald & Breckler's [1985] ego-task analysis; Schlenker's [1986] theory

Address correspondence to: Stephen G. Harkins, Psychology Department, Northeastern University, 360 Huntington Avenue, Boston, MA 02115. E-mail: valentine@neu.edu

of self-identity; Tesser's [1988] theory of self-esteem maintenance). More pertinent to our present interest, the opportunity for self-evaluation also has been
hypothesized to play a central role in motivating task performance. For example,
Festinger's (1954) theory of social comparison suggests that, at least under some
circumstances, people are motivated to do their best in order to evaluate their
ability on a given task.

Self-categorization theory (e.g., David & Turner, this volume) would make
the same prediction. According to David and Turner (this volume): "Self-categorization theory is a general analysis of group processes in terms of the distinction between personal and social identity (Turner, 1982; Turner, Hogg, Oakes,
Reicher, & Wetherell, 1987, p. 293)." This approach suggests that people expect to agree with others categorized as similar to self (ingroup), and that disagreement with these similar others produces uncertainty. "To reduce such uncertainty one can recategorize self and others as different in relevant respects,
redefine the objective stimulus situation as one that is not shared . . . or engage
in mutual influence to produce the expected agreement (i.e., persuade and/or
be persuaded)" (David & Turner, this volume, p. 293). On the other hand, is
disagreement with others categorized as the outgroup creates no psychological
pressure because the difference in and of itself is enough to account for the
discrepancy. As David and Turner (this volume) note, this approach is consistent with Festinger's (1954) social comparison theory in its emphasis on the use
of similar others as a means of judging the validity of opinions, although these
authors do not agree with Festinger's contention that people turn to social comparison only in the absence of some physical criterion.

In the current volume, the self-categorization approach is used as a means
of understanding majority and minority influence in conformity (David &
Turner), the attitude-behavior relationship (Terry & Hogg), the effect of social
influence on stereotype change (Stangor, Sechrist, & Jost), and deindividuation
(Spears, Postmes, Lea, & Watt). So, for example, in their analysis of minority
and majority influence in conformity, David and Turner (this volume) argue
that "persuasion can only be effected by people who are psychological ingroup
members on a relevant dimension. Any evidence that psychological outgroup
membership can produce influence is contrary to the theory" (p. 293). It should
be noted that this ingroup/outgroup process is engaged simply by exposing the
participants to the views of the ingroup or outgroup members. Our own work
focuses on task performance rather than on attitudes, but there is no reason to
believe that self-categorization processes would not apply to abilities as well as
attitudes. In fact, social comparison theory explicitly encompasses both attitudes and abilities (Festinger, 1954). Thus, self-categorization theory would
predict that the opportunity to compare one's performance to the performance
of a similar other should be motivating.

However, even though the potential for self-evaluation may be sufficient
to motivate task performance, opportunities to make such judgments of one's
abilities in isolation are rare. Task performance most often takes place in social
contexts in which one is subject to evaluation by others. For example, in situa-

tions in which an individual can self-evaluate by comparing his or her performance to the performances of coactors, it is often the case that these coactors also have the opportunity to compare their performances to that of the individual. In addition, an individual's performances are often evaluated by nonparticipants whose judgments are particularly salient. For example, in school, we are evaluated by teachers, in sports by coaches, and at work by supervisors.

Thus, even though the potential for self-evaluation may be a potent source of motivation in isolation, to assess its contribution to task performance we also must know what effects it has in the social contexts in which such judgments are most often made. Previous research does not allow us to distinguish among the joint and independent effects of the potential for self-evaluation and the potential for external (social) evaluation because, in this work, their effects have been confounded. For example, Sanders, Baron, and Moore (1978) argued that it was the potential for self-evaluation afforded by the opportunity to compare one's performance to the performances of one's fellow participants that produced the coaction effects observed in their research. However, in that research, it also was the case that the experimenter could compare a given participant's performance to the performances of the coactors, and the given participant also could have been motivated by the coactors' abilities to compare their performances to the participant's. Locke and Latham (1990a) argued that goal setting effects are produced by the potential for self-evaluation, but in the great majority of their studies, there is not only the potential for self-evaluation, but also the potential for evaluation by the experimenter. In social loafing research (e.g., Latané, Williams, & Harkins, 1979), participants could loaf because they could not evaluate their own performances, because the experimenter could not evaluate the participants' performances, and/or because their performances could not be evaluated by their fellow participants.

In our research, we have employed a paradigm that allows us to examine the motivational potency of self-evaluation independently and in combination with the potential for evaluation by external sources. Participants are asked to work on simple tasks by an experimenter who either tells them to "do their best" (e.g., generate as many uses as you can, detect as many dots as you can), or sets a specific, stringent criterion that the participants are urged to strive to attain (i.e., a stringent goal). In this work the experimenter represents a potent source of external evaluation in just the same way that teachers, coaches, and supervisors do in the "real world." Consistent with the predictions of social comparison (Festinger, 1954) and self-categorization theories (David & Turner, this volume), this work has shown that participants given "do your best" instructions are motivated by the potential for self-evaluation alone. In fact, the potential for self-evaluation motivates participants to the same extent as the potential for evaluation by the experimenter (Harkins & Szymanski, 1988; Szymanski & Harkins, 1987). However, when stringent goals are set, the potential for evaluation by the social source leads to *better* performance than the potential for self-evaluation (Harkins, White, & Utman, 2000; White, Kjelgaard, & Harkins, 1995). Moreover, this research has shown that whether the experimenter gives do your best or goal instructions, when there is the potential for evaluation by both sources, concern over the potential for evaluation by a social source supersedes interest in the potential for self-evaluation (Harkins et al., 2000; Harkins & Szymanski, 1988; Szymanski & Harkins, 1993).

Taken together, these findings suggest that concern over social evaluation supersedes interest in self-evaluation in a range of settings, demonstrating the potency of social evaluation as a source of social influence and calling into question the importance of the role of social comparison/self-categorization processes in motivating task performance in situations in which there is also the potential for evaluation by an external (social) source. In the following pages, we summarize this program or research, suggest possible motives underlying these effects, and propose some boundary conditions.

THE PARADIGM

To examine the independent and interactive effects of external and self-evaluation on task performance, we have used the social loafing paradigm. Social loafing refers to the finding that people put out less effort when working together than when working alone (Latané et al., 1979). Harkins (1987) has argued that this reduction in effort is a consequence of the fact that when participants work together in the loafing paradigm, their outputs are pooled (combined). Thus, individual outputs are "lost in the crowd," and participants can receive neither credit nor blame for their performances. Consistent with this notion, Williams, Harkins, and Latané (1981; see also Kerr & Bruun, 1981) found that when participants were led to believe that their individual outputs could be monitored even when they performed "together" (i.e., pooled outputs), they performed as well together as when they performed individually (i.e., no loafing). Also, when participants were led to believe that interest centered on group performance and their individual outputs were to be pooled, they loafed as much when they performed individually as when they performed together. These findings suggest that people are motivated to work when their outputs can be evaluated. When outputs are pooled, evaluation is not possible and it is this aspect of "working together" that leads to loafing. Thus, the "pooled condition" of the loafing paradigm provides a "no" or "minimal" evaluation baseline.

Given this minimal evaluation baseline, to study the impact of the potential for evaluation by a given source on performance, we manipulate that source's access to the two pieces of information necessary for evaluation: 1) a measure of the participant's task output; and 2) an evaluative criterion against which this task output can be compared. In our work, we have used two types of evaluative criteria. In the do-your-best paradigm, participants are asked to produce as much as they can (e.g., generate as many uses for an object as they can, detect as many signals in a vigilance task, etc.). Participants in the self-evaluation conditions are told that at the end of their performance they will be provided with a criterion (e.g., the average performance of previous participants). If they know their task output, they then have the means for self-evaluation. In the second basic paradigm, participants are provided with the criterion prior to performance, most often in the form of a "goal." That is, they are asked to strive to reach a given level of performance prior to undertaking the task. In this case, the goal serves as the evaluative criterion against which their task output can be compared.

DO-YOUR-BEST PARADIGM

Social Criterion

To test the possibility that the opportunity for self-evaluation would be sufficient to eliminate the loafing effect, we (Szymanski & Harkins, 1987) asked participants to generate as many uses as they possibly could for a common object, regardless of the creativity of these uses. Pilot work had shown that, after completing the task, participants felt that they knew how many uses they had generated, a measure of their task output. To manipulate the potential for self-evaluation, we provided or withheld an evaluative criterion. We told one-third of the participants that at the end of their performance they would be given the average number of uses generated by participants in a previous version of the experiment (social criterion). We told another third of the participants that to ensure confidentiality, we would not be able to give them this average (no social criterion), and a final third were told nothing about the criterion (no information). When the participants were provided with the social criterion, they were presented with the opportunity for self-evaluation by social comparison.

This manipulation of the potential for self-evaluation was crossed with a manipulation of the potential for experimenter evaluation. One-half of the participants were told that at the end of the experimental session, the experimenter would come in and count the number of uses that they had generated (experimenter evaluation), whereas the other half were told that the experimenter was interested in average performance, and so their individual outputs would be pooled with those of the others and would not be examined (no experimenter evaluation).

Descriptions of the tasks used in loafing research (Brickner, Harkins, & Ostrom, 1986; Harkins, Latané, & Williams, 1980) suggest that taking part in these tasks would be sheer drudgery and that, in the absence of external evaluation pressures, there would be little reason to perform well since the tasks are devoid of inherent interest. Nonetheless, we found that the opportunity for self-evaluation alone (no experimenter evaluation/social criterion) was sufficient to motivate participants to produce more uses than the number found in the no experimenter evaluation/no criterion and no experimenter evaluation/no information conditions. In fact, the opportunity for self-evaluation led to performance equivalent to that produced when participants were subject to experimenter evaluation.

In this research participants were led to believe that the criterion (the average performance of previous participants) was based on the performance of other students at the same university who were taking the same course at about the same time. Thus, the students on whose performances the criterion was based would have seemed very similar to the participants themselves. Both self-categorization (e.g., David & Turner, this volume) and social comparison (Festinger, 1954) theories would suggest that it is the fact that the criterion is based on the performance of similar others that motivates the participants. Criteria based on the performance of dissimilar others would not be expected to have this effect.

Similarity of Comparison Other

To test the similarity hypothesis, Harkins, White, and Utman (2000, Exp. 2) manipulated the composition of the group on whose performance the criterion was based. Participants were led to believe that their performances either would (experimenter evaluation) or would not (no experimenter evaluation) be evaluated by the experimenter. Crossed with this manipulation, participants were asked to do their best, or they were asked to do their best and told that afterward they would learn the average performance of other undergraduates at their university (similar-undergraduate criterion), the average performance of ninth-grade students (dissimilar-ninth-grade criterion), or the average performance of 3rd-year Ph.D. students (dissimilar-Ph.D. criterion).

As shown in Table 16.1, Harkins, White, and Utman (2000) replicated the social loafing effect: Participants in the experimenter evaluation/do your best condition produced more uses than did participants in the no experimenter evaluation/do your best condition. Harkins et al. also replicated Szymanski and Harkins' (1987) finding: No experimenter evaluation participants who could self-evaluate by comparing their performances to the average performance of their fellow undergraduates (similar) produced as many uses as did participants in the experimenter evaluation/do your best condition.

However, consistent with self-categorization (e.g., David & Turner, this volume) and social comparison (Festinger, 1954) theories, this do-your-best level of performance was produced by participants in the no experimenter evaluation condition only when the criterion was based on the performance of similar

TABLE 16.1. Mean Uses for a "Knife:" Exp. 2, Harkins et al. (2000)

	Criterion condition			
	Do your Best	Dissimilar (ninth-graders)	Similar (undergraduates)	Dissimilar (3rd-year Ph.D.s)
Experimenter evaluation	28.4[a]	26.1[a]	26.6[a]	28.6[a]
No experimenter evaluation	13.8[c]	18.2[b,c]	28.9[a]	20.3[b]

Means not sharing a common superscript are significantly different, $p < .05$

others. When the criterion was based on the performance of dissimilar others, whether ninth-grade students or 3rd-year Ph.D. students, the performance of no experimenter evaluation participants dropped significantly below that of experimenter evaluation/do your best participants. Participants were not motivated by the opportunity to compare their performances against the performances of dissimilar others because they did not provide a valid means of self-evaluation.

When the criterion is based on the performance of similar others, the opportunity for self-evaluation provides the participants with two incentives. They can learn something about how well they can perform the particular task, and they also can take pleasure from the fact that they have surpassed the performance of the average previous participant. These two incentives correspond to two sources of motivation that Goethals and Darley (1987) have termed self-knowledge and self-validation, respectively. As long as a social standard is used as the criterion, both incentives are available. However, by using an optimizing task in which participants are asked to attempt to achieve some criterion level of performance (e.g., number of answers correct, number of signals detected), rather than a maximizing task, in which participants are asked to produce as much as they can (Steiner, 1972), the contribution of self-validation can be removed. If only an objective criterion is provided, there is no opportunity for self-validation, because there is no information about how other people have performed; there is only the opportunity for self-knowledge. Of course, social comparison theory (Festinger, 1954) would predict that the opportunity for self-knowledge alone should be sufficient to motivate performance.

Objective Criterion

Harkins and Szymanski (1988) sought to determine whether the opportunity to compare one's performance against an objective standard was sufficient to motivate performance. Participants worked on a simple vigilance task that required them to try to detect as many signals as they could while minimizing false alarms. Participants performed the task knowing that, at its conclusion, they would be told how many signals had been presented, or that this information would be withheld. As noted previously, at the conclusion of the use-generation task, participants think that they know their task output (i.e., the number of uses they have generated). However, on the vigilance task, pilot testing indicated that participants do not think that they know how many signals they have detected (the measure of task output). Thus, in this experiment, we were able to manipulate the two components of evaluation—task output and evaluative criterion—independently. The participants could be evaluated by the experimenter or could not, the task output was displayed or not, and participants were told that the objective criterion would be provided at the end of the task or not.

As Table 16.2 shows, the potential for experimenter evaluation motivated performance; however, when the experimenter could not evaluate individuals, but individuals could evaluate themselves (task output plus the objective crite-

TABLE 16.2. Number of Errors: Harkins & Szymanski (1988)

| | Evaluative criterion | | No evaluative criterion | |
	Output feedback	No output feedback	Output feedback	No output feedback
Experimenter evaluation	2.4[a]	2.4[a]	2.5[a]	2.3[a]
No experimenter evaluation	2.7[a]	3.3[a]	6.1[b]	6.7[b]

Means not sharing a common superscript are significantly different, $p < .05$

rion), the same level of performance was achieved, a self-evaluation effect. These findings suggest that, consistent with social comparison theory, self-knowledge alone is sufficient to motivate performance.

When participants who were not subject to experimenter evaluation were missing one or both of the necessities for evaluation (task output and criterion), performance fell significantly, with one interesting exception: No experimenter evaluation participants who were provided *only* with the criterion performed as well as the experimenter evaluation participants. Even though these participants were missing one of the pieces of information required for evaluation (task output feedback), they achieved the same level of performance as participants subject to experimenter evaluation. Follow-up research (Szymanski, 1988) showed that these participants were so motivated by the prospect of self-evaluation that they went to the trouble of keeping track of the number of signals that they had detected in order to do so.

This research has shown that when participants are asked to do their best, the potential for self-evaluation motivates participants to the same extent as the potential for evaluation by the experimenter. Each of these designs incorporated orthogonal manipulations of the potential for evaluation by the experimenter and the self, and, in each experiment, we found that, whether the criterion was social or objective, the joint action of these sources produced performance no better than that achieved by either source taken alone. This failure of the motivation stemming from the two sources to summate could have resulted from a ceiling effect. The potential for evaluation by either source could have put the participants at peak motivation, eliminating the possibility of greater output. For example, the "motivated" participants detected 86% of the signals in the vigilance task. However, the same pattern of findings was produced on the use-generation task for which there is no meaningful ceiling. In addition, in follow-up research Szymanski (1988) showed that participants were able to generate more uses and detect more signals when offered a financial incentive, demonstrating that they were not at a performance ceiling.

Instead of a ceiling effect, we argue that the combination of these sources did not produce greater output than the potential for evaluation by either taken alone because concern over the potential for experimenter evaluation superseded interest in the potential for self-evaluation. Thus, the effect of the combination of the two sources was no greater than either taken alone, because, in effect, there was no combination. We were seeing the effect of experimenter evaluation alone. This interpretation is suggested by another finding in Harkins and Szymanski's (1988) vigilance experiment. As noted previously, participants in the no experimenter evaluation condition went to the trouble of keeping track of the number of signals that were presented so that they could self-evaluate. Participants in the experimenter evaluation counterpart of this condition were presented with the same opportunity but they did not take advantage of it. That is, they would have had the opportunity for self-evaluation had they kept track of the signals (task output), but they did not, suggesting that their concern over the impending evaluation by the experimenter may have supplanted their interest in self-evaluation.

The Choice Experiment

Szymanski and Harkins (1993) generated additional evidence consistent with this argument in a choice paradigm in which participants selected the conditions under which they would work. Participants were presented with one of three experimental conditions, each of which involved a choice. In the first condition, participants were given a choice between working on a task that was arranged so that participants could be evaluated by the experimenter only, or working on a task that was arranged so that no one could evaluate them. The participants chose reliably more often to be evaluated by no one. Thus, participants avoided the potential for experimenter evaluation. In a second condition participants could choose between an experiment that afforded the opportunity for self-evaluation alone or evaluation by no one. Consistent with our earlier findings, participants chose the former, the opportunity for self-evaluation. In a third condition, participants chose between evaluation by both experimenter and self or evaluation by no one. They opted for the latter, evaluation by no one. This pattern of findings both reinforces and extends the interpretation of the previous research (Harkins & Szymanski, 1988; Szymanski, 1988). The overall pattern of data suggests that the dominance of experimenter over self-evaluation stems from apprehension regarding evaluation by the experimenter, rather than interest in impressing the experimenter.

Power of the Social Source

Our research has shown that the potential for evaluation by the experimenter, a powerful source, overpowers interest in the potential for self-evaluation. One could argue that the ascendancy of social evaluation depends on the power of the source of social evaluation. I note that even if this were so, our findings would be relevant for the wide range of real world settings in which task performance is judged by powerful sources (e.g., teachers, coaches, supervisors). However, Szymanski, Garczynski, and Harkins (2000) have found evidence that is consistent with the view that the potential for evaluation by a lower status source, a classmate, has the same effect on self-evaluation as the potential for evaluation by the experimenter. Szymanski et al. eliminated the potential for evaluation by the experimenter and then randomly assigned participants to one of four conditions in a 2 (self-evaluation vs. no self-evaluation) × 2 (coactor evaluation vs. no coactor evaluation) design. Just as has been the case in previous research in which the experimenter was the source of social evaluation (e.g., Harkins & Szymanski, 1988; Szymanski & Harkins, 1987), the potential for evaluation by each of the sources (self and coactor) led to better performance than was found in the "no evaluation" condition. And, just as in the previous research, the combination of the two sources led to no better performance than either one taken alone.

In a follow-up experiment, Szymanski et al. (2000) arranged matters so that participants could not self-evaluate, and then randomly assigned participants to one of the four conditions in a 2 (experimenter evaluation vs. no experimenter evaluation) × 2 (coactor evaluation vs. no coactor evaluation) design. Replicating previous research, each of the sources taken alone led to better performance than was found in the "no evaluation" condition. However, unlike past research in which one of the sources was always self, when there was the potential for evaluation by both external sources, performance was reliably better than that produced by either source taken alone. These findings suggest that the potential for evaluation by external sources, whether experimenter or coactor, have the same effect on the potential for self-evaluation. In addition, the finding that the impact of the potential for evaluation by the experimenter and the coactor sum is consistent with Latané's (1981) theory of social impact, the static precursor to dynamic social impact theory described by Latané and Bourgeois in the current volume.

Simple Versus Complex Tasks

One could argue that although external evaluation appears to be more potent on the simple types of tasks that we have used in our research, if we used more complex tasks, we would find an advantage for the potential for self-evaluation. For example, Szymanski and Harkins's (1987) use-generation task required participants to generate as many uses for an object as they could. Perhaps if participants were asked to generate uses that were as creative as possible instead, one would find that the potential for self-evaluation led to better performance than the potential for external evaluation. In fact, however, Bartis, Szymanski, and Harkins (1988) and Szymanski and Harkins (1992) found that when participants were asked to be as creative as possible, the potential for self-evaluation produced the same effect as the potential for external evaluation. Whether it was the potential for external evaluation (Bartis et al., 1988) or the potential for self-evaluation (Szymanski & Harkins, 1992), the potential for evaluation undermined performance. Participants who would be evaluated by no one produced the most creative uses. Thus, even with more complex tasks, there is no advantage for self-evaluation.

THE GOAL SETTING PARADIGM

In the research described thus far, participants have been asked to do their best (e.g., "generate as many uses as you can," "detect as many signals as you can"). Locke and Latham (1990a) report that participants urged to strive to attain a specific, difficult level of performance do even better than participants asked to do their best. They argue that this goal setting effect is the result of the potential for self-evaluation. Just as Szymanski and Harkins (1987) argued that for self-evaluation to be possible, participants must have access to some measure of task output and a criterion, Locke and Latham (1990b) argued that the goal setting effect requires that participants have knowledge of their task output (feedback, in Locke & Latham's terminology). Goals then "provide them with a yardstick for determining whether the feedback they are given reveals acceptable or unacceptable performance. Without a goal or standard, people do not appraise feedback as significant and thus do not take action in response to it" (Locke & Latham, 1990b, p. 241). Thus, it is the opportunity for self-evaluation provided by comparing the performance to a specific, difficult criterion that is supposedly responsible for the goal setting effect.

Self-Evaluation Versus Social Evaluation

If the potential for self-evaluation is responsible for producing goal setting effects, it would suggest that interest in the potential for self-evaluation is not superseded by concern over social evaluation when one is asked to strive to reach a stringent criterion instead of only being asked to do one's best. However, our research shows that the potential for self-evaluation is not responsible for the goal setting effect. White, Kjelgaard, and Harkins (1995) used the social loafing paradigm to test the contribution of self-evaluation processes to the goal setting effect by giving participants 12 minutes to generate as many uses as possible for a knife. They were told either that their uses would be individually counted by the experimenter (experimenter evaluation), or that their uses would be combined with those of the previous participants because the researchers were interested in average performance (no experimenter evaluation). Crossed with this manipulation, in the conditions on which we will focus, participants were asked to do their best, or were told to strive to achieve a goal of 40 uses which they were told was based on the performance of participants in a prior version of the experiment (goal).

The "do your best" conditions correspond to the basic conditions included in social loafing research. That is, in loafing research, participants are told to produce as much as they can (i.e., to do their best). As shown in Table 16.3, the social loafing effect was replicated: Participants subject to experimenter evaluation outperformed participants who were not subject to experimenter evaluation (Latané et al., 1979). In the goal setting literature (Locke & Latham, 1990a), when testing for goal setting effects the performance of participants in the goal condition is compared to the performance of participants who are asked to do their best. In this research, the experimenter typically has access to the participants' task outputs. Replicating the goal setting effect reported in the literature (Locke & Latham, 1990a), White et al. (1995) found that participants who were subject to the evaluation of the experimenter and were provided a stringent goal produced more uses than participants who were subject to experimenter evaluation and asked to do their best.

Locke and Latham (1990a) suggest that it is the potential for self-evaluation that produces goal setting effects. White et al.'s (1995) finding does not support or refute this view, because (as in almost all goal setting research) the potential for experimenter evaluation was confounded with the potential for self-evaluation. In White et al.'s (1995) paradigm, the effect of experimenter evaluation was removed in the no experimenter evaluation/goal condition. If the potential for self-evaluation alone is sufficient to produce a goal setting effect, then it should be seen here, but, as can be seen in Table 16.3, it was not.

However, providing a goal did have some effect on the performance of participants in the no experimenter evaluation/goal condition—their performance exceeded that of participants in the no experimenter evaluation/do your best condition (i.e., exceeded the loafing level), and equaled the performance of participants subject to experimenter evaluation who were asked to do their best. In subsequent research, Harkins, White, and Utman (2000) argued that White et al.'s (1995) no experimenter evaluation/goal participants may have seen the goal as a means of judging their performance (a yardstick), rather than as a level of performance that they had to achieve. That is, these participants did their best to see how this level of performance compared to the yardstick represented by the stringent goal.

As a result, even though the potential for self-evaluation alone may not have been sufficient to produce a goal setting effect, one could argue that the goal setting effect found in the experimenter evaluation/goal-40 (uses for a knife) condition was produced by the combination of the motivation produced by the potential for experimenter and self-evaluation. The potential for experimenter evaluation alone provided one source of motivation, as shown by the difference between performance in the experimenter evaluation/do your best condition and performance in the no experimenter evaluation/do your best condition. Providing a goal to participants in the no experimenter evaluation condition provided another source of motivation (i.e., better performance under goal instructions than under do your best instructions), and the two sources of motiva-

TABLE 16.3. Mean Uses for a "Knife:" Exp. 1, White et al. (1995)

	Do your best	Goal-40
Experimenter evaluation	25.1[a]	35.6[b]
No experimenter evaluation	17.6[c]	26.5[a]

Means not sharing a common superscript are significantly different, $p < .05$

tion combined to produce the goal setting effect (an additive model). Consistent with the argument that an additive model can account for these results, a 2 (experimenter evaluation vs. no experimenter evaluation) × 2 (do your best vs. goal instructions) analysis of variance yielded two robust main effects and no interaction.

Goal Setting and Social Evaluation

Harkins, White, and Utman (2000, Exp. 3) argued that the potential for self-evaluation did not contribute to White et al.'s (1995) goal setting effect at all. Instead, based on the research that suggests that concern over the potential for evaluation by the experimenter supersedes interest in the potential for self-evaluation (e.g., Harkins & Szymanski, 1988; Szymanski & Harkins, 1993), Harkins et al. (2000) argued that the goal setting effect was produced by the potential for experimenter evaluation alone. To test this hypothesis, Harkins et al. (2000) randomly assigned participants to one of ten conditions in a 2 (striving vs. no striving) × 2 (criterion based on the performance of similar vs. dissimilar others) × 2 (experimenter evaluation vs. no experimenter evaluation) + 2 (experimenter evaluation/do your best vs. no experimenter evaluation/do your best) design. Participants in the 2 × 2 × 2 portion of the design were provided a criterion of 40 uses (for a knife) before they began performing. Half of them were asked to strive to achieve this criterion (striving instructions), whereas the other half were told that they were provided the criterion because they might be interested in knowing that our prior research showed that participants could produce this number of uses (no striving instructions). Crossed with this manipulation, half of these participants were told that this criterion was based on the performance of other undergraduates at their university (similar others), whereas the other half were told that the criterion was based on the performance of 3rd-year Ph.D. students (dissimilar others). Crossed with these manipulations, half of the participants were led to believe that their outputs would be evaluated by the experimenter (experimenter evaluation), whereas the other half were led to believe that they would not be evaluated by the experimenter (no experimenter evaluation).

Participants in the two do your best conditions were not provided with a criterion. They simply were asked to do their best to generate as many uses as they could on the task. Half of these participants were led to believe that they would be evaluated by the experimenter, whereas the other half were led to believe that they would not be evaluated.

Harkins, White, and Utman (2000) reasoned that if experimenter evaluation alone is important, then the validity of the criterion (the goal) should not matter. If the experimenter has directed them to strive to reach the goal, they should attempt to do so. So, whether participants in the experimenter evaluation condition were given an invalid criterion (goal based on the performance of dissimilar others) or a valid criterion (goal based on the performance of similar others), they should produce a goal setting effect (i.e., performance greater than that found in the experimenter evaluation/do your best condition). In contrast, if the goal setting effect requires motivation stemming from the potential for self-evaluation (additive model), then there should be a goal setting effect when the criterion is valid, but not when it is invalid, because in the latter case the contribution of self-evaluation has been eliminated.

As shown in Table 16.4, Harkins et al. (2000) found that no experimenter evaluation participants in the striving condition worked at the do-your-best level (performance equal to that found in the experimenter evaluation/do-your-best condition) when the criterion was based on the performance of similar others, but not when the criterion was based on the performance of dissimilar others. Once again consistent with social comparison and self-categorization theories, participants were motivated by the opportunity to compare their performances to the performances of similar, but not dissimilar, others.

But the crucial question is whether the potential for experimenter evaluation was sufficient to produce a goal setting effect in the absence of the contribution of the potential for self-evaluation. As shown in Table 16.4, it was. Consistent with the "experimenter evaluation only" interpretation, goal setting effects were obtained whether the goal was based on the performance of similar or dissimilar others.

Harkins, White, and Utman (2000) pitted the experimenter evaluation only interpretation against the additive model in a second way. Participants in the experimenter evaluation/do your best condition outperform participants in the no experimenter evaluation/do your best condition because of the potential for experimenter evaluation. There is no opportunity for self-evaluation, because the participants have no criterion against which to compare their performances. The additive model would suggest that the improvement from this level of performance to the level required for a goal setting effect reflects the influence of motivation stemming from the potential for self-evaluation provided by the goal. No striving instruction should be required, because whether or not the experimenter asks the participants to strive, the goal provides a criterion for self-evaluation. In contrast, the experimenter evaluation only interpretation suggests that it is simply the experimenter's instruction to strive to reach the stringent goal that produces the additional performance. Without this striving instruction, there should be no goal setting effect, only a do-your-best effect. Once again, consistent with the experimenter evaluation only interpretation, when participants were provided a stringent criterion only as a piece of information (no striving

TABLE 16.4. Mean Uses for a "Knife": Exp. 3, Harkins et al. (2000)

		Striving instructions		No striving instructions	
	Do your best	Similar	Dissimilar	Similar	Dissimilar
Experimenter evaluation	31.6[a]	39.3[b]	39.3[b]	32.9[a]	32.6[a]
No experimenter evaluation	19.7[c]	32.05[a]	22.53[c]	30.2[a]	22.9[c]

Means not sharing a common superscript are significantly different, $p < .05$

instructions), Harkins et al. (2000) found do-your-best effects, whether the criterion was based on the performance of similar or dissimilar others (see Table 16.4).

Thus, when participants were asked to strive to reach the criterion, whether the goal was based on the performance of similar or dissimilar others, participants subject to the evaluation of the experimenter produced the same level of performance, a goal setting effect. Eliminating the potential for self-evaluation through the use of an invalid criterion left the goal setting effect unaffected. In the no striving conditions, participants subject to experimenter evaluation who were provided a criterion based on the performance of similar others (valid criterion) performed at the same do-your-best level as participants provided a criterion based on the performance of dissimilar others (invalid criterion). In this case, adding the potential for self-evaluation had no effect. Taken together, these findings provide strong support for the argument that concern over the potential for experimenter evaluation supplants interest in self-evaluation.

Self-Set Goals

In this research, participants have been asked to strive to reach goals set by the experimenter. One could argue that the ascendancy of social evaluation would be eliminated if participants were allowed to set their own goals. After all, the goal setting literature is unequivocal in its suggestion that when participants are asked to set their own goals, goal setting effects are produced. As Locke and Latham (1990b) write

> A surprising finding of research on goal commitment is that assigning goals to individuals generally leads to the same level of commitment and performance as letting individuals participate in the setting of their goals or letting them set their own goals (Latham & Lee, 1986; Locke & Latham, 1990a). Participation is not less effective than most social scientists (including ourselves) assumed it would be; rather assigned goals are more effective than predicted (p. 241).

That is, the surprise is not that participatively-set and self-set goals produce goal setting effects; rather, the surprise is that assigned goals lead to performance *as good as* participatively-set and self-set goals. In fact, Locke and Latham (1990a) believe that the literature is so compelling on this point that they write: "Further research on the motivational effects of different goal setting methods would appear to have limited value" (p. 171).

However, White, Kjelgaard, and Harkins (1995) found that when participants were asked to set their own goals, they set them far too low to produce goal setting effects. When the experimenter suggested appropriately stringent goals (Harkins & Lowe, 2000; White et al., 1995), participants set their goals only at the do-your-best level, far short of the level necessary to produce goal setting effects. Participants who were subject to experimenter evaluation did produce goal setting effects, but they did so by working past the goals that they set.

To resolve the discrepancy between these findings and the claims of the literature (e.g., Locke & Latham, 1990b), Harkins and Lowe (2000) undertook a meta-analysis of the self-set goal literature. They found that self-set goal effects were produced only when participants had taken part in a pretest equal in length to the experimental session *and* were subject to evaluation by the experimenter. Consistent with these findings, Harkins and Lowe (2000) successfully produced a self-set goal effect under these conditions. However, the potential for self-evaluation alone was not sufficient to motivate participants enough to set stringent goals or to generate goal setting effects even when they had the requisite experience. Thus, it is not the fact that participants have been asked to strive to reach experiment-set rather than self-set goals that accounts for the ascendancy of social evaluation.

Ego-Involvement

One could argue that the potential for experimenter evaluation appears to be more potent than self-evaluation because we have used tasks that participants performed simply because they were told to do so. Utman and Harkins (1996) increased the participants' ego-involvement in the task by leading participants to believe that the task was a test of intellectual ability and then set goals for performance. We found that if the participants were ego-involved, the potential for self-evaluation led to a goal setting effect, just like the potential for external evaluation. These findings suggest that the potential for self-evaluation can be as potent as the potential for experimenter evaluation when participants have a stake in their performance.

But this goal setting effect was produced by the potential for self-evaluation in the absence of the potential for social evaluation. In another experiment, Utman and Harkins (1996) sought to determine whether concern over the potential for experimenter evaluation supersedes interest in self-evaluation when ego-involvement is high. In fact, it is here that we find the most striking support for the ascendancy of social evaluation. Harkins, White, and Utman (2000) found that striving instructions had no effect on participants who were not subject to experimenter evaluation. As long as the criterion was valid (based on the performance of similar others), they produced do-your-best effects whether the experimenter asked them to strive to reach the criterion or supplied the criterion only as a piece of information in which they might be interested. As shown in Table 16.5, Utman and Harkins (1996) found that when ego-involvement was high, once again striving instructions made no difference to no experimenter evaluation participants. But, in this case, high ego-involvement participants produced goal setting effects whether they were asked to strive or not. Given this finding, if interest in the potential for self-evaluation has an effect when there is the potential for experimenter evaluation and ego-involvement is high, we should see it in the experimenter evaluation/no striving condition. But we do not. Whether ego-involvement was high or low, experimenter evaluation/no striving participants worked only at the do-your-best level. Thus, even when ego-in-

TABLE 16.5. Mean Uses for a "Knife:" Exp. 3, Utman & Harkins (1996)

	Low ego-involvement			High ego-involvement		
	Do-your-best	No striving	Striving	Do-your-best	No striving	Striving
Experimenter evaluation	30.6[a]	31.5[a]	39.4[b]	30.6[a]	30.7[a]	40.1[b]
No experimenter evaluation	21.2[c]	27.7[a]	32.7[a]	30.1[a]	40.1[b]	41.8[b]

Means not sharing a common superscript are significantly different, $p < .05$

volvement was high, the potential for external evaluation maintained its ascendancy.

RESEARCH SUMMARY

Our research suggests that there are some situations in which the potential for self-evaluation motivates performance to the same extent as the potential for external evaluation (e.g., when the experimenter only asks participants to do their best). In fact, the potential for self-evaluation can lead to better performance than the potential for external evaluation. For example, as shown in Table 16.5, Utman and Harkins (1996) found that under high ego-involvement with no striving instructions, no experimenter evaluation participants produced a goal setting effect whereas experimenter evaluation participants only produced a do-your-best effect. However, our findings also show that the potential for social evaluation motivates performance more than the potential for self-evaluation under a wide variety of conditions. For example, when goals are experimenter-set and the experimenter can evaluate performance, goal setting effects are produced whether or not the participants have had previous experience with the task (Harkins & Lowe, 2000), whether or not the participants are ego-involved (Utman & Harkins, 1996), and whether or not the goals are based on the performance of similar others (Harkins, White, & Utman, 2000). In fact, the experimenter can produce goal setting effects by only suggesting goal levels (Harkins & Lowe, 2000; White et al., 1995).

Szymanski, Garczynski, and Harkins (2000) have shown that these effects do not depend on the power of the experimenter. The potential for evaluation by a coactor, a less powerful source, has the same effect on self-evaluation as the potential for evaluation by the experimenter. These effects also do not depend on the fact that, in most of this research, participants have been asked to perform simple, uninteresting tasks. Whether participants are asked to produce as much as possible without regard to quality, or to be as creative as possible without regard to quantity, the potential for evaluation, whether by the experimenter (Bartis et al., 1988) or by the self (Szymanski & Harkins, 1992), has the same effect on performance: Quantity is increased whereas quality (creativity) is decreased.

Although we have not conducted research that shows this, we also speculate that effort is more likely to be sustained when participants are motivated by
the potential for external evaluation, rather than by the potential for self-evaluation. Initially participants may be interested in seeing how well they can perform the task. However, once they have gained this information, their interest
may wane, and their performance may deteriorate. On the other hand, faced
with external evaluation, participants may sustain their efforts because slacking
off at any point could lead to a negative judgment from the external source.

In our research, we have used the bell jar provided by the laboratory to
examine separately the effects of experimenter and self-evaluation. It is under
these special conditions that we can find some few instances in which the potential for self-evaluation is as potent as, or even more potent than, the potential for social evaluation. However, in the real world, the potential for social and
self-evaluation most often coexist. Our research suggests that, under these circumstances, concern about the potential for social evaluation supersedes interest in self-evaluation (Harkins & Szymanski, 1988; Harkins, White, & Utman,
2000; Szymanski & Harkins, 1993), even when ego-involvement is high (Utman
& Harkins, 1996).

POSSIBLE MOTIVES UNDERLYING THESE EFFECTS

Geen (1991) has suggested that concern about evaluation produces social anxiety,
and it is this anxiety (or its absence) that produces these performance effects.
Geen argues that the social anxiety produced by evaluation apprehension results from "a more basic motive of individuals to present themselves to others in
such a way that a favorable impression is created and approval is obtained" (p.
378. Geen, 1991). Geen goes on to write: "It can be argued further that the self-
presentation motive is a facet of a still more basic need for inclusion and for role
fulfillment within society" (p. 378, Geen, 1991).

Geen's (1991) emphasis on the importance of belonging is consistent with
sociometer theory, which "proposes that the self-esteem system evolved as a
monitor of social acceptance, and that the so-called self-esteem motive functions not to maintain self-esteem per se but rather to avoid social devaluation
and rejection" (Leary, 1999, p. 32). Thus, "self-esteem is essentially a psychological meter, or gauge, that monitors the quality of people's relationships with
others" (Leary, 1999, p. 33). It follows from this view of the function of self-
esteem that public events would affect self-esteem more strongly than private
events. As Leary writes: "The sociometer perspective explains why events that
are known (or potentially known) by other people have much greater effects on
self-esteem than events that are known only by the individual him- or herself"
(1994, p. 34).

One of the key inputs to this meter is information about competence, and
it is exactly this kind of information that is provided when one performs the
tasks used in our research. Of course, we do not have measures of self-esteem,

but we do have evidence that participants are more motivated by, and attend more to, the potential for social evaluation (a public event) than to the potential for self-evaluation (a private event). The theory also suggests that the potential for self-evaluation will affect performance, because one's performance can have an impact on acceptance or rejection at some later point. However, in most cases, one would not expect the participants to be as motivated under these circumstances as they would be when social evaluation is possible, and this is what we have found.

Thus, our findings are certainly consistent with sociometer theory's account, but we can say no more than this. We have no evidence that the need to belong is the basic motive underlying these performance effects. Tedeschi has developed a social interactionist theory of coercive actions that "focuses on the exercise of power and influence by an actor who is motivated to achieve social goals" (Tedeschi, this volume). According to Tedeschi, "a basic motive of human social behavior is a desire to maximize one's potential for influencing others (i.e., social power)" (Tedeschi & Norman, 1985, p. 294). This approach suggests that "self-esteem can be viewed as a barometer (and generalized reinforcer) of potential power derived from evaluations of self against ideal identities" (Tedeschi & Norman, 1985, p. 317). Thus, as in sociometer theory, self-esteem serves as a meter, but in this case, instead of measuring belongingness, the meter measures one's success in exerting power and influence. Of course, this formulation also would suggest that public events would affect self-esteem more than private events, because public events will have more impact on one's ability to exert power and influence.

So, the participants' motivation could stem from a basic need to belong (Leary, 1999), from a desire to maximize influence potential (Tedeschi, this volume), or from some other source. Whatever the source, our findings suggest that the resulting concern about the potential for social evaluation supersedes interest in self-evaluation.

INDIVIDUAL VERSUS GROUP PERFORMANCE

In the work that we have summarized, participants have worked on the tasks as individuals. Although this paradigm appears functionally equivalent to David and Turner's (this volume) conformity paradigm, one's *social* identity would be expected to be more salient when one works as a member of a group of similar others facing a common task than when one works alone. And, in fact, Harkins and Szymanski (1989) have provided evidence that suggests that the potential for social evaluation may not maintain its ascendancy when there is the opportunity for evaluation at the level of the group rather than at the level of the individual.

Harkins and Szymanski (1989) noted that previous social loafing research focused on the individual, even though participants worked together to produce a group product. In this research, the group was unable to evaluate its performance because it was missing either one or both of the pieces of information required for evaluation: task output and a criterion. For example, Latané, Williams, and Harkins (1979) told participants that they would be shown their group scores at the end of the session, but there was no criterion against which this group output could be compared. In two experiments, one with an optimizing task and one with a maximizing task (Steiner, 1972), Harkins and Szymanski (1989) found that providing a criterion that allowed the group to evaluate its performance eliminated the loafing effect.

For example, in the experiment with a maximizing task (Harkins & Szymanski, 1989, Exp. 2), participants in the group evaluation condition were told that their outputs would be pooled, and that, at the end of the session, they would be provided with their group's total output as well as the average performance of previous groups (pooled-standard). Participants in the other pooled output conditions were told either that we knew the average of the performance of previous groups but we couldn't tell them what this average was because this information could affect the performance of later participants (pooled-no standard condition), or were told nothing about a standard (pooled-social loafing replication). Despite the fact that participants in each of the groups in which outputs were pooled acknowledged that the experimenter could evaluate their group's performance, the participants worked harder only when they themselves could evaluate the group's performance. Thus, at the level of the group, participants did not care whether or not the experimenter could evaluate their group. They only cared whether or not they could. Only when there was the potential for the group to evaluate itself was the social loafing effect eliminated.

In this paradigm, strangers came together for a brief time with no promise of future interaction. There was little in the procedure itself to make the participants feel that they were part of a group. There was no interaction during the experiment; the participants were not invited to compete with other groups, or even to try to outdo their own group's last effort. However, a group product was generated, and when a criterion was provided, there was the potential for group evaluation. In addition, participants who made up the groups also were likely to have seen themselves as highly similar to one another. These features alone were sufficient to motivate performance in these minimal groups.

CONCLUSION

In future research, the limits of this group-level effect should be examined. For example, self-categorization theory would predict that if participants were led to believe that their fellow group members were dissimilar from them or that the participants whose outputs comprised the social standard were dissimilar from them, there would be no group evaluation effect. In the former case, the participants should no longer feel part of an ingroup; in the latter, the criterion would not provide meaningful information.

The potency of the group evaluation effect also could be tested. For example, using the goal setting paradigm, Harkins, White, and Utman (2000) found that participants who were provided a stringent goal but were not subject to experimenter evaluation did not produce a goal setting effect, but performed at the level of participants in the experimenter evaluation/do your best control group. Perhaps leading participants to believe that they are part of a group striving to reach a group goal would be sufficient to motivate them to produce a goal setting effect instead of a do-your-best effect. Making individual contributions to the group known would provide an even more telling test. That is, in the Harkins and Syzmanski (1989) research and the research proposed thus far, individual contributions are not known. The situation could be arranged so that the group is instructed to strive for a group goal, but individual contributions are known to the experimenter, to the other group members, or to both the experimenter and the other group members. Will the potency of social identity be sufficient to overcome concern over the potential for evaluation by these sources?

Additional research, such as that described above, will be required to understand the complex ways in which sources of evaluation, task characteristics, and personal and social identity interact to produce task performance. Perhaps the potential for social evaluation does not maintain its ascendancy when there is the opportunity for evaluation at the level of the group rather than at the level of the individual. However, the present research does demonstrate the potency of social evaluation as a source of social influence at the level of the individual, and raises questions about the role that self-evaluation processes are hypothesized to play in theory in social psychology.

REFERENCES

Bandura, A. (1986). *Social foundations of thought and action: A social cognitive theory.* Englewood Cliffs, NJ: Prentice-Hall.

Bartis, S., Szymanski, K., & Harkins, S. (1988). Evaluation of performance: A two-edged knife. *Personality and Social Psychology Bulletin, 14,* 242–251.

Brickner, M., Harkins, S., & Ostrom, T. M. (1986). Effects of personal involvement: Thought-provoking implications for social loafing. *Journal of Personality and Social Psychology, 51,* 763–769.

Deci, E. L., & Ryan, R. M. (1985). *Intrinsic motivation and self-determination in human behavior.* New York: Plenum.

Festinger, L. (1954). A theory of social comparison processes. *Human Relations, 7,* 117–140.

Geen, R. (1991). Social motivation. *Annual Review of Psychology, 42,* 377–399.

Goethals, G., & Darley, J. (1987). Social comparison theory: Self-evaluation and group life. In B. Mullen & G. Goethals (Eds.), *Theories of group behavior* (pp. 21–47). New York: Springer-Verlag.

Greenwald, A., & Breckler, S. (1985). To whom is the self presented? In B. Mullen & B. Schlenker (Eds.), *The self and social life* (pp. 126–145). New York: McGraw-Hill.

Harkins, S. (1987). Social loafing and social facilitation. *Journal of Experimental Social Psychology, 23,* 1–18.

Harkins, S., Latané, B., & Williams, K. (1980). Social loafing: Allocating effort or taking it easy? *Journal of Experimental Social Psychology, 16,* 456–465.

Harkins, S., & Lowe, M. (2000). The effects of self-set goals on task performance. *Journal of Applied Social Psychology, 30,* 1–40.

Harkins, S., & Szymanski, K. (1988). Social loafing and self-evaluation with an objective standard. *Journal of Experimental Social Psychology, 24,* 354–365.

Harkins, S., & Szymanski, K. (1989). Social

loafing and group evaluation. *Journal of Personality and Social Psychology, 56*, 934–941.

Harkins, S., White, P., & Utman, C. (2000). The role of internal and external sources of evaluation in motivating task performance. *Personality and Social Psychology Bulletin, 26*, 100–117.

Higgins, T., Strauman, T., & Klein, R. (1986). Criteria and the process of self-evaluation: Multiple affects from multiple stages. In R. Sorrentino & T. Higgins (Eds.), *Handbook of motivation and cognition* (pp. 23–63). New York: Guilford.

Kerr, N., & Bruun, S. (1981). Ringelmann revisited: Alternative explanations for the social loafing effect. *Personality and Social Psychology Bulletin, 7*, 224–231.

Latané, B. (1981). The psychology of social impact. *American Psychologist, 36*, 343–356.

Latané, B., Williams, K., & Harkins, S. (1979). Many hands make light the work: The causes and consequences of social loafing. *Journal of Personality and Social Psychology, 37*, 823–832.

Latham, G., & Lee, T. (1986). Goal setting. In E. Locke (Ed.), *Generalizing from laboratory to field settings*. Lexington, MA: Lexington Books.

Leary, M. (1999). Making sense of self-esteem. *Current Directions in Psychological Science, 8*, 32–35.

Locke, E., & Latham, G. (1990a). *A theory of goal setting and task performance*. Englewood Cliffs, NJ: Prentice Hall.

Locke, E., & Latham, G. (1990b). Work motivation and satisfaction: Light at the end of the tunnel. *Psychological Science, 1*, 240–246.

Masters, J., & Keil, L. (1987). Generic comparison processes in human judgment and behavior. In J. Masters & W. Smith (Eds.), *Social comparison, social justice, and relative deprivation* (pp. 11–54). Hillsdale, NJ: Erlbaum.

Sanders, G., Baron, R., & Moore, D. (1978). Distraction and social comparison as mediators of social facilitation effects. *Journal of Experimental Social Psychology, 14*, 291–303.

Schlenker, B. (1986). Self-identification: Toward an integration of the private and public self. In R. F. Baumeister (Ed.), *Public self and private self* (pp. 21–62). New York: Springer-Verlag.

Steiner, I. (1972). *Group processes and productivity*. New York: Academic.

Szymanski, K. (1988). *Social loafing and self-evaluation*. Unpublished dissertation, Northeastern University, Boston, MA.

Szymanski, K., Garczynski, J. & Harkins, S. (2000). The contribution of the potential for evaluation to coaction effects. *Group Processes and Intergroup Relations, 3*, 269–283.

Szymanski, K., & Harkins, S. (1987). Social loafing and self-evaluation with a social standard. *Journal of Personality and Social Psychology, 53*, 891–897.

Szymanski, K., & Harkins, S. (1992). Self-evaluation and creativity. *Personality and Social Psychology Bulletin, 18*, 259–265.

Szymanski, K., & Harkins, S. (1993). The effect of experimenter evaluation on self-evaluation within the social loafing paradigm. *Journal of Experimental Social Psychology, 29*, 268–286.

Tedeschi, J., & Norman, N. (1985). Social power, self-presentation, and the self. In B. Schlenker (Ed.), *The self and social life* (pp. 293–322). New York: McGraw-Hill.

Tesser, A. (1988). Toward a self-evaluation maintenance model of social behavior. In L. Berkowitz (Ed.), *Advances in experimental social psychology*, (Vol. 21, pp. 181–227). New York: Academic.

Utman, C., & Harkins, S. (May, 1996). The effect of ego-involvement on the use of goals in self-evaluation. Midwestern Psychological Association, Chicago.

White, P., Kjelgaard, M., & Harkins, S. (1995). Testing the contribution of self-evaluation to goal setting effects using the social loafing paradigm. *Journal of Personality and Social Psychology, 69*, 69–79.

Williams, K., & Harkins, S., & Latané, B. (1981). Identifiability as a deterrent to social loafing: Two cheering experiments. *Journal of Experimental Social Psychology, 40*, 303–311.

17

Self-Categorization Principles Underlying Majority and Minority Influence

BARBARA DAVID
JOHN C. TURNER

*I*n the early 1970s Moscovici and his colleagues (Moscovici, 1976) launched a broadside against the dominant "dependence" theory of social influence (see Turner, 1991). They criticized the idea that power was the basis of influence and that influence was the exertion of power. They argued that power (reflecting people's dependence on others) and influence (persuasion, the capacity to change private attitudes) were alternative and opposed means of changing people's behavior. Empirically, they demonstrated the fact of minority influence, that a minority within a group could change the judgments of the majority to some degree even if they had less power by all the normal criteria. Moscovici (1976) also rejected the dualism within traditional theory which contrasted nor-

Address correspondence to: Barbara David and John C. Turner, Division of Psychology, Australian National University, Canberra ACT 0200, Australia. E-mail: barbara.david@anu.edu.au

293

mative and informational processes of influence (Deutsch & Gerard, 1955). He suggested that there was one fundamental process of influence (separate from power) related to the production, avoidance, and resolution of social conflict, and that all members of a group (whether majority or minority) had the capacity for influence.

In 1980 Moscovici rejected or at least substantially modified this "genetic" theory. Now he argued that the influence of majorities was based on a power process, producing compliance and conformity (but not private attitude change), but that the influence of minorities was based on conversion, representing true influence, persuasion, and private acceptance. Thus he reintroduced the dualism of normative and informational influence and linked these processes to the nature of the influence source as a majority or minority group.

His "conversion" theory (Moscovici, 1980) argues that majorities tend to produce influence by means of a comparison process and that such influence tends to be immediate but short-term, public rather than private, and direct rather than indirect (specific rather than more general), whereas minorities tend to produce influence by means of a validation process and that such influence tends to be long-term rather than immediate (appearing at a delay), private rather than public, and indirect rather than direct. Thus true influence has become the preserve of minorities. Only minorities can convert. Majorities on the other hand apparently only have power. Over the last 20 years many studies have appeared exploring the differences between majority and minority influence and many variants of Moscovici's ideas as well as other ideas have appeared to make sense of the findings. The idea that majority and minority influence are in some essential way different or that they produce different outcomes has come to be widely accepted.

The aim of this chapter is to outline and test a different analysis of majority and minority influence, based on self-categorization theory (Turner, 1985; Turner, Hogg, Oakes, Reicher, & Wetherell, 1987; Turner, Oakes, Haslam, & McGarty, 1994). We briefly summarize the basic theoretical principles underlying social influence as specified by self-categorization theory (e.g., Turner, 1991; Turner & Oakes, 1986, 1989), indicate their relevance to majority and minority influence, and outline a series of studies testing the analysis (David & Turner, 1996, 1999, in press). We try to show that the various outcomes of majority and minority influence can be explained by means of the same set of general theoretical principles. Self-categorization theory holds that people define themselves at different levels of abstraction. Under some conditions they may tend to define themselves as individual persons different from other ingroup members (personal identity). Under other conditions they may tend to define themselves as group members, as members of some social category in contrast to some other social category (social identity). Self-categorization theory argues that where some shared social identity becomes salient people will tend to accentuate the degree to which they see themselves as similar to other ingroup members and different from outgroup members. It is assumed that shared social identity is the basis of mutual influence between people. The creation of mutually perceived similarity between ingroup members not only leads to more consensual behavior in terms of the norms and values that define one's group, but also produces shared expectations of agreement between ingroup members. Where the latter are disconfirmed (i.e., where there is disagreement within the group), subjective uncertainty about the validity (appropriateness, correctness, etc.) of one's judgments is produced, which has to be resolved. The uncertainty is created by individuals' implicit awareness that people who are similar and who are judging a similar (shared, publicly invariant) stimulus situation ought to agree (i.e., react in the same way). Furthermore, where they do agree, the agreement provides evidence that ingroup members' responses reflect an external, objective reality, rather than personal biases or idiosyncrasies. If some response to the stimulus situation is depersonalized, shared with similar others, if it is consensual and normative for the group, then it can be attributed to external reality, it provides information about reality. In fact, the response is experienced as subjectively valid and appropriate precisely because it is perceived in some sense as "objectively demanded" by reality. By the same token, disagreement within the group raises basic questions that have to do with the perceived cause of one's response, which amount to the experience of uncertainty: Do we differ in some relevant way after all? Are we confronting the same reality, approaching it from the same perspective? Am I (or are they) wrong?

Thus the basic principles are (1) that people expect to agree with others that they categorize as similar to themselves in relevant respects (as perceivers) when they are judging the same stimulus reality ("If we are the same and are judging the same thing, then we ought to agree."), and expect to disagree with people they categorize as different from themselves in relevant respects (or where judging a different stimulus), (2) that such agreement with similar others or disagreement with different others produces subjective validity (certainty, confidence in the objective correctness of one's judgment), (3) that disagreement with similar others about the same stimulus or agreement with different others produces uncertainty, and (4) that uncertainty (which will vary with strength of self-categorization, relevance and importance of issue to group identity, extent of agreement/disagreement, etc.) motivates efforts to reduce uncertainty by recategorizing the self and others, redefining the stimulus situation, or engaging in mutual influence (in which one seeks to persuade and also is open to persuasion). The traditional distinction between "informational" and "normative" influence (see Turner, 1991) is rejected in this formulation. One's own judgment or behavior is subjectively validated (as correct, appropriate, informative of reality) to the degree that it participates in and exemplifies an ingroup norm. Others' responses exert informational force and embody persuasive, valid arguments, to the degree that they exemplify an ingroup normative stance. It is assumed that ingroup norms induce private acceptance rather than merely public compliance because they provide information about appropriate behavior. They define congruent responses as informationally valid for members, as shared within the ingroup, and hence as reflecting reality rather than personal bias or the incompetence or prejudice of outgroups. Informational influence is influence as a function of the perceived validity of information, and here perceived validity is a function of the degree to which the message (judgment, response, etc.) is consensual (i.e., normative) within the ingroup. Thus for self-categorization theory, informational and (ingroup) normative influence represent the same process. Compliance, on the other hand, going along with social norms as a function of the social power of the source, rather than its capacity for persuasive influence, is seen as specifically a reaction to the norms and power of an outgroup.

Our argument is that both majority and minority influence are mediated by self-categorization processes. What do we mean by this? We do not mean that majorities and minorities always produce the same outcomes. On the contrary we do not dispute that majorities sometimes produce compliance but not conversion and that minorities sometimes produce conversion but not compliance. Our reading of the literature, however, suggests that there is no exclusive link between majorities and compliance, or minorities and conversion. We think the evidence is clear (see Turner, 1991) that both majorities and minorities can produce a whole variety of outcomes. Sometimes majorities produce compliance without conversion; sometimes they produce both. Minorities can produce conversion without compliance, or both; indeed in one study a minority produced compliance without conversion (see Perez & Mugny, 1987, as discussed by Turner, 1991, p. 109). We do not yet know of a study in which a majority has produced conversion without compliance, but theoretically we think it is perfectly possible. When we say that majority and minority influence are based on the same influence process, we mean that the same general theoretical principles outlined above can be used to make sense of all the varying outcomes by taking into account the specific influence conditions. We do not mean that majorities and minorities do not produce qualitatively different effects under many conditions. Nor do we mean that there is no difference between influence and power or that people will not sometimes accept or reject influence easily, superficially, with little thought, and at other times accept or reject it with much cognitive elaboration and mental effort.

From this perspective, then, influence is fundamentally about social identity and ingroup-outgroup membership. One expects to agree with ingroup members and disagree with outgroup members; one feels confident to the degree that one does so and uncertain to the degree that one disagrees with ingroup members and agrees with outgroup members. Accepting or engaging in influence is both informational and (ingroup) normative, a matter of social comparison and validation; it is related to the production and reduction of uncertainty and is a means of reducing uncertainty. The relevance of majority/minority group membership (which is manipulated in the literature in many different ways) to these processes varies. Sometimes in the context of society at large majority status is used to indicate ingroup membership (people like us), and minorities are seen as outgroup members (deviants, marginalized, outsiders). Thus sometimes majority/minority status functions as a direct cue to ingroup-outgroup membership. At other times, it is clear that researchers are taking for granted that the majorities and minorities they are studying are both members of the same ingroup (e.g., they expect people to agree with the majority, defining it as implicitly normative and ingroup, but disagree with a deviant minority from the same social category). Within a group, majority or minority status can provide information about the degree to which some judgment is consensual, normative or prototypical; thus a majority ingroup judgment is likely to be perceived as consensual, normative, informational, and persuasive; whereas ingroup minority or outgroup majority response are likely to be perceived as counternormative and incorrect. Also majority/minority status often provides information about the degree to which some group is extreme or moderate in attitudes in relation to the social context. This is important for self-categorization theory in that it bears on the issue of how easy it is to recategorize a majority or minority as similar to self or different from self in different social contexts. The effects of majority and minority in the literature are likely to operate in all these ways as well as through more subtle ways, discussed below.

All of these potential but often implicit effects of manipulating numerical status can, in turn, impact on whether targets are influenced lastingly, temporarily, or not at all, whether little or considerable cognitive effort is required, and whether the effort is focused primarily on the source or its message. In all cases, however, we argue that it is the perceived social and self-categorical relationship between source and target, rather than fixed, reified qualities of majorities or minorities that determines the course of the influence process.

Contrary to self-categorization theory most minority influence researchers seem to endorse the idea that there are two distinct kinds of influence, one that is determined primarily by social concerns such as whether a target wants to be seen agreeing with a particular source ("normative" influence in the traditional sense), and another determined by a concern for the objective factual information contained in an influence message ("informational" influence in the traditional sense). In line with Moscovici (1980; Moscovici & Mugny, 1983), some suggest that majorities exert the former kind of superficial influence, through stimulating a comparison and conformity process, and that minorities stimulate a validation process that focuses attention on the informational content of their message. Others (e.g. Mackie, 1987) argue on the other hand that it is majority messages that are closely scrutinized for informational content.

The normative/informational dichotomy also is reflected in theories that, although not initially concerned with majorities and minorities, have been applied to this area of research. In the area of persuasion, researchers have suggested that communications from a would-be persuasive source are either given careful scrutiny—"systematic" processing in terms used by Chaiken (1980, 1987) and "central" processing in terms used by Petty and Cacioppo (1981, 1986)—or one searches for social cues in order to determine the objective correctness of the communication—"heuristic" processing (Chaiken, 1980, 1987) and "peripheral" processing (Petty & Cacioppo, 1981, 1986). Most researchers applying these cognitive-processing theories to models of minority and majority influence (e.g., Baker & Petty, 1994; Crano & Alvaro, 1998; Crano & Hannula-Bral, 1994; Martin & Hewstone, in press, this volume) propose that "message processing is contingent upon source status and one or more additional variables" (Martin & Hewstone, this volume), that is, targets will sometimes process majority more than minority messages, and sometimes minority more than majority messages, depending on circumstances.

From our perspective the problem with these "contingency" models is that they still assign majority/minority numerical status the fundamental theoretical role in determining the nature of influence. Our view is that the influence process must be understood from the point of view of its targets and that from different points of view majorities and minorities have different natures and different effects. We suggest that many of the apparent contradictions and inconsistencies in the literature (see Wood, Lundgren, Ouellette, Busceme, & Blackstone, 1994) can be resolved by attempting to understand the point of view of the targets of influence and, in particular, by taking into account how these targets perceive themselves and their relationship to the source. While it is unarguable that in some influence encounters attention will be focused on the source while in others it will be focused on the message, that some influence messages are more deeply processed than others, and that influence may be fleeting or lasting, we think there is no direct correspondence between source status as objectively defined by an experimenter, and any influence process or outcome.

The first two studies in our research program addressed the fundamental idea of the self-categorization analysis of influence, that, all things being equal, it is the social categorization of others into ingroup and outgroup that determines whether there will be acceptance or rejection of influence from those others on a relevant topic. The studies not only illustrate the classic pattern of majority compliance and minority conversion when these are ingroup majorities and minorities, but also demonstrate that when a source, be it majority or minority, is outgroup in relation to the topic of the influence attempt, its only effect is to cause targets to move further away from the advocated position than they were initially. Our third and fourth studies offer an explanation for the "conversion" pattern of ingroup minority influence in terms of the role of the social context in determining whether the same minority is categorized as ingroup or outgroup. A fifth and sixth study, described in more detail, examine the role of social identity in determining the cognitive elaboration and processing of majority and minority messages.

MINORITIES AS OUTGROUPS

In a series of studies (e.g., Moscovici & Lage, 1976, 1978; Moscovici, Lage, & Neffrechoux, 1969; Moscovici & Neve, 1973) based on his "genetic" theory Moscovici (1976), observed that numerical majorities influence in public, in the short term, and on direct measures (compliance), while minorities exert influence in private, at a temporal delay, and on indirect measures (conversion). His explanation assumes that majorities, by definition, tend to be perceived as normative and correct and are positively valued, while minorities tend to be perceived as deviant and incorrect and are negatively valued. When a target of influence finds him- or herself disagreeing with the normative majority, the conflict is unexpected and disturbing and the target turns to social comparison to explain the discrepancy. Social comparison with the normative source produces immediate compliance, but inhibits close examination of the message content, and therefore prevents conversion. On the other hand, conflict with the negatively valued minority is neither unexpected nor disturbing. One does not agree with it, because by definition it is seen as wrong, but one does attempt to understand its strange point of view. To this end one validates the minority message and the resultant deep processing of the message content results in delayed influence.

In our third and fourth studies we tested an alternative explanation of conversion. In the first two studies we focused on the contention that the influence of a normative reference group (the "majority" according to Moscovici's characterization) will only be temporary and public, while people we see as deviant (the "minority") can have a lasting influence on our private beliefs. This is in direct conflict with self-categorization theory's assertion that the perception of social deviance in a would-be source is an alternative to influence. If a source is deviant, that is, an outgroup or different from self, one expects to disagree with it , there is no uncertainty to be resolved, and no change needs to be made to one's existing beliefs. Thus we disagree with the claim that "shared social identity actually reduces true influence while categorization of others as outgroup may increase it " (Mugny, Perez, & Sanchez-Mazas, 1993, p. 10).

In these studies the targets of influence were either conservationists and therefore against the felling of Australian old-growth forests, or individuals identified with the timber industry who were against the implementation of tighter controls on the logging of forests. Participants were exposed to a prologging or proconservation message from "Friends of the Forest" or "Friends of the Timber Industry," who purportedly represented a minority or majority of conservationists or the timber industry. Thus participants received a message from either an ingroup majority, ingroup minority, outgroup majority, or outgroup minority source.

In the first study (David & Turner, 1996, Study 1) participants indicated their attitudes to logging the rainforest prior to, immediately after, and three weeks after the influence message. In all conditions where the source was outgroup (i.e., Friends of the Timber Industry for conservationists and Friends of the Forest for prologgers), participants' attitudes shifted *away from* the position advocated by the would-be source of influence. The strengthening of participants' original positions was immediately evident, did not decrease three weeks later, and was equally strong whether the source was majority or minority. In the ingroup source conditions (i.e., where source and targets shared the same and a relevant social identity), the pattern predicted by Moscovici (1980) was obtained. Targets' attitudes shifted towards the position advocated by the majority in the short term and back towards their original position three weeks later; those in the minority conditions showed greater long-term than short-term influence.

The second study (David & Turner, 1996, Study 2) employed the same ingroup/outgroup × majority/minority source design, but used public or private responses rather than short- or long-term responses as the measure of compliance versus conversion. The same pattern of results was obtained. Targets moved away from the outgroup majority and outgroup minority sources in both public and private, but more toward the ingroup majority in public than private, and more toward the ingroup minority in private than public.

Thus it appears that majority and minority sources can produce different patterns of influence under certain conditions, but only where they are categorized as ingroup rather than outgroup. Outgroup sources, whether majority or minority, do not produce influence, or rather produce only negative influence. One cannot explain the conversion effect of minorities in terms of their being judged as deviant, inherently incorrect, negatively valued, different from self, and so forth, since it was precisely in conditions where the majority and minority sources were categorized as different from the targets (where participants should have felt most free from social comparison, see Turner, 1991) that no (positive) influence at all was evident. These data raise the question of why ingroup majorities and minorities produce different patterns of influence under certain conditions. The following studies tested an explanation of minority conversion. The final two studies are relevant to majority compliance.

SOCIAL CONTEXT, RECATEGORIZATION, AND MINORITY CONVERSION

The first two studies affirmed the principle that only people perceived as similar to oneself in terms of some relevant social identity will influence. However, self-categorization theory takes for granted that the same people can be categorized as similar to self at one time and different from self at another, solely as a function of the social context within which they are defined (Turner et al., 1994). The theory suggests that perceived self-other similarity flows from self-categorization and that self-categorizing is inherently comparative and always relative to a frame of reference. In particular the theory suggests that self-categories form in such a way as to maximize the perceived differences between self- and nonself categories compared to the differences within them (the principle of metacontrast, Turner, 1985). It follows that an outgroup perceived as different from one's ingroup in the context of comparison between the ingroup and outgroup may be recategorized as part of a more inclusive ingroup when the comparative field extends to include even more discrepant people.

There is indeed evidence that people who have been perceived as different from self in a restricted context, comprising moderately similar people, can come to be perceived as similar to self in a more extended context, comprising more different people (e.g., Haslam & Turner, 1992, 1995; Hensley & Duval,

1976; Wilder & Thompson, 1988). We suggest that ingroup majority members (who are the unnamed targets of influence in most of the literature) can perceive an ingroup minority as different from self (and therefore as a negative reference group to be rejected and disagreed with) when the field of comparison is limited to the sociological ingroup, or similar to self (and therefore as part of a positive reference group to be accepted and agreed with) when compared to some more fundamentally different outgroup.

How does such a context-dependent variation in ingroup-outgroup categorization relate to conversion? We suggest that when an ingroup minority attempts to influence the majority, immediate, direct, and public measures make the discrepancy between the ingroup majority and minority highly salient. This is to say that when required to openly indicate whether or not one agrees with a minority position, when given no time to consider the response, and when the directness of the question requires a yes or no answer, one's attention is focused on the difference between the new suggestion and what is assumed to be correct by definition, that is, the ingroup majority position. On the other hand, because they remove participants from the need to confront the ingroup conflict directly, we suggest that delayed, indirect, and private measures attenuate the salience of the factional conflict. In other words, measures of delayed, private, and indirect influence allow the frame of reference to broaden and include the more fundamental conflict with the outgroup. Thus one fails to be influenced by the ingroup minority who are different from self on immediate, public, and direct measures, but is influenced by them when delayed, private and indirect, measures lead them to be perceived as similar to self.

To test this idea, David and Turner (1999, Study 1) employed moderate feminist participants and used separatist feminists, espousing radical feminism, as the ingroup minority source of influence. Participants indicated their attitudes to feminism on a questionnaire that was administered before and immediately after an influence message from separatist feminists, and again at a delay of three weeks. We manipulated the context in which the message was presented by informing participants that "a typical group of participants" had produced a statement to be evaluated. In the intragroup context this statement endorsed moderate feminist views, and in the intergroup context it endorsed anti-feminist views. We expected that the intragroup context statement, endorsing the values of the moderate feminist majority, would cause the radical feminist minority to be seen as different (outgroup) and thus their message to be rejected. Conversely, we expected that the intergroup context statement, by bringing outgroup values into the frame of reference, would cause the ingroup minority (different from moderates only in the extremity with which they endorsed ingroup values), to be perceived as similar to the majority in the essential correctness of their views. Thus in the intergroup context we expected the ingroup minority to exert influence.

Since our proposed explanation of conversion is that time (inter alia) attenuates the salience of intragroup conflict, we introduced conditions in which the context was repeated immediately prior to the delayed posttest. If we are correct about the effect of time, participants in the intragroup context conditions should fail to be influenced in the short term but only those for whom the context is restated prior to the posttest should remain uninfluenced, since the delay of three weeks should have returned the other intragroup participants to the "default" intergroup context in which the ingroup minority is influential. We expected that controls who received the influence message without an explicit context, would evince an immediate rejection of the message, comparable to participants in the intragroup context conditions. Further, we expected no-context controls to evince delayed acceptance (i.e., to "convert"), as would subjects in the intergroup *restated* context condition.

As can be seen from Table 17.1, our predictions were strongly supported. Participants for whom no context was explicitly induced (i.e., those in the "normal" minority influence situation) evinced no immediate, but a significant delayed, influence. This conversion pattern also was exhibited by intragroup context participants who had the context induced before the immediate measure only. For them, explicit induction of an intragroup context caused an initial move away from the source, but the passing of time ameliorated the conflict of comparison with the ingroup majority, resulting in acceptance of the ingroup minority's message. That such a delayed acceptance was not merely a product of increased familiarity with the repeated measure was made clear by participants for whom the intragroup context was restated immediately prior to the delayed measure: They evinced no positive immediate *or* delayed influence. Comparison of the ingroup minority message with the outgroup (the intergroup context) also led to the effect we predicted, with participants shifting towards the ingroup minority source.

Our fourth study was a replication of the third, using a simpler induction

TABLE 17.1. Study 3: Mean Immediate and Delayed Shift for Control and Experimental Conditions

Condition	n	Shift°	
		Immediate	Delayed
Intragroup Context single statement	19	−0.71[a]	0.18
	(−0.82)	(1.07)	
Intragroup Context repeated statement	18	−0.86[a]	−0.78 [a]
	(0.82)	(0.85)	
Intergroup Context single statement	18	1.69[a]	1.63[a]
	(0.86)	(0.76)	
Intergroup Context repeated statement	19	1.78[a]	1.85[a]
	(0.86)	(0.79)	
No-context Control	19	−0.06	0.53[a]
	(0.71)	(0.56)	
Irrelevant-message Control	21	0.07	0.08
	(0.32)	(0.29)	

Numbers in parentheses are standard deviations.
°Shift is the difference on a 9-point feminism scale between pretest and either immediate or delayed posttest.
[a]exceeds Bonferroni critical t at .01 significance level.

of context: Participants received a Likert-type scale on which was indicated the mean attitude to feminism of "most women who have taken part in the study so far." To create an intragroup context the supposed mean position was moderately profeminist and to create an intergroup context the mean was moderately anti-feminist.

Results largely replicated those of our third study with some minor exceptions (see David & Turner, 1999, Study 2). Thus, while we acknowledge that evidence for changes in self-categorization are inferential rather than direct, our data from both studies are fully consistent with predictions. We were able both to replicate and prevent conversion, and to foster compliance (i.e., immediate influence) by manipulating the context in which a minority presented its message. Since studies to which we have already referred (Haslam & Turner, 1992, 1995; Hensley & Duval, 1976; Wilder & Thompson, 1988) have demonstrated that restricted contexts foster perceptions of difference and broader contexts foster perceptions of similarity, and since it was only in the broader (intergroup) contexts that participants in Studies 3 and 4 were influenced by the minority source, we can certainly claim that our studies are inconsistent with the contention that it is the perceived deviance and difference of minorities that enable them to convert. We now turn to the issue of how minority and majority messages are processed.

UNCERTAINTY AND THE COGNITIVE PROCESSING OF MAJORITY AND MINORITY MESSAGES

Both Chaiken's (1980, 1987) Heuristic-Systematic Model and Petty and Cacioppo's (1981, 1986) Elaboration Likelihood Model of persuasion propose a lazy, cue-based mode of processing a persuasive communication (heuristic or peripheral) and one which is more careful and focused on scrutinizing the informational content of the message (systematic or central). There is little disagreement in the literature that the latter kind of processing, where attention and energy are devoted to understanding a communication, has a more profound and lasting effect on deeply-held beliefs than the former, more superficial kind of processing. There is, however, considerable disagreement about who stimulates which process, why this is so, and what outcome the processing has.

Researchers have argued that majorities stimulate superficial processing because disagreement with the majority is unexpected while minorities stimulate deep processing because expecting to disagree with the majority frees one to consider their point of view (Moscovici, 1980; Moscovici & Mugny, 1983). Majority messages are shallowly processed because they are normative (Axson, Yates, & Chaiken, 1987; Chaiken, 1980; Chaiken & Stangor, 1987; DeVries, DeDreu, Gordijn, & Schurman, 1996; Kelman, 1961); and that majority messages are deeply processed because they are normative (Mackie, 1987; see also Baker & Petty, 1994, Study 1; DeDreu & DeVries, 1993). The picture becomes even more complex when we consider researchers who do not link one type of process to one type of source. Nemeth (1986) suggests that majorities stimulate both social comparative and validational processing, but that this focuses strictly on their message, while minorities foster a broader contemplation of the issue. Petty and Cacioppo (1979) suggest that it is personal involvement in the issue at hand, rather than the source of communication about the issue, that fosters thinking about message content. Baker and Petty (1994) produce evidence that level of processing is not a simple product of source status. They show that both majority and minority messages are closely scrutinized when they are not what participants expect from the source (this runs contrary to Moscovici's (1980) proposal that the unexpectedness of conflict with a majority leads attention away from contemplation of its message).

Amidst the richness, complexity, and contradictions of the literature addressing the processing of influence messages it seemed to us that an important group of participants had been largely overlooked—those who are doing the processing. Targets of influence seem to exist only as a generalized abstraction rather than as a specific social group in a specific social location. While some attention has been given to individual differences such as involvement with the issue (Petty & Cacioppo, 1979), susceptibility to subtle manipulations (Petty, this volume), and mood (Forgas, this volume; Schwarz, Bless, & Bohner, 1991; Wegener & Petty, 1996), little appears to have been given to *targets'* social identity or numerical status, even by researchers who address the social identity and numerical status of sources of influence (for a notable exception see Crano & Hannula-Bral, 1994). This creates important problems for any theory that makes claims about the effects of majority and minority sources in isolation, since such theories are usually based on the normative nature of majorities and counternormative nature of minorities. Only a moment's consideration is needed to realize that majorities are normative and minorities counternormative only if the targets of influence are ingroup majority members. Would, for example, a white Protestant majority set the norms for members of a black Muslim minority?

In order to deal with the implicit assumption in the literature that targets are majority members of the same ingroup as the source, an assumption which reifies majority and minority sources as normative and counternormative respectively, our fifth study used politically active and committed moderate feminists as targets, who could be argued to be minority members in the context of society at large, and our sixth study used separatist feminists, a minority of the minority. We manipulated various forms of source-message balance and imbalance to test the idea that when deviant people (in this case anti-feminists) present a deviant message, it will be dismissed out of hand rather than processed, and the converse, that when the same deviant source presents a normative message, the need to explain a flouted expectation may result in increased message elaboration or increased thinking about the identity of the source. We differ here from Baker and Petty (1994) in that they predict that the increased cognitive effort elicited by source-message imbalance will be devoted quite specifically to the message, leading to influence. We return later to the general issue of how our analysis differs from their model of source-position discrepancy.

We expected that for our (societal) minority targets, members of the same minority (moderate and separatist feminists) would be ingroup and that, when they presented a normative (feminist) message, it would be accepted relatively uncritically and unthinkingly, whereas, when they presented a counternormative message, cognitive effort would be needed to explain the discrepancy and reduce uncertainty. We did not suppose that this effort would be confined to consideration of the message, and we did not suppose that cognitive elaboration of any message would necessarily lead to its acceptance. Our main aim was to show that uncertainty, cognitive elaboration, and influence are driven by the self-categorical relations between sources and targets and the perceived norms of sources and targets, and that, within this context, majorities and minorities are both capable of producing compliance or conversion, certainty or uncertainty, and uncritical or cognitively effortful acceptance or rejection of the message.

Even before we began the studies, our participants illustrated for us the importance of not making assumptions about how they would perceive group status. Prior to distributing influence messages and response sheets (to be completed privately), participants were asked to try to come to consensus as a group about the numerical status of moderate feminists, separatist feminists, and anti-feminists. As can be seen from Table 17.2, moderate feminists did not endorse our suggestion that they are a minority group, seeing themselves as a majority, and seeing both separatists and anti-feminists as minorities. When it came to

TABLE 17.2. Studies 5 & 6. Mean agreement, total elaboration, and number of additional thoughts devoted to reinterpreting a statement and questioning the identity of the source

Participants' self-categorization	Source and perceived source status†							
	Modfem *majority*		Sepfem *minority*		Antifem *minority*		Control	
Modfem (Study 5)	Norm	Counter	Norm	Counter	Norm	Counter	Norm	Counter
agreement	7.8	6.3[b]	7.2	5.9[b]	6.8[a]	1.4	7.8	1.2
elaboration	1.6	8.6[a]	6.4[b]	9.7[b]	7.1[b]	1.3[a]	1.2	4.6
reinterpret statement	0.0	3.3[a]	0.0	7.1[b]	1.8[a]	0.0	0.0	0.0
question source identity	0.0	5.1[b]	0.0	2.1[a]	5.0[b]	0.0	0.0	0.0
Sepfem (Study 6)	*Mainstream minority*		*Minority*		*Majority*			
	Norm	Counter	Norm	Counter	Norm	Counter	Norm	Counter
agreement	8.0	5.4[b]	7.9	7.1[b]	4.0	1.0	8.4	1.0
elaboration	5.3[b]	8.9	0.7	8.7	8.8[b]	0.5[b]	0.7	8.9
reinterpret statement	0.1	0.5	0.0	7.3[b]	7.7[b]	0.0	0.0	0.0
question source identity	0.2	8.1[b]	0.0	0.8[a]	0.4	0.0[b]	0.0	4.0

†italics indicate the status of the source as consensually defined by participants.
modfem = moderate feminists; sepfem = separatist feminists; norm = normative statement; counter = counternormative statement
[a]comparison with control exceeds Bonferroni critical *t* at .05
[b]comparison with control exceeds Bonferroni critical *t* at .01

Study 6, separatists indicated that they were a minority, as were moderate feminists (although they distanced themselves from moderates by indicating that moderates were "mainstream"), and they emphasized their own embattled status by indicating that the outgroup, anti-feminists, were a majority. Thus separatists saw themselves as an extremist minority within a minority and the moderates as a majority within the feminist minority.

Two influence messages were pretested and found to be normative (i.e., profeminist, an argument promoting women's right to abortion) and counternormative (i.e., anti-feminist, an anti-abortion argument) for both groups of feminists. In both studies participants received either the normative or the counternormative message which was attributed to either moderate feminists, separatist feminists, or anti-feminists, or no source attribution was made. Participants indicated, on a scale from 1 (total disagreement) to 9 (complete agreement), the extent to which they endorsed the message. Participants were then asked to list any additional thoughts they had on the matter (the mean number of these is referred to in Table 17.2 as "elaboration"). The additional thoughts were content analyzed. Originally we wanted merely to ascertain whether elaboration focused on message content or on the source but the data suggested a more precise understanding: Most participants, when focusing on the source, did so in order to question it ("are these people really who they say they are?") and, when focusing on the message, did so in order to reinterpret it ("they can't really mean what they say they mean"). In Table 17.2 the mean number of thoughts directed to reinterpreting the statement are listed as "reinterpret statement," and mean number of thoughts directed to questioning the source as "question source identity."

In Study 5, it can be seen that moderate feminists indicated that they agreed with the normative statement in the control condition, and, in fact, in all source conditions, although it should be noted that they agreed with it significantly less when it was endorsed by the outgroup. It appears that when the normative statement issued from the appropriate reference group (moderate feminists themselves), little additional thought was necessary, but when it issued from either the ingroup minority (separatists) or the outgroup, a significant amount of extra thinking was generated. In the latter case, where there is a source-position imbalance (anti-feminists arguing for women's right to abortion), the elaboration seemed mainly to be devoted to making sense of the discrepancy, by suggesting that the position was not what it appeared to be, or by questioning whether the source was really who they said they were.

Whereas moderate feminists always endorsed the normative message, the source variable determined whether or not they rejected the counternormative message. They indicated that they disagreed with an anti-abortion stance in the control condition, and when the position was presented by anti-feminists, but indicated that they agreed with it when it was presented by either separatists or by moderate feminists, which reinforces the basic principle that like-minded people will exert positive influence. Interestingly, attribution of the message to the outgroup led to a significant decrease in elaboration—supporting our earlier contention that when a deviant source presents a message with which one disagrees, the source explains the disagreement and no additional attention needs to be devoted to the matter. In the cases of the counternormative message from the ingroup majority (moderates) and minority (separatists) almost all of the significant amount of elaboration was devoted to explaining the discrepancy by reinterpreting the statement or questioning the source: With a moderate feminist source there was more questioning of the source's identity, and with a separatist source, more reinterpretation of the statement.

Turning now to Study 6, and contemplation of agreement with the normative message, it can be seen from Table 17.2 that separatists did not follow the same pattern as moderate feminists who accepted the message in all conditions. The control condition shows us that separatists are basically very strong in their support for women's right to abortion, and this support also is seen in the moderate and separatist source conditions. However, and somewhat surprisingly for such an identity-defining topic, separatists indicated that they did not agree with such rights when they were promoted by anti-feminists. It would appear that, more important than being correct in attitudes to abortion, was being correct in attitude to the outgroup majority, as defined by disagreeing with anything they might propose. If we examine the amount of elaboration stimulated by this denial of a basic feminist principle, we see that it was costly in terms of cognitive effort, and when we examine the form taken by the elaboration, we see that, rather than questioning who made the statement, separatists questioned what was said (if they did not accept that the source were anti-feminists, they would not have needed to disagree with their message). For example one respondent wrote "Anti-feminists wouldn't understand why women need the right to abortion, they probably look on it as a kind of contraception that allows men to °— around as much as they want to without having to take responsibility" and another that "Anti-feminists weren't thinking of women when they said this, they were thinking of the big fat fees the surgeons would get," or "In their eyes making abortion legal is just another way to get women's bodies under the control of the patriarchy again."

When it came to the counternormative message, separatists showed the same pattern as moderate feminists, although they were more extreme in their rejection of it in the control and outgroup conditions and stronger in their acceptance when it was endorsed by themselves, the essential ingroup. It can be seen that, as for moderates, even in the control condition, separatists elaborated the counter-normative message, and about half of this elaboration was devoted to questioning the identity of the source, even though none had been given explicitly. This took the form of such statements as "The blokes must have got pissed round the bar one night to produce this —, unless Freddy got his girls to learn to read and write" (the latter referring to the female congregation of a well-known Australian fundamentalist preacher) and "Who reckons this! The chauvinist pig brigade!?". Once again following the moderates' pattern, separatists showed a significant decrease in elaboration of the counternormative message in the outgroup condition, where its source attribution explained it.

Again this was more extreme than for moderate feminists. In the ingroup conditions separatists indicated bare neutrality (5.4 on a 9-point scale) when the counternormative statement was endorsed by moderate feminists, but clear agreement with it when endorsed by themselves. In both conditions they devoted considerable cognitive effort to explaining the discrepancy. In the moderate source condition this took the form of questioning the source identity, and in the separatist source condition of reinterpreting the statement.

Earlier we suggested that targets of influence and their relationships with sources must be taken into account. This is quite clear when we compare Studies 5 and 6 and see that separatists, while presenting basically the same patterns of acceptance and rejection of the influence messages and of degree and focus of cognitive elaboration as moderate feminists, were in all instances more extreme. Clearly we cannot refer to the objective status of the sources, to the normative or counternormative nature of the messages, to the strength or weakness of the arguments, or even to the consonance or dissonance between source and message, to explain separatists' distinctive responses, since source and message variables were the same for separatists and moderate feminists. It seems that the most significant difference between the groups was in the way in which they saw themselves, and consequently their relationships with different sources.

It will be remembered that moderate feminists believed they were a majority; separatists believed that they were a minority. Separatists gave us a clue to the fact that they saw themselves not only as a minority but also as marginalized and embattled, when they emphasized that moderate feminists, while also a minority, were part of the mainstream, and that the "enemy," anti-feminists, were in the majority. A number of studies suggest that social identity is more salient for minorities than for majorities (Mullen, 1991; Simon & Brown, 1987) and we might surmise that this will be particularly true when a minority perceives itself as threatened and victimized. The self-categorization explanation for the salience of minority identity is inter alia that "as a group becomes smaller within a given comparative context it will tend to be making more intergroup comparisons than intragroup ones" (Haslam, Turner, Oakes, McGarty, & Hayes, 1992, p. 5) while the reverse is true for majorities. Since intergroup comparisons focus on the differences between categories compared to the differences within them, it follows from the metacontrast principle (Hogg & Turner, 1987; Hogg, Turner, & Davidson, 1990; Turner, 1985, 1991; Turner et al., 1994) that minorities are more likely than majorities to perceive themselves as a unified group, devote effort to maximizing their positive distinctiveness, and to act in terms of prototypical ingroup norms (for links with the literature on extremists and polarized judgment, see Haslam & Turner, 1995, 1998).

Thus separatists in the control conditions were more extreme than moderate feminists in their endorsement of the normative message and their rejection of the counternormative message, and in the latter case produced more cognitive elaboration. The impact of ingroup and outgroup status of sources had more effect on separatists, leading them to reject even the normative message when endorsed by anti-feminists and to agree more strongly with the counternormative message as endorsed by themselves. When a source-position discrepancy led separatists to search for meaning, they were more "black and white" than moderate feminists in focusing on either the statement or the source.

Our post hoc interpretation of separatists' social identity as minority and extremist and of the effects this may have on perception of and reaction to influence attempts from particular social sources is something we will pursue in the future. Other important findings from Studies 5 and 6 are not as speculative.

When targets receive the messages they expect, they respond to the message unthinkingly, showing scant evidence of cognitive elaboration. When source-message relationships are unexpected, there is evidence of considerable cognitive elaboration that may focus on the source or the message and may be aimed at either accepting or rejecting the message. Most notably, for example, separatists put in a great deal of cognitive work scrutinizing the message both in order to accept an anti-abortion message from other separatists (their ingroup minority) and to reject a proabortion message from anti-feminists (outgroup majority). In a sense they engaged in message elaboration to turn what was for them a normally weak message into a strong one and a strong message into a weak one. The processing involved both social cues to the correctness of the message (elsewhere equated with normative influence) and focus on message content (elsewhere equated with informational influence), strongly suggesting, as do all our data, that informational and social comparative processing are interrelated (for a more detailed discussion of the dual-process model, see David & Turner, 1999, in press; Turner, 1991).

It also is important to note that the effects of these studies cannot be reduced to the nature of the source as perceived majority or minority. In the different target-source conditions we can find unthinking acceptance (compliance) of both majority and minority sources, unthinking rejection of both majority and minority sources, effortful acceptance of both sources, and effortful rejection of a majority, as defined by the targets. All these responses depend on the self-categorical relations between target and source. These data, however, cannot be summarized by a contingency model along the lines of Baker and Petty (1994). These authors suggest that message-processing arises when there is source-message imbalance, defined as disagreeing with a majority or agreeing with a minority (it is assumed that one expects to agree with a majority and to disagree with a minority). Suffice to say that Studies 5 and 6 show that agreeing with a majority can produce either certainty or uncertainty, that disagreeing with a majority can produce either certainty or uncertainty, that agreeing or disagreeing with a minority can also produce either certainty or uncertainty. It all depends on who we are and who they are in terms of ingroup-outgroup membership and subgroups of ingroup and outgroup. No contingency model that ignores the fact that social identity is theoretically more fundamental than the numerical status of the source is likely to prove viable.

CONCLUSION

At the beginning of the chapter we suggested that a greater understanding of the influence process might be achieved by paying attention to the targets of influence, and to their relationship with the source, rather than by focusing largely on the objectively defined majority or minority status of sources of influence. In the program of studies presented here we have demonstrated some of what we believe are the underlying social psychological principles involved.

The first and most important principle is that influence is the product of disagreement with others categorized as similar to self in terms of the social identity relevant to the specific judgment. The first two studies demonstrated that the numerical status of a source makes no impact when it is socially categorized as different from self, but that participants respond differently to ingroup majority and minority sources. Testing an explanation for the "conversion" pattern of response to an ingroup minority was the focus for the following two studies.

Studies 3 and 4 demonstrated that an ingroup minority could elicit different responses to its influence attempts: immediate rejection that did not change with time; immediate rejection followed by influence (the classic "conversion" pattern); and immediate influence that did not wane. The responses were consistent with influence being a product of perceived similarity (occurring in the intergroup context, which defines the ingroup majority and the ingroup minority as more similar than different) and rejection of influence being a product of perceived dissimilarity (occurring in the intragroup context, which defines ingroup majority and minority as more different than similar).

In Studies 5 and 6 we addressed the reification of sources of influence and their connection with specific kinds of processing and saw that when a normative message came from a moderate feminist source, moderate feminist targets endorsed the message with little cognitive elaboration which, given that moderates believe themselves to be a majority, is an illustration of majority "compliance." However, when the same message was attributed to separatists, separatist targets also endorsed it relatively unthinkingly and this, given their belief that they are a minority, is minority "compliance." Clearly there is little need to think about the correctness of our essential reference groups unless they say something unexpected (no more than the incorrectness of our outgroups), but majorities only serve the function of reference group for ingroup majority members, as witnessed by our separatist respondents' rejection of anything the antifeminist (perceived) majority had to say.

When a reference group does say something unexpected (i.e., when people who are similar to us say something we do not agree with or when outgroup members agree with us), self-categorization theory assumes that we will seek to resolve the conflict by recategorizing ourselves or the source, reinterpreting the object of judgment (reinterpreting the meaning of the message), engaging in efforts at mutual influence, or some combination of these. Participants in our last two studies gave graphic illustrations of this when they devoted cognitive resources to questioning the identity of the source (e.g., "Real feminists wouldn't say this!"; "These women probably think they're feminists because their husbands let them go to work.") and the meaning of the influence message (e.g., "They say that abortion is wrong but they probably mean that if contraception was more readily available, there would be no need for abortion. After, all it can't be good for women to have their bodies ripped up."). These processes went on as ways of actively agreeing or disagreeing with the message, both in the service of reducing uncertainty and producing self-categorical consonance.

In sum, self-categorization theory proposes that the influence process begins with the conflict created when we disagree with people who are similar to us or agree with people who are different, on a relevant dimension of identity. We search for ways to maintain current beliefs, focus on the source (i.e., process in a supposedly "heuristic" or "peripheral" manner) and inquiring if we might have been mistaken in perceiving the source as similar or different to self. We also may focus (alternatively or at the same time) on the message (i.e., process in a supposedly "systematic" or "central" manner) and inquire if there is a less conflictual way we can interpret it. Whether we employ both strategies equally, or use one more than the other, is not a straightforward function of source identity, but of interactions between our relevant, salient self-categorization (the social identity that is situationally salient), whether we are majority or minority within our ingroup (consensual, prototypical, moderate, or extreme), our representation of the source in relation to self (ingroup or outgroup, majority or minority, moderate, or extreme), and the perceived nature of the message (normative, counternormative, irrelevant). If cognitive elaboration does not explain away the conflict, we are likely to move in our opinions toward or away from the message, including it in our latitude of acceptance or rejection. In the world beyond the laboratory, this may mean that we ourselves shift from being merely the targets of influence to becoming active and passionate sources of social change, creating our own messages, in harmony with our understanding of ourselves and social reality, as we reject those that make no sense to us.

REFERENCES

Axson, D., Yates, S., & Chaiken, S. (1987). Audience response as a heuristic cue in persuasion. *Journal of Personality and Social Psychology*, 53, 30–40.

Baker, S. M., & Petty, R. E. (1994). Majority and minority influence: Source-position imbalance as a determinant of message scrutiny. *Journal of Personality and Social Psychology*, 67, 5–19.

Chaiken, S. (1980). Heuristic versus systematic processing and the use of source versus message cues to persuasion. *Journal of Personality and Social Psychology*. 39, 752–766.

Chaiken, S. (1987). The heuristic model of persuasion. In M. P. Zanna, J. M. Olson, & C. P. Herman (Eds.), *Social influence: The Ontario Symposium* (Vol. 5, pp. 3–39). Hillsdale, NJ: Erlbaum.

Chaiken, S., & Stangor, C. (1987). Attitudes and attitude change. *Annual Review of Psychology*, 38, 575–630.

Crano, W. D., & Alvaro, E. M. (1998). The context/comparison model of social influence: Mechanisms, structure, and linkages that underlie indirect attitude change. *European Review of Social Psychology*, 8, 175–202.

Crano, W. D., & Hannula-Bral, K. A. (1994).

Context/categorization model of social influence: Minority and majority influence in the formation of a novel response norm. *Journal of Experimental Social Psychology, 30,* 247–276.

David, B., & Turner, J. C. (1996) Studies in self-categorization and minority conversion: Is being a member of the out-group an advantage? *British Journal of Social Psychology, 35,* 179–199.

David, B., & Turner, J. C. (1999). Studies in self-categorization and minority conversion: The ingroup minority in intragroup and intergroup contexts. *British Journal of Social Psychology, 38,* 115–134.

David, B., & Turner, J. C. (in press). Majority and minority influence: A single-process self-categorization analysis. In C. K. W. DeDreu & N. K. DeVries (Eds.), *Group consensus and innovation: Fundamental and applied perspectives.* Oxford, England: Blackwell.

DeDreu, C. K. W., & DeVries, N. K. (1993). Numerical support, information processing and attitude change. *European Journal of Social Psychology, 23,* 647–663.

Deutsch, M., & Gerard, H. B. (1955). A study of normative and informational social influences upon individual judgment. *Journal of Abnormal and Social Psychology, 51,* 629–636.

DeVries, N. K., DeDreu, C. K. W., Gordijn, E., & Schurman, M. (1996). Majority and minority influence: A dual role interpretation. *European Review of Social Psychology, 7,* 145–172.

Haslam, S. A., & Turner, J. C. (1992). Context-dependent variation in social stereotyping 2: The relationship between frame of reference, self-categorization and accentuation. *European Journal of Social Psychology, 22,* 251–277.

Haslam, S. A., & Turner, J. C. (1995). Context-dependent variation in social stereotyping 3: Extremism as a self-categorical basis for polarized judgment. *European Journal of Social Psychology, 22,* 341–371.

Haslam, S. A., & Turner, J. C. (1998). Extremism and deviance: Beyond taxonomy and bias. *Social Research, 65,* 435–448.

Haslam, S. A., Turner, J. C., Oakes, P. J., McGarty, C., & Hayes, B. K. (1992). Context-dependent variation in social stereotyping 1: The effects of intergroup relations as mediated by social change and frame of reference. *European Journal of Social Psychology, 22,* 3–20.

Hensley, V., & Duval, S. (1976) Some perceptual determinants of perceived similarity, liking and correctness. *Journal of Personality and Social Psychology, 34,* 159–168.

Hogg, M. A., & Turner, J. C. (1987). Intergroup behavior, self-stereotyping and the salience of social categories. *British Journal of Social Psychology, 26,* 325–340.

Hogg, M. A., Turner, J. C., & Davidson, B. (1990). Polarized norms and social frames of reference: A test of the self-categorization theory of group polarization. *Basic and Applied Social Psychology, 11,* 77–100.

Kelman, H. C. (1961). Processes of opinion change. *Public Opinion Quarterly, 25,* 57–78.

Mackie, D. M. (1987). Systematic and non-systematic processing of majority and minority persuasive communications. *Journal of Personality and Social Psychology, 53,* 41–52.

Martin, R., & Hewstone, M. (in press). Conformity and independence in groups: Majorities and minorities. In M. A. Hogg & R. S. Tindale (Eds.), *Blackwell handbook of social psychology, Volume 1: Group processes.* Oxford, England: Blackwell.

Moscovici, S. (1976). *Social influence and social change.* London: Academic Press

Moscovici, S. (1980). Towards a theory of conversion behavior. In L. Berkowitz (Ed.), *Advances in experimental social psychology, 13* (pp. 209–239). New York: Academic Press.

Moscovici, S., & Lage, E. (1976). Studies in social influence III; Majority versus minority influence in a group. *European Journal of Social Psychology, 6,* 148–174.

Moscovici, S., & Lage, E. (1978). Studies in social influence IV: Minority influence in a context of original judgment. *European Journal of Social Psychology, 8,* 349–365.

Moscovici, S., Lage, E., & Neffrechoux, M. (1969). Influence of a consistent minority on the responses of the majority in a colour perception task. *Sociometry, 32,* 365–380.

Moscovici, S., & Mugny, G. (1983). Minority influence. In P. B. Paulus (Ed.), *Basic group processes,* (pp. 43–64). New York: Springer.

Moscovici, S., & Neve, P. (1973). Studies in social influence II: Instrumental and symbolic influence. *European Journal of Social Psychology, 3,* 461–471.

Mugny, G., Perez, J. A., & Sanchex-Mazas, M. (1993). *Changing attitudes: Conflict elaboration and social influence in xenophobia and racism.* Paper presented to the Summer School on "Migration Conflicts," University of Muenster, Germany, July.

Mullen, B. (1991). Group composition, salience and cognitive representations: The phenomenology of being in a group. *Journal of Experimental Social Psychology, 27,* 1–27.

Nemeth, C. J. (1986). Differential contributions of majority and minority influence. *Psychological Review, 93,* 1–10.

Perez, J. A., & Mugny, G. (1987) Paradoxical effects of categorization in minority influence: When being an outgroup is an advantage. *European Journal of Social Psychology, 17,* 157–169.

Petty, R. E., & Cacioppo, J. T. (1979). Issue involvement can increase or decrease persuasion by enhancing message-relevant cognitive responses. *Journal of Personality and Social Psychology, 37,* 1915–1926.

Petty, R. E., & Cacioppo, J. T. (1981). *Attitudes and persuasion: Classic and contemporary approaches.* Dubuque, IA: Wm C. Brown.

Petty, R. E., & Cacioppo, J. T. (1986). The elaboration likelihood model in persuasion. In L. Berkowitz (Ed.), *Advances in experimental social psychology* (Vol. 19, pp. 123–205). New York: Academic.

Schwarz, N., Bless, H., & Bohner, G. (1991). Mood and persuasion: Affective states influence the processing of persuasive communications. In M. P. Zanna (Ed.), *Advances in experimental social psychology* (Vol. 24, pp. 161–201). San Diego: Academic.

Simon, B., & Brown, R. J. (1987). Perceived intergroup homogeneity in minority-majority contexts. *Journal of Personality and Social Psychology, 53,* 703–711.

Turner, J. C. (1985). Social categorization and the self-concept: A social cognitive theory of group behavior. In E. J. Lawler (Ed.), *Advances in group processes* (Vol. 2, pp. 77–122). Greenwich, CT: JAI.

Turner, J. C. (1991). *Social influence.* Milton Keynes: Open University Press and Pacific Grove, CA: Brooks/Cole.

Turner, J. C., Hogg, M. A., Oakes, P. J., Reicher, S. D., & Wetherell, M. S. (1987). *Rediscovering the social group: A self-categorization theory.* Oxford, England/New York: Basil Blackwell.

Turner, J. C., & Oakes, P. J. (1986). The significance of the social identity concept for social psychology with reference to individualism, interactionism and social influence. *British Journal of Social Psychology, 25,* 237–252.

Turner, J. C., & Oakes, P. J. (1989). Self-categorization theory and social influence. In P. B. Paulus (Ed.), *The psychology of group influence* (2nd ed., pp. 233–275). Hillsdale, NJ: Erlbaum.

Turner, J. C., Oakes, P. J., Haslam, S. A., & McGarty, C. A. (1994) Self and collective: Cognition and social context. *Personality and Social Psychology Bulletin, 20,* 454–463.

Wegener, D. T., & Petty, R. E. (1996). Effects of mood on persuasion processes: Enhancing, reducing and biasing scrutiny of attitude-relevant information. In L. L. Martin & A. Tesser (Eds.), *Striving and feeling: Interactions between goals and affect* (pp. 329–362). Mahwah, NJ: Erlbaum.

Wilder, D. A., & Thompson, J. E. (1988). Assimilation and contrast effects in the judgements of groups. *Journal of Personality and Social Psychology, 54,* 62–73.

Wood, W., Lundgren, S., Ouellette, J. A., Busceme, S., & Blackstone, T. (1994). Minority influence: A meta-analytic review of social influence processes. *Psychological Bulletin, 115,* 323–345.

18

Determinants and Consequences of Cognitive Processes in Majority and Minority Influence

ROBIN MARTIN
MILES HEWSTONE

Empirical Studies
Conclusion

Thee is growing evidence that majority and minority influence are determined by different cognitive processes that affect the type of social influence that occurs (Wood, Lundgren, Ouellette, Busceme, & Blackstone, 1994), although there is dispute concerning the nature of the underlying processes (Martin & Hewstone, in press). In particular, there is disagreement concerning which source condition (majority versus minority) elicits the most cognitive scrutiny of the message. While some theorists have adopted a main effects approach (i.e., one source leads to greater message processing than the other

The writing of this chapter was facilitated by a grant from the Economic and Social Research Council (R000236149). It was completed while Miles Hewstone was a Fellow at the Center for Advanced Study in the Behavioral Sciences, Stanford, for which he gratefully acknowledges financial support provided by the William and Flora Hewlett Foundation.

Address correspondence to: Robin Martin, School of Psychology, University of Queensland, Brisbane, QLD 4072, Australia. E-mail: r.martin@psy.uq.edu.au

source), others have adopted a contingency approach (i.e., message processing is contingent upon source status and one or more additional variables).[1] These are briefly described below.

There are three main effect models. The first, Moscovici's (1980, 1985) conversion theory, has been the most influential perspective in this area. According to Moscovici, majority influence generates a comparison process that leads to a focus on the relationship between source and target; because agreement is derived from a need for consensus and not from a change in understanding of the issue, it is most likely to be manifest at a public level. In contrast, minority influence triggers a validation process, that instigates closer attention to, and detailed evaluation of, the issue. As a consequence of the validation process, individuals are unlikely to agree publicly with the minority (for fear of also being categorized as having deviant status) but the cognitive processing of the message can lead to attitude change on a private or indirect level (conversion). Moscovici's dual-process model highlights the different amounts of thinking instigated by minorities and majorities. In particular, Moscovici predicts that minorities induce perceivers to pay closer attention to the stimulus than do majorities; and minorities instigate more cognitive activity than do majorities.

The second main effect model is the objective consensus approach (Mackie, 1987, see also DeVries, DeDreu, Gordijn, & Schuuman, 1996). In contrast to conversion theory, the objective consensus approach proposes that individuals are more likely to systematically process a majority-endorsed message. Two main reasons are given for this. First, people assume that the majority view reflects reality and "informs recipients about the probable validity of the arguments presented, directs attention to them, and results . . . in the majority messages receiving considerable processing" (Mackie, 1987, p. 50). Second, people believe they share similar attitudes to the members of the majority and hold different attitudes from those in the minority and, as a consequence, they expect to agree with the majority and disagree with the minority (termed the false consensus effect; cf., Ross, Greene, & House, 1977). When faced with a disagreeing majority the consensus expectation is broken, which is surprising. This motivates people to analyze the majority arguments in an attempt to understand this discrepancy. By contrast, exposure to a discrepant minority is consistent with the consensus heuristic and therefore is not surprising, and consequently one is less likely to process the minority's message. Baker and Petty (1994) have suggested other reasons why a majority might lead to greater message processing, other than by violating the consensus heuristic. People often assume that the majority position is more likely to be adopted than that of the minority and therefore they may believe it is more important to process the

---

1. It should be noted that some theorists have advocated that majority and minority influence are determined by the same process (e.g., David & Turner, 1999; Doms, 1983; Latané & Wolf, 1981; Tanford & Penrod, 1984). However, since these theories do not make specific hypotheses concerning the level of message processing associated with each source, they are not considered in detail.

majority's arguments. Another reason is that individuals wish to identify with the majority group and process the majority message in order to discover what their own attitudes should be. In direct contrast to conversion theory, the objective consensus approach proposes that it is a majority source that results in greater message processing.

The third main effect model we consider arises from research conducted by Nemeth and her colleagues (see Nemeth, 1986, 1995). According to Nemeth's convergent-divergent theory, majority and minority influence result in different types of thinking styles, each of which requires cognitive capacity. A determining factor in influence is the level of stress experienced by the target of influence when exposed to persuasive attempts from others. In line with the principles of the objective consensus approach, Nemeth argues that exposure to a disagreeing majority is stressful as it is unexpected and threatens one's position. Since stress is known to reduce focus of attention (Easterbrook, 1959), this is likely to result in convergent thinking which is characterized by a "convergence of attention, thought, and the number of alternatives considered" (Nemeth, 1986, p. 25). In the case of minority influence, experienced stress is less than is the case with a majority and this permits divergent thinking that involves "a greater consideration of other alternatives, ones that were not proposed but would not have been considered without the influence of the minority" (Nemeth, 1986, p. 25).

While Nemeth avoids explicitly stating which source condition is associated with more cognitive activity, her theory is widely interpreted as either showing no difference in the level of cognitive activity between majority and minority influence or as not specifying the relationship (see DeDreu & DeVries, 1996). However, Nemeth does give a clear indication of the direction of thinking by predicting "message-specific cognitive activity in response to a majority and issue-specific activity in response to a minority" (1996, p. 284) and furthermore, stating that "cognitive activity induced by the minority is *not about the message but, rather, about the issue*" (1996, p. 284). Thus, one can interpret Nemeth's theory as indicating greater message processing for a majority source.

A number of contingency theories have been developed to explain majority and minority influence (e.g., context/comparison model [Crano & Alvaro, 1998]; conflict elaboration theory [Mugny, Butera, Sanchez-Mazas, & Pérez, 1995; Pérez & Mugny, 1996]) However, Baker and Petty's (1994) source/position congruity approach is the most relevant with respect to the issue of message processing. According to Baker and Petty's (1994) source/position model, the degree of message processing is determined by the status of the source (majority versus minority) and whether its position breaks the consensus heuristic. When the source/position is expected or 'balanced' (proattitudinal majority or counterattitudinal minority) this situation is unsurprising and therefore it is unlikely to lead to message processing. However, when the source/position is unexpected or imbalanced (counterattitudinal majority or proattitudinal minority) this is surprising and it motivates individuals to process the message in order to understand the incongruity. Alternative congruency factors, that predict when a majority or minority source will lead to greater message processing, have been identified (e.g., source/message content, Maheswaran & Chaiken, 1991).

In summary, there is disagreement amongst researchers concerning which source condition (majority versus minority) should elicit the most cognitive scrutiny of the message and consequently the types of social influence that may occur, with some advocating superior message processing associated with a majority (e.g., Mackie, 1987; Nemeth, 1986), others advocating this for a minority source (e.g., Moscovici, 1980) and, finally, others proposing that both a majority and minority can lead to enhanced message processing under different circumstances (e.g., Baker & Petty, 1994).

In order to determine whether message processing has occurred several researchers have utilized a technique originally developed in the persuasion literature that varies the quality of arguments in the message (see Petty & Cacioppo, 1986). If individuals systematically process a message, then one that contains strong and persuasive arguments should lead to greater attitude change than one that contains weak and nonpersuasive arguments. A reliable difference in posttest attitude scores between a strong and weak message—which we refer to as the argument quality effect—can be interpreted as indicating that individuals have systematically processed the message. By crossing source status (majority versus minority) and argument quality (strong versus weak) it is possible to determine whether either, neither, or both source conditions lead to systematic processing of the message.

Several studies have crossed source status and message quality but inconsistent findings have been found. These studies have shown that an argument quality effect (i.e., strong message having greater influence than weak message indicating systematic processing) has been found (1) with a counterattitudinal majority but not a counterattitudinal minority source (e.g., Baker & Petty, 1994, Exp. 1; Gordijn, 1998, Exp. 1) which, at first sight, supports the objective consensus approach (Mackie, 1987); (2) a majority and minority source in different circumstances (e.g. Baker & Petty, 1994, Exp. 2; DeDreu & DeVries, 1993, Exp. 2) supporting a contingency approach; and, (3) for *both* a majority and minority source (e.g., Bohner, Frank, & Erb, 1998; Crano & Chen, 1998, Exp. 3).

Although there have been inconsistent results in the studies noted above, it is possible to explain some of these findings with reference to participants' motivation to process the message. Of the studies that showed that a majority led to greater message processing than a minority, the source advocated a position that could be interpreted as being against its own (and the participants') interests and therefore would be undesirable (e.g., the introduction of a community service program for students, Baker & Petty, 1994, Exp. 1). Under this atypical situation, it is not surprising that a counterattitudinal majority arguing against its self-interest invoked greater message scrutiny than did a minority. When a majority endorses such a position it is likely to raise suspicion or curiosity in the participants ("why are the majority arguing against my, and their, interest?") and this may result in closer examination of the message. By contrast, when the minority argues against its self-interest, it's message may not be scrutinized for a number of reasons, such as the minority's deviancy being attributed to an underlying bias, because lowly supported positions are unlikely to be adopted, or to protect ones self-interest beliefs.

The studies showing message processing for both a majority and minority either used topics that were high in personal relevance (e.g., increase in tuition fees, Crano & Chen, 1998, Exp. 3) or introduced a manipulation to focus attention on the source (e.g., information concerning source distinctiveness, Bohner et al., 1998) that is know to increase systematic processing (Petty & Cacioppo, 1986). Not withstanding the importance of these studies, it is noticeable that they typically employed topics that had a high impact upon the participants, that encouraged systematic processing and, coupled with source status, could lead to a range of processing biases. Thus, our first research aim is to examine which source condition leads to systematic processing of the message under conditions that avoid the potential processing biases noted above—which we refer to as the 'default' situation.

Since we know that systematic processing typically requires both motivation and ability (Eagly & Chaiken, 1993; Petty, Priester, & Wegener, 1994) and is adversely affected by situational variables that usurp people's capacities for in-depth processing, it follows that majority and minority influence should vary as a function of processing instructions. Therefore, our second research aim is to manipulate task variables that influence systematic versus nonsystematic processing. Specifically, we manipulated cognitive and motivational variables designed to enhance or reduce processing of persuasive messages by majorities or minorities.

We present a summary of five studies from our research program. Each study manipulated both source status (majority versus minority) and message quality (strong versus weak) in order to determine which source condition is associated with systematic processing. The studies are grouped into two categories. The first category of studies examined which source condition is associated with systematic versus nonsystematic processing. The second category of studies employed a range of tasks designed to increase or decrease systematic processing.

EMPIRICAL STUDIES

Methodology

Unless otherwise stated, a standard procedure was employed in all the studies. The participants were either university undergraduates or students at colleges of higher education. Participants were tested either individually or in small groups and received three booklets. In the first booklet, participants were asked to indicate their attitude to six issues on 9-point Likert scales. One of these issues concerned the topic of influence and served as a screening item to ensure that only participants were selected that met sample selection criteria. The second booklet informed participants of a recent survey of people at their college concerning the topic of influence. In all the studies, participants were told that either 82% (majority) or 18% (minority) of those surveyed held a particular attitude towards the issue and the participants were given the main arguments this group had used to support their position. The participants either read the strong or weak version of the message. We undertook extensive pretesting to generate attitude materials (following standard procedures described by Eagly & Chaiken, 1993, p. 311 and Petty & Cacioppo, 1986, p. 133). This established carefully pretested strong and weak arguments on the social issues employed in these studies (namely, animal experimentation, voluntary euthanasia, introduction of a single European currency, and introduction of oral examinations). The third booklet contained the dependent measures that typically included careful manipulation checks on the efficacy of the independent variables, a thought-listing task where participants reported their thoughts to the message (with each thought being subsequently rated as in favor, against, or neutral towards the topic), and a reliable multi-item scale of attitudes (consisting of six, 9-point semantic differential scales).

Results

Statistical analysis. Our main analyses focused on the two dependent variables, namely, the posttest attitude score (an index of the semantic differential scales) and the thought-listing responses. In line with previous research, a message-congruent thought ratio was computed by dividing the number of thoughts in favor of the position advocated by the source by the total number of thoughts in favor and against the source's position. This ratio indicates the proportion of message-congruent thoughts in the direction of the source's position. For each dependent variable, ANOVA analyses were conducted, and, where appropriate, hypotheses were tested using planned comparison. To explore the potential mediating role of thought elaborations in determining attitudes, regression procedures outlined by Baron and Kenny (1986) were employed.

Majority and minority influence and the 'argument quality effect.' The key prior study for our research was by Baker and Petty (1994) who claim that message processing occurs when the consensus heuristic is broken (such as in a counterattitudinal majority). Notwithstanding the theoretical importance of this paper, a number of methodological issues led us to question its findings. We sought to improve on the original experiment in several ways. In particular, we did not assume (as did Baker & Petty, 1994) that the consensus heuristic was broken. Study 1 used the topic of attitudes towards animal experimentation (AE), and used a pro-AE message. Source status was manipulated via false feedback from a student survey (82% for majority and 18% for minority conditions). At pretest, participants were asked to indicate the percentage of people they thought were in favor of, against, or undecided on this issue. We then selected as participants (1) those whose pretest attitude was against AE and who thought more people were against than in favor of AE, and (2) those whose pretest attitude was pro-AE and who thought more people were in favor of than against AE. Thus we ensured that participants thought the majority shared their attitude and the minority were against it.

The design was 2 (message direction: pro- vs. counterattitudinal) × 2 (source: majority vs. minority) × 2 (argument quality: strong vs weak). Baker and Petty (1994) would predict message quality to affect attitudes in the imbalanced conditions (i.e., counterattitudinal majority and proattitudinal minority). In contrast to this prediction, we found the argument quality effect for attitudes (strong message having greater influence than weak message) in the minority conditions, regardless of balance or imbalance (see Fig. 18.1). Moreover, regression analyses showed that attitudes in the minority conditions was mediated by the degree of message-congruent thinking suggesting that participants had systematically processed the message. Furthermore, message quality had no effect for the majority source for either the attitude or message-congruent thoughts measures. This pattern of results does not replicate the original Baker and Petty (1994) nor does it support either Mackie (1987) or Nemeth's (1986) theories that would have expected message processing only in the majority condition. However, the results offers support for Moscovici's (1980) conversion theory showing that a minority source leads to systematic processing of the message.

In our first study we had participants give their thoughts in response to the persuasive message *prior* to filling in their attitudes; this is the logical order of tasks, given the theoretical model explicit in the cognitive theories of persua-

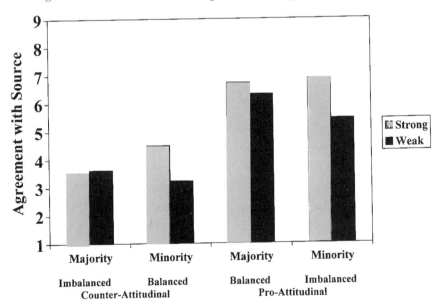

FIGURE 18.1. Message: Pro-animal experimentation; Counterattitudinal condition (pretest anti-animal experimentation) and proattitudinal condition (pretest). The higher the score the more favorable to animal experimentation.

sion that thoughts cause (and therefore must precede) attitudes (see Wood, Pool, Leck, & Purvis, 1996). However, it is noticeable that in the Baker and Petty (1994) studies and in the others reported in our review, attitude measurement preceded thought listing while it was the reverse in our first study. This might account for the difference in findings. To eliminate this methodological issue as a rival explanation, we varied the order in which thoughts and attitudes were measured; the design of Study 2 (which employed an anti-voluntary euthanasia counterattitudinal text) was 2 (order of tasks: thoughts-attitudes vs. attitudes-thoughts) × 2 (source: majority vs. minority) × 2 (argument quality: strong vs. weak). We replicated the argument quality effect only for the minority source, regardless of the order of tasks (see Fig. 18.2; scores were reverse coded such that high scores indicate greater agreement with the source). As for Study 1, the regression analyses showed that the attitude scores in the minority condition were mediated by the level of message-congruent thinking supporting the view that attitudes had been determined by systematic processing of the message.

These two studies provide consistent support for Moscovici's (1980) view that minorities, rather than majorities, instigate validation of (thinking about) the message, and challenge the reliability of Baker and Petty's (1994) findings. However, in these studies we explicitly chose message topics that did not introduce the types of processing bias observed in previous research. More specifically, studies showing a majority leading to systematic processing have tended to use a counterattitudinal message that advocated an undesirable outcome that was likely to be perceived as against the participants' (and the source's) self-

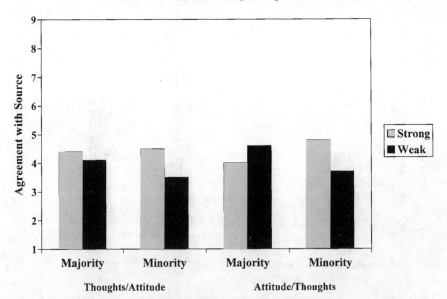

FIGURE 18.2. Counterattitudinal message: Anti-voluntary euthanasia. Attitude scores were reverse coded, higher scores more anti-voluntary euthanasia.

interest. We have argued that this unusual situation introduces a source/self-interest processing bias that can lead to greater message processing for a majority than for a minority. In Study 3 we sought to manipulate this processing bias by employing different message topics. From piloting studies we were able to identify two counterattitudinal messages that varied with respect to the extent they argued against participants' self-interest. The first message argued an anti-voluntary euthanasia position, that was not seen as being against the self-interests of the participants. This message is the same as that employed in Study 2 and we predicted similar findings, namely message processing only for the minority condition. By contrast, our piloting showed that a message that was in favor of the UK adopting the European currency (the ECU) was viewed as being against the participants' self-interest. We predicted that this message would induce a processing bias, similar to that observed in other studies, leading to message processing only for the majority condition.

In this study participants either received the anti-voluntary euthanasia (no processing bias) or the pro-ECU (processing bias) message. The procedure was the same as employed in Study 2 with thought-listing preceding the attitude measures. The design was 2 (processing bias: yes vs. no) × 2 (source: majority vs. minority) × 2 (argument quality: strong vs. weak). The results supported our predictions (see Fig. 18.3; scores for voluntary euthanasia conditions were reverse coded). When the topic did not induce the self-interest processing bias, the results were the same as for the first two studies, namely an argument quality effect only for the minority source. However, when the topic induced the

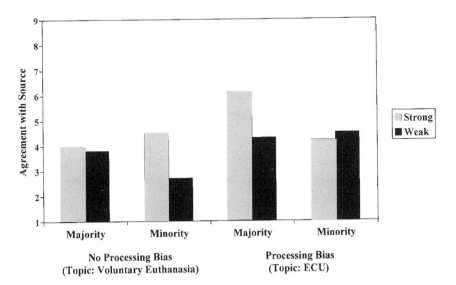

FIGURE 18.3. Counterattitudinal messages: Anti-voluntary euthanasia (no processing bias) or Pro-ECU (processing bias); Attitude scores were reverse coded for voluntary euthanasia topic. Higher scores more anti-voluntary euthanasia (no processing bias) or more in favor of ECU (processing bias).

self-interest processing bias the reverse effect was found, namely an argument quality effect only for the majority. Unlike the first two experiments, message-congruent thoughts did not mediate the attitude scores.

The results from these three studies show that either a majority or a minority source can lead to systematic processing of the message. One factor that can determine which source leads to systematic processing is the nature of the topic and the impact it has upon participant's self-interest. With neutral topics, that are not associated with processing biases, and that we refer to as a default situation, it is the minority, that leads to message processing. However, when the topic introduces a processing bias (such as when arguing against participants' self-interest) then the majority leads to message processing. These results help to explain the contradictory findings in the literature and indicate the importance of understanding participants processing motivation in determining the outcomes of majority and minority influence. We address this issue in the next group of studies, which introduced manipulations to vary the ability and motivation of participants to process the message.

When, not whether, source status instigates message processing.   The results of the above studies, together with the literature review, led us to propose that whether a majority or minority leads to systematic processing is dependent upon the ability and motivation of individuals to process the message. According to contemporary models of persuasion, such as the Elaboration Likelihood Model (ELM; Petty & Cacioppo, 1986) and the Heuristic/Systematic Model (HSM; Chaiken, Liberman, & Eagly, 1989), source status will have an effect under conditions of low elaboration, will differentially affect message processing under moderate elaboration, and have no or little effect under conditions of high elaboration. While the direction of the cue effect under low elaboration conditions is not specified by the ELM, previous research suggests that it is a majority source that would act as a peripheral cue because of the assumption that consensus implies correctness (Erb, Bohner, Schmälzle, & Rank, 1998). When there is moderate elaboration levels, which is similar to our default situation, we predict that the minority source is likely to lead to greater message processing than a majority source (see also Heesacker, Petty, & Cacioppo, 1983; Petty, Fleming, & White, 1999). Finally, when the elaboration level is high, we predict that the effects of message cues diminishes and persuasion is determined by the quality of the arguments.

In our studies on this issue, we employed task variables, which should influence systematic versus nonsystematic processing. Specifically, we tested the hypotheses that (1) under conditions of low elaboration there should be heuristic acceptance of the majority (shown by a significant source effect but nonsignificant message quality effect); (2) under medium elaboration conditions there should be message processing for only the minority source (shown by a significant interaction between source and message quality); and, (3) under high elaboration conditions there should be message processing for both a majority and minority source (shown by a significant argument quality effect).

In Study 4 the participant's ability to process the message was manipulated by means of a number of processing instructions. In this study, the anti-voluntary euthanasia message was employed and segments of the text were reproduced next to the message. The participants were required to perform one of three tasks: indicate whether the segments were of the same font and size as the same segment in the main message (low level of processing), indicate whether the segments contained any spelling errors (medium level of processing), or rewrite the segment using different words but retaining the meaning (high level of processing). A variety of manipulation checks (including recall of message content) indicated that these tasks had achieved the desired level of message processing. The design of the study was: 3 (processing condition: low vs. medium vs. high) × 2 (source: majority vs. minority) × 2 (argument quality: strong vs. weak). The results showed that under high message processing (paraphrase condition) there was an argument quality effect for both source conditions indicating close scrutiny of the message (see Fig. 18.4; attitude scores were reverse coded). Under the medium processing (spelling condition), which parallels the situation in Studies 1 and 2, there was an argument quality effect only for the minority condition. As in our previous studies, the regression analyses showed that the argument quality effect observed in both processing conditions was mediated by the degree of message-congruent thoughts. When there was low message processing (font condition), there was no effect of argument quality but, as predicted, a reliable source effect showing greater majority than minority influence. The latter finding shows that under situations of low message

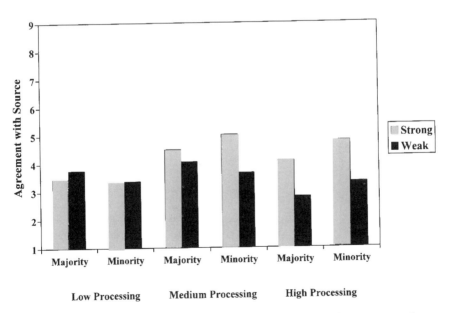

FIGURE 18.4. Counterattitudinal message: Anti-voluntary euthanasia; Attitude scores were reverse coded. Higher scores more anti-voluntary euthanasia

processing there can be heuristic acceptance of the majority position without detailed scrutiny of the contents of its message (Erb et al., 1998).

The results of Study 4 show that message processing depends upon the processing demands. More specifically, the results suggest that a minority is more likely to lead to message processing than a majority when either no processing load is instigated or it is relatively moderate. A majority will only lead to message processing when the task calls for deeper processing. To compliment Study 4, which used cognitive-based tasks, in Study 5 we employed a motivation-based task designed to increase or decrease message processing. We used the topic of whether oral exams should be introduced in universities, and we manipulated relevance by saying these new exams would be introduced either into the participants' own college or another one. Thus the design of the study was 2 (personal relevance: high vs. low) × 2 (source: majority vs. minority) × 2 (argument quality: strong vs. weak). Under high relevance, which we anticipated should increase message processing, we found an argument quality effect for both sources and this effect was mediated by the degree of message-congruent thinking which is consistent with Study 4 (see Fig.18.5). Furthermore, there was a main effect for source showing greater majority than minority influence. This finding was not observed in Study 4, which also used a task to increased message processing (paraphrase), and therefore appears inconsistent. However, Crano and Chen (1998) predict that a majority can have greater influence than

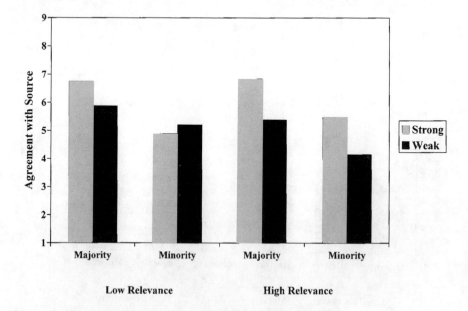

Figure 18.5. Counterattitudinal message: Pro-oral exams; Higher scores more in favor of oral exams.

a minority under conditions of high processing demands if it makes salient the importance of ingroup membership. It is possible that the motivational task used in this study might increase participants' attention to their own and other group memberships to a greater degree than the cognitive tasks used in Study 4, which focused attention more on the content of the message. In the low-relevance condition, that we anticipated would lead to low message processing, we found, as predicted, no argument quality effect, but a main effect of source (greater influence for majority than minority). As for Study 4, when message processing was low there was heuristic acceptance of the majority position without detailed message scrutiny.

CONCLUSION

The aim of this research program was to explore the extent to which individuals will process a persuasive communication that is endorsed by either a majority or minority. This issue has important implications as theories differ with respect to the processes they propose underlie majority and minority influence and the types of social influence that occurs. In the studies reported in this chapter we used the argument quality effect (greater influence following a strong rather than weak message) as an indicator of systematic processing of the message (Petty & Cacioppo, 1986).

A review of the previous research suggests that there is more evidence of systematic processing for a majority than a minority source, although both can lead to message processing under specific circumstances (e.g., Baker & Petty, 1994; Crano & Chen, 1998; DeDreu & DeVries, 1993; Gordijn, 1998). A careful analysis of this prior research shows that these studies often employed messages that advocated a position that might be seen as undesirable to the source and the participants and therefore may have introduced a processing bias. It is therefore important to examine which source leads to greater message processing when employing a message that does not invoke such a bias. To meet this objective, the first two studies in this chapter employed a topic that was seen by the participants as being interesting and important, but neither directly affected their self-interest nor was associated with an undesirable outcome for the source or participants (namely, animal experimentation and voluntary euthanasia). This situation (default condition), does not induce either low or high message elaboration and represents the most likely persuasion context (Petty et al., 1999).

The results of Studies 1 and 2 were consistent in showing an argument quality effect for the minority but not the majority source.[2] In addition, mediational analyses showed that the argument quality effect found for the minority

---

2. Research in the persuasion literature also supports the view that, under moderate processing conditions, majority group members are more likely to process an outgroup or stigmatized minority source (Heesacker et al., 1983; Petty et al., 1999; White & Harkins, 1994).

source was mediated by message-congruent thoughts, providing further evidence of systematic processing. On the other hand, Study 3 demonstrated that the extent to which the message argued against participant's self-interest moderates which source leads to message processing. When the message did not argue against participant's self-interest, a situation similar to Studies 1 and 2, then there was message processing only for the minority source. However, when the message did argue against participant's self-interest, a situation akin to previous research, then it was only the majority source that led to systematic processing. Taken together this pattern of results not only shows support for conversion theory (Moscovici, 1980) in what we refer to as default conditions (that is, situations where there are no processing biases) but also shows that there are contingency variables that can lead either source to engage in systematically processing.

Our second group of studies (4 and 5) employed a number of processing tasks designed to either decrease or increase message processing. Based upon current dual process models of persuasion, we predicted that processing of a majority or minority message would be contingent upon an individual's ability and motivation to engage in message elaboration. The results from these studies provide support for these hypotheses. Tasks which led to a low level of message processing resulted in no effect of message quality indicating that systematic processing had not occurred although there was a source effect (majority greater than minority) indicating heuristic processing (Study 4, font and Study 5, low relevance conditions). In a situation that can be characterized as instigating a moderate level of message processing, and similar to Studies 1 and 2, there was systematic processing of only the minority source (Study 4, spelling condition). Finally, processing tasks which led to a high level of message processing led to systematic processing of *both* a majority and minority source (Study 4, paraphrase; and Study 5, high relevance conditions). In both these studies, mediational analyses showed that the level of message-congruent thinking mediated the argument quality effect.

In conclusion, the systematic variation of source and argument quality effects across task conditions, chosen to encourage or constrain particular types of processing, gives the strongest support yet for the idea that different processes underlie majority and minority influence (Kruglanski & Mackie, 1990). Contrary to Moscovici's (1980) conversion theory, Mackie's (1987) objective consensus approach, or Nemeth's (1986) convergent-divergent theory, neither source exclusively leads to more processing but whether a message from a majority or minority source will be processed, and the consequences of that processing for attitude change, depends upon the processing demands that prevail when the message is encountered. Taken together, our consistent findings underline an important change in the questions we should ask about social influence. We should no longer ask *whether* the majority or minority can instigate systematic processing but *when* either source does so. It seems that neither the majority nor the minority can persuade all of the people all of the time. Rather, it is processing conditions that have that power. Our research, using a range of attitude topics, suggests that systematic processing is the default in the minority condition, but that either source can, in principle and in practice, trigger systematic processing.

REFERENCES

Baker, S. M., & Petty, R. E. (1994). Majority and minority influence: Source-position imbalance as a determinant of message scrutiny. *Journal of Personality and Social Psychology, 67,* 5–19.

Baron, R. M., & Kenny, D. A. (1986). The moderator-mediator variable distinction in social psychological research: Conceptual, strategic, and statistical considerations. *Journal of Personality and Social Psychology, 51,* 1173–1182.

Bohner, G., Frank, S., & Erb, H. P. (1998). Heuristic processing of distinctiveness information in minority and majority influence. *European Journal of Social Psychology, 28,* 855–860.

Chaiken, S., Liberman, A., & Eagly, A. H. (1989). Heuristic and systematic information processing within and beyond the persuasion context. In J. S. Uleman & J. A. Bargh (Eds.), *Unintended thought: Limits of awareness, intention and thought* (pp. 212–252). New York: Guilford.

Crano, W. D., & Alvaro, E. M. (1998). The context/comparison model of social influence: Mechanisms, structure, and linkages that underlie indirect attitude change. In W. Stroebe & M. Hewstone (Eds.), *European review of social psychology* (Vol. 8, pp. 175–202). Chichester: John Wiley.

Crano, W. D., & Chen, X. (1998). The leniency contract and persistence of majority and minority influence. *Journal of Personality and Social Psychology, 74,* 1437–1450.

David, B., & Turner, J. C. (1999). Studies in self-categorization and minority conversion: The ingroup minority in intragroup and intergroup contexts. *British Journal of Social Psychology, 38,* 115–134.

DeDreu, C. K. W., & DeVries, N. K. (1993). Numerical support, information processing and attitude change. *European Journal of Social Psychology, 23,* 647–663.

DeDreu, C. K. W., & DeVries, N. K. (1996). Differential processing and attitude change following majority and minority arguments. *British Journal of Social Psychology, 35,* 77–90.

DeVries, N. K., DeDreu, C. K. W., Gordijn, E., & Schuurman, M. (1996). Majority and minority influence: A dual interpretation. In W. Stroebe & M. Hewstone (Eds.), *European review of social psychology* (Vol. 7, pp. 145–172). Chichester: John Wiley.

Doms, M. (1983). The minority influence effect: An alternative approach. In W. Doise & S. Moscovici (Eds.), *Current issues in European social psychology* (Vol. 1, pp. 1–31). Cambridge: Cambridge University Press.

Eagly, A. H., & Chaiken, S. (1993). *The psychology of attitudes.* Fort Worth, TX: Harcourt Brace Jovanovich.

Easterbrook, J. A. (1959). The effect of emotion on the utilization and the organization of behavior. *Psychological Review, 66,* 183–201.

Erb, H. P., Bohner, G., Schmälzle, K., & Rank, S. (1998). Beyond conflict and discrepancy: Cognitive bias in minority and majority influence. *Personality and Social Psychology Bulletin, 24,* 620–633.

Gordijn, E. H. (1998). *Being persuaded or persuading oneself: The influence of numerical support on attitudes and information processing.* Unpublished Doctoral dissertation, University of Amsterdam, The Netherlands.

Heesacker, M., Petty, R., & Cacioppo, J. (1983). Field dependence and attitude change: Source credibility can alter persuasion by affecting message-relevant thinking. *Journal of Personality, 51,* 653–666.

Kruglanski, A. W., & Mackie, D. M. (1990). Majority and minority influence: A judgmental process analysis. In W. Stroebe & M. Hewstone (Eds.), *European Review of Social Psychology* (Vol. 1, pp. 229–261). Chichester: John Wiley.

Latané, B., & Wolf, S. (1981). The social impact of majorities and minorities. *Psychological Review, 88,* 438–453.

Mackie, D. M. (1987). Systematic and

nonsystematic processing of majority and minority persuasive communications. *Journal of Personality and Social Psychology, 53*, 41–52.

Maheswaran, D., & Chaiken, S. (1991). Promoting systematic processing in low-motivation settings: Effects of incongruent information on processing and judgment. *Journal of Personality and Social Psychology, 61*, 13–25.

Martin, R., & Hewstone, M. (in press). Conformity and independence in groups: Majorities and minorities. In M. A. Hogg & R. S. Tindale (Eds.), *Blackwell handbook of social psychology, Vol. 1: Group processes*. Oxford, England: Blackwell.

Moscovici, S. (1980). Toward a theory of conversion behavior. In L. Berkowitz (Ed.), *Advances in experimental social psychology* (Vol. 13, pp. 209–239). New York: Academic.

Moscovici, S. (1985). Social influence and conformity. In G. Lindsey & E. Aronson (Eds.), *The handbook of social psychology*, (Vol. 2, 3rd ed., pp. 347–412). New York: Random House.

Mugny, G., Butera, F., Sanchez-Mazas, M., & Pérez, J. A. (1995). Judgments in conflict: The conflict elaboration theory of social influence. In B. Boothe, R. Hirsig, A. Helminger, B. Meier, & R. Volkart (Eds.), *Perception-evaluation-interpretation* (pp. 160–168). Göttingen: Hogrefe and Huber.

Nemeth, C. (1986). Differential contributions of majority and minority influence. *Psychological Review, 93*, 23–32.

Nemeth, C., (1995). Dissent as driving cognition, attitudes and judgements. *Social Cognition, 13*, 273–291.

Pérez, J. A., & Mugny, G. (1996). The conflict elaboration theory of social influence. In E. H. Witte & J. H. Davis (Eds.), *Understand-ing group behavior: Small group processes and interpersonal relations* (Vol. 2, pp. 191–210). Hillsdale, NJ: Erlbaum.

Petty, R. E., & Cacioppo, J. T. (1986). *Communication and persuasion: Central and peripheral routes to attitude change*. New York: Springer-Verlag.

Petty, R. E., Fleming, M. A., & White, P. H. (1999). Stigmatized sources and persuasion: Prejudice as a determinant of argument scrutiny. *Journal of Personality and Social Psychology, 76*, 19–34.

Petty, R. E., Priester, J. R., & Wegener, D. T. (1994). Cognitive processes in attitude change. In R. S. Wyer, Jr. & T. K. Srull (Eds.), *Handbook of social cognition* (Vol. 2, pp. 69–142). Hillsdale, NJ: Erlbaum.

Ross, L., Greene, D., & House, P. (1977). The "false consensus effect": An egocentric bias in social perception and attribution processes. *Journal of Experimental Social Psychology, 13*, 279–301.

Tanford, S., & Penrod, S. (1984). Social influence model: A formal integration of research on majority and minority influence processes. *Psychological Bulletin, 95*, 189–225.

White, P. H., & Harkins, S. G. (1994). Race of source effects in the Elaboration Likelihood Model. *Journal of Personality and Social Psychology, 67*, 790–807.

Wood, W., Lundgren, S., Ouellette, J. A., Busceme, S., & Blackstone, T. (1994). Minority influence: A meta-analytic review of social influence processes. *Psychological Bulletin, 115*, 323–345.

Wood, W., Pool, G. J., Leck, K., & Purvis, D. (1996). Self-definition, defensive processing, and influence: The normative impact of majority and minority groups. *Journal of Personality and Social Psychology, 71*, 1181–1193.

19

A SIDE View
of Social Influence

RUSSELL SPEARS
TOM POSTMES
MARTIN LEA
SUSAN E. WATT

*A*lthough the lament "what ever happened to the group in social psychology?" is probably less relevant today than it was 10 years ago, it might still be appropriate to the domain of social influence. Reintroducing the group not only focuses our attention on an important dimension of the influence process, but also extends influence beyond the head and brings it into the social world. Once we do this it probably is legitimate to ask ourselves "what ever happened to the social context in the study of social influence?" Focusing on group influence opens the door to assessing the influence of the social con-

Some of the research reviewed in this chapter was financially supported by the ESRC 'Virtual Society?' Research Program, the British Council UK—Dutch Joint Scientific Research Program, and the Kurt Lewin Institute. We would like to thank the editors and in particular Kip Williams for insightful feedback on an earlier version of the chapter.

Address correspondence to: Russell Spears, Department of Social Psychology, University of Amsterdam, Roetersstraat 15, 1018 WB Amsterdam, The Netherlands. E-mail: sp_Spears@macmail.psy.uva.nl

text in which group influence is embedded. Considering the context of group influence also addresses the key themes of this volume, namely the direct and indirect forms that influence can take. The group might be considered a direct source of influence whereas, as we will try to show, the impact of context can often be indirect, and even counterintuitive. The question of how social context can moderate group influence is the subject of the present chapter.

With social context we mean, broadly, any feature of the social situation that is beyond and apparently incidental to the identity of the source or target of influence or the content of the message. In this chapter we focus on two such related features of social context, namely the anonymity and isolation among group members. These two features should a priori be expected to have little logical relation to the influence process: They are simply part of the context in which the key players impart and receive the information that is the substance of influence. However, we will try to show that these features can significantly influence the influence process, and sometimes in counterintuitive ways. There are good reasons to expect that anonymity and isolation, if they have any effect at all, will weaken the bond and thus the influence between members of a group. We will argue, and provide empirical evidence that just the reverse may be the case.

If we look at the history of social influence research we can probably detect a shift in emphasis, reflecting developments in the discipline more broadly. That is, research has increasingly examined the cognitive processes involved in persuasion. This is a positive development that has brought welcome specification, and understanding. For example the work on dual process models (e.g., Elaboration Likelihood Model (ELM) and the Systematic-Heuristic Model (HSM)) provides many insights into the cognitive and affective mechanisms underlying attitude change, and the different routes it can take (see e.g., Eagly & Chaiken, 1993; Petty & Cacioppo, 1986). However, it also probably is true to say that the focus on the actual cognitive processes (e.g., on elaboration of the message) has gone hand in hand with a shift away from considering the social circumstances of social influence. For example, much early social influence research, such as the classic studies of Sherif, Asch, and another sort of dual process model of Deutsch and Gerard (1955), were all concerned with these circumstances, and primarily how the group effected influence. To be sure, the influence of the group has been integrated into the new dual process models. However, in these approaches it can be seen as part of the source (a "source characteristic"), rather than a principal mechanism of influence in itself.

The group as a basis of social influence has not entirely disappeared from view however. Researchers from the field of intergroup relations, and notably self-categorization theorists, have investigated how our group memberships impinge on the social influence process. Much progress has been made in showing how ingroup and outgroup information is processed differently and can have different impacts. Within this tradition, the way in which we categorize the source is more than an input, but may actually change the way we see the same message, and even whether we process it systematically, if at all (e.g., Mackie, Worth, & Asuncion, 1990; Turner, 1982, 1991). In this sense, self-categorization theory (SCT) moves beyond earlier group-based explanations of social influence in offering an approach that also focuses on processes of cognitive elaboration of information. However, once again there has been minimal emphasis on the effects of context, in the sense of the social setting in which source and recipient are embedded, on the process of influence.

One of the aims of the present contribution is to build on self-categorization theory, and to show that the group relation between source and receiver is indeed critical to social influence (the "direct" path, so to speak). The second major aim is to show how this process can also be critically moderated by the social context (an "indirect" influence). The influence of context is indirect because, as we have defined it above, it is often incidental or irrelevant to the message, and even the relation between group and individual (see also Knowles, Butler, & Linn, this volume; Ng, this volume). To make this case we present data from a program of research using the "SIDE" model: The Social Identity model of Deindividuation Effects. We elaborate this model further below. However, because it develops the self-categorization theory of social influence, and examines how features of the context may affect the influence process we begin by briefly outlining the self-categorization theory of social influence.

SELF-CATEGORIZATION: AN INTEGRATION OF GROUP AND COGNITIVE BASES OF SOCIAL INFLUENCE?

The self-categorization theory of social influence is sometimes called the theory of referent informational influence and is elaborated in greater detail elsewhere (Turner, 1985, 1987, 1991; see also David & Turner, this volume and also Terry & Hogg, this volume). It is a theory of group influence in which the group forms the link between others (potential sources) and the self. We belong to many social groups and categories, and we are influenced in what we feel and think by these groups, at least to the extent that we identify with them. A basic assumption is that we are primarily influenced by members of ingroups. The group is particularly important because it provides social validation for our views and even our perceptions. People expect to agree with others from their own group or category. Indeed, when we find that we disagree, this opens up a space for (mutual) social influence (see Latané & Bourgeois, this volume).

The self-categorization explanation of social influence differs in important respects from many of the earlier approaches to group influence. In the earlier work, and in particular the dual process model of Deutsch and Gerard (1955), group influence was set in contrast in important respects to the more cognitive processes of influence that have developed into the persuasion tradition. Thus normative influence (group-based) was seen as distinct from informational influence (cognitive). Indeed, to the extent that normative influence related to group dynamics (promoting social acceptance and avoiding ridicule or rejection by group members) it was not conceptualized as influence in the sense of internalization and conversion to agreement with the source. In other words, the gap between actual beliefs and overt behavior is generally greater for normative than informational influence.

The self-categorization theory of social influence, however, represents an integration of both group and cognitive bases of influence. To the extent that we already define the group as part of the self, group influence is not external pressure to comply. The notion of referent informational influence proposed in self-categorization theory in one sense represents a unification of informational and normative elements in a common process. In other words, like the contemporary dual process models, the self-categorization process moves away from the notion that influence is necessarily negative or imposed (as implied in earlier conceptualizations of "compliance") and implicates cognitive processes of elaboration and internalization of information leading to private as well as public attitude change. Unlike other cognitive approaches to influence, this process is seen as intrinsically related to the social self. The reconceptualization of the group as a dimension the self (Turner, 1982, 1985) has important implications here. It means that while the group is external to the self (a source of information from others and a basis for social validation) it is also internal to it (a source of self-definition). The group therefore provides both a medium and a mechanism of social influence. Because our relation to the source defines how we perceive the message we might characterize this as a relational or interactionist approach. The constituent elements (source, message, recipient) cannot be considered independent but instead interact and codefine each other.

Unless the nature of the message is so outlandish as to bring the whole question of group self-definition into question, we will tend to shift towards the group's position. What defines the group's position? This is the prototypical position, and is not a fixed property of the group, but varies with the social comparative context. In contexts where there is a clear and relevant outgroup present, the prototypical position is that which simultaneously maximizes similarity to the ingroup, and difference from the outgroup. However, the self-categorization analysis of group influence can also be applied when no explicit outgroup is present. This is the case in the group polarization paradigm (Turner, 1991; Wetherell, 1987). The fact that people have to provide their response to an attitude item or choice dilemma on a scale often provides some contextual information about what the group is and what it is not.

For example, if group members come to find out that they are mostly clustered on one side of the scale, this scale provides a frame of reference defining their position. They can then see themselves as the relatively risky (or cautious) group, or as the relatively pro (or con) group. On this basis we would predict them to conform to the most prototypical position in the group, this time defined by emphasizing similarity to other discussion group members and difference from the scale positions avoided by the group (e.g., those opposite to the preferred side of the scale). When people have a preference for positions on either side of the scale, the prototypical position will tend to be more extreme (i.e., further from the midpoint of the scale) than the mean position of the group (Turner, 1991; Wetherell, 1987). This is the logical consequence of differentiating the ingroup from the outgroup (or more broadly from noningroup positions). This analysis helps to explain the puzzle of group polarization—the fact that people actually shift beyond the group mean to a more extreme position.

We return to this paradigm in our own research below. First, however, we examine how this analysis of the social influence process may be further affected by variations in the features of the social context. The SIDE model provides one framework designed to address this question.

THE SIDE MODEL

SIDE stands for the Social Identity model of Deindividuation Effects. It is concerned with, amongst other things, understanding contextual influences on the social influence process in group contexts. As its name indicates the model grew out of social identity theory (Tajfel, 1978; Tajfel & Turner, 1986), and also self-categorization theory (Turner, 1985, 1987). Specifically, SIDE draws on this theoretical tradition to provide a critique and alternative explanation for a range of deindividuation phenomena associated with anonymity in the group. More generally, SIDE attempts to extend and supplement SCT with an analysis of the effects of a range of contextual factors on self-definition and self-expression. The first way in which SIDE extends SCT is in providing an analysis of specific contextual conditions that can affect the salience of self-categorization. This analysis has been referred to as the cognitive dimension of SIDE. This is in order to distinguish it from the strategic dimension of the model, which is concerned with the patterns of behavior that flow from the combination of these salient identities and the contextual constraints on their expression. Although this strategic dimension can be relevant to the realm of social influence it is beyond the scope of the present chapter (see Reicher, Spears, & Postmes, 1995).

The roots of SIDE can be traced back to Reicher's work on crowd behavior (e.g., Reicher, 1984, 1987). In our research we have applied and extended this approach to understanding the effects of social influence in the domain of computer-mediated communication (CMC; Lea & Spears, 1991; Lea, Spears, & De Groot, in press; Postmes, Spears, & Lea, 1998, in press; Postmes, Spears, Sakhel, & De Groot, in press; Spears & Lea, 1992, 1994; Spears, Lea, & Postmes, in press; Spears, Lea, & Lee, 1990). This is where we focus most of our attention in this chapter. We develop our argument shortly. Both of these domains have certain contextual features in common relevant to the focus on social context, namely the relative anonymity of group members (although it can be argued that this is clearer in the case of CMC than in crowds). An additional contextual feature of CMC not present in crowds, however, is the high degree of isolation. This has interesting implications for the social influence process that we consider below. However, it is first necessary briefly to consider the critique of deindividuation theory and the research modeling social influence in crowds that laid the foundations for the SIDE model, before proceeding to develop the relevance of these lines of argument for the CMC domain.

Successive generations of deindividuation theorists had proposed that immersion and anonymity in the group could result in reduced self-awareness or even a "loss of self," leading to uninhibited and anti-normative behavior (e.g., Diener, 1980; Dipboye, 1977; Festinger, Pepitone, & Newcomb, 1952; Prentice-Dunn & Rogers, 1989; Zimbardo, 1969). Reicher proposed that anonymity in the group does not produce a loss of identity or reduced self-awareness, but actually promotes a *switch* to social identity such that the salience of group identity becomes enhanced (e.g., Reicher, 1987).[1] An early study by Reicher (1984) made this point and set out the principle underlying the cognitive dimension of the SIDE model. This study involved university students from science and social science students. The salience of these group identities was manipulated by separating the groups and seating them at two different tables (high group salience) or interspersing them around a single table (low group salience). Moreover, a classic deindividuation/anonymity manipulation was introduced by dressing people in masks and overalls (à la Zimbardo, 1969), or leaving them identifiable and individuated in their normal clothing. The idea was that this manipulation would accentuate the effects of group salience by reinforcing group distinctions when group salience was already high (i.e. by eliminating a focus on interpersonal difference), but not when group salience was low (where group boundaries were not distinguishable in any case). Group

---

1. It is important to note that the proposal made by SIDE theorists that deindividuating conditions can lead to greater group influence is subtly but clearly distinct from the argument made by classical deindividuation theorists that such conditions lead to the enhanced influence of environmentally available cues, and the reduced influence of internal standards (e.g., Diener, 1980; Zimbardo, 1969; see also Postmes & Spears, 1998 for a discussion of this issue). First, as the earlier discussion of self-categorization theory should make clear, a group norm is not just (if at all in some cases) an external cue, it is also an internal standard (i.e., relating to a group self-categorization or social identity). Defined in these terms, responsiveness to a group norm is not a mindless or irrational process reflecting a reduced sense of self, as is implied in deindividuation theory, but may be a conscious and rational process relating to a meaningful sense of identity. These two routes may be sometimes difficult to distinguish on the surface, but not impossible. First, the group normative account suggests that the influence of the environmental cues will not be general, but will be strictly limited to the confines and constraints of a group identity. For example, classical deindividuation theory would suggest that people become more aggressive when exposed to a violent cue (e.g., a gun) under deindividuating conditions, whereas the SIDE model proposes that people will only become aggressive if this behavior is defined as normatively appropriate by the group identity for the situation. Related to this point, the impact of environmental cues implies an individual and virtually automatic process (somewhat akin to priming), while the group normative explanation suggests that the group is an important mediator of the influence effect (see Postmes et al., 1998 Study 2, described below). In short, the higher impact of cues in the environment under deindividuating conditions is mediated and constrained by identity according to the SIDE model, but not according to classical deindividuation theory.

salience was maintained in the high salience condition by using overalls of different colors for the two groups, but not in the low salience condition.

The effects of this deindividuation manipulation were not strong or general across conditions in this study. However, there was some evidence that when group boundaries were clear (high group salience), and people were anonymous in their group, this led to more social influence in a group normative direction (specifically for the science students). The argument here is that anonymity enhances the salience of group identity by depersonalizing self and social perception, thereby stimulating group related behavior (see also Reicher, Spears, & Postmes, 1995). Science students therefore became more provivisection (a science norm) when group identity was salient and they were anonymous.

This point was important because it was the first study to question the accepted wisdom of previous deindividuation research. Rather than behavior becoming *deregulated* under deindividuation conditions, it seemed to be highly socially *regulated*, and indeed normative at the group level (see footnote 1). Although some conceptual and methodological question marks have been raised about this study (see Spears, Lea, & Lee, 1990), it motivated a reappraisal of apparently robust evidence for deindividuation effects. A meta-analytic review of the deindividuation literature (Postmes & Spears, 1998b) provides support for a SIDE analysis of the effects produced in this literature. This meta-analysis showed that: 1) there is little or no evidence for "anti-normative" behavior increasing as a function of deindividuation conditions as predicted by deindividuation theory, and 2) classical deindividuating conditions (group immersion, anonymity, group size) lead to increased conformity to *local* group norms when these norms are measured and coded. In short, evidence from deindividuation studies provides strong indications that the SIDE analysis of social influence has some validity in this domain.

We have subsequently formalized the theoretical framework that developed out of the crowd and the CMC research relating to the cognitive components of the model (Spears & Lea, 1992). Specifically, we propose that the effects of anonymity within the group will tend to deflect attention from individual differences, thereby depersonalizing perception and rendering the relevant group identity more salient and influential (Reicher et al., 1995; Spears & Lea, 1992). Anonymity in the group therefore emphasizes a common group self-categorization at the expense of other identities (e.g., personal identity, or superordinate identities). However, as we show in more detail below, if personal identity is salient a priori, the effects of anonymity may be further able to reduce the salience of group distinctions based on category membership (see also Reicher, 1984). In short, contextual features such as anonymity, can serve to vary the salience of the group self, thereby affecting the strength of group influence.

The purpose of our subsequent research program was twofold. First we aimed to extend the SIDE analysis to another domain where issues of anonymity and identifiability are also central, namely computer-mediated communication (CMC). Second, we wanted to develop this analysis in order to gain more insight into the underlying process, and plot the limits of social influence. In this respect, CMC formed an interesting testing ground and test case. Unlike crowd contexts where people derive their anonymity (to others at least) from their close proximity in the mass, anonymity in CMC is derived from physical isolation. Many traditional models of social influence would predict the influence of others to be strengthened by copresence and proximity and (inter alia) the enhanced social presence, interdependence, cohesion, surveillance, and social impact that these imply (Deutsch & Gerard, 1955; Latané, 1981; Lewin, 1948/1997; Lott & Lott, 1965; Short, Williams, & Christie, 1976; see also Latané & Bourgeois, this volume). Deindividuation theory notwithstanding, the case for social influence in the crowd seems quite compelling given the presence of numerous coacting others. The presence of others can also reduce or remove the restraints on behavioral expression or the fear of sanction, which is also a form of social influence (Reicher et al., 1995; Wheeler, 1966). To argue that social influence can be enhanced under conditions of anonymous isolation therefore seems to fly in the face of both much knowledge of group dynamics as well as common sense. Demonstrating that influence can be enhanced under conditions of anonymous isolation would therefore provide a conservative test, and a counterintuitive demonstration, of the power of social influence.

EXTENDING SIDE TO COMPUTER-MEDIATED COMMUNICATION

We now focus on how some of our own research picked up on these leads and applied these ideas to the realm of CMC. Our first study was a group polarization study (Spears, Lea, & Lee, 1990; see also Lea & Spears, 1991) and in certain respects this was a conceptual replication of the 1984 study by Reicher described earlier. However in this case we replaced the classic Zimbardo deindividuation manipulation with the isolation and lack of visibility characteristic of CMC. This study also implicated a single group (of psychology students) rather than trying to model an explicitly intergroup context. We manipulated the salience of personal identity by telling participants that we were only interested in them as individuals and that the study concerned personality differences in communication styles (personal identity salient). By contrast, in the group identity salient condition we informed them that we were interested in them as psychology students. Additionally, participants were either isolated in separate rooms, or were located in the same room and thus visible to each other, resulting in a 2 × 2 factorial design.

Our assumption was that group polarization on the discussion topics would reflect conformity to an extremitized group norm as described earlier (Turner, 1991; Wetherell, 1987). We reinforced this norm by providing participants with representative feedback about the (progressive) views of student on the discussion topics gleaned from students in the previous cohort. In line with the cognitive dimension of SIDE we predicted most group polarization in the direction of the group norm when group identity was salient and anonymous. In this condition we expected the most depersonalization in terms of group identity (little individuation between participants would be possible) and thus enhanced group salience and conformity to group norms. When personal identity was salient, however, anonymity might increase the sense of being an isolated individual, resulting in least normative polarization. The visible conditions were predicted to lie somewhere in between. These predictions were confirmed. Polarization in the normative direction was strongest when the group identity was salient and when participants were anonymous and thus depersonalized. When personal identity was salient, anonymous participants actually exhibited depolarization away from the group norm. We interpreted this as evidence of people accentuating their individuality, in contrast to the group norm, when personal identity is accentuated by anonymous isolation.[2]

In subsequent studies we have concentrated on situations where a group identity is clearly salient in context, and thus where anonymity tends to strengthen group influence. However, from the above study it should be remembered that this effect is not generic, but depends of this level of identity being salient (in this sense identity salience moderates the effect of anonymity on influence). A recent study provided further support for the idea that anonymity in the group strengthens rather than weakens social influence when group identity is salient, while addressing some of the methodological weaknesses of earlier research. Postmes and colleagues primed group norms surreptitiously in order to assess whether these norms would have more impact in anonymous groups (Postmes, Spears, Sakhel, & De Groot, in press). As in the previously described study, groups were anonymous and thus depersonalized, or identifiable and thus individuated. In this study all participants were isolated in separate cubicles and individuation was manipulated by having a scanned picture of the participants displayed on the computer screen during discussion.

Participants were presented with a dilemma in which they had to propose solutions to problems of patient care confronting a hospital. We primed group norms relating to efficiency or prosocial behavior using a scrambled sentence procedure (Srull & Wyer, 1979; Dijksterhuis et al., 1998; see also Dijksterhuis, this volume and Petty, this volume). As predicted, behavior followed group norms most strongly in anonymous/deindividuated groups with these groups propos-

---

2. In this study social influence was operationalized as conformity to the progressive student norm as reinforced by the graphical feedback. Although providing a powerful manipulation, strictly speaking, this information undermines the possibility that the effects of information contained in such norms is the product of a group transmission process (e.g., as opposed to individual thoughts). We address this issue in a subsequent study described below (Postmes et al., in press, Study 2). However, if this were the case, this would not be able to account for the interaction obtained. The fact that anonymity produced more norm directed influence when group identity was salient, but less when personal identity was salient, only makes sense if such information is perceived as group normative (see also Lea & Spears, 1992).

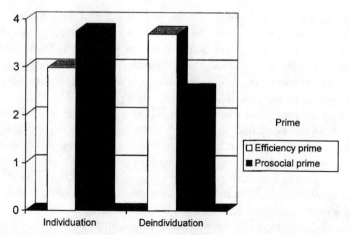

FIGURE 19.1. Solutions proposed after discussion as a function of deindividuation and priming condition.

ing solutions that emphasized either efficiency or more prosocial patient care in line with the norm that was manipulated. This pattern was not evident for the individuated groups however (there was even a nonsignificant reversal; see Fig. 19.1). The words used in the discussion transcripts also reflected the primed norms for the anonymous/depersonalized groups, with participants more likely to use efficiency related words in the efficiency prime condition and prosocial words in the prosocial prime condition. Once again there was little evidence of this in the individuated conditions.

This study showed that the social influence effect generalized beyond the group polarization paradigm and held up when group norms were subtly manipulated rather than simply being imposed (cf. Spears et al., 1990). However, it is conceivable that the priming effect in this study simply reflects an individual cognitive process (i.e., priming) rather than representing a true group influence process (see Dijksterhuis, this volume; Petty, this volume; Spears, 2000; see footnotes 1 & 2). A follow-up study by Postmes et al. (in press) therefore attempted to show that this norm was actually actively transmitted *within* the group. In this study we primed two members of four person groups with the efficiency prime as in the previous study, and gave the remaining two group members a neutral prime. The second factor consisted of the anonymity/identifiability manipulation as before. If group influence really is occurring the primed norm should transfer to other neutrally primed group members, and especially so in the anonymous groups. This prediction was supported: More efficiency-oriented solutions and efficiency related words were generated in the anonymous conditions, and these generalized equally to the neutral group members. Levels for both efficiency-primed and neutrally-primed participants in the individuated groups were lower.[3]

---

3. One might ask why the neutral prime does not transfer to the other two (efficiency primed) group members, and more so under anonymous/deindividuated conditions?

We also found some evidence in this study for the mediating process. A key issue in SIDE, and one that continues to generate research, is the question of the precise mediating process. Recall that we proposed that making groups anonymous increases group salience by shifting attention away from the perception of interpersonal differences. Here we used group identification as an indicator of group salience. We found evidence that this measure did indeed mediate the direct effect of anonymity on social influence (Postmes et al., in press; Study 2). In other words, group identification increased in the anonymous conditions, and when this effect of identification was entered into the regression equation, the direct effect of anonymity on influence was reduced to nonreliability (Baron & Kenny, 1986).

In another study (Lea, Spears, & De Groot, in press) we attempted to gain further evidence for the mediating processes involved by showing that visual anonymity in the group depersonalizes social perception. This can have a range of consequences beyond social influence: It should strengthen group effects in general. One effect of depersonalization is that it increases social attraction defined as attraction to the group (Hogg & Hains, 1997; Turner, 1982). This then leads to the somewhat counterintuitive prediction that anonymity can increase attraction to the group.

In this study, participants interacted in what they thought were groups of three. In fact the other two participants were confederates of the experimenter who responded according to a standard script during the group discussions (their attitudes were held constant). The study was presented as an investigation of Internet communication with people in different locations. Participants were told that the other two group members were students in Germany (Berlin, Munich). Common membership of the discussion group was emphasized by means of group identifiers, and reference in the instructions to the group. Identifiability was manipulated by means of a quickcam on the computers in the identifiable conditions that produced a streaming online picture of the three participants, which was absent in the anonymous conditions.

During the session the groups discussed a number of topics, although we were not primarily concerned with social influence in this study (there were not clear norms associated with these issues). Rather, these topics were used as a basis for developing in vivo group identity and identification. The main aim here was to examine the relation between anonymity, self-categorization processes, and attraction to the group. We measured self-categorization and stereo-

---

The answer is that it may well have done so, but because this norm is irrelevant to the dependent measure here (namely the number of efficiency related words used) the effects of this would likely be diffuse and would go undetected by this measure. In this regard it is important to note that neutral here does not mean counterefficiency, but simply that the prime was orthogonal to and irrelevant to the efficiency dimension. There could well have been bidirectional influence such that neutral and efficiency primed members influenced each other on both dimensions, but because only the efficiency norm had a clear directional form tapped by the dependent variable, only this effect was detectable.

typing of other group members in terms of the local group identity. The SIDE model proposes that anonymity, by depersonalizing social perception, will enhance both self-categorization and group stereotyping of others, and that these should increase attraction to the group. More specifically we expected anonymity to enhance self-categorization in terms of the group and that this would mediate an effect of anonymity on group attraction.

The effect of group stereotyping of others was expected to be contingent on self-categorization, however. That is, categorizing oneself as a group member is likely to increase the probability of seeing other participants as fellow group members rather than as unrelated individuals. Or put in other terms, if the perceivers themselves are not depersonalized in terms of group membership, the perception of others thus is also unlikely (recall the contrasting effects of anonymity for personal identity in Spears et al., 1990). In short, we hypothesized an additional path from self-categorization to group stereotyping of others, which in turn should increase attraction to the group.

To test these predictions we developed reliable measures of self-categorization, group stereotyping, and group attraction and administered these after the group discussion. We then contrast coded the anonymity manipulation and constructed a model of the relations between this and the measured variables in line with the paths outlined above. The predicted model provided a very good fit with the data (see Lea, Spears, & De Groot, in press, for further details). In line with the SIDE model these findings offer further support for the proposed intragroup dynamics that result from anonymity within a salient group that then help to explain the effects of social influence.

Other studies have extended the SIDE analysis in CMC to intergroup contexts, similar to Reicher's (1984) study. For example, Postmes, Spears, and Lea (1999) and Lea, Spears, Watt, & De Groot (in press) have conducted research involving groups in Amsterdam and Manchester in which visibility to the outgroup (Postmes et al., 1999) and to both the ingroup and outgroup (Lea, Spears, Watt, & De Groot, in press) were manipulated. These studies generally support the contention that anonymity enhances group salience and influence. However this does not apply to the category of gender (Lea, Spears, Watt, & De Groot, in press; Watt, Lea, & Spears, in press). Social categories that are characterized by clear visual cues (e.g. race, gender), may be rendered as much if not more salient by identifiability, because visibility draws attention to these markers of category membership.

To summarize, we have shown how some apparently incidental aspects of the context, in this case the anonymity or identifiability of the participants, can have significant effects on the direction and degree of social influence in the group. Building on self-categorization theory, the relation between the individual and the source of influence is crucial. Indeed we have shown that self-categorization and group identification are critical mediators of influence and related group processes. However this relation (and the resulting influence) is not fixed but is dependent on context as well as the (a priori) salience of group identity. Contextual features that intensify group salience should increase social influence. In this case we have shown that anonymity in the group is one factor that can have this effect, but there are likely to be others (Spears, in press).

Let us pause for a moment to consider the implications of these studies. The idea that anonymity and isolation can induce greater influence as shown in the CMC studies is in many ways counterintuitive and contradicts many assumptions contained in the group influence literature. Concepts such as "social presence," "social impact," "normative influence," and "interdependence" theories of the group, all seem to imply that influence should be greater to the extent that the bonds between individuals are emphasized. These would presumably be most evident when group members are visible to each other and copresent rather than isolated. According to this view, sources should be better able to exert their influence when other (nonverbal) channels to communication are open, because a visible source is more vivid, or because targets are under surveillance. Recall that the theory of normative influence suggests that people go along to get along (Deutsch & Gerard, 1955); influence should disappear when the surveillance of face to face interaction is replaced by the anonymity of CMC (see Turner, 1991). Visibility and thus identifiability also enhances accountability to others (as in the strategic dimension of SIDE; see also Prentice-Dunn & Rogers, 1989). Yet group influence in the research described above was (with some interesting exceptions) consistently stronger under conditions of anonymity. This points to one of the theoretical strengths of the relational approach of SCT and the cognitive dimension of SIDE. It would seem that social influence in this research is codetermined by social relations (and psychological bonds) together with physical parameters (anonymity, isolation), that interact in such a way as to contradict the expected impact of physical parameters considered on their own. In other words, the fact that anonymity and isolation can increase social influence in the way they do, only makes sense if we view social influence primarily as the product of a psychological relation, rather than a physical contingency.

Does this mean that social influence is always strengthened when people are anonymous with respect to one another? Not necessarily. We have already pointed to the case of salient personal identity reversing this effect. We also have indicated some groups whose visibility makes them salient because of obvious markers to category membership (e.g., gender). It also may be that there are other forms of influence that do not rely primarily on the depersonalizing effects of anonymity to enhance group salience. The studies described until now have all been concerned with the influence of the groups or social categories that are defined as such by virtue of a shared social identity (psychology students, science students, the in vivo task group). Following self-categorization theory it makes sense that the conditions that emphasize the salience of the group or category should therefore facilitate influence. However, in many real life groups the group may be characterized by differentiated roles or by interpersonal bonds between individuals rather than primarily in terms a shared social identity. Take for example a work team, or a group of friends. These kinds of groups are not so much characterized by a common attribute (unless we define this broadly as the work task, or the fact of friendship, respectively), but more by the roles and relationships within the group. This raises the question of whether these other sorts of group will respond to contextual features such as anonymity in quite the same way, leaving aside for the moment the obvious point that anonymity may be more difficult to achieve in such groups.

This issue speaks to a distinction in the group literature between the classic Lewinian interdependence definition of the group (as the sum of its interpersonal bonds; e.g., Lewin, 1948/1997), and the definition of the group as a shared social identity (as in the social identity and self-categorization tradition; see e.g., Turner, 1982, 1987). Most recently this has been captured in the distinction between common-bond and common-identity groups respectively (Prentice, Miller, & Lightdale, 1994). Common-identity groups correspond to groups defined by a shared identity (e.g., social categories), whereas common-bond groups are groups defined by the sum of interpersonal bonds between group members (e.g., as in friendship groups). Indeed, from a self-categorization perspective there is a question about whether we should think about a common-bond group as a group in the sense of a psychological self-category, or whether it is more accurately an interpersonal network (see also Latané & Bourgeois, this volume). One answer is that it *can* be a psychological group in the sense of SCT, to the extent that members define their interpersonal bonds as making them one (hence psychological group). In this respect, and from a self-categorization perspective, there need not be a psychological discontinuity between these types of group. Rather they can simply be distinguished by the contents (norms or social structure) that define them (i.e., in terms of bonds or in terms of attributes). Durkheim's distinction between "organic" and "mechanical" solidarity refers to a similar distinction in the basis for the group (see Haslam, 2001).

The more relevant question for us here is whether and how this distinction might be affected by our central contextual variable of anonymity. It may well be the case that the effects of anonymity will be moderated by the kind of group in question. We know that the predictions of the SIDE model seem to hold for common-identity groups. This makes sense because the depersonalizing effects of anonymity tend to draw attention to common properties and deflect attention from individual differences. However, there are good reasons to suppose that this effect might be eliminated or even reversed in the case of common-bond groups. For these groups we would expect influence to be enhanced when the members of a discussion group are visible to each other. This is because visibility should emphasize the bonds that characterize this group by emphasizing the intimacy, accountability, reciprocity, and so forth between individual group members.

Note that we are not arguing that the process of social influence (and the mediating mechanism of group salience) is fundamentally different in this type of group. Rather we are arguing that the defining features of this kind of group may mean that a different aspect of social context will enhance group salience and facilitate influence (in this case identifiability rather than anonymity). This is analogous to our argument that the visibly marked categories such as gender may have different relations to contextual moderators such as anonymity than those that are not so marked. In both cases we assume that the process of group influence is broadly the same, even though the facilitiating conditions vary.

We tested this idea in an experiment in which we randomly assigned groups of three people to four conditions in a 2 × 2 design (Postmes & Spears, 1999; see also Spears & Postmes, 1998). In the identifiable conditions participants were visible and could see digital photos of all the participants on their computer screen. In the anonymous conditions these photos were not displayed. Furthermore, the type of group identity was manipulated. In the common-bond group condition participants were told that they were assigned to "personal bond groups based on pretest questionnaires, and that personal bond groups exist because group members like and value each other: members have a mutual bond, as in a group of friends for example." Participants in the common-identity group were told that they were assigned to common-identity groups based on pretesting and that such groups exist "because its members share a common outlook or unite behind a common goal, as is the case in political parties for example."

After some further elaboration and manipulation checks, participants proceeded to engage in group discussion on the first of two topics on then-relevant issues that were pretested for their relevance to this student group and to establish the student group norms. The first topic was concerned with whether government policy should introduce temporary contracts to limit the payment of social security benefits in order to extend the flexibility and reduce costs of employers in their hiring practices. The second discussion topic concerned government proposals to build a new airport in the sea, off the coast of the Netherlands, and the potential environmental implications of this. Piloting indicated that the student norm was opposed to temporary contracts and the airport development scheme. Discussion of the topics was separated by dependent measures, some of which were administered after the second discussion.

To recap predictions, we expected greater group salience and normative polarization in *common-identity* groups when members were *anonymous*; similar effects were expected for *common-bond* groups whose members were *identifiable*. Two measures provide some support for our rationale. A measure of individualism/collectivism showed that while anonymous common-identity groups were perceived as more collectivist (consistent with their group identity being salient), identifiable common-bond groups were perceived as more collectivist. This is consistent with the idea that common-bond group identity was strengthened under conditions of identifiability. A two-item measure of the ability to form an impression of the other group members (I could form an impression of the members of my group; I do not have a clear image of the people I just communicated with [reverse code]) also resulted in a similar interaction. Anonymity tended to hinder the ability of common-bond groups to form an impression of their fellow group members (as one might expect), but the anonymity of common-identity groups actually facilitated the formation of impressions of others. This suggests that common-bond group members base their impressions of other group members on individual characteristics, but common-identity group members do not.

The predicted cross-over interaction also was obtained for social influence. Specifically, on both topics there was most group polarization in the direction of the norm for common-bond groups when participants were identifiable and thus individuated. However, for common-identity groups this pattern was reversed, with influence being strongest when these groups were anonymous. Interestingly the interaction on the second discussion topic was mediated by the group impression measure (taken after the first discussion topic). These different impressions reflect the different forms of group: common-bond vs. common-identity respectively.

CONCLUSION

In this chapter we have tried to extend the relational model of social influence proposed in self-categorization theory by examining how contextual features influence the influence process. We have used the SIDE model to analyze how features typically examined in deindividuation research, notably anonymity versus identifiability, can moderate the effects of group influence. We argue that this occurs by influencing the salience of group identity, thereby strengthening the relation of the individual to the group. Under conditions of anonymity, perception of oneself and other group members becomes depersonalized and the influence of this group identity is correspondingly greater. This assumes of course some identification with this group (as we saw, identification and self-categorization were crucial mediators). This also assumes that this group identity is already salient to some extent.

Even with these caveats in mind it would be misleading to claim a general theoretical rule, however. The evidence of exceptions emphasizes the importance of specifying not only context and identity, but of analyzing how these may interact. Thus when personal identity is salient, the relation of the individual to the group is broken and anonymity can undermine group influence (Spears et al., 1990). For certain groups whose essence is captured in visual cues (such as gender) identifiability may actually enhance salience (Watt et al., 2000). Moreover, if the group is defined in terms of interpersonal relations (as in common-bond groups), rather than a shared attribute, then identifiability rather than anonymity may strengthen the path to group salience and social influence (Postmes & Spears, 1999).

To summarize, in order to understand the pattern of social influence occurring within groups and between individuals, a general analysis needs to take into account:

1. The salient level of self-definition (personal vs. group);
2. The form and content of these levels of self-categorization (e.g., do they emphasize interdependence, or shared attributes, as in common-bond versus common-identity groups?), and their contextual properties (e.g., are they denoted by visible cues); and
3. The contextual factors that can moderate the relation between individual and group (e.g., anonymity, identifiability, isolation; see Spears, in press).

These considerations suggest that social influence may be a complex social process as well as a complex cognitive process. Taking into account the social relations and the social circumstances of social influence may help to enrich our understanding of the factors at play in explaining the variety of influence in social situations defined by a range of contextual features. In terms of the theme of this volume, this analysis speaks both to the direct and the indirect nature of social influence. The effects of context in terms of their impact on social perception and social influence can be quite direct in the sense of being immediate as illustrated most clearly in the priming studies described above. The influence of such implicit manipulations also can be seen as indirect, in the sense of being able to bypass awareness. However, these effects also are mediated by identity, and in this sense clearly refer to a *social* influence process grounded in the group. The influence process also is indirect in the sense that context may often only be incidentally related to the topic of influence, if at all (see Knowles, Butler, & Linn, this volume; Ng, this volume). These properties help to explain both the power and diversity of influence effects.

We are not suggesting that the SIDE model provides the only way in which to extend our understanding of the role of contextual inputs into the influence process. This framework also is open to extension beyond the range of deindividuating conditions and effects considered here (Reicher, in press; Spears, in press). However, it does provide one framework with which to understand the variety of these effects and one that makes sometimes counterintuitive predictions with respect to existing theories and assumptions. It is also a framework that, to pick up a theme raised in the introduction, takes us outside the head of the social perceivers and into the social world in which they are embedded. In focusing on the psychological process of social influence it is sometimes easy to neglect the social and contextual factors that can "influence" this process. One of the most interesting paradoxes of the present research is to show that social influence can often be strengthened by anonymity and isolation, when common sense, along with much research, tells us that these are the very conditions that could weaken our links to others. This consistent finding underlines the point that the relation between the individual and the influencing group is an internal psychological relation, and not one merely built on physicality, be this defined in terms of proximity or coercion.

REFERENCES

Baron, R. M., & Kenny, D. A. (1986). The moderator-mediator variable distinction in social psychological research: Conceptual, strategic, and statistical considerations. *Journal of Personality and Social Psychology, 51,* 1173–1182.

Deutsch, M., & Gerard, H. (1955). A study of normative and informational social influences upon individual judgment. *Journal of Abnormal and Social Psychology, 51,* 629–36.

Diener, E. (1980). Deindividuation: The absence of self-awareness and self-regulation in group members. In P. B. Paulus (Ed.), *The psychology of group influence* (pp. 209–242). Hillsdale, NJ: Lawrence Erlbaum.

Dijksterhuis, A., Spears, R., Postmes, T., Stapel, D. A ., Koomen, W., van Knippenberg, A., & Scheepers, D. (1998). Seeing one thing and doing another: Contrast effects in automatic behavior. *Journal of Personality and Social Psychology, 75,* 862–871.

Dipboye, R. L. (1977). Alternative approaches to deindividuation. *Psychological Bulletin, 84,* 1057–1075.

Eagly, A. H., & Chaiken, S. (1993). *The psychology of attitudes.* Fort Worth, TX: Harcourt Brace Jovanovich.

Festinger, L., Pepitone, A., & Newcomb, T. (1952). Some consequences of de-individuation in a group. *Journal of Abnormal and Social Psychology, 47,* 382–389.

Haslam, S. A. (2001). *Psychology in organizations: The social identity approach.* Philadelphia: Psychology Press.

Hogg, M. A., & Hains, S. C. (1997). Intergroup relations and group solidarity: Effects of group identification and social beliefs on depersonalized attraction. *Journal of Personality and Social Psychology, 70,* 295–309.

Latané, B. (1981). The psychology of social impact. *American Psychologist, 36,* 343–356.

Lea, M., & Spears, R. (1991). Computer mediated communication, de-individuation, and group decision-making. *International Journal of Man-Machine Studies, 34,* 283–301.

Lea, M., & Spears, R. (1992). Paralanguage and social perception in computer-mediated communication. *Journal of Organizational Computing, 2,* 321–341.

Lea, M., Spears, R., & De Groot, D. (in press).

Knowing me, knowing you: Effects of visual anonymity on self-categorization, stereotyping and attraction in computer-mediated groups. *Personality and Social Psychology Bulletin.*

Lea, M., Spears, R., Watt, S., & De Groot, D. (in press). Inside stories: Building a model of anonymity effects using structural equation modeling. In T. Postmes, R. Spears, M. Lea, & S. D. Reicher (Eds.), *SIDE issues centre stage: Recent developments of de-individuation in groups.* Amsterdam: Proceedings of the Dutch Royal Academy of Arts and Sciences.

Lewin, K. (1997). *Resolving social conflicts and field theory in social science* (G. Weiss Lewin, ed.). Washington, DC: APA. (*Resolving social conflict* was originally published in 1948 by Harper & Row; *Field theory in social science* was originally published in 1951 by Harper & Brothers and reissued in 1976 by the University of Chicago Press)

Lott, A. J., & Lott, B. E. (1965). Group cohesiveness as interpersonal attraction: A review of relationships with antecedent and consequent variables. *Psychological Bulletin, 64,* 259–309.

Mackie, D. M., Worth, L. T., & Asuncion, A. G. (1990). Processing of persuasive ingroup messages. *Journal of Personality and Social Psychology, 58,* 812–822.

Petty, R. E., & Cacioppo, J. T. (1986). The elaboration likelihood model of persuasion. In L. Berkowitz (Ed.), *Advances in experimental social psychology* (Vol. 19, pp. 123–205). New York: Academic.

Postmes, T., & Spears, R. (1998). Deindividuation and anti-normative behavior: A meta-analysis. *Psychological Bulletin, 123,* 238–259.

Postmes, T., & Spears, R. (1999). *Anonymity in computer-mediated communication: Different groups have different SIDE effects.* Manuscript submitted for publication.

Postmes, T., Spears, R., & Lea, M. (1998). Breaching or building social boundaries? SIDE-effects of computer mediated communication. *Communication Research, 25,* 689–715.

Postmes, T., Spears, R., & Lea, M. (1999). *The effects of anonymity in intergroup discussion: Bipolarization in computer-mediated groups.* Manuscript submitted for publication.

Postmes, T., Spears, R., & Lea, M. (2000). The emergence and development of group norms in computer-mediated communication. *Human Communication Research, 26,* 341–371.

Postmes, T., Spears, R., Sakhel, K., & De Groot, D. (in press). Social influence in computer-mediated groups: The effects of anonymity on social behavior. *Personality and Social Psychology Bulletin.*

Prentice, D. A., Miller, D. T., & Lightdale, J. R. (1994). Asymmetries in attachments to groups and to their members: Distinguishing between common-identity and common-bond groups. Special Issue: The self and the collective. *Personality and Social Psychology Bulletin, 20,* 484–493.

Prentice-Dunn, S., & Rogers, R. W. (1989). Deindividuation and the self-regulation of behavior. In P. B. Paulus (Ed.), *The psychology of group influence* (2nd ed., pp. 86–109). Hillsdale, NJ: Lawrence Erlbaum.

Reicher, S. D. (1984). Social influence in the crowd: Attitudinal and behavioral effects of de-individuation in conditions of high and low group salience. Special Issue: Intergroup processes. *British Journal of Social Psychology, 23*(4), 341–350.

Reicher, S. D. (1987). Crowd behavior as social action. In J. C. Turner, M. A. Hogg, P. J. Oakes, S. D. Reicher, & M. S. Wetherell (Eds.), *Rediscovering the social group: A self-categorization theory* (pp. 171–202). Oxford: Basil Blackwell.

Reicher, S (1999). Refuting relativism and pathology in group psychology: Two SIDEs of the same coin. In T. Postmes, R. Spears, M. Lea, & S. D Reicher (Eds.), *SIDE issues centre stage: Recent developments of de-individuation in groups.* Amsterdam: Proceedings of the Royal Netherlands Academy of Arts and Sciences.

Reicher, S. D., Spears, R., & Postmes, T. (1995). A social identity model of deindividuation phenomena. *European Review of Social Psychology, 6,* 161–198.

Short, J. A., Williams, E., & Christie, B. (1976). *The Social Psychology of Telecommunications.* Chichester, England: Wiley.

Spears, R. (in press). The interaction between the individual and the collective self: Self-categorization in context. In C. Sedikides &

M. B. Brewer (Eds), *Individual self, relational self, and collective self: Partners, opponents or strangers?* Philadelphia: Psychology Press.

Spears, R. (2000). Automatic intergroup behavior: Social identity meets social cognition. Invited Keynote address at the Society of Australasian Social Psychologists annual meeting, Fremantle, Perth, Western Australia, April.

Spears, R., & Lea, M. (1992). Social influence and the influence of the 'social' in computer-mediated communication. In M. Lea (Ed.), *Contexts of computer-mediated communication* (pp. 30–65). Hemel-Hempstead: Harvester-Wheatsheaf.

Spears, R., & Lea, M. (1994). Panacea or panopticon: The hidden power in computer-mediated communication. *Communication Research, 21,* 427–459.

Spears, R., Lea, M., & Lee, S. (1990). De-individuation and group polarization in computer-mediated communication. *British Journal of Social Psychology, 29,* 121–134.

Spears, R., Lea, M., & Postmes, T. (in press). Social psychological theories of computer-mediated communication: Social pain or social gain? In P. Robinson & H. Giles (Eds.), *The handbook of language and social psychology* (2nd ed.). Chichester, England: Wiley.

Spears, R., & Postmes, T. (1998). Anonymity in computer-mediated communication: Different groups have different SIDE effects. Paper presented in "Social psychology on the web" symposium (Kipling Williams), Society for Experimental Social Psychology, Lexington, Kentucky, October.

Srull, T. K., & Wyer, R. S., Jr. (1979). The role of category accessibility in the interpretation of information about persons: Some determinants and implications. *Journal of Personality and Social Psychology, 37,* 1660–1672.

Tajfel, H. (Ed.) (1978). *Differentiation between social groups: Studies in the social psychology of intergroup relations.* London: Academic.

Tajfel, H., & Turner J. C. (1986). The social identity theory of intergroup behavior. In S. Worchel & W. G Austin (Eds.), *Psychology of intergroup relations* (pp. 7–24). Chicago: Nelson Hall.

Turner, J. C. (1982). Towards a cognitive redefinition of the group. In H. Tajfel (Ed.),

Social identity and intergroup relations (pp. 15–40). Cambridge, UK: Cambridge University Press.

Turner, J. C. (1985). Social categorization and the self-concept: A social cognitive theory of group behavior. In E. J. Lawler (Ed.), *Advances in group processes: Theory and research* (Vol. 2). Greenwich, CT: JAI.

Turner, J. C. (1987). A self-categorization theory. In J. C. Turner, M. A. Hogg, P. J. Oakes, S. D. Reicher, & M. S. Wetherell (Eds.), *Rediscovering the social group: A self-categorization theory* (pp. 42–67). Oxford, England: Basil Blackwell.

Turner, J. C. (1991). *Social influence.* Milton Keynes, UK: Open University Press.

Watt, S. E., Lea, M., & Spears, R. (in press.). How social is Internet communication? Anonymity effects in computer-mediated groups. In S. Woolgar (Ed.), *Virtual society? The social science of electronic technologies.*

Wetherell, M. (1987). Social identity and group polarization. In J. C. Turner, M. A. Hogg, P. J. Oakes, S. D. Reicher, & M. S. Wetherell (Eds.), *Rediscovering the social group: A self-categorization theory* (142–170). Oxford, England: Basil Blackwell.

Wheeler, L. (1966). Toward a theory of behavioral contagion. *Psychological Review, 73,* 179–192.

Zimbardo, P. G. (1969). The human choice: Individuation, reason, and order vs. deindividuation, impulse, and chaos. In W. J. Arnold & D. Levine (Eds.), *Nebraska symposium on motivation* (Vol. 17, pp. 237–307). Lincoln, NE: University of Nebraska Press.

Author Index

351

Subject Index